During the summer of 1800, slaves in and around Richmond conspired to overthrow their masters and abolish slavery. This book uses Gabriel's Conspiracy and the evidence produced during the repression of the revolt to expose the processes through which Virginians of African descent built an oppositional culture. Sidbury portrays the rich cultures of eighteenth-century Black Virginians and the multiple, and sometimes conflicting, senses of identity that emerged among enslaved and free people living in and around the rapidly growing state capital. The book also examines the conspirators' vision of themselves as God's chosen people and the complicated African and European roots of their culture. In so doing, it offers an alternative interpretation of the meaning of the Virgin

Fathers of the United States.

spectives of Black and enslav

as a counterpoint to more co

Ploughshares into swords

Ploughshares into swords
Race, rebellion, and identity
in Gabriel's Virginia, 1730–1810

JAMES SIDBURY

University of Texas at Austin

CAMBRIDGE
UNIVERSITY PRESS

PUBLISHED BY THE PRESS SYNDICATE OF THE UNIVERSITY OF CAMBRIDGE
The Pitt Building, Trumpington Street, Cambridge CB2 IRP, United Kingdom

CAMBRIDGE UNIVERSITY PRESS
The Edinburgh Building, Cambridge CB2 2RU, United Kingdom
40 West 20th Street, New York, NY 10011-4211, USA
10 Stamford Road, Oakleigh, Melbourne 3166, Australia

First published 1997

Printed in the United States of America

Typeset in Ehrhardt by Graphicraft Typesetters Ltd., Hong Kong

Library of Congress Cataloging-in-Publication Data
Sidbury, James.
Ploughshares into swords : race, rebellion, and identity in
Gabriel's Virginia, 1730–1810 / James Sidbury.
p.   cm.
Originally presented as the author's thesis – Johns Hopkins
University.
Includes bibliographical references and index.
ISBN 0-521-58454-X (hc). – ISBN 0-521-59860-5 (pbk.)
1. Slavery – Virginia – Richmond Region – Insurrections, etc.
2. Richmond Region (Va.) – Race relations.   3. Slavery – Virginia –
Insurrections, etc.   4. Virginia – History – 1775–1865.   5. Prosser,
Gabriel, ca. 1775–1800.   I. Title.
F234.R59N477   1997
975.5'45100496073 – dc21   96-51787
                                                        CIP

*A catalog record for this book is available from
the British Library.*

ISBN 0 521 58454 X hardback
ISBN 0 521 59860 5 paperback

To the memory of
Alice Lucas Rayle Sidbury,
and for
James Buren Sidbury

Contents

vii

Acknowledgments

Many people contributed to the writing of this book. It started as a dissertation at Johns Hopkins University. A number of professors and (then) graduate students – Philip Curtin, Christine Daniels, Toby Ditz, Lige Gould, John Higham, Cathy Jurca, Kurt Nagel, J. G. A. Pocock, William Rowe, John Russell-Wood, Ronald Walters, Steve Whitman, Stephen Young, and Larzer Ziff – helped me think through various problems that they have long forgotten. I remain grateful for their help.

A smaller group of people began making suggestions and offering critiques at the beginning and have remained engaged through multiple drafts. Jeff Bolster, Julie Hardwick, Mieko Nishida, and Robert Olwell have seen so many versions of this material that they may be as relieved to see it in print as I am. Their questions have improved this book immeasurably, and I am as grateful for their friendship as for their advice. Philip Morgan and Sylvia Frey have also provided advice, criticism, and support that have greatly improved this book.

Two historians were especially important in the development of this project and have continued to be great teachers and good friends. In William Freehling's undergraduate class on the coming of the Civil War, I first thought about the possibility of becoming a historian, and his example continues to influence me. Jack Greene supervised my dissertation. The standards that he and his students set in his research seminar and his delight in and openness to the various perspectives and approaches that his students brought to early American history helped to shape my approach to history.

Many archivists have also helped. The staffs at the Virginia Historical Society, Duke University's Perkins Library, the University of Virginia's Alderman Library, the Southern Historical Collection at the University of North Carolina, and the manuscripts reading room at the Library of Congress were all helpful. Most of the archival work for this book was done in the Virginia State Library (now the Library of Virginia), and I owe special thanks to Conley

Edwards, Robert Clay, Minor Weisigar, Christian Kolbe, Lyndon Hart, and others who worked there.

Three other people helped to make my time in Richmond more enjoyable. David Allmendinger, Philip Schwarz, and Michael Lee Nicholls welcomed me to the historical profession when I was far from sure I belonged and shared their knowledge and research. Mick, especially, generously gave me printouts of some of his notes. All three have also read and commented on various drafts of my work over the years.

Many people have commented on conference papers or individual chapters, or have given me copies of their work that have proven helpful. They include John Boles, Kathleen Brown, Reginald Butler, Douglas Egerton, David Barry Gaspar, Gwendolyn Midlo Hall, Larry Hudson, Michael Johnson, Susan Juster, Wilma King, Jan Lewis, Robert Paquette, Charles Royster, Julius Scott, Fredrika Teute, and the late Armstead Robinson.

Many colleagues in the history department at the University of Texas have made it a harmonious and collegial place for me to work. I am especially grateful to Robert Abzug, Antonia Casteñeda, Neil Foley, Richard Graham, Michael Hall, Neil Kamil, Gunther Peck, and Michael Stoff, who have either commented on individual chapters or participated in seminars in which chapters were discussed. Shearer Davis Bowman, Sally Clarke, Kevin Kenny, and Sandra Lauderdale have read all or much of the manuscript and have made extensive and helpful comments. I am grateful to Frank Smith at Cambridge University Press for his advice and for his support of this book, and to Helen Wheeler and Shirley Covington for their help as production editor and copyeditor, respectively.

For funding my work I thank Johns Hopkins University and, at the University of Texas, the University Research Institute and the Center for African and African American Studies. The Rockefeller Foundation funded a year at the University of North Carolina's Institute for the Arts and Humanities, and James Peacock, Ruel Tyson, and Lloyd Kramer did much to make that year productive and enjoyable.

I would also like to thank the following people whose friendship and support over the course of this project have made the work worth doing: Ellen Goellner, Viranjini Munasinghe, Patty and Bill Haley, Anne Sidbury and Scott Menella, Mercy Sidbury, Robert Sidbury, and Scott Hutchinson. Astrid Oesmann has lived with and contributed to this book, for six years. It and I are better for her help.

Introduction

This book is not about Gabriel's Conspiracy. It is, instead, about the Black and White worlds of late-eighteenth-century Virginia, the worlds in which that conspiracy grew. People of recognized African descent who lived in Gabriel's Virginia, even those who were not enslaved, suffered enormous legal and social disadvantages associated with chattel slavery. This book illustrates many of those hardships, but it is not about them either. It focuses, instead, upon the ways that Blacks living in eighteenth-century Virginia made sense of their world, of their relationships to their own pasts, and of their relationships to the revolutionary tradition that White Virginians held so dear but also held to be irrelevant to "their" slaves. It uses Gabriel's Conspiracy and the evidence produced in the trials of alleged conspirators to open a window on the perceptions of people of African descent in Richmond at the turn of the nineteenth century. Blacks in Gabriel's Virginia forged a collective identity and a vibrant living culture of resistance through creative acts of appropriation that reconstituted Virginian culture. They turned their new creation, their new Virginian culture, into a weapon in their battle for the end of slavery and the genesis of racial justice.

These processes occurred at specific times and in specific places. Much of the best social history written during the last three decades has examined individual localities or communities and has tried to reconstruct the social and cultural forces that influenced people's day-to-day lives. The best of these works avoid the danger of antiquarianism by asking important general questions about historical change and about the nature of American society in the small localities in which the vast majority of early Americans lived. Studies of Andover, Massachusetts, or Sugar Creek, Illinois, or Middlesex County, Virginia, speak to issues with resonance far beyond those small communities.[1]

[1] Philip Greven, *Four Generations: Population, Land, and Family in Colonial Andover, Massachusetts* (Cambridge, Mass., 1970); John Mack Faragher, *Sugar Creek: Life on the*

They illustrate at once the important peculiarities of individual localities and
the ways that general historical forces played out in the communities in which
people lived.

Historians of slavery and of eighteenth- and nineteenth-century African
Americans have been less drawn toward local studies, opting more often for
broad, cohesive arguments about the emergence of slave communities and
African American culture that have generally been applied at the level of a
single state (or colony) or else at even broader regional and national levels.[2]
Most of these works fall into a broad "community and culture" school, and
they have immeasurably enriched our understanding of slaves' lives, but they
have done so by portraying a powerful composite picture of "the slave experience," "the slave community," and in the end of "the slave."[3]

This book benefits from and asks some of the same questions as do these
broad works, but by seeking answers in a more localized place it uncovers the

Illinois Prairie (New Haven, 1986); Darrett B. Rutman and Anita H. Rutman, *A Place in
Time: Middlesex County, Virginia 1650–1750* (New York, 1984). These are three excellent examples of a large historiographical genre.

[2] This includes many excellent books dealing with slavery and slave culture throughout the
South: Eugene D. Genovese, *Roll, Jordan, Roll: The World the Slaves Made* (New York,
1972); Lawrence Levine, *Black Culture and Black Consciousness: Afro-American Folk
Thought From Slavery to Freedom* (New York, 1977); John W. Blassingame, *The Slave
Community: Plantation Life in the Antebellum South*, rev. ed. (New York, 1979); Sterling
Stuckey, *Slave Culture: Nationalist Theory and the Foundations of Black America* (New
York, 1987), esp. ch. 1. It also includes studies of slavery in individual states or colonies:
Peter H. Wood, *Black Majority: Negroes in Colonial South Carolina from 1670 through the
Stono Rebellion* (New York, 1974); Norrece T. Jones, *Born a Child of Freedom, Yet a
Slave: Mechanisms of Control and Strategies of Resistance in Antebellum South Carolina*
(Hanover, N.H., 1990); Gerald W. Mullin, *Flight and Rebellion: Slave Resistance in
Eighteenth-Century Virginia* (New York, 1972); Robert McColley, *Slavery and Jeffersonian
Virginia*, 2d ed. (Urbana, 1973); Allan Kulikoff, *Tobacco and Slaves: The Development of
Southern Cultures in the Chesapeake, 1680–1800* (Chapel Hill, 1986); Mechal Sobel, *The
World They Made Together: Black and White Values in Eighteenth-Century Virginia*
(Princeton, 1987); Gwendolyn Midlo Hall, *Africans in Colonial Louisiana: The Develop-
ment of Afro-Creole Culture in the Eighteenth Century* (Baton Rouge, 1994). Several local
studies constitute important exceptions: Charles Joyner, *Down by the Riverside* (Urbana,
1984); Winthrop D. Jordan, *Tumult and Silence at Second Creek: An Inquiry into a Civil
War Slave Conspiracy* (Baton Rouge, 1993); Janet Sharp Hermann, *The Pursuit of a Dream*
(New York, 1981).

[3] Perhaps the best emblem of this tendency, as well as one of the most important and valuable contributions of this school of historical work, is the collected depression-era interviews of ex-slaves compiled by George Rawick: George P. Rawick, ed., *The American
Slave: A Composite Autobiography*, 41 vols. (Westport, Conn., 1972–9), which includes
his important book-length introduction that was published separately as *From Sundown
to Sunup: The Making of the Black Community* (Westport, Conn., 1972).

dynamic processes through which enslaved Richmonders sought meaning in their lives and freedom from their masters. Rather than offering a composite picture of "the slave," it portrays many enslaved people living, working, playing, and struggling within the developing town in which they lived. Rather than compiling evidence that slaves built rich plantation communities, it portrays the contours of the specific communities in which enslaved people in and around Richmond lived, and it uncovers some of the tensions, as well as the bonds of affection, that held these communities together. Placing the Black people of early Richmond in their local context and examining the ways that they lived offer a richer picture than can more geographically dispersed studies of the ways that early Americans of African descent came to conceive of themselves as a people. This book also uncovers the contradictory senses of identity that enriched the culture that they built, while paradoxically straining the bonds of solidarity. And it presents the complicated textures of daily life in the city in order to contextualize these crosscutting senses of identity.

This offers a new picture of late-eighteenth-century Virginia that complements and complicates traditional interpretations of Jeffersonian Virginia. While recent historians of Virginia in the age of the American Revolution have consistently confronted the importance of slavery and of Black people for the state's history, they have generally put Whites' experiences in the foreground. Focusing on Gabriel's Virginia – rather than on the roles of Black people and the meanings of slavery in Jeffersonian Virginia – brings new questions to the fore and broadens perspectives on old questions.[4] It entails struggling to come to grips with the divergent meanings of Revolutionary Virginia's history for those who lived in it and for those who have been influenced by it during the ensuing two centuries.

Three potentially ambiguous terms are central to my attempt to make sense of Gabriel's Virginia – community, corporate identity, and cultural appropriation. I use community and identity to denote the ways that people perceived

---

[4] I am not the first to foreground Black experiences in writing of early Virginia. See, for example, Mullin, *Flight and Rebellion*, and Sobel, *The World They Made Together*. Sobel's is an especially powerful attempt to recover the interior worlds of enslaved Virginians with the subtlety and scope that have characterized studies of White Virginians. Compare it with Kulikoff's important *Tobacco and Slaves*, which includes an insightful discussion of the demographic basis of the cultures of Blacks in the Chesapeake but which foregrounds the study of Whites. Also compare the main text of Rhys Isaac, *The Transformation of Virginia, 1740–1790* (Chapel Hill, 1982), which focuses on the worlds of White Virginians, to the brilliant "Discourse on Method" with which Isaac closes the book, a thirty-page essay in which Black experiences and perceptions take center stage. Isaac's is one of the most important explorations of the mental worlds of eighteenth-century Black Virginians in the historical literature.

themselves to belong to various social groups. An important ambiguity is inherent in these concepts: while group identity and community are, on one level, about drawing boundaries to delineate who is and is not a part of the group, most people simultaneously consider themselves part of several groups. Thus a single person can consider him or herself to be a part of two seemingly contradictory communities at the same time.

My approach can best be demonstrated by discussing the various senses of community and identity that influenced a set of events that I discuss in Chapter 5. During the 1790s a free Black woman named Angela Barnett and a free Black man named William Anthony began to build a family. Their family included at least five children – four daughters and a son. Late one evening, two white men broke into their house and found a runaway slave whom Barnett and Anthony were hiding. The next night, the same slave-catchers again broke into the house, and Barnett responded to this aggression by hitting one of them with an adze and killing him. She was convicted of murder, sentenced to be hanged, and locked in jail to await execution. While there she was impregnated by Jacob Valentine, a White man thrown in jail for debt, and she received a stay of execution to spare the life of the fetus. During that stay, a group of prominent White Richmonders petitioned the governor for a pardon, which was granted, and Barnett was set free. She died in Henrico County in 1810.

The only documents with which Barnett's life can be constructed are court records, so her sense of identity must be inferred from her behavior. She likely conceived herself to be part of a community of free Black Richmonders, a group that defined itself in part through the exclusion of unfree people. But her membership in that group did not stop her from sheltering runaway slaves, suggesting that she also considered herself a part of the Richmond Black community, most of whose members were enslaved. And her relationship with Jacob Valentine, while perhaps purely a matter of desperation, might also indicate a feeling of identity that crossed racial lines between these two poor residents of Richmond's waterfront. Valentine was later arrested for attempting to foment an insurrection among slaves in the city, a fact that enhances the possibility that their relationship involved issues more complicated than lust and desperation.

Had Barnett left an extensive diary, then perhaps these sometimes contradictory identities could be untangled, and one could rank the communities with which she felt a sense of belonging. Such is not, however, the case. Instead, a wide range of behavior by various White and Black people in the Richmond area has survived and can be analyzed. Not surprisingly, "race" proves to be the most consistently powerful determinant of group identity, but showing that obvious point is not the major goal of this book. Rather, I try to show the way various theoretically contradictory identities – called within the text "crosscutting identities" – were played out in eighteenth-century Virginia. The third term – cultural appropriation – is less familiar. Richmond-area Blacks built an oppositional culture through a process of cultural appropriation. Appropriation, as I use it, is not, however, a mimetic act in which enslaved appropriators copied the European (or "White," or "Western") culture of their masters. Cultures are clusters of ideas about how people should relate to one another, to nature, and to the supernatural. It can be useful to break cultures into their component parts – to study beliefs about kinship, for example – and to trace their provenance (Africa, Europe, or America), their function (subversive or stabilizing), and the degree to which they change over time and space. But these component belief systems (sometimes called institutions) do not have stable meanings independent of one another. They become a culture precisely through their integration into a way of understanding the world that appears, at least to those who hold it, coherent. Cultural appropriation occurs when one group is inspired to make use of the ideas and practices of another but perceives those practices and ideas to have a relation to other cultural values that differs from that of the originating group.

Such cultural borrowing takes place whenever different groups come into contact, often in trivial ways, and it is almost inevitably a reciprocal process in which both (or all) groups borrow from each other. The Black and White cultures of Revolutionary Virginia were built in part out of such exchanges. Cultural appropriation takes on heightened importance, however, when the borrowing group more actively and creatively alters the relation of the borrowed beliefs to fundamental values. As Edmund Morgan showed more than twenty years ago, in late-eighteenth-century Virginia, slavery and racism constituted core political values, and the meanings of other core beliefs – republicanism, equality, manhood, independence – took much of their meaning through their relationship to slavery and racial degradation. Thus, when enslaved Virginians appropriated traditional "Virginian" emblems of social and political authority, emblems that had intertwined roots stretching back to Europe and Africa, and used them to formulate attacks on slavery, they fundamentally changed the meanings associated with that which they appropriated. In doing so they did not copy an existing culture; they began to build a new one.[5]

---

[5] Edmund S. Morgan, *American Slavery, American Freedom: The Ordeal of Colonial Virginia* (New York, 1974). Two analogies might clarify the argument. Slave narratives clearly appropriate the narrative structure of conversion narratives but by altering the primary

This book is divided into four parts. The analysis begins with a prologue that traces the emergence of racial identity in eighteenth-century Virginia. The "Prologue" recasts accepted visions of the history of eighteenth-century Virginians by viewing creolization through the lens of the emergence of different stages in the development of collective consciousness among people of African descent. It enlarges on Gerald Mullin's discussion of slave-quarter-based local communities and then analyzes the disparate forces – demographic and political, local and international – that pushed Black Virginians to broaden their sense of identity, first geographically and then ideologically. Following the demographic shift from the Tidewater to the Piedmont, the influence of the American and Haitian Revolutions, and the effects of successive waves of evangelical fervor, Black Virginians displayed increasingly complicated collective identities – at once local (Virginian) and Atlantic (racial).

The three chapters that constitute Part I move away from a broad provincial analysis to a finer-grained representation of the cultural processes revealed in the course of Gabriel's Conspiracy. That conspiracy began during the spring and summer of 1800, when a group of slaves living in and around Richmond began to conspire to fight for their freedom. By early August, Gabriel, a blacksmith who belonged to Thomas Henry Prosser and lived about six miles outside Richmond, emerged as the leader of the plot. He planned for his followers to meet, divide into three columns, and enter Richmond after midnight on a Saturday. The first column would slip through the streets while the residents slept and set fire to warehouses in the southeastern end of town. When White townsmen, awakened by the firebell, rushed to fight the fire, the other two columns would enter Richmond's west end. One would seize the guns in the state armory, while the other would occupy the executive mansion and take Governor James Monroe hostage. The newly armed rebels would slaughter the exhausted White townsmen who returned from fighting the fire, fortify the town, and demand the abolition of slavery.[6]

goal toward which the subject of the text moves (secular instead of, or in addition to, spiritual deliverance), authors of slave narratives created a new genre. Similarly, jazz musicians constantly appropriate musical phrases, but it makes no sense to suggest that a Sonny Rollins solo that incorporates passages from sources as diverse as European classical music and advertising jingles is a "copy" of anything.

[6] Standard modern accounts of Gabriel's Conspiracy are Mullin, *Flight and Rebellion*, ch. 5; Douglas R. Egerton, *Gabriel's Rebellion: The Virginia Slave Conspiracies of 1800 and 1802* (Chapel Hill, 1993). An extensive but incomplete collection of source material is in H. W. Flournoy, ed., *Calendar of Virginia State Papers and other Manuscripts from January 1, 1799, to December 31, 1807; Preserved in the Capitol at Richmond* (hereafter *CVSP*), (Richmond, 1890), v. 9, pp. 140–74.

Gabriel and his chief lieutenants – his brother Solomon, a blacksmith named Thornton, Jack Ditcher, Ben Woolfolk, George Smith, and Sam Byrd – traveled around Richmond and the surrounding counties recruiting slaves to join their conspiracy. They sought potential rebels at numerous Baptist religious meetings, a slave's funeral, barbecues, and fish fries. The conspiracy centered in Henrico County and stretched north into Hanover and Caroline Counties. It may also have extended west into Powhatan and Goochland Counties and south into Chesterfield County and the town of Petersburg. Monroe believed there was "good cause to believe that the knowledge" of the conspiracy "pervaded other parts, if not the whole, of the State."[7] There is no way to know how many men joined the conspiracy or how many would have taken part had the insurrection occurred.

As the day appointed for the insurrection drew near, rumors of the slaves' plan began to reach White ears, but when August 30 dawned, White authorities had done nothing to protect the town from insurrection. Toward the end of that Saturday morning Pharoah and Tom, two slaves of the Sheppard family of Henrico County, slipped into the counting room of Mosby Sheppard and told him that the slaves planned to take Richmond that evening. He dashed off a frantic note warning Governor Monroe, who scrambled to mobilize a militia force to patrol the neighborhood surrounding Prosser's plantation. As evening fell, the skies unleashed a violent rainstorm, and rising water rendered impassable a bridge that the slaves would have had to cross to enter Richmond. Gabriel sent out word that the insurrection would occur on Sunday evening instead, but the militia patrolled all day Sunday, and the slaves did not gather that evening either.

By Monday morning Monroe decided that the scare was more rumor than reality and sent the patrols home. But William Mosby, one of the patrollers, received a warning from one of his enslaved women when he got home. He relayed her warning to Monroe, who decided the conspiracy was real and sent magistrates to visit the plantation where Gabriel lived. The magistrates did not find Gabriel, but they began interrogating a young man named Ben ("Prosser's Ben" in the records) – probably an apprentice in Gabriel's blacksmith shop and privy to much of the plan – and the conspiracy unraveled. Authorities mobilized the militia from Richmond City and surrounding counties, set up military processions throughout the capital, and rounded up suspects. On Thursday, September 11, almost two weeks after the insurrection

[7] James Monroe to The Speakers of the General Assembly, December 5, 1800, Virginia Executive Papers, Governor's Letter Book, 1800–1803 (hereafter ELB), Library of Virginia, Richmond.

had been scheduled to occur, Henrico County magistrates first met to try slaves for conspiracy and insurrection. During the next two months, area courts tried approximately seventy men and convicted forty-four. Twenty-six or twenty-seven men were hanged in public executions; others were either pardoned by the governor and his council, or their sentences were commuted to transportation outside of the United States.

Gabriel escaped the first sweep for alleged conspirators and remained at large for over a month. He spent the first week hiding in the Richmond area, and he may have retained hope that he could rally his followers for an insurrection. He finally gave up, however, and tried to escape on a sloop traveling from Richmond to Norfolk. In one of the cruel ironies of the conspiracy, the White captain of the boat appears to have helped Gabriel, but two enslaved shiphands turned the famous Gabriel in to Norfolk magistrates. He was transported back to Richmond, tried, and hanged on Friday, October 10. The conspiracy scare began winding down, and old patterns of life in Richmond began to reassert themselves.

Chapter 2 of this book uses the evidence produced by the trials of alleged conspirators to uncover the creative appropriations through which Gabriel and his followers transformed Virginia's culture, a creole culture that had developed out of African and European roots as refracted through American experiences. They seized culturally sanctioned symbols of authority and reconfigured their meanings, making them tools in a struggle against slavery rather than bulwarks of White privilege. Gabriel and his followers had been born and raised in Virginia, and their conspiracy was deeply embedded in Virginia's culture even as it attempted to overthrow the state's social system. Chapter 3 examines the important but sometimes neglected role of informers in the conspiracy in order to explore the tensions between communalism and individuality and between resistance and accommodation in Gabriel's Virginia. Chapter 4 outlines the White repression of Gabriel's challenge, first recounting the theater of power through which Governor James Monroe sought to overawe potentially rebellious slaves and reassure uncertain Whites. It then analyzes the way White Virginians fit the story of the conspiracy into their narratives of the state's history. The chapter closes with an examination of traces of the alternative picture of Virginia's history – and especially of the projected end of Virginia's history – into which Black Virginians fit their stories of Gabriel.

Part II steps back from the conspiracy to look at the social structures that characterized early Richmond and helped to create the context within which the culture of resistance took its meanings. Here the book addresses many, though not all, of the standard questions posed by social historians studying early American towns. Chapter 5 examines the growth of early Richmond from a small Piedmont tobacco town into the political and manufacturing center of the new state. The chapter argues that, during the first decade after the state legislature moved the government from Williamsburg to Richmond, the town grew and developed into a place with patterns of social and race relations that were qualitatively different – by virtue of being urban – from those that had long prevailed in rural Virginia. These new patterns of urban social relations offered Virginians of African descent more chances to pursue individual autonomy and advancement than Blacks had experienced in Virginia since the third quarter of the seventeenth century. Elite Virginians periodically expressed unease over the social and cultural space that Black people and working White people carved out along the wharves and the warehouses of Richmond's riverfront.

Elites did not, however, engage in sustained attempts to close down the social and cultural openings created within the growing town, because those spaces emerged out of the economic processes through which elite Richmonders enriched themselves. Chapter 6 examines the work that Black and White people did in the early town. It begins by examining the business of slave hiring to uncover the dynamic economic adaptations through which White Richmonders shaped slavery to fit their needs. The chapter then turns to more important questions about the ways that free and enslaved Black people influenced the evolving institution of urban slavery, and it untangles some of the knotted evidence regarding on-the-job relations between enslaved people and the free people beside whom they frequently worked. Chapter 7 continues, through a careful analysis of the meanings of gender in early Richmond, to trace constructions of the urban norms that governed daily life. It reveals the emptiness of elite Whites' suggestions that Black Virginians failed to make significant gender-based distinctions, by showing the various meanings that Richmonders of different socioeconomic standing came to associate with masculinity and femininity. Different overlapping groups – Black and White, enslaved and free, wealthy and poor – built sometimes contrasting notions of "acceptable" behavior for women and of the "proper" relations between men and women. Part II taken whole represents a complicated urban world in which people of different racial background and people of different status interacted with one another in inconsistent and sometimes surprising ways. In so doing, it provides an important perspective on the crosscutting identities that played such a vital role in Gabriel's Conspiracy.

The "Epilogue" moves away from Richmond in 1800 to ask how people, especially African Americans, made sense of Gabriel's world in the ensuing years. It argues that remembering Gabriel offered an alternate focus for Black

Virginians', and later for broader groups of Black Americans', history of Virginia during the age of the American Revolution. Enslaved Virginians structured their memories of Gabriel into songs and stories, imperfect traces of which have survived into the present. Those songs and the more formal journalistic and literary texts that used them as sources kept the memory of Gabriel's struggle alive and embedded the changing story of that struggle in a prophetic narrative of redemption and racial justice. Understanding the meanings of Gabriel's world and of the conspiracy that provides a window on that world involves tracing the ways that Black Virginians negotiated their way through life in a slave society and the ways that they understood and chose among the strategies open to them, but it also involves tracing the changing meanings of their struggle for people fighting for racial equality and justice into the twentieth century. Only by paying attention to both of these distinct issues can we begin to see the limitations of our understanding of Jeffersonian Virginia and begin to recognize that comprehending Virginia in the age of the American Revolution requires paying as much attention to Gabriel's Virginia as to that of Jefferson.

PROLOGUE

From Blacks in Virginia to Black Virginians

P EOPLE OF AFRICAN DESCENT lived, worked, and struggled in Virginia throughout most of the seventeenth century, but prior to the 1680s they never constituted a very large percentage of the population or of the colony's laboring people. In the decades following 1680 wealthy White Virginians began to turn increasingly toward Africa and Africans to fill their labor needs, rapidly transforming Virginia into a slave society. The people whose forced migration and labor fueled colonial Virginia's development came from a variety of settings, including various African backgrounds and Britain's Caribbean slave societies. Most were bought by White Virginians and set to work growing tobacco on farms and plantations. Though enslaved people of African descent may appear in retrospect to have shared a racial identity, in fact they were separated by linguistic, religious, and other cultural differences as deeply rooted in their experience as were national differences in Europeans' experience. During the first half of the eighteenth century, enslaved Virginians drew on what they brought from their African pasts and what they confronted in their American present to build close-knit, plantation-based local communities. A series of disruptions, including White Virginians' decisions to expand settlement into Virginia's Piedmont, the American Revolution, and the evangelical revivals of the second half of the century, created conditions that encouraged enslaved Virginians to broaden their definitions of community – both geographically and ideologically – to include an ever expanding percentage of Black Virginians. This incipient racial identity was bolstered during the 1790s by the Haitian Revolution, which offered Black Virginians both a nonracial model of revolution and natural equality and a reason to begin conceiving of themselves as participants in a history of African peoples that transcended Virginia and each person's particular genealogical homeland. Through the confluence of these forces and through Black Virginians' powerful sense of their difference from the enslaved refugees from Saint Domingue whom they met during the 1790s, Virginians of African descent began to develop the crosscutting sense of racial, religious, and provincial identity that lay at the base of the rich and contradictory oppositional cultures that animated their struggles for equality.

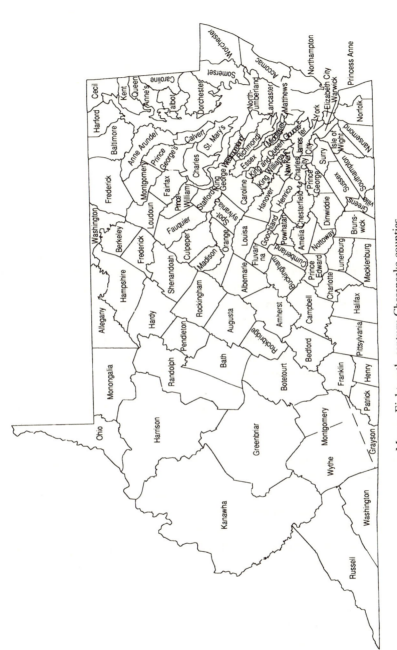

Map 1. Eighteenth-century Chesapeake counties.

1

The emergence of racial consciousness in eighteenth-century Virginia

In 1756 an eleven-year-old Igbo boy was kidnapped from the interior of present-day Nigeria, transported to the coast, and sold into the Atlantic slave trade. After the harrowing Middle Passage, he was offered for sale in Barbados, but sugar planters apparently found him too small to suit their purposes. The slavers packed him back into the ship, fattened him up a bit while sailing to Virginia, and sold him to a tobacco planter. In Virginia, Olaudah Equiano encountered a strange world. He witnessed an enslaved cook wearing an iron muzzle to prevent her from eating the food she prepared for her master. He was ordered to fan his indolent sleeping master, and he feared that a ticking clock was a machine to report to "the gentleman any thing . . . [Equiano] might do amiss." And he saw a portrait that he suspected was something the Whites did "to keep their great men when they died." While he attempted to adjust to this incomprehensible world, his master assigned him a Western name: Jacob.[1]

Equiano found himself in a "forlorn, and much dejected state" in Virginia, for he had been separated from anyone with whom he could speak. He was relieved, at least in retrospect, to be removed from this lonely land by a ship captain named Michael Henry Pascal, who bought the young slave and took him to sea. Pascal, like every other White who had claimed ownership of Equiano, assumed the right to name his chattel and told Equiano that he would henceforth be called Gustavus Vassa. The young man, perhaps beginning to

[1] Olaudah Equiano, *The Interesting Narrative of the Life of Olaudah Equiano, or Gustavus Vassa, The African*, in Henry Louis Gates Jr., ed., *The Classic Slave Narratives* (New York, 1987 [1789]), 39. Gates, *The Signifying Monkey: A Theory of African-American Literary Criticism* (New York, 1988), 154–6 analyzes Equiano's double-voiced narration of this incident, a narrative technique that gives expression to both the naive perceptions of the child and the sophisticated understanding of the older man. David Barry Gaspar, *Bondmen and Rebels: A Study of Master–Slave Relations in Antigua With Implications for Colonial British America* (Baltimore, 1985), 131–2 discusses this incident when analyzing naming.

overcome the disorientation caused by the horrors he had witnessed and the fears he had experienced, refused the new name. However, he fought a battle different from what one might expect. He did not insist that Pascal call him Olaudah Equiano, or even Michael, the first Western name the slavers had assigned; instead, he told the captain "as well as [he] could, that [he] would be called Jacob," and only after "many a cuff" was he forced to submit and accept the name by which he was known to Whites for the rest of his life.[2]

Equiano's text does not comment on the oddity of his attempt to preserve his Virginia name. His temporary preference for "Jacob" does not represent a serious rejection of his African name or past, for he pointedly titled the autobiography he wrote three decades later "The Life of Olaudah Equiano or Gustavus Vassa, the African"; many of the meanings of his act of self-assertion are unrecoverable. The lost meanings and ambiguities of Equiano's early struggle over his name, however, contain a powerful emblem of the uncertainty inherent in attempts to comprehend the cultural change and adaptation that occurred when Africans and Europeans interacted in early Virginia. And his later decision to reclaim his unadorned Igbo name, while adding the modifying "the African" to his Western name, suggests an incipient diasporic racial identity.[3]

Countless individuals from African and British localities came into contact with and adjusted to one another within the brutal power relations of slavery. Thousands of these meetings had occurred by the time Equiano arrived in Virginia. The peculiarities of each encounter cannot be re-created, but the patterns through which the Black and White cultures of Virginia evolved can be approached with more certainty. For it was out of encounters in specific times and places like Equiano's that enslaved Virginians came to define the boundaries of their communities and their collective identities. Neither the boundaries nor the identities were static: both changed in response to the interaction between local New World conditions and cultural inheritance.

This chapter explores the ways that Africans and people of African descent responded to the conditions they found and created in eighteenth-century Virginia to develop a new sense of corporate identity. It begins with an exploration of the experiences of the first groups of Africans brought in

---

[2] Gates, *Classic Slave Narratives*, 40.
[3] Lorena S. Walsh, "A 'Place in Time' Regained: A Fuller History of Colonial Chesapeake Slavery Through Group Biography," in Larry E. Hudson, ed., *Working Toward Freedom: Slave Society and Domestic Economy in the American South* (Rochester, New York, 1994), 1–32 (esp. p. 14). Compare Marvin L. Michael Kay and Lorin Lee Cary, *Slavery in North Carolina, 1748–1775* (Chapel Hill, 1996), ch. 6.

large numbers to Virginia and of the ways they forged plantation-based communities. Interpreting the new world into which they were sold in light of the values they brought from their old world, enslaved Africans built relationships and identities that revolved around the plantations where they lived, worked, struggled, and began to build new families. This chapter traces the ways these local communities expanded geographically and demographically during the westward shift of Virginia's slave population. The chapter then turns to the American and Haitian revolutions and to the large-scale conversion of slaves to Christianity, all of which accelerated and changed the terms of the geographic expansion of enslaved Virginians' communities. Together they created increasingly powerful reasons for Black people in Virginia to think of themselves first as Black Christian Virginians and then as people sharing a racial identity with Black people of diverse African origins throughout plantation America.[4] The tensions inherent in these developments are elaborated through an analysis of the impact of the Haitian Revolution upon Black Virginians during the 1790s. Between 1680 and 1810 Blacks in Virginia became African Americans. They developed the crosscutting identities that comprise much of the feeling of twoness that W. E. B. DuBois later argued lay at the heart of African American identity.

Plantation-based communities

People of African descent were among the earliest settlers of colonial Virginia, but for most of the seventeenth century White indentured servants dominated Virginia's labor force. Blacks brought to Virginia before 1680 generally worked beside English indentured servants in tobacco fields, and some Blacks discovered possibilities for social advancement that disappeared when slavery became the colony's central source of labor.[5] Though some individual Africans who arrived in Virginia during the seventeenth century sought to

---

[4] Sylvia R. Frey, *Water from the Rock: Black Resistance in a Revolutionary Age* (Princeton, 1991), chs. 1, 2, 7, 9 and throughout for overview of this throughout the southern United States.

[5] T. H. Breen, *Puritans and Adventurers: Change and Persistence in Early America* (New York, 1980) 127–48; T. H. Breen and Stephen Innes, *"Myne Owne Ground": Race and Freedom on Virginia's Eastern Shore* (New York, 1990); and J. Douglas Deal, *Race and Class in Colonial Virginia: Indians, Englishmen, and Africans on the Eastern Shore during the Seventeenth Century* (New York, 1993). For race relations in slave-owning and slave societies see Philip D. Morgan, "British Encounters with Africans and African-Americans, circa 1600–1780," in Bernard Bailyn and Philip D. Morgan, eds. *Strangers in the Realm: Cultural Margins of the First British Empire* (Chapel Hill, 1992), 157–219.

re-create (or at least commemorate) their African past – free Black planter John Johnson, for example, named his forty-four-acre farm "Angola" in 1677[6] – demographics militated against Black Virginians' creating a distinct culture. Only when wealthy White Virginians turned toward slavery as a labor system and toward Africa as their primary source of labor did Black Virginians begin to live in concentrations high enough to develop and perpetuate a creole culture.[7]

Between 1680 and 1720 wealthy Virginians turned from indentured servitude to slavery in response to economic incentives. For reasons whose causes lay outside of Virginia, the prices planters had to pay for English indentured servants rose relative to the prices they had to pay for African slaves.[8] Increasing numbers of tobacco planters responded by investing in slave labor, and the racial composition of the colony changed rapidly. Between 1687 and 1699 the percentage of Middlesex County's population composed of Black people grew from 8 to 22 percent, and slaves overtook servants in the county's bound labor force. By 1750 people of African descent comprised more than 40 percent of the residents of Middlesex County. Other counties in Virginia's Tidewater region followed similar demographic patterns, and by 1755 Black people comprised majorities of a large swath of counties from the Chesapeake west to the Blue Ridge Mountains.[9]

Those whom White Virginians labeled "Negro" did not, however, come from the same place, nor did they speak the same language or share the same

[6] Breen and Innes, *"Myne Owne Ground,"* 17. Ira Berlin places the experiences of these Virginia "Atlantic Creoles" in broad perspective in "From Creole to African: Atlantic Creoles and the Origins of African American Society in Mainland North America," *The William and Mary Quarterly* [hereafter *WMQ*] 3d Ser., 53 (1996): 251–88 (276–79 for Chesapeake).

[7] Edmund S. Morgan, *American Slavery, American Freedom: The Ordeal of Colonial Virginia* (New York, 1975); Russell R. Menard, "From Servants to Slaves: The Transformation of the Chesapeake Labor System," *Southern Studies* 16 (1977): 355–90; Darrett B. Rutman and Anita H. Rutman, *A Place in Time, 1650–1750* (New York, 1984), ch. 6; Allan Kulikoff, *Tobacco and Slaves: The Development of Southern Cultures in the Chesapeake, 1680–1800* (Chapel Hill, 1986), chs. 8 and 9; Mechal Sobel, *The World They Made Together: Black and White Values in Eighteenth-Century Virginia* (Princeton, 1987), 3–11.

[8] Menard, "From Servants to Slaves"; David Galenson, "White Servitude and the Growth of Black Slavery in Colonial America," *Journal of Economic History* 41 (1981): 39–49; and "The Rise and Fall of Indentured Servitude in the Americas: An Economic Analysis," *Journal of Economic History* 44 (1984): 1–26.

[9] Rutman and Rutman, *Place in Time*, 166; Rutman and Rutman, *A Place in Time: Explicatus* (New York, 1984), 30; Kulikoff, *Tobacco and Slaves*, ch. 8; Richard S. Dunn, "Black Society in the Chesapeake, 1776–1810," in Ira Berlin and Ronald Hoffman, eds., *Slavery and Freedom in the Age of the American Revolution* (Charlottesville, 1983), 54–9.

religion. Accepting the racial designations assigned by White Virginians implicitly presupposes an at least latent racial identity on the part of Virginians of African descent, an identity that did not exist at the beginning of the
eighteenth century. Most of the Black men and women who increasingly
dominated the colony's labor force were transported to Virginia along one of
two distinct trade routes, each of which included representatives of an indeterminate number of African ethnic groups. A substantial majority – about
80 percent according to Herbert Klein's calculations – arrived on slavers that
sailed from the west coast of Africa to Virginia.[10] Though White Virginians
displayed little sensitivity to African ethnicity, the best estimates are that a
large plurality of the Africans brought directly to Virginia, perhaps approaching 40 percent, left from trading stations along the Bight of Biafra. Many
of these people, probably most, would, like Olaudah Equiano, have been
Igbos, but there were also Ibibio, Igala, and other neighboring peoples. And
Igbo society itself was, during this era, "strikingly variegated" in language,
social institutions, and religion. In addition, significant numbers of Africans
from Senegambia, the Angola region, and the Gold Coast were transported
to Virginia.[11]

  Perhaps a fifth of those sold into slavery in Virginia did not travel directly
from Africa to the American mainland. They were brought into Virginia
from slave societies in the Caribbean. No doubt many traveled a path similar to Equiano's, undergoing the Middle Passage to the islands, only to be
packed back into the slave ship and taken on to Virginia. Others lived and
worked in the islands before being sold to White Virginians. Regardless of the
path traveled, the people sold into Virginia through this inter-American trade
probably represented a variety of African ethnic groups as well as people born
in the Americas. None of these peoples can be presumed to have had a natural

---

[10] Herbert S. Klein, *The Middle Passage: Comparative Studies in the Atlantic Slave Trade*
(Princeton, 1978), 125–8.

[11] James A. Rawley, *The Transatlantic Slave Trade: A History* (New York, 1981), 335; Philip
D. Curtin, *The Atlantic Slave Trade: A Census* (Madison, 1969), 156–7, 188, 228; A. E.
Afigbo, *Ropes of Sand: Studies in Igbo History and Culture* (Ibadan, Nigeria, 1981), ch. 4
(p. 123 for "strikingly variegated"; Afigbo notes, however, that there was "striking uni-
formity" in the primacy of the village and in the religious and political *structures* in each
village); David Northrup, *Trade Without Rulers: Pre-Colonial Economic Development in
South-Eastern Nigeria* (Oxford, England, 1978), 58–62; Walsh, " 'Place in Time' Regained,"
14–15. Michael Mullin, *Africa in America: Slave Acculturation in the American South and
the British Caribbean, 1736–1831* (Urbana, 1992), ch. 1. If these rough numbers are accurate, then about 30 percent (38% of 80%) of those sold into Virginia were exported from
Africa through the Bight of Biafra.

predisposition to perceive other enslaved Virginians as members of a common race any more than would Russians and Englishmen of the same period.[12] The surviving evidence allows scarcely a glimpse into newly enslaved people's experiences after arriving in Virginia. Scholars have attempted to overcome this lack through imaginative approaches to masters' advertisements for runaway slaves, through painstaking demographic analyses of the opportunities for family and community formation among enslaved people, through careful counting of names in inventories and bills of sale, through discussions of linguistic change, and through the ethnographic reconstruction of the worldviews that residents of early Virginia must have brought to their new world.[13] Some who purchased slaves in Virginia, unlike masters in most other British slave societies, intended from the beginning that their human property perpetuate itself through natural reproduction.[14] Nonetheless, newly arrived Africans had few children, and it was not until several decades into the eighteenth century that large numbers of enslaved Virginians were able to build stable families. Once Virginia-born (or creole) people came to dominate the colony's Black population – between 1730 and 1740 for much of the Tidewater – slaves began having larger families, and Blacks in Virginia began to build stable creole communities.[15]

[12] Klein, *Middle Passage*, 125–8; Kulikoff, *Tobacco and Slaves*, 319–23. Sterling Stuckey, *Slave Culture: Nationalist Theory and the Foundations of Black America* (New York, 1987), ch. 1, roots pan-African nationalism in slaves' experiences, arguing that the key lies in "African 'tribalism,'" the memory of which "enabled them to go back to the sense of community in the traditional African setting and to include all Africans in their common experience" (p. 3). I agree with Stuckey that racial consciousness is an outgrowth of the slaves' experience but emphasize the historical experiences of people of different African heritages in their new world as much as memories of their old.

[13] Gerald W. Mullin, *Flight and Rebellion: Slave Resistance in Eighteenth-Century Virginia* (New York, 1972), ch. 2; Kulikoff, *Tobacco and Slaves*, chs. 8 and 9; Mullin, *Africa in America*, Part 1; and Sobel, *World They Made Together*; Rutman and Rutman, *Place in Time: Explicatus*, ch. 12; and Walsh, "'Place in Time' Regained" are the most important attempts to overcome the scarcity of evidence. What follows draws on them in ways that go beyond the specific citations.

[14] William Byrd I to Sadler & Thomas, February 10, 1686; Marion Tinling, ed., *The Correspondence of The Three William Byrds of Westover, Virginia, 1684–1776* (Charlottesville, 1977), 50 (Byrd asked for "4 Negro's, 2 men 2 women not to exceed 25 years old & to bee likeley."); William Fitzhugh to Ralph Wormely, July 14, 1681; Richard Beale Davis, ed., *William Fitzhugh and His Chesapeake World* (Chapel Hill, 1963), 104 (Fitzhugh asked Wormely to buy "five or six, whereof three or four to be boys, a man & woman or men & women). Also see Thomas Starke to James Westomore, November 1702, in Elizabeth Donnan, ed., *Documents Illustrative of the Slave Trade to America* 4 vols. (New York, 1932–5), v. 4, pp. 71–2.

[15] Kulikoff, *Tobacco and Slaves*, chs. 8 and 9; Berlin, "From Creole to African."

These communities grew within a legal context that assumed all Black people to be slaves. Early-seventeenth-century Virginia laws did not reify racial difference into an automatic marker of servitude, but as the gentry turned to slavery during the last decades of the century, the House of Burgesses passed explicitly racist laws that legally stigmatized all people of recognizably African heritage.[16] Slaves can be presumed to have recognized that, at least in their masters' eyes, they shared some kind of kinship with other African peoples in Virginia. But the abstract and imposed quality of racial similarity held less sway than the concrete ties of kinship and friendship that enslaved people created in Virginia's quarters.

Little is known about the experiences of these early victims of slavery in Virginia. Africans sold into early-eighteenth-century Virginia were generally purchased in small groups (two, three, or four slaves) and marched to a new plantation home – a final journey that took a day or two and often included slaves purchased by several masters who lived in a single neighborhood. After arriving at their masters' quarters, these people were put to work in tobacco fields and expected to begin learning to speak English.[17] At that point they disappear from the record except as property on tax lists, unless they ran away, used violence against a White person, were caught stealing, or became subject to White observation for some other unusual reason. A key transition in the development of plantation communities occurred when the growing number of Virginia-born slaves began to balance sex ratios in the quarters. As the number of enslaved women caught up with the number of men, a larger percentage of adults could form permanent unions, and increasing numbers of Blacks became incorporated into local kinship networks. Once enslaved people could form lasting unions, have children, and develop kinship networks, slave communities could take shape, and cultures with American as well as African roots began to grow.

Historians have shown that prior to the second third of the century many enslaved Virginians lived in neighborhoods that lacked a reliable demographic base for strong Black communities.[18] And they agree that, over the course of

---

[16] Jane Purcell Guild, comp., *Black Laws of Virginia: A Summary of the Legislative Acts of Virginia Concerning Negroes from Earliest Times to the Present* (Richmond, 1936), 45–55, 94, 130–32, 151–5; Morgan, *American Slavery, American Freedom*, 329–37 is the best secondary account.

[17] Kulikoff, *Tobacco and Slaves*, 322–31; Mullin, *Flight and Rebellion*, 39–62; Walsh, " 'Place in Time' Regained."

[18] Allan Kulikoff, "The Origins of Afro-American Society in Tidewater Maryland and Virginia, 1700–1790," *WMQ* 3d. ser., 35 (1978): 226–58; Kulikoff, *Tobacco and Slaves*, ch. 8; Jean Butenhoff Lee, "The Problem of Slave Community in the Eighteenth-Century Chesapeake," *WMQ* 3d. ser., 43 (1986): 333–61.

the middle two quarters of the eighteenth century, increasing numbers of neighborhoods in Virginia became more heavily settled by slaves, creating conditions that favored the evolution of cohesive local identities among slaves. Such conditions appeared first in regions dominated by great planters, many of whose slaves lived together on home plantations. Slaves who lived on these large quarters and others who lived nearby and could visit the larger group in the limited free time masters "granted" them, first forged the plantation-based identities and local communities that grounded Virginia slave cultures prior to 1750.[19] This happened quite early in some localities as enslaved people, despite diverse origins, forged local cohesive cultures. Whites sometimes expressed fear of these cultures, but such expressions rarely shed light on the characteristics of those local cultures.[20]

The uncertain ethnic origins of Africans sold into Virginia further clouds the lens through which scholars can view the beliefs of Blacks in early-eighteenth-century Virginia.[21] A plurality of the enslaved people brought directly into Virginia through the African slave trade originated in the region bounded by the Niger and Cross river valleys, a region dominated by "stateless" people. Among the Igbo, for example, "sense of 'country' was very narrow . . . , so narrow that it could at times be limited to the village group." Slavers also sold people from Senegambia and the Angola region into Virginia, creating a multicultural mix too complicated to permit any but the most general extrapolation from "African" values to Afro-Virginian worldviews.[22]

When these African peoples came together on tobacco plantations, they melded diverse and sometimes conflicting traditions to develop mores that could govern their lives together. Despite deeply rooted differences, all came from village-oriented cultures in which kinship served as a primary link among

---

[19] Kulikoff, *Tobacco and Slaves*, 332; Rutman and Rutman, *Place in Time*, 164; Lee, "Problem of Slave Community," 356–61 for large holdings. John Randolph Barden, "'Flushed With Notions of Freedom': The Growth and Emancipation of a Virginia Slave Community, 1732–1812" (Ph.D. dissertation, Duke University, 1993), 215–16, n. 17 for neighborhood parties among enslaved Virginians by the middle of the eighteenth century.

[20] *Correspondence of the Three William Byrds*, 32, 487–8 for expressions of this fear by William Byrd I in 1685 and William Byrd II in 1736.

[21] John Thornton, *Africa and Africans in the Making of the Atlantic World, 1400–1680* (Cambridge, England, 1992), 187–92 argues African cultural diversity has been overstated, but the trade to Virginia was characterized by qualities that he argues were unusual in the whole African slave trade and increased the significance of diversity.

[22] Rawley, *Transatlantic Slave Trade*, 335; Curtin, *Atlantic Slave Trade*, 156–7, 188, 228; Robin Horton, "Stateless societies in the history of West Africa," in J. F. A. Ajayi and Michael Crowder, eds., *History of West Africa* (New York, 1972), v. 1, pp. 78–119; Afigbo, *Ropes of Sand*, 150 ("sense of country").

members of local societies. The construction of new kinship networks, new communal webs within which enslaved individuals could define a meaningful existence, constituted a first step in the formation of a creolized Afro-Virginian culture. Given the profound degree of cultural simplification that European settlers experienced upon coming to America, despite their incomparably larger control over their destinies, enslaved people in early Virginia must have had to adapt the beliefs they brought to America to make sense of what they endured in Virginia. Many probably expected to make such adjustments, since they came from societies with long-standing slaveholding traditions that offered integration into the dominant society in return for assimilation.[23] While White Virginians offered little incentive for such adaptation, ethnically heterogeneous slave communities must have required innovative melding of cultures. This creative adaptation of inherited cultural pasts to present Virginia experiences resulted in plantation-based identities.[24]

As various Africans settled into Virginia and struggled to make sense of their new homes, important parts of their original home cultures inevitably lacked utility, and atrophied. Thus, while Igbo slaves no doubt remembered the judicial, commercial, and military ways of Igboland, they had few opportunities to exercise them.[25] They did, however, have immediate opportunities to forge relationships with those among whom they were forced to live, and they appear to have done so by re-creating the kin-based lineages that had structured their lives in their former homes. These lineages constituted the social skeleton of their developing community-centered identities.[26]

---

[23] Onwuka Dike and Felicia Ekejiuba, *The Aro of South-eastern Nigeria: A Study of Socio-Economic Formation and Transformation in Nigeria* (Ibadan, Nigeria, 1990), 74–8.

[24] My approach to creolization relies upon T. H. Breen, "Creative Adaptations: Peoples and Cultures," in Jack P. Greene and J. R. Pole, eds., *Colonial British America: Essays in the New History of the Early Modern Era* (Baltimore, 1984), 204–5; Sidney Mintz and Richard Price, *The Birth of African-American Culture: An Anthropological Perspective* (Boston, 1992 [1976]), chs. 4, 5, and throughout; Jack P. Greene, *Pursuits of Happiness: The Social Development of Early Modern British Colonies and the Formation of American Culture* (Chapel Hill, 1988), 166–9.

[25] Equiano, *Classic Slave Narratives*, 11–28 for his memory of Igbo institutions. There were exceptions: when fifteen newly arrived Africans escaped to the mountains to establish a maroon settlement in 1729, they presumably used military and political traditions from their homeland(s), but in Virginia such occasions were rare. See Lt. Governor William Gooch to the Board of Trade, June 29, 1729, in Michael Mullin, ed., *American Negro Slavery: A Documentary History* (Columbia, S.C., 1976), 83.

[26] Afigbo, *Ropes of Sand*, ch. 4. For an unusually well-documented example of an early kinship network, see Dickson J. Preston, *Young Frederick Douglass: The Maryland Years* (Baltimore, 1980), esp. pp. 3–21, 205–7. Barden, "'Flushed With Notions of Freedom,'"

By 1724 Hugh Jones reported that Blacks in Virginia were "very prolifick among themselves," and less than a decade later a visitor traveling up the York River saw plantations that looked like "little villages" composed of "7 or 8 distinct Tenements." The Black residents were "allow[ed] . . . little Platts [plots] for potatoes or Indian pease," a sure sign that they had begun to struggle to increase their control over their own lives.[27] No evidence of the rules governing the ownership or exchange of the produce of the plots survives, but the slaves probably developed such rules in line with those that governed markets and production in their homelands. And though little evidence of these people's perceptions of the boundaries of their communities has survived, at least one member of the gentry had already begun to refer to "his families" of slaves and to conceive of them as grouped into different quarter communities. A visitor to nearby Maryland thought that masters allowed a good deal of liberty to slaves in their quarters and reported the persistence of African polygynous marital practices within these communities.[28]

Many early struggles in these emerging communities took place over the pace and nature of work. Conflicts over labor began when newly arriving Africans were ordered to the fields. Edward Kimber, upon visiting Maryland in 1745, saw newly arrived Africans insisting upon taking wheelbarrows by the wheel and hoes by the bottom, despite repeated demonstrations of the

69, n. 57 shows that "recent arrivals" from Africa declined rapidly from a high of 37.8 percent of Virginia's black population in 1719–29, to 10 percent in 1740–49, and less than 5 percent by 1750–9. Kay and Cary, *Slavery in North Carolina*, ch. 7 (esp. pp. 155–60).

[27] Jones quoted in Willie Lee Rose, ed., *A Documentary History of Slavery in North America* (New York, 1976), 37–8; William Hugh Grove Diary, Selections, 1732 (typescript), April 17, 1732, pp. 4, 8, Alderman Library, University of Virginia, Manuscripts Department, Charlottesville, Virginia (hereafter U.Va.). Grove noted that slaves received corn for subsistence, so garden plots supplemented necessities. See Mullin, *Africa in America*, ch. 6 for the importance of slave control over growing food, though he highlights the limited importance of Virginia garden plots relative to Caribbean provision grounds. See Ira Berlin and Philip D. Morgan, eds., *Cultivation and Culture: Labor and the Shaping of Slave Life in the Americas* (Charlottesville, 1993); and Hudson, *Working Toward Freedom* for case studies that reinforce the importance of "self-subsistence."

[28] Robert Carter to ?, March 3, 1721, in Louis B. Wright, ed., *Letters of Robert Carter, 1720–1727: The Commercial Interests of a Virginia Gentleman* (San Marino, Cal., 1940), 87. Carter discussed mortality "in my families" at Corotoman, and then in "all my families in Westmoreland and at the Falls." Also Carter to John Johnson, June 22, 1721, ibid., 105–6. "Eighteenth Century Maryland as Portrayed in the 'Itenerant Observations' of Edward Kimber," in *Maryland Historical Magazine* 51 (1956): 327. Barden, " 'Flushed With Notions of Freedom' " is the most complete reconstruction of a colonial Virginia slave community from arrival in Virginia through the eighteenth century.

proper way to use these tools. Men and women with more experience under plantation regimes often moved from individual to collective struggles to restrain masters' rates of exploitation, and slave communities were forged in battles over the rate of work.[29]

The prickly Landon Carter, always incensed that his slaves, neighbors, or family might be evading "obligations" to him, engaged in a constant struggle with his slave communities over their labor. On frequent inspections of his quarters he painstakingly counted rows of crops hoed, hills of tobacco or corn made, stacks of hay cut, and amounts of corn or tobacco harvested. He invariably discovered that "his" people were lazy, useless wretches who were failing to do their duty. He sought to overcome his slaves' communal efforts to control work by dividing up gangs that had coordinated their efforts, by collectively punishing unproductive gangs, and by devising ways to observe and measure the amount of work done.[30] Regardless of his success in extorting extra labor from his slaves – and he was convinced he had little – his efforts and frustrations reveal that slaves in Virginia engaged in a perpetual low-level battle to lessen their masters' demands upon their labor. And they often pursued these struggles collectively, countering masters' access to coercive power with a determination to resist this "industrial regimentation" together.[31] Such battles reinforced a developing collective identity.

The communal nature of this conflict extended even to running away – a form of resistance that might seem wholly individual. Thus Carter, like most masters, considered himself plagued by individuals who resented his oppression and ran from Sabine Hall. Rhys Isaac's masterful reconstruction of an incident in which an oxcarter named Simon ran away from Carter's home quarter uncovers the communal cooperation that made running to the woods (*petit marronage*) possible. In March 1766 Simon ran to the woods and, fed and concealed by members of his quarter community, remained at

---

[29] "'Itenerant Observations' of Edward Kimber," 328. See Ira Berlin and Philip D. Morgan, "Labor and the Shaping of Slave Life in the Americas," in Berlin and Morgan, *Cultivation and Culture*, 1–45; James C. Scott, *Weapons of the Weak: Everyday Forms of Peasant Resistance* (New Haven, 1985); and Scott, *Domination and the Arts of Resistance: Hidden Transcripts* (New Haven, 1990) for approaches to the way struggles over labor influence community formation.

[30] Jack P. Greene, ed., *The Diary of Colonel Landon Carter of Sabine Hall, 1752–1778* (Charlottesville, 1965), 138, 147, 357, 362, 369, 429, 534.

[31] Mullin, *Africa in America*, 88–94; Sobel, *World They Made Together*, ch. 5 for elite struggles to enforce slaves' efficiency. Robert William Fogel, *Without Consent or Contract: The Rise and Fall of American Slavery* (New York, 1989), ch. 1 for "industrial regimentation" in slavery. Also Barden, "'Flushed With Notions of Freedom,'" chs. 4, 5.

large for over a month. The kin and friends with whom he lived incurred
great risk to protect Simon from a vengeful master. Isaac's analysis also suggests the limits of racial solidarity in pre-Revolutionary Virginia, for the overwhelming support of the people with whom Simon lived did not mean that
all of Landon Carter's slaves aided the runaway. Simon got caught because
Carter could call on the aid of Talbot, Mangorike Will, and George, slaves
who lived on a different quarter from Simon's and proved willing to cooperate in his capture.[32] Simon was for them part of a different community and
thus someone whose conflict with the master created an opportunity to court
favor with Carter. Both Simon's ability to remain at large in and around
Sabine Hall and his eventual capture reveal the degree to which enslaved
Virginians' identities centered around their kin-based quarter communities.

Battles rooted in quarter identities could escalate to more open resistance
and collective violence when masters tried to win back concessions that a
slave community believed had been granted. New overseers were often focal
points of such conflicts, because they entered into areas of disputed terrain
without knowing the history of the community they were to supervise. A
newly appointed overseer trying to execute his employer's instructions sometimes found that his predecessor had allowed the slaves "to Impose on him
very much," and thus failed to keep "them to their duty." The slaves, having achieved a state in which they were "almost free," were unwilling to give
up their "privileges," and "fell on every plan they possibly could to get . . .
[the new overseer] turned off." This might involve choosing an older man
to run from the quarter to the master's home plantation to petition the "just"
patriarch for protection against the inhumane "outsider."[33]

A community aware that the master stood behind an attempt to revoke hard-
won customary rights could respond violently. During the five-day Christmas
break in 1769, Blacks belonging to the Hanover County plantation of Bowler
Cocke resisted the new steward hired to end the "indulgence" to which Cocke
thought the slaves had grown accustomed. When the steward's deputy rep-
rimanded an insolent slave, the victim struck back. The deputy steward began
to get the better of the fight, so other slaves came to the slave's assistance
and "beat the young man severely" before chasing him off the quarter. The

[32] Isaac, *Transformation of Virginia*, 328–44 (esp. pp. 335–6, 340–41).
[33] John Blair Jr. to Charles Dabney, April 1, 1769, in Mullin, ed., *American Negro Slavery*,
70–1 (also pp. 72–4). For later examples: Robert Carter to Trustees in behalf of the
Creditors of Robert Bladen Carter, Sept. 9, 1784; Robert Carter to Mr. George Howe,
Sept. 10, 1784; entry for November 15, 1784, Day Books and Letters, v. 6, pp. 31–4;
Councilor Robert Carter of Nomini Hall Papers (typescript), Perkins Library, Duke
University, manuscripts, Durham, N C. (hereafter Duke).

---

community then subjected the new steward (and a neighboring White man who foolishly intervened in this internal struggle) to the same humiliating torture that he no doubt had used to break their "insolent and unruly" spirit: they tied him up and whipped him until he was "raw from the neck to the waistband." Eventually the deputy steward returned with armed reinforcements, released the "unhappy sufferers," and forced the slaves into a barn. The quarter community refused to surrender. Armed with clubs and staves, the slaves rushed the armed force, almost killing two Whites, before guns triumphed over clubs and the community was suppressed.[34]

Enslaved Virginians' profoundly local, plantation-based identities were revealed again when the colony's last royal governor, Lord Dunmore, issued his famous proclamation of 1775 offering freedom to bound laborers owned by disloyal Virginians and willing to fight to maintain royal authority. Dunmore's proclamation precipitated many important events, some of which will be dealt with later,[35] and it opens a window on the communal values of Black Virginians at the time of the Revolution. Many of the slaves who ran to Dunmore or to the British privateers who cruised the Chesapeake Bay after Dunmore was expelled from Virginia were individual men or small groups of men. Blacks who lived near the bay on Virginia's great rivers, however, had opportunities that would not reappear until the Civil War to run away not as individuals or small groups but as whole communities.[36]

Robert Carter of Nomini Hall recognized the potential appeal such an opportunity might have to the people who lived at his Coles Point quarter, which looked out upon the Potomac and was several miles away from Nomini Hall. In 1776 Carter visited the quarter and told the community of Dunmore's offer, warning that any who joined the British fleet might find themselves sold to "white people living in the West [Indian] Islands." When the people of Coles Point expressed their unwillingness to enter into Lord Dunmore's

[34] Mullin, *American Negro Slavery*, 94–5. The account originates in the *Virginia Gazette*, January 25, 1770. It may contain inaccuracies, but there is no reason that Whites would have invented the quarter-based nature of the event.

[35] Benjamin Quarles, *The Negro in the American Revolution* (Chapel Hill, 1961), 19–32; Mullin, *Flight and Rebellion*, 130–6; Sylvia Frey, "Between Slavery and Freedom: Virginia Blacks in the American Revolution," *Journal of Southern History* 49 (1983): 375–98; Frey, *Water From the Rock*, ch. 2 are starting points for events surrounding Dunmore's proclamation.

[36] *Diary of Landon Carter*, 1049–57, 1075–81 for two small groups of men. For similar resistance during the Civil War, see Benjamin F. Butler to Winfield Scott, May 27, 1861, in Ira Berlin, Barbara J. Fields, Steven F. Miller, Joseph P. Reidy, and Leslie S. Rowland, eds., *Free at Last: A Documentary History of Slavery, Freedom, and the Civil War* (New York, 1992), 8–11.

service, Carter told them what to do should a British fleet land. The "black men [were to] take . . . [their] wives, Children, male and female acquaintances," run into the woods, and send a messenger to Nomini Hall to tell of the community's whereabouts.[37] Carter expected the people of Coles Point to make a collective decision about how to respond to the British presence and to follow the leadership of male heads of families.

He proved right in his expectation about communal decision making, though he was sorely disappointed by the decision the residents of Coles Point made. In 1781 a privateer landed near the quarter, and thirty-two members of the community chose to "put themselves under the care and direction" of the king of England rather than to hide in the woods and send word to their master. Carter recognized the danger that slaves living at other quarters might follow the example of the Coles Point community, so he immediately began "removing to different plantations the remainder of the Negroes and Stocks" in the area.[38] Dunmore's appeal to enslaved Virginians was contradictory, and he lacked any commitment to emancipation or to the Black people he invited to fight under his banner.[39] The moral failures of Dunmore's offer notwithstanding, it offered slave communities that bordered the Chesapeake Bay a rare opportunity to strike out for freedom as communities.

The demographic preconditions for multigenerational communities did not develop in all regions of the Chesapeake by the era of the American Revolution.[40] But long before that period enslaved people living on and near the

---

[37] July 12, 1776 entry, Day Books and Letter Books, v. 13, p. 175–9, Carter Papers, Duke.

[38] Robert Carter to John Sutton, April 14, 1781; Robert Carter to the Commanding Officers who Now have the care of Sundry negroes Slaves lately under the protection of part of the British army, Oct. 30, 1781, Day Books and Letters, v. 4, pp. 55, 137–8, Carter Papers, Duke. Of the four people Carter named in the letter to the "Commanding Officers," three were women. Barden, "'Flushed With Notions of Freedom,'" ch. 6 explores this event and the effect of the Revolution on all of Carter's slaves. He is more cautious than I about inferring a communal decision-making process, though he strongly suggests one (p. 247). For other slaves running in groups, see Thomas Newton to Governor Benjamin Harrison, August 23, 1782, Virginia Executive Papers, Letters Received (hereafter "Executive Papers"), Library of Virginia (hereafter "LiVa"), microfilm. Newton reported that "Coll Godfrey lost 35 [slaves,] Jno Willoughby upwards of 90" and "others in proportion" in the Norfolk area. Harrison himself "lost thirty of" his "finest slaves" (Harrison to the Honorable Virginia Delegates in Congress, August 9, 1783, Virginia Executive Papers, Governor's Letter Book (hereafter "Executive Letter Book"), LiVa, microfilm).

[39] Frey, "Between Slavery and Freedom," 375–98. Barden, "'Flushed With Notions of Freedom,'" Appendix 13 provides a geographical breakdown of the Virginia origins of slaves evacuated to New York by the British Army in 1783.

[40] Lee, "Problem of Slave Community," 333–61.

large plantations along Virginia's major rivers had built relatively autonomous communities. White Virginians showed little interest in the mental world of the residents of those communities, so surviving records provide only fleeting glimpses of the early slave culture(s) of these great plantations. Viewing those glimpses from the perspective of the cultural background most common to those Blacks sold into slavery in Virginia suggests that the Africans who were settled in Virginia made sense of their new surroundings – awful as they were – by forging ties that linked the residents of the slave quarters of Virginia into village communities similar to those in the hinterland of the Bight of Biafra.

Residents of these communities struggled – usually semisecretly but sometimes openly and violently – to influence the pace of work, to protect one another, and to increase their autonomy. Little evidence survives of the divisions within quarter communities that surely emerged along lines determined by place of birth (Africa or America) or task allocation.[41] As long as slaves in Virginia spurned (and were spurned by) Christian churches, Whites rarely described their religious practices, but Blacks probably continued to perceive the world in animist terms, with quarters developing similar but slightly different patterns and objects of worship.[42] Among the methods of worship and the recreational activities common to these quarters were surely the "dances . . . without any method or regularity" that Andrew Burnaby reported White Virginians had "borrowed . . . from the Negroes."[43] In short, these early communities, like the villages of Igboland, shared a broadly similar culture, but their residents' collective identity centered on local quarters and real and fictive kinship networks.

---

[41] Barden, "'Flushed With Notions of Freedom,'" 162–4 reveals internal status divisions within Robert Carter's slave community by showing that "artisans and domestic servants preferred to choose one another as spouses when numbers and circumstances permitted," though he overstates his important discovery by referring to the "outlines of a caste system" within the community.

[42] In 1724 Hugh Jones reported that the "religions and customs" of "new Negroes" were those described in a book by "Mr. Bosman." William Bosman, *A New and Accurate Description of the Coast of Guinea: Divided into The Gold, The Slave, and The Ivory Coasts*, John Ralph Willis, J. D. Fage, and R. E. Bradbury, eds. (London, 1967 [1705]), 145–61, 367a–73 describes the religions of the coast in terms compatible with my broad generalizations. Also see Charles Ball, *Fifty Years in Chains* (New York, 1970 [1837]), 264–5. Different Igbo villages worshipped different deities, so different Afro-Virginian communities almost surely did (Afigbo, *Ropes of Sand*, 123).

[43] Andrew Burnaby, *Travels through the Middle Settlements in North-America in the years 1759 and 1760 with observations upon the state of the Colonies* (Ithaca, 1960 [1775]), 26.

Toward a Black Virginian identity

There is no reason to believe that an internal cultural dynamic would have pushed Black Virginians from a local toward a more broadly defined sense of identity had they controlled their own destiny. But they did not. During the second half of the eighteenth century, these local communities were disrupted by forces over which enslaved Virginians had little control. Blacks did, however, control the way they made sense of their charging world, and during this period slave communities began to expand geographically and then ideologically to include all Virginians of African descent.

Geographic expansion provided the initial impetus toward a broadening corporate identity. In West African stateless societies, relatives settled on land contiguous to one another, and ties forged through kinship were reinforced through settlement patterns.[44] Africans in Virginia might have replicated this archetype had they been able to determine where they lived, but during the third quarter of the eighteenth century White Virginians began forcibly moving their bonded laborers onto "virgin" land in the Piedmont. By 1755 Black people comprised a majority of the populations of most counties on each side of Virginia's major rivers from the Chesapeake Bay all the way west to the Blue Ridge Mountains, and by 1782 the Piedmont was the geographic center of the state's rapidly growing slave population (see Map 2).[45]

This shift occurred after the height of Virginia's participation in the Atlantic slave trade, so the rapid growth of the Piedmont slave population involved the forced movement of people who had become settled or else grown up in the Tidewater. Sometimes these forced moves resulted from Tidewater masters selling slaves to people in the west, or from the children of Tidewater planters taking the people they inherited to found new family seats out west.[46]

---

[44] Horton, "Stateless societies in the history of West Africa" 84–91. The village-centered nature of the culture was not among the many things that changed in Igboland over the course of the nineteenth century (Afigbo, *Ropes of Sand*, pp. 183–4).

[45] Dunn, "Black Society in the Chesapeake," 54–9.

[46] Philip D. Morgan and Michael L. Nicholls, "Slaves in Piedmont Virginia, 1720–1790," *WMQ* 3d ser., 46 (1989): 211–51 for movement west. Lathan A. Windley, ed., *Runaway Slave Advertisements: A Documentary History from the 1730s to 1790* (Westport, Conn., 1983), v. 1, pp. 35, 36, 37, 41, 43, 47 (slaves sold west who ran back to their old quarters); John Davis, *Travels of Four Years and a Half in the United States of America During 1798, 1799, 1800, 1801, and 1802*, A. J. Morrison, ed. (New York, 1909 [1803]), 258–9 (family dispersed through sale), 424–5 (plantation settled by the daughter and son-in-law of an eastern planter).

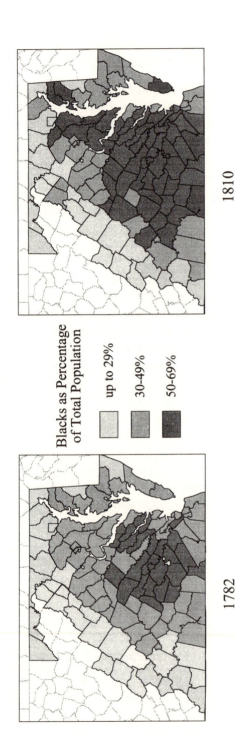

Blacks as Percentage
of Total Population

☐ up to 29%

▨ 30-49%

■ 50-69%

1782

1810

Map 2. During the final quarter of the eighteenth century, as a result of the westward push of settlement and the forced migration of many enslaved people, the demographic center of the Black population of Virginia shifted from the Tidewater to the Piedmont. Source: Richard S. Dunn, "Black Society in the Chesapeake, 1776–1810," in Ira Berlin and Ronald Hoffman, eds., *Slavery and Freedom in the Age of the American Revolution* (Charlottesville, 1983).

Even enslaved people belonging to masters who tried to avoid selling slaves, however, were not exempt from the westward drift of Virginia's population. During the 1780s, Councilor Robert Carter, who was uncomfortable selling people and who later manumitted more than 450 slaves, began to move many Blacks who lived in Tidewater communities to new quarters in Loudon County and the Shenandoah Valley about 80 to 100 miles away. Carter gave them no choice – at least one man ran away rather than accept the move – but he sought a humane way to carry out the forced migration by moving people "young and old in families."[47] Nonetheless he chose young people for the arduous work of clearing new land – other than one forty-seven-year-old woman, no one as old as thirty was sent – so he separated people from their close kin. And he put together on one quarter people who had previously lived on several different ones, forcing them to form new connections and a new group identity.[48]

This movement from the Tidewater to the Piedmont entailed a process of cultural adaptation that may appear analogous to that through which Virginia's first slave communities were forged. But the differences far outweigh the similarities. In addition to obvious differences – most who were moved west spoke the same language, and the forced march to new western land, while rough, was nothing like the Middle Passage – enslaved Virginians who lived in the Piedmont did not lose contact with the kin and communities that they left in the Tidewater. Masters who advertised for runaways frequently believed that the fugitives had fled to their former homes in the east, indicating that connections to the old quarters remained strong.[49] As new quarter communities composed of enslaved people with strong connections to several different eastern quarters developed, many Blacks' sense of collective

---

[47] Robert Carter to George Smith, Jan. 5, 1788; Carter to John Sutton, May 18, 1782, Day Books and Letters, v. 5: p. 15; v. 8, p. 62, Robert Carter Papers, Duke. Barden, "'Flushed With Notions of Freedom,'" ch. 8 discusses Carter's movement of people.

[48] Robert Carter to George Newman, Oct. 23, 1787; Carter to George Smith, Jan. 5, 1788, Day Books and Letters, v. 8, pp. 18, 62–3, Carter Papers, Duke.

[49] Windley, *Runaway Slave Advertisements*, v. 1, pp. 35–48 has ads for the return of 55 runaway slaves published in the *Virginia Gazette* (Hunter, Royle, or Purdie) between 1761 and 1766. Masters of nine slaves suspected they had run east to a former home; masters of three thought they had run north, west, or south toward a former home. Most did not hazard guesses, and those who did guessed that slaves ran to former homes more frequently than any other destination. Philip D. Morgan and Michael L. Nicholls, "Runaway Slaves in Eighteenth-Century Virginia," (unpublished paper), Table 9, have analyzed extant runaway advertisements in colonial Virginia and found that almost half of runaways advertised during the 1760s and 1770s were believed to be running to a former home or hiding with family members. I am grateful to Morgan and Nicholls for giving me their paper.

identity must have widened to include a growing percentage of Virginia's Black population.[50]

The dynamics behind this expanding sense of identity are revealed in the makeup of the new community on one of Carter's western quarters. In 1791, when he registered a deed of manumission freeing his slaves, Carter's Aquarius quarter in the Shenandoah Valley (Frederick County) was home to Ned, the fifteen-year-old son of Molly at Virgo; Gregory, the sixteen-year-old son of Rachel at Virgo; James, the seventeen-year-old son of Beck at Cancer; Betty and Judith, two fourteen-year-old girls from Old Ordinary; and Grace, a nineteen-year-old woman from Cancer. Virgo and Aquarius, two of Carter's six Frederick County quarters, were home to forty-three enslaved people; Cancer, just to the east in Prince William County, was home to twenty-three blacks; and forty-four blacks lived on Old Ordinary, one of the Councilor's Tidewater quarters (in Westmoreland County).[51] Other residents of Aquarius whose original homes remain unknown would presumably have linked quarter residents to other slave communities. Thus, if we assume that the people who lived at Aquarius began to build their own strong quarter community tied together through marriage and collective struggles over work, they would have developed kinship ties spreading east through Prince William County to the Chesapeake Bay. The quarters definitely linked in this way included 110 people, and quarter communities also included many enslaved people living in surrounding neighborhoods. As a result of the westward shift in Virginia's population, by the 1790s, many enslaved Virginians had developed networks of kinship and friendship that extended east to west along the state's rivers. The sense of identity behind these expanding networks operated, however, on the same principles as had earlier, more local communities.

The American Revolution offered enslaved Virginians new practical reasons to expand their sense of identity ideologically in ways that paralleled the geographical expansion already underway. Lord Dunmore's promise of freedom

[50] Gail S. Terry, "Sustaining the Bonds of Kinship in a Trans-Appalachian Migration, 1790–1811: The Cabell-Breckinridge Slaves Move West," *Virginia Magazine of History and Biography* 102 (1994): 458–62 traces the maintenance of kinship connections within a slave community moving to western Virginia.

[51] Robert Carter of Nomini Hall, Deed of Manumission, *Records of Ante-Bellum Southern Plantations from the Revolution Through the Civil War*, Ser. F, Pt. 3, Reel 32; Louis Morton, *Robert Carter of Nomini Hall: A Virginia Tobacco Planter of the Eighteenth Century* (Charlottesville, 1941), Table 9 (tables are in unpaginated section at end of book). Barden, "'Flushed With Notions of Freedom,'" ch. 8, Appendix 17 provides a full analysis of Carter's movement of slaves to the west. Though identity formation is not Barden's primary interest, he notes that "the migration of people among the Nomony Hall plantations forced the creation of expanded networks and renewed communities" (p. 324).

to "all indented Servants, Negroes, or others, (appertaining to Rebels)" who helped "more speedily" reduce White Virginians to "a proper Sense of their Duty," while providing a chance for slaves to run away as communities, also provided impetus toward a new racial identity. Men of African descent from various quarter communities rallied to the governor's banner. Upon arriving at British camps near Norfolk, they were organized into Lord Dunmore's Ethiopian Regiment – a segregated unit – to fight for the king.[52] While an enslaved man need only have desired to escape bondage in order to join Dunmore, upon joining he was assigned a racial identity – neither these men nor their immediate ancestors would, after all, ever have been to Ethiopia – and this racial identity offered a pathway to freedom.

Dunmore's proclamation and organization of the Ethiopian Regiment are specific examples of a more general erosion of order and authority in Virginia during the Revolutionary War. The war did not create conditions conducive to slave insurrection – armed Whites remained on alert throughout the period – but it offered enslaved people chances to strike out for freedom if they were willing to leave their quarter communities.[53] Black Virginians sought freedom by running to French as well as British armies. Even patriot militia units included slaves serving as substitutes for their masters; the state legislature granted freedom following the war to such Blacks.[54] Other Black Virginians served the state as "public slaves," while still others took advantage of social chaos to leave their masters and seek work elsewhere. So many individuals left their home quarters that the state legislature passed a law stipulating that wandering slaves be committed to jail for three months.[55]

As enslaved people moved or were moved within the state, the networks linking communities continued to expand. Many transient people acted in

---

[52] Ivor Noël Hume, *1775: Another Part of the Field* (London, 1966), 389–459 for fullest retelling of the story of Dunmore's regiment.

[53] Frey, *Water from the Rock*, ch. 5.

[54] Benjamin Harrison to Count Rochambeau, [June] 26, 1782; Harrison to Virginia Delegates in Congress, July 6, 1782, Executive Letter Book, 1781–2; Rochambeau to Harrison, June 28, 1782; Thomas Read to Harrison, March 22, 1782, Executive Papers, microfilm (French). Benjamin Harrison to Colonel Charles Dabney, October 7, 1783; Harrison to the Speaker of the House of Delegates, October 20, 1783, Executive Letter Book, 1783–86 (microfilm); Guild, *Black Laws of Virginia*, 191 (patriot militia).

[55] Requisitions by General Greene from the State of Virginia, n.d. [1781], Executive Papers (microfilm); Rochambeau to Harrison, June 28, 1782; Major Charles Dick to William Davies, Jan. 14, 1782, Executive Papers (microfilm). Most runaways whose masters advertised presumed destinations in the 1780s were believed to be running to freedom (Morgan and Nicholls, "Runaway Slaves in Eighteenth-Century Virginia," Table 9). Compare n. 49. Guild, *Black Laws of Virginia*, 190.

response to promises of freedom or heard the language of natural rights as they worked in French or patriot armies. From Dunmore's proclamation and the threats White Virginians issued in response, to the different armies' recruiting efforts and the whispered discussion of emancipation during the postwar revisions of Virginia's law codes, Black Virginians were occasionally addressed not as residents of individual slave quarters but as a cohesive people who shared a racial identity.[56] By the end of the revolutionary period, Whites' projection of a racial identity onto Virginians of African descent would develop a pervasively derogatory meaning, but during the war it sometimes offered an enhanced opportunity for freedom. The disorder of the Revolution in Virginia created social conditions and ideological forces conducive to a Black Virginian identity.

Nonetheless, the Revolution's impetus to racial identity remained ambivalent. The manumission law of 1782 was the most impressive benefit that Virginians of African descent acquired through the Revolution, a benefit effectively revoked in 1806. The 1782 law repealed the prohibition on private acts of manumission by allowing slaveowners to free their slaves by will or deed. A few people, deeply troubled by slavery's iniquity, freed all their slaves, but many more slaveowners used manumission to reward favored slaves or allowed enslaved individuals to hire their own time, promising to sell the slave freedom for an agreed-upon price. In this way owners used the promise of freedom to extort greater profits from their human property.[57] It is hardly surprising that slaveowners used the laws they passed to their own advantage, and despite complexities in the practice of manumission the 1782 law represents a small, temporary, but important improvement in Virginia law. Those complexities, however, influenced the law's (and thus the Revolution's) effect upon Black Virginians' racial consciousness. The main avenues to freedom opened by the 1782 law encouraged individual rather than collective pursuit of freedom. Individual strategies did not necessarily subvert collective struggles, though the course of Gabriel's Conspiracy shows that they could do so. Nonetheless, the fact that the manumission law – one of the few concrete benefits that Black Virginians got from the Revolution – was so oriented toward individuals highlights the limits of the American Revolution's promise to enslaved Virginians.

Those limits are further underscored by the state's response to one jurist's attempt to reconcile the contradictory messages of the Revolution. The

---

[56] Frey, *Water from the Rock*, 50, and chs. 2 and 5.
[57] Ira Berlin, *Slaves Without Masters: The Free Negro in the Antebellum South* (New York, 1974), ch. 1.

manumission law of 1782 created recognized claims to freedom for many Virginians of African descent, but those claims were fragile because black skin remained a presumed marker of servitude. Unscrupulous Whites kidnapped and enslaved free Black people, while others refused to recognize legitimate claims to freedom, many of which predated the Revolution. In 1786 and 1795 the legislature offered a remedy by allowing people who believed themselves illegally detained as slaves to sue for their freedom. Many enslaved Virginians sought to use this statute to make good the claims to freedom that they traced to maternal ancestors who were Native Americans or White servants. The celebrated jurist George Wythe ruled in one such case that the Virginia Bill of Rights created the presumption that freedom was the birthright of all people and put the burden of proof in all freedom suits upon the person who "claim[ed] to hold another in slavery."[58]

An appellate court accepted Wythe's ruling in the specific case, a ruling rooted in the claimants' Native American genealogy, but it rejected Wythe's reasoning in language that emphasized White Virginians' insistence that the libertarian promises of the Revolution did not apply to Black people. The court insisted that "the first clause of the Bill of Rights . . . was notoriously framed with a cautious eye to" slavery and that it only "embrace[d] the case of free citizens, or aliens." Enslaved Virginians, the court maintained, lacked "concern, agency or interest" in the Revolution. Black Virginians did not have to accept elite notions about the limits of the Revolution's promise of equality, and Sylvia Frey emphasizes Black agency during the War.[59] Nonetheless the notorious care with which Virginia's founders excluded native Africans and their descendants attenuated the tendency of the Revolution to foster a sense of racial identity. Most of the improvements that the Revolution ultimately offered Black Virginians, it offered to individuals despite their race, rather than to "Black Virginians."

Evangelical Christianity constituted a second and more powerful ideological force that encouraged Virginians of African descent to broaden their collective identity.[60] Beginning with Presbyterian Samuel Davies's 1740s revivals

[58] Helen T. Catterall, ed., *Judicial Cases Concerning Slavery and the Negro*, 5 vols. (Washington, D.C., 1926–37), v. 1, pp. 94–5, 101–2, 105, 112–13 includes a sample of Virginia freedom suits from the Revolutionary era. Ibid., 112–13 (Wythe).

[59] Ibid. Frey, *Water from the Rock*, esp. ch. 5.

[60] Sobel, *World They Made Together*, Part Three; and Sylvia Frey, "'The Year of Jubilee Is Come': Black Christianity in the Plantation South in Post-Revolutionary America," in Ronald Hoffman and Peter J. Albert, eds., *Religion in a Revolutionary Age* (Charlottesville, 1994), 90–95; Frey, "Shaking the Dry Bones: The Dialectic of Conversion," in Ted Ownby, ed. *Black and White Cultural Interaction in the Antebellum South* (Jackson,

in Hanover County and continuing through the rest of the century, evangelical preachers sought to bring the word of God to the unchurched. Enslaved
people were prominent among the evangelists' listeners during the Great
Awakening, and they joined the Baptist and Methodist churches in great
numbers. The Christian love that infused these congregations created a new
community among believers, a sense of belonging determined by belief in
the Bible more than lineage or place of residence. Robert Carter of Nomini
Hall, the richest Virginian to join the early Baptists, illustrated the egalitarian potential of these new communities when addressing questions to "Black
Brother Billy," one of his slaves.[61] If slaves and masters could become true
brothers in Christ, then perhaps the new state could turn away from slavery.

Masters and slaves could not, however, remain true brothers in Christ no
matter how sincere the professions of faith from each side. A few exceptionally principled Whites, like Robert Carter, responded to this situation by
manumitting all their slaves, but even Carter unthinkingly included a racial
marker when addressing his fellow believer. Most masters fell far short of
Carter's attempt to reconcile his belief in spiritual equality with the inequity
he found on Earth. Thus, while White Baptists referred to enslaved people
who joined their congregations as brothers and sisters, many segregated the
membership lists of their integrated churches according to race.[62] Such segregation did not arise spontaneously out of a transcendent racist ideology but
out of differences in the lives and status of Black and White members,
differences that all but inevitably found their way into churches. On lists of
enslaved members, for example, churches included a column in which to
register the name of the person to whom they belonged, and churches had
to organize special meetings for Black members who did not have it in their
power to attend the regularly scheduled Saturday disciplinary meetings.[63]

Miss., 1993), 30–34 for Virginia slaves' conversion to Christianity. For a convincing interpretation of the mechanism of conversion that differs from Sobel's see Thornton, *Africa
and Africans*, ch. 9.
[61] Carter to Black Brother Billy, June 10, 1789, "Day Books and Letters," v. 8, p. 286,
      Carter Papers, Duke.
[62] Boar Swamp/Antioch Baptist Meeting House Minute Book, 1787–1828, Virginia Bapt-
      ist Historical Society, Richmond, Virginia (hereafter VBHS); Robert Carter kept "A
      List of the White Members belonging to the Nomony Baptist Church of Christ," n.d.
      [1778–1791], Robert Carter Manuscripts, VBHS. John Boles, *Black Southerners, 1619–
      1869* (Lexington, KY., 1983), 156–64 discusses many of these issues in a survey of slave
      Christianity. He acknowledges the barrier that racism raised to the creation of biracial
      fellowship but argues that "what is more remarkable is the degree to which there existed
      a biracial religious community in the Old South" (162).
[63] Boar Swamp Minute Book, 1787–1828, "A List of Black Members," and entry for August
      1793.

And, as numerous scholars have pointed out, evangelical churches had to confront how to enforce biblical strictures against adultery and divorce when enslaved members' families were divided through their masters' callousness or the state's inheritance laws.

This list of ways that racial and status differences intruded into relations between free White and enslaved Black members of Virginia's Baptist churches is not an indictment of race relations in Baptist churches. Mechal Sobel has shown that "awakenings in Virginia were a shared black and white phenomenon," and that the effect of "shared spiritual experiences . . . was deep and lasting in both communities."[64] Black and White Baptists who called one another brother and sister developed emotional ties of remarkable power, considering the racial chasm that such ties had to cross, but Baptists did not fill the chasm, so the religious communities that they built remained split along racial lines. Thus, while enslaved Baptists and Methodists developed ties to their integrated churches, they conceived of themselves, as White Baptists and Methodists clearly conceived of them, as a distinct and racially defined group within those congregations.

Beginning in the 1780s, Virginians of African descent in several of the state's towns acted on that belief and began to build separate Black Baptist churches.[65] Some of those churches, like the African Baptist Church in Williamsburg,[66] adopted titles that included racial designations, and all represent the development of racial consciousness among Black Virginians. Black Baptists' conflicting desires for segregation from and fellowship with White Baptists led the Black church members in Norfolk to consider requesting an independent vote in the Portsmouth Association but instead to accept the association's preference to "consider the Black people as a wing of" the White church, at least at district meetings. Nonetheless, after 1795 Norfolk's Black Baptists met separately and followed the leadership of Jacob Bishop, a free Black preacher.[67]

[64] Sobel, *World They Made Together*, 180 and throughout.

[65] This discussion of separate Black churches draws on Sobel, *World They Made Together*, Part 3; Frey, *Water from the Rock*, 284–8; Luther P. Jackson, "Religious Development of the Negro in Virginia from 1760 to 1860," *Journal of Negro History* 14 (1931): 170–203; Douglas R. Egerton, *Gabriel's Rebellion: The Virginia Slave Conspiracies of 1800 and 1802* (Chapel Hill, 1993), 7–10.

[66] Jackson, "Religious Development of the Negro," 188; Frey, " 'Year of Jubilee Is Come,' " 93–5. Because few records have survived from these early Black churches, it is sometimes difficult to know when they took on racially specific names.

[67] Lemuel Burkitt and Jesse Read, *A Concise History of the Kehukee Baptist Association, from its Original Rise Down to 1803* (New York, 1980 [1850]), 264. The Dover Baptist Association recognized the Williamsburg African Baptist Church (though not by that name),

During and immediately following the era of the Revolution, Virginians of African descent turned to evangelical Christianity and transformed its meaning and practice in Virginia. Their turn to Baptist and Methodist churches also involved a reconceptualization of the bounds of their communal lives. As they entered into congregations professing a universal creed, they necessarily expanded their sense of kinship to include, at least in theory, all people. On a less theoretical level, they began to develop presumptions of kinship with fellow worshippers – Black and White – in expanding concentric circles from the congregation, to the district association, to the denomination. Black Baptists also began leaving traces of a growing racial consciousness that cut through, without eliminating, this crossracial community. While little direct evidence of the content of this growing racial consciousness has survived, Black Baptist ministers like Gowan Pamphlet and Jacob Bishop probably developed the vision of enslaved African Americans as God's chosen people that would eventually help to fuel Gabriel's Conspiracy and play such a prominent role in antebellum slave religion.

By the 1790s, as a result of the forced moves westward that so many enslaved people had experienced, the transience and disorder associated with the Revolutionary War, the ideological changes associated with natural rights arguments during the Revolution, and numerous conversions to Christianity during the Great Awakening Virginians of African descent increasingly viewed one another as sharing a racial identity – an identity based on skin color and a shared African heritage.[68] This new and broader identity did not displace the earlier local one, nor did it invariably win over other ways that Blacks could conceive themselves to be members of social groups. Given the role of Christianity, a tension between racial and crossracial identity was inherent in this emerging worldview; similarly, local slave communities remained strong and cohesive through the Civil War. Neither the continuities nor the contradictions, however, should obscure the degree to which political, religious, and demographic changes between 1750 and 1790 encouraged Black Virginians to broaden the local identities that prevailed in the first half of the eighteenth century – a way of seeing the world rooted in

and the black preacher Gowan Pamphlet represented the church at the annual meetings (Dover Baptist Association Minutes, 1793, 1794, 1795, 1796, 1797, 1798, 1799, 1801, 1803, VBHS).

[68] My analysis foregrounds developments within Black Virginians' communities because these developments have received less scholarly attention. White racial attitudes certainly accelerated these trends. See Winthrop D. Jordan, *White Over Black: American Attitudes Toward the Negro, 1550–1812* (Chapel Hill, 1968); and Duncan J. MacLeod, *Slavery, Race and the American Revolution* (London, 1974).

many different African pasts – and begin to presume kinship with all other Black Virginians.[69]

Saint Domingue and double consciousness

This new racial consciousness had roots in the Great Awakening and in the language of the American Revolution. Prior to the 1790s, however, the sacred impetus took precedence, for reasons easy to discern. Though natural rights philosophy and the language of the Declaration of Independence offered Virginians of African descent practical tools for asserting claims to freedom, the prominence of property rights in the revolutionary ideology and the degree to which both parties in the Revolutionary War exploited Black Virginians must have caused many enslaved Virginians to doubt whether their masters' Revolution could be extended in ways that would benefit them.[70]

The beginning of the Haitian Revolution in the French colony of Saint Domingue, however, provided Black Virginians a narrative of revolution in which race played a different role than it had in Virginia's revolution. The effects of this narrative can be traced through the appearance and elaboration of a new idiom that Black Virginians increasingly used when discussing attempts to win freedom. The 1790s witnessed a sharp increase in reported slave conspiracies in the state, and participants in several of these conspiracies used what might best be called tropes of "frenchness" when discussing the possibility of overthrowing slavery. The revolution in Saint Domingue played the central role in slaves' consciousness and use of "French" themes, for the French Revolution was neither an abstract nor a distant event: following the 1793 fall of Cap Français to the revolutionary forces, thousands of White French colonists fled the city with slaves, and many ended up in Virginia. In enslaved Virginians' sometimes contradictory attempts to respond to a "french" presence and to invoke "frenchness" in acts of resistance, they elaborated upon a central and creative tension in North American slave cultures. This tension between local (in this case Virginian) identities and an Afro-Atlantic identity developed during the 1790s and remained powerful through the Civil War. It further complicated Black Virginians' sense of identity.[71]

---

[69] The ironic way in which an "African" identity represented an adaptation to the "Virginia" present modifies Sterling Stuckey's general point that pan-African nationalism developed first in the New World rather than the Old (*Slave Culture*, ch. 1). Also Kwame Anthony Appiah, *In My Father's House: Africa in the Philosophy of Culture* (New York, 1992), chs. 1–3.

[70] Frey, *Water from the Rock*, ch. 5; Frey, "Between Slavery and Freedom."

[71] For a fuller development and documentation of this argument and an interpretation of the role of ideologies of revolution in slave resistance, see my "Saint Domingue in Virginia:

Enslaved Virginians were not unaware of France prior to the revolution
in Saint Domingue. As mentioned, some slaves had sought freedom by attach-
ing themselves to the French army in Virginia during the Revolutionary War.
In addition, the French Revolution itself was widely discussed in Virginia
and certainly helped to shape the meanings of "frenchness" among both White
and Black Virginians. Citizens of the new United States remained passion-
ately attached to Europe, and the French Revolution and the wars it spawned
dominated news from the Old World throughout the 1790s. Attitudes toward
the new French Republic became a crucial pole around which Hamiltonians
and Jeffersonians organized their incipient partisan organizations. Jeffersonians, who came to dominance quickly in Virginia and then throughout most
of the nation, favored France and believed the French Revolution to be
an extension of the struggle for human liberty unleashed by the American
Revolution.[72]

The French Revolution was discussed in newspapers, speeches, and private conversations in Virginia, so Black Virginians surely knew about it.[73]
Nonetheless, it was the slave rebellion in Saint Domingue that transformed
the meaning of "frenchness" among Black Virginians into a concrete realization of the radical possibilities for revolution in a slave society. This transformation helped alter the ways that Black Virginians thought of themselves
as a people.

White Virginians recognized the dangers posed by news of the slave rebellion in Saint Domingue, but they did little to quarantine their slaves from
the contagion of this strain of liberty. Virginia newspapers printed occasional
letters detailing atrocities and pointing out commercial opportunities arising
from the struggle there, and Black mariners who traveled to the West Indies
surely carried news of the conflict to Virginia, as they carried it to the rest
of Afro-America.[74] A more direct source of news materialized when White

Ideology, Local Meanings, and Resistance to Slavery, 1790–1800," *Journal of Southern History* (forthcoming, Aug., 1997).

[72] Henry F. May, *The Enlightenment in America* (New York, 1976), 245–50.

[73] Especially because the Revolutionary government abolished slavery. See David Geggus, "Racial Equality, Slavery, and Colonial Secession during the Constituent Assembly," *American Historical Review* 94 (1989): 1290–1308 for fights over abolition in France. Kenneth Roberts and Anna M. Roberts, transl. and eds., *Moreau de St. Méry's American Journey [1793–1798]* (New York, 1947), 17.

[74] Julius S. Scott, "'The Common Wind': Currents of Afro-American Communication in the era of the Haitian Revolution" (Ph.D. dissertation, Duke University, 1986); and W. Jeffrey Bolster, "African American Seamen: Race, Seafaring Work, and Atlantic Maritime Culture, 1750–1860," (Ph.D. dissertation, Johns Hopkins University, 1992).

French colonists, chased away by the violence of the Haitian Revolution, fled the island in search of refuge. Many traveled to the United States, and a sizable group landed in Norfolk, beginning in 1793. White Virginians probably would have preferred these ships and the experience with slave rebellion they carried to bypass Virginia entirely, but authorities also sympathized with these victims of a slaveholder's worst nightmare and assured the "Indigent french people" that (White) Virginians shared their distress. Within days of the refugees' arrival, the Norfolk Common Hall extended an emergency loan to cover the "Necessities of the Sufferers," and the state government soon added to the relief fund.[75] By contributing to the "cause of humanity" and simultaneously acknowledging their remembrance of the important aid France had given the United States during the American Revolution, White Virginians accepted not just White refugees from the Haitian Revolution but an unspecified number of slaves who accompanied their owners.[76] Suddenly Virginia ports – especially Norfolk, but others as well – gained direct sources of information about the Haitian Revolution to supplement the stories Black Virginians had heard from mariners.

Saint Domingue's revolution had a remarkably immediate impact on slave resistance in Virginia. A full year before refugees began arriving, rumors surfaced of a conspiracy among the slaves of Norfolk, Portsmouth, and the surrounding countryside as well as the lower Eastern Shore. Among the causes White Virginians offered for this unrest were "the . . . severing [of] husband, wife and children," and "the example in the West Indies," a combination that connects the effects of westward movement and the ideological spur of Saint Domingue.[77] During the next few years, Whites frequently invoked the arrival of Blacks from Saint Domingue to make sense of Black Virginians' expressions of discontent.[78]

---

[75] Brent Tarter, ed., *The Order Book and Related Papers of the Common Hall of the Borough of Norfolk, Virginia, 1736–1798* (Richmond, 1979), 337–8 (9 July 1793); Governor James Wood to Miles King, July 8, 1793, Executive Letter Book, 1792–4, 215.

[76] Quotations from Henry Lee to the Speaker of the House of Delegates, October 24, 1793, Executive Letter Book 1792–4, 290–1.

[77] Thomas Newton to Governor Henry Lee, May 10, 1792, Executive Papers, Box 74, 1–10 May folder. Lee to Colonel Robert Goode, May 17, 1792, Executive Letter Book 1792–4, 5–7. One must be careful with White perceptions of slave conspiracies. Apparently White fear greatly magnified this alarm – a magistrate from Northampton County reported that the "danger is not so great as . . . was apprehended" (Smith Snead to Lee, May 21, 1792, Executive Papers Box 74, 21–31 July folder) – but Lee's suspicion that news of Saint Domingue contributed to the slaves' unrest seems reasonable.

[78] Willis Wilson to Lee, August 21, 1793, Executive Papers Box 80, 21–30 August folder; Langham to Lee, August 3, 1793, Executive Papers Box 80, 1–10 August folder; Richard

The revolution in Saint Domingue also helped to inspire talk of an incipient general attempt to rally slaves throughout the southern mainland to a
revolution against slavery. On August 8, 1793, William Nelson reported that
"Garvin a black itinerant preacher" had dropped a letter on a Yorktown street.
The preacher, presumably Gowan Pamphlet, the free Black minister of Williamsburg's African Baptist Church, dropped a letter from the Secret Keeper
in Richmond to the Secret Keeper in Norfolk.[79] It promised that the "great
secret" that had long been kept by "our colour" was nearly ready to "come
. . . to a hed." The Secret Keeper told his Norfolk counterpart that their
"friend in Charleston" had written a letter reporting the enlistment of "near
six thousand men." The conspirators, he promised, would "be in full possession of the hole country in a few weeks."[80]

The letter made no mention of Saint Domingue, but other evidence points
toward Haiti as an influence upon the plan. Late in the evening of July 21,
1793, John Randolph was asked by his wife to go to the window to quiet a
group of slaves making noise outside their Richmond house. While there,
Randolph overheard two slaves discussing plans "to kill the white people,"
plans that White Virginians believed to be part of the Secret Keeper conspiracy. After one slave specified when the event would occur, the other
attempted to call his bluff by questioning "whether the plot wou'd" actually
be "put in Execution." The leader responded by pointing to the houses that
he would claim once the insurrection succeeded and by reminding the skeptic
"how the blacks *has* kill'd the whites in the French Island . . . a little while
ago."[81] Later, Peter Oram reported to the governor of South Carolina that

Cary to Lee, November 25, 1793, Executive Papers Box 82, 21–30 November folder;
Robert Mitchell to John Marshall, 23 September 1793, Executive Papers Box 81, 20–30
September folder; Miles King to Lee, September 10, 1793, Executive Papers Box 81,
1–10 September folder; Extract from Council Journal, July 14, 1795, Executive Papers
Box 90, 11–20 January folder.

[79] William Nelson to Lee, August 8, 1793, Executive Papers Box 80, 1–10 August folder.
Pamphlet, however, had a permanent position in an organized congregation, so if he was
"Garvin," then Nelson wrongly called him an itinerant.

[80] Lt. Gov. James Wood (of Virginia) to Governor William Moultrie, August 1793, (no.
577), South Carolina Department of Archives and History, Records of the General
Assembly, Governor's Messages 1783–1830 (hereafter SCDAH, Governor's Messages).
Wood wrote Moultrie to inform him of the letter and included a copy. Robert A. Olwell
kindly gave me a copy of this letter.

[81] Deposition of John Randolph, July 22, 1793, Executive Papers Box 80, 21–30 August
folder (emphasis in original). That the plot that Randolph heard discussed was believed
to be related to the Secret Keeper letter was made explicit in T. G. Peachy, et al. to
Lee, August 17, 1793, Executive Papers Box 80, 11–20 August folder.

Richmond's Secret Keeper had disclosed that Charleston slaves were to be "furnished by a person from the West Indies with arms and ammunition." Authorities in Norfolk, responding to this scare, warned that 200 or more "Negroes from Cape Francois" would join rebellious Black Virginians if the insurrection broke out.[82]

   Much about the Secret Keeper conspiracy must remain shadowy and ultimately unknowable, but several important assertions can be made with reasonable assurance. In 1793 at least some slaves in Virginia's towns conceived of themselves as sharing enough of a corporate identity with slaves from South Carolina to speak of forming a joint conspiracy to take "the hole country." Participants in this conspiracy spoke of the ties among potential rebels in racial terms: it was a secret held among "our colour." The key to the importance of the conspiracy lies less in unanswerable questions about the "reality" or extent of the conspiracy than in the clear evidence that the letter provides that Black Virginians felt what Julius Scott calls the "common wind" of news of the Haitian Revolution.[83] The Revolution on Saint Domingue served at least as a confidence-inspiring example for these Virginians, a model of revolution that offered them the freedom that the American Revolution had denied. And Saint Domingue may have meant more. The "French" slaves in Virginia may have participated in the plan, and a West Indian in Charleston may have promised arms. The language used by the Secret Keepers displayed Black Virginians' evolving sense of themselves as African Americans who shared interests with people of African descent at least in South Carolina and perhaps throughout some greater portion of the maritime Atlantic. This awareness reflected the intensification of contact among people of African descent along all Atlantic trade routes.

   An emerging racial identity is a crucial part of what Black Virginians spoke of when they invoked "frenchness," but it is only a part. Glimpses of slaves telling stories of the Haitian Revolution as a part of the process through which they spoke of overthrowing slavery must be balanced by equally compelling glimpses of Virginia slaves defining a more local identity specifically through their differences from island refugees. For if Toussaint Louverture and his followers provided powerful inspiration through their triumphs against

---

[82] Peter Oram to William Moultrie, August 16, 1793, SCDAH, Governor's Messages. The Secret Keeper's letter mentioned "a gentlemen" who would arm the slaves but never said he was from the West Indies. How Oram made (or invented) this connection is unclear. Thomas Newton to James Wood, August [13?] 1793, SCDAH, Governor's Messages (copy courtesy of Robert Olwell). Wood responded on August 16, 1793, Executive Letter Book 1792–4, 230–1.

[83] Scott, " 'Common Wind' "; Bolster, "African American Seamen."

European powers, the slaves who accompanied their French colonial masters
to Virginia brought another culture forged under circumstances strikingly
different from those they found in Virginia. While most Virginia slaves were
creoles by the 1790s, roughly "two-thirds of the . . . slaves in Saint Domingue were African-born" in 1789.[84] Partially as a result, the languages and
religions that grounded the cultures of these two peoples differed radically.
During the 1790s, new-light Christian churches continued their outreach toward
and accommodation to enslaved Virginians, and Baptists probably predominated among slaves in the Norfolk area.[85] Slaves from Saint Domingue, on
the other hand, brought different vodûn (voodoo) and Catholic traditions from
their African and island homelands.[86] And, perhaps most fundamentally, refugee
slaves would have spoken some mix of French and African languages, while
enslaved Virginians generally spoke English.

Conflicts arose quickly, in part because the refugees from Saint Domingue
were divided among themselves. On August 20, 1793, Willis Wilson found
four slaves hanging from a tree twenty steps from his house in Portsmouth.
Wilson suspected that the lynching reflected conflicts between slaves who
had supported the revolution in Haiti and "the household family negroes . . .
[who were] trusty and well disposed" to the masters who had brought them
to Virginia. In grappling with these murders Wilson revealed a perception
of the growing diversity among Blacks within the town. Portsmouth was full,
he said, of "strange Negroes, foreign and domestick," and the hanging was
evidence for his general observation that they had "already begun hostilit-
ies upon themselves."[87] In his perception that Portsmouth, after the influx
of Caribbean refugees, was not divided along straightforward racial lines
and that divisions among Blacks were creating a confusing, disordered, and
potentially explosive cultural mix, Wilson struggled to comprehend the ways
in which the short-term immigration from Saint Domingue underscored the
cultural differences between Virginia's overwhelmingly creole slaves and
slaves from the more immediately African worlds of the islands.

[84] Sobel, *World They Made Together*, 6; Carolyn E. Fick, *The Making of Haiti: The Saint
Domingue Revolution from Below* (Knoxville, Tenn., 1990), 25.
[85] Sobel, *World They Made Together*, Part 3; Frey, *Water From the Rock*, chs. 8, 9; Jackson,
"Religious Development of the Negro," 170–80.
[86] Fick, *Making of Haiti*, 40–45 (defines voodoo), ch. 4 (voodoo in Revolution). Africans
from the Kingdom of Kongo would have been members of the Catholic Church prior
to getting caught in the Atlantic slave trade, but no evidence of a persisting Catholic tradition among Virginians from the Angola region has survived. See John Thornton, *The
Kingdom of Kongo: Civil War and Transition, 1641–1718* (Madison, 1983), ch. 5.
[87] Wilson to Lee, August 12, 1793, Executive Papers Box 80, 21–30 August folder. The
letter does not specify who hanged whom.

These conflicts intensified during the next few months. In November an anonymous letter writer warned "Mr Pennack" of trouble that threatened Virginia's coastal ports. The informer claimed to be a ringleader of a "mob of more than 80 . . . blacks concernd to burn both Norfolk and Portsmouth," but the towns themselves do not appear to have been the chief targets of these men. The anonymous source threatened to burn the "French ships also," and this self-proclaimed ringleader seemed to hope above all to get rid of the French: "the plot is to take place shortly without the French leaves the place," he claimed. "Disperse the French or burn all is the word." This letter was probably written by a White man – it claimed that "34 white men be sides a number of blacks" were participating in the plot, and it referred to "the negroes" in the third person as "very hot for beginning soon." But its threat to "drive the French or burn all," delivered in the name of Blacks and Whites, was believed plausible enough for Pennack to forward the letter to the governor.[88] This suggests that, while the revolution on Saint Domingue encouraged Virginia slaves to perceive the interests that they shared with enslaved people throughout the hemisphere, the encounter of those who lived in Virginia's port towns with "strange negroes" – to use a White Virginian's description – reinforced their "Virginia-ness." The enslaved people of Saint Domingue had solemnized their agreement to overthrow slavery with "a voodoo ceremony" that invoked the gods to direct and help" the rebellion.[89] Such people were different from a group of King William County, Virginia, slaves who organized their opposition to oppression by meeting and talking of "Chusing Delegates and a high Sheriff."[90] The point is not that one approach was more radical or authentic than the other but that they reflected different traditions. Some Virginians of African descent, when confronted with these "French" slaves and their masters, conspired with poor Whites to expel the interlopers from Norfolk.

These two influences of Saint Domingue on Virginia slaves' consciousness were analytically distinct, but they were not chronologically sequential. The order in which they appear here is not an implicit argument that the inspirational effect of Saint Domingue created a moment when Virginia slaves recognized their kinship with other enslaved peoples, a recognition that was dashed when they confronted the culturally distinct refugees from the island.

[88] Anonymous to Mr Pennack [William Pennock?], n.d., Executive Papers Box 82, 21–30 November folder.
[89] Fick, *Making of Haiti*, 93.
[90] Robert Richardson to Lee, June 5, 1792, Executive Papers Box 74, 1–10 June folder. Richardson described "large Night meetings" among "Negroes" that occurred "at some white persons house."

In fact, the incidents illustrating the incipient Afro-Atlantic identity occurred at the same times, were sometimes reported in the same letters, as the incidents that reveal Virginia slaves' sense of their difference from the refugees. Of course, only a small percentage of Black Virginians ever met refugees from Saint Domingue. Thus, the alienating effect that raised the latent local Virginian identity to the level of consciousness remained a minority experience. Its importance lies in what it reveals about slaves' culture in Virginia rather than in its influence upon it.

The 1790s, then, brought into sharp relief the paradoxical relationship between local and racial identities that developed out of enslaved Virginians' increasingly intense connections to the communicative webs of the Atlantic world. They had always been enmeshed in these webs – African slavery in the New World was an outgrowth of the same processes that created them – but the development of several mercantile towns, the intensification and diversification of the state's trade in the Atlantic economy (especially to the Caribbean), and the presence of revolutionary doctrines among the goods moving through the seas in the 1790s allowed Black Virginians greater concrete experience with both that which they shared with other people of West African descent in the Americas and that which set them apart. As the decade wore on, tension between Black Virginians' diasporic and local identities became less immanent. Presumably the slaves from Saint Domingue blended into the Virginia slave population, for there was not a steady flow of refugees that would have created conditions conducive to the development of a "French" subculture among Black Virginians. Events lessened the frequency with which Black Virginians interacted with Blacks from Saint Domingue, so encounters underscoring the specificity of Black Virginians' worldview decreased. That did nothing, however, to change the distinctive local identity rooted in the history of people of African descent in Virginia.

Nor did these events render Saint Domingue irrelevant to enslaved Virginians. It remained a powerful symbol of Black liberation and helped to transform "frenchness" into a trope with which Virginians communicated ideas about freedom and revolution. In 1798, at the height of the undeclared naval war between the United States and France that was known as the Quasi War, a remarkable incident underscored the complicated relationships between Virginians' implicit understandings of "frenchness" and events in Saint Domingue. In July 1798 White Virginians heard rumors that vessels were heading toward the Chesapeake with emigrants from Saint Domingue composed of Frenchmen and armed Blacks. Governor James Wood ordered local officials to prevent such vessels from docking in Virginia. At the same time a Major General Meade declared, in the presence of several persons, his inten-

tion, should Virginia be "invaded by a French Army," to "repair to their
Standard, with the black people who he could enlist."[91] All this occurred
during a period when France's relations with the Black armies in Saint
Domingue wavered somewhere between being very strained and openly hostile.[92] At least during the Quasi War, the meanings of "frenchness" among
Virginians apparently became less closely tied to the rapidly shifting alliances
and reversals on the island of Hispaniola and more closely defined as a general signifier – positive for some, negative for others – of Black liberation.

Most important for understanding the evolution of group consciousness
among Virginians of African descent, uses of "frenchness" came to embody
a complex racial identity. In the context of the Atlantic world in the 1790s,
any combined invocation of "frenchness," race, and resistance inevitably and
intentionally drew meanings from the revolution then taking place on Hispaniola. When Black Virginians referred to "frenchness" and revolution, they
implicitly described an Atlantic system of slavery in which people of African
descent shared an identity constituted through their common oppression. As
they developed peculiar local meanings for these tropes of "frenchness," they
simultaneously if unconsciously developed a language of resistance whose
meaning was specific to Virginia.[93] Ultimately, then, not only was there a
doubleness to the consciousness of Black Virginians (both Black or African,
and Virginian), there was a doubleness internal to the racial consciousness
of Black Virginians (Black Virginian and African American).[94] Of course, crosscutting identities were not peculiar to slaves, or Black Virginians, or African

[91] Wood to Otway Byrd, July 5, 1798, Executive Letter Book 1794–1800, 243–4 ("Vessels");
Wood to Capt. Archibald McRae, July 16, 1798, ibid., 244–5 (Meade).

[92] C. L. R. James, *The Black Jacobins: Toussaint L'Ouverture and the San Domingo Revolution*, 2nd rev. ed. (New York, 1989 [1963]), 215–23; Fick, *Making of Haiti*, ch. 8.

[93] This is analogous to the way that the language of "Britishness" came to mean something
different to English and American subjects of Britain prior to the American Revolution.
See Bernard Bailyn, *Ideological Origins of the American Revolution* (Cambridge, Mass.,
1967); Jack P. Greene, *Peripheries and Center: Constitutional Development in the Extended
Polities of the British Empire and the United States, 1607–1788* (New York, 1990 [1986]),
chs. 5–7; Jack P. Greene, *Imperatives, Behaviors, and Identities: Essays in Early American
Cultural History* (Charlottesville, 1992), chs. 6, 7.

[94] People most frequently express a sense of identity – to themselves as well as others – in
contrast with people whom they perceive to be different. Thus, black Virginians more
frequently conceived of themselves in racial terms (in opposition to the White Virginians
with whom they interacted daily) than in provincial "Virginian" terms (in opposition to
people who brought other cultures from other places). Nonetheless, a specific "Black
Virginian" identity, rooted in a shared century of history, existed implicitly even when
external events failed to spur its explicit expression.

Americans. Understanding the particular mix of identities that enslaved Virginians developed through the course of the eighteenth century, however, creates a fuller cultural context within which to understand their resistance to their masters and to slavery as a system.

Toward Gabriel's conspiracy

People of African descent lived in Virginia from early in the state's history, but "Black Virginians" – if the term is taken to reflect the self-perceptions of those to whom it refers – did not. Enslaved people who were sold into Virginia came from various societies and displayed no natural tendency to perceive one another as sharing a racial identity. Nor did a racial identity emerge whole out of the experience of slavery, though the racial basis of slavery in Virginia surely pushed various African peoples toward a shared identity. Enslaved people in Virginia, like other settlers in new societies, developed a changing culture and a shifting sense of identity by struggling to understand their new world using the cultural vocabularies they brought from their old world. Parts of those vocabularies lacked utility in the new world, and much had to be altered, so the building of a creole slave culture involved a constant dialectic between cultural inheritance and social experience.[95]

Before 1780 few people from Africa were brought to Virginia. Those who were spent most of their time with settlers from Europe, so little opportunity for the elaboration of a distinct subculture existed. From roughly 1680 to 1750, however, White Virginians bought many people from Africa, and the colony's bound labor force came to be dominated by Africans or creoles of African descent. A plurality of these people came from the Bight of Biafra and shared a view of the world that privileged local identity, a view that proved effective in making sense of the decentralized world of plantation Virginia. During the first half of the century, they developed a quarter-centered culture tied together through kinship and shared experience. They surely recognized that slavery followed a color line, but the relatively concrete lines of kinship and friendship dominated more abstract and imagined ties of race. This would have been especially true of people arriving from Africa, because their personal histories, rooted in their home societies, would have had no place for conceptions of identity based on blackness.[96]

---

[95] Free Virginians' (and other Americans') cultures were built through analogous processes. See Greene, *Pursuits of Happiness*.

[96] See Thornton's discussion of slavery in African societies: *Africa and Africans*, ch. 3. Also Appiah, *In My Father's House*.

During the second half of the century, however, events disrupted these cohesive local worlds. White Virginians moved west onto new land, taking slaves with them and forcibly extending the tightly bound communities. The American Revolution created disorder in Virginia, creating conditions in which many enslaved people tried to escape bondage and in which others were pulled away from their home quarters by various armies, thus breaking down local ties. The Revolution also increased the frequency and intensity with which White Virginians spoke of slavery as a system and of the possibility of ending it, a development that provided an ideological stimulus to a more broadly defined identity. Evangelical Christianity provided more potent ideological encouragement for Virginians of African descent to see themselves as part of communities that transcended quarters or neighborhoods. Finally, the revolution of the people of Saint Domingue offered a powerful way to incorporate the unfulfilled promises of freedom inherent in some of the language of the American Revolution into a racial consciousness with elastic boundaries.

The disruptions of the eighteenth century did not, however, lead in a *simple* way to a stronger racial identity. Both the religious and secular forces pushing Black Virginians toward racial consciousness included countervailing tendencies that either reinforced more local identities or underscored values enslaved Virginians shared with their masters. The crosscutting identities that Black Virginians developed were expressed in the largest and most important slave conspiracy of the Revolutionary era – Gabriel's Conspiracy – in which Richmond-area slaves used strikingly Virginian idioms to discuss an attempt to overthrow slavery and White supremacy, the central props of Virginia's dominant culture.

PART I

Cultural process

Creolization, appropriation, and collective identity in Gabriel's Virginia

D URING THE SUMMER of 1800, creole slaves from the Richmond
area built a fraternal movement to overthrow slavery. The
planned insurrection was betrayed and crushed, but the trials
of conspirators created an unusual forum in which enslaved
Virginians' discussions about their history, their present lives, and
their future possibilities were recorded in official records. By the
end of the eighteenth century, Virginians of African and European
descent had developed overlapping and distinctly Virginian ways of
communicating authority, of interpreting the state's revolutionary
tradition, and of understanding their relations to the supernatural.
These cultures with complicated and intertwined roots in Africa,
America, and Europe had grown in a society built on racial
inequality and slavery. Gabriel and his followers engaged in
creative acts of cultural appropriation through which they
reconstituted the meanings associated with shared elements of these
cultures, building a movement to destroy the racist foundations
of Virginia's society. Ultimately, however, two members of the
brotherhood turned on the conspiracy, informed White Virginians
of the approaching insurrection, and were granted freedom.
To understand Gabriel's Virginia entails understanding the
conspirators' attempt to win freedom, but it also entails
understanding the betrayers' relationship to the world that spawned
the conspiracy. The informers' lives uncover the rich and
contradictory tension between communal and individualistic
impulses among Virginians of African descent. The betrayers won
their freedom but at the cost of their comrades' lives and of a place
within enslaved Virginians' communal memories. Understanding
Gabriel's Virginia also entails making sense of the White reaction
to the conspiracy – the way Whites used military power to crush

the conspiracy and the way they used cultural power to inscribe
the conspiracy into their sense of Virginia's history – and of Black
Virginians' response to that reaction. For if Gabriel's Conspiracy
was defeated militarily, it survived in the memories and oral
traditions of Black Virginians, becoming an inspiring moment in a
communal history that promised to culminate with God's chosen
people finding justice on Earth.

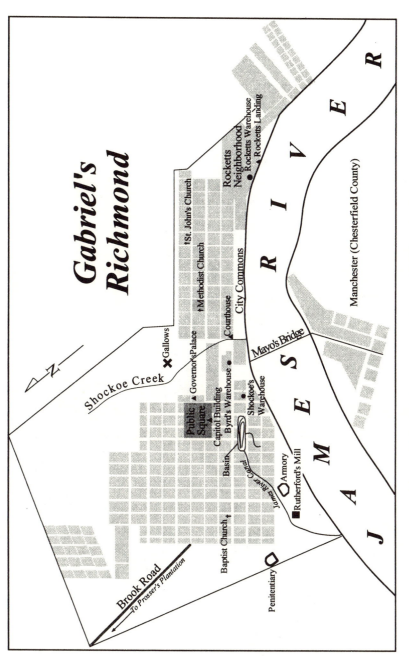

Map 3. Richmond, Virginia, at the time of Gabriel's Conspiracy.

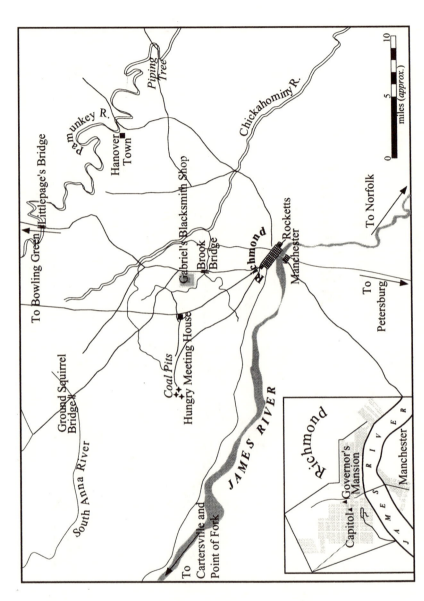

Map 4. Much of the activity associated with Gabriel's Conspiracy occurred in the countryside surrounding Richmond.

2

Forging an oppositional culture

Gabriel's Conspiracy and the process
of cultural appropriation

In the fall of 1799 Gabriel, later to become the famous leader of a slave conspiracy, initiated a less well-publicized act of resistance. He and his brother
Solomon, both blacksmiths and well-entrenched members of the Prosser
plantation's slave community, joined a man named Jupiter to steal a pig from
the nearby farm on which Jupiter worked. The farmer, a former overseer and
a newcomer who had just begun renting in Henrico County, saw the brothers
making off with his pig, confronted them, and a fight ensued. Apparently
Gabriel was bigger and stronger than Johnson, for he got the better of their
fight. By the time the two were separated Gabriel had bitten off part of Absolam
Johnson's left ear.

Gabriel was tried by a court of Oyer and Terminer composed of justices
who served on the Henrico County Court, just as he would later be tried for
attempting to foment a slave rebellion. Like most trials of slave defendants,
Gabriel's first encounter with the Henrico County Court produced a meager
documentary record, a record full of suggestive but inconclusive hints about
the contexts that gave meaning to his decision to fight Absolam Johnson.[1]
That three slaves from two different farms joined together to steal the hog
suggests but does not prove that the neighborhood surrounding Thomas Henry
Prosser's plantation was home to the kind of tight-knit slave community that
had developed around Virginia plantations over the course of the eighteenth
century. Perhaps the three defendants had been planning a barbecue for the
Black community. That they targeted a relatively transient newcomer's livestock suggests but does not prove that they may have been punishing him for
failing to respect norms that had evolved through local struggles over work,

---

[1] Henrico County Court Order Book (hereafter HCCOB) #9, 94–5. Philip J. Schwarz,
"Gabriel's Challenge: Slaves and Crime in Late Eighteenth-Century Virginia," *Virginia
Magazine of History and Biography* 90 (1982): 283–309 reads this incident within a broad
sociolegal context.

food, or leisure. Their attempt to stay and fight rather than fleeing when Johnson caught them may indicate that they sought to make a point beyond stealing the pig. Though these three men faced temporary imprisonment, trials, the threat of hanging (in Gabriel's case), and physical brutality (lashes and branding), one might guess that they returned to their communities as heroes who had stood up to a White man's attempt to transgress hard-won community rights. One might guess that Johnson's missing ear served as a constant reminder within the Black community of the need to defend customary rights, while serving as a reminder within the White community of the cost of infringing upon them. Understanding the historical development of enslaved Virginians' communities and resistance can render such guesses much more productive, but it cannot ultimately make up for the sparseness of the record.

Too much that would shed light upon the meaning of this incident remains lost to the record, in part because no one recorded any of the discussions that preceded the three enslaved men's decision to take the pig. It is impossible to know what combination of conscious protest, hunger, youthful rebelliousness, personal animosity, and communal antagonism lay behind this (or most any other) act of resistance. One can safely assert that Gabriel's attempt to steal a pig and the fight that grew out of it would have remained buried in Henrico County's local records had he learned the lesson that the court intended him to learn from the thirty-nine lashes and the branded thumb that it meted out to him as punishment. Rather than learning his lesson, however, Gabriel walked away from his encounter with Virginia's court system with his determination to resist intact. Within a year he had played a leading role in organizing one of the most extensive insurrectionary conspiracies in the history of North American slavery.

Gabriel's Conspiracy merits historical attention for its remarkable ability to reveal how some enslaved Virginians perceived and sought to change their world.[2] The conspirators' attempt to overthrow slavery frightened White

[2] It has received extensive historical attention for other reasons. From the nineteenth century through the first half of the twentieth, historians examined the conspiracy to argue that African Americans resisted slavery. See Thomas Wentworth Higginson, *Travelers and Outlaws: Episodes in American History* (Boston, 1889); Joseph C. Carroll, *Slave Insurrections in the United States, 1800–1865* (New York, 1973 [1938]); Herbert Aptheker, *American Negro Slave Revolts* (New York, 1987 [1943]); Marion D. Kilson, "Towards Freedom: An Analysis of Slave Revolts in the United States," *Phylon* 25 (1964): 175–87. More recently historians have analyzed the conspiracy in light of task allocation and the conspirators' assimilation to Euro-American norms (Gerald W. Mullin, *Flight and Rebellion: Slave Resistance in Eighteenth-Century Virginia* [New York, 1972], ch. 5), or

Virginians and led to a much deeper and better-documented inquiry into the motivations behind the slaves' decision to fight their oppression and the ways that they went about organizing against their masters. Such records are complicated, because they were produced in power-laden encounters in which many of the lives of those testifying were at risk. If read with care, however, the documents produced during the trials of Gabriel and his alleged conspirators reveal the processes through which enslaved Virginians constructed a movement to end slavery.[3] They uncover a process of cultural appropriation near the center of this movement – a process through which these men who were born and raised in Virginia used local symbolic idioms to communicate their conception of status and authority, their belief in themselves as God's chosen people, and their desire for freedom.

This process of appropriation through which Gabriel and his followers reconstituted the meanings associated with powerful symbolic structures that they shared with other Virginians provides a key to understanding the ways in which enslaved Virginians were at once of the dominant culture yet crucially apart from it. These fragmentary pictures of slaves discussing – sometimes debating – the path to liberty provide an intense snapshot of the processes of resistance and the sense of identity that undergirded "routine" acts of resistance like Gabriel's attempt to steal Absolam Johnson's pig, as well as fueling more spectacular acts of resistance like Gabriel's attempt to end slavery.

placed the conspiracy within the context of the revolutionary movements of the late eighteenth-century Atlantic world (Eugene D. Genovese, *From Rebellion to Revolution: Afro-American Slave Revolts in the Making of the Modern World* [Baton Rouge, 1979], ch. 1; Sylvia R. Frey, *Water from the Rock: Black Resistance in a Revolutionary Age* [Princeton, 1991], ch. 9), or argued that it represented a flowering of one variety of the artisanal republicanism that developed among working people in many northern urban centers (Douglas R. Egerton, *Gabriel's Rebellion: The Virginia Slave Conspiracies of 1800 and 1802* [Chapel Hill, 1993]).

[3] An extensive collection of official papers relating to the conspiracy is in *Calendar of Virginia State Papers and Other Manuscripts, 1652–1869, Preserved in the Capitol, at Richmond* (hereafter *CVSP*) 11 vols., ed. by William Price Palmer and Henry W. Flournoy (Richmond, 1875–93), v. 9, pp. 140–74. Executive Communications to the Legislature, Box 24 (hereafter Executive Communications) contains a paginated collection of documents from the conspiracy trials which Monroe had copied and sent to the General Assembly. When possible I refer to this source because it is accurate and relatively complete, and because of the convenience of providing a page reference. To find all surviving material from the original trials, see the original copies made for Monroe and stored in the Virginia Executive Papers, Letters Received (hereafter Executive Papers), Boxes 114, 115. Executive Communications and Executive Papers are at the Library of Virginia (hereafter LiVa) in Richmond.

Favorable conditions and traditions of resistance

Virginia slaves faced dauntingly prohibitive odds against a successful insurrection. Throughout most of its history, the state maintained a substantial White majority, and Whites always commanded virtually all the firearms. They maintained control – at least in theory – over communications and transportation, and they held a monopoly over governmental and most social institutions. Despite this, Virginia slaves discussed rebellion throughout the early national period. White Virginians frequently heard this talk and sometimes reported it to authorities. As many Whites recognized, such discussions did not always signal an immediate danger of rebellion: slaves who met among themselves often held "conversation relative to what hath not only already happened, but what may hereafter come to pass, without having a real intention of puting the same into Execution." Such talk, even without an immediate intention to rebel, did however keep alive traditions of resistance among the enslaved, traditions that could fuel real conspiracies when conditions proved favorable.[4]

Some conditions favored potential slave rebels in 1800, at least by Virginia's standards. According to the 1800 federal census, slaves comprised about 48 percent of Virginia's population, and counting free Blacks the Commonwealth was slightly more than half Black. Probably never before and certainly never again would Virginia have a Black majority. The number of Blacks was even larger near Richmond, where Gabriel and his fellow conspirators lived. Richmond City's population was almost exactly half Black, though the freedom enjoyed by a fifth of town Blacks meant that only 40 percent of the town was enslaved. In the surrounding area slaves were even more numerous. Slaves from five jurisdictions – Richmond City, Henrico County, Hanover County, Chesterfield County, and Caroline County – almost certainly took part in the conspiracy, and of the 61,000 people who lived in those jurisdictions, almost 60 percent were Black. Eighteenth-century census-takers, like their twentieth-century counterparts, may well have undercounted Black residents, so Blacks may have comprised an even larger majority of the area's population.

Gabriel and his followers believed that other factors left Richmond unusually vulnerable to a slave insurrection during the summer of 1800. Some

---

[4] Pardon petition, May 24, 1802, Executive Papers, Box 120. This petition signed by twenty-two White residents of Hanover County sought pardons for two slaves, both of whom belonged to Paul Thilman, some of whose slaves participated in Gabriel's Conspiracy, who were convicted of conspiring to "raise an insurrection." Aptheker, *American Negro Slave Revolts*, chs. 8–15.

United States army troops who had been stationed in the state capital were disbanded that June. More important, the Commonwealth chose that summer to take stock of the public arms in response to long-standing complaints by local leaders about the readiness of the militia. Monroe ordered all county militia officers to collect their regiments' arms, count them, and send them to Richmond, and he set John Clarke to work cleaning the old arms. The state also purchased 4,000 new muskets from a Philadelphia gunsmith. By the end of the summer, all these arms sat stored in Richmond awaiting the governor's distribution order. If Gabriel and his followers could have seized the armory, they would not only have armed themselves, they would effectively have denied arms to many of the militia men who would inevitably have been called to repress the insurrection. As Gabriel's brother Martin pointed out when arguing against delaying the rebellion: "the Soldiers were discharged, and all the Arms all put away."[5]

Just as important, the patrols charged with catching and punishing slaves who left their home quarters without their masters' permission do not appear to have been vigilant during the summer of 1800. Although it is difficult to document precisely when patrols rode or how carefully they policed their beats, most evidence suggests they were rarely very vigilant. Apparently they grew especially lax during the summer of 1800, for Martin claimed "there was no patroling in the Country."[6] In all the trips made by conspirators to recruit and organize followers, no one reported an encounter with a slave patrol.

Gabriel noted two other factors that made the summer of 1800 an unusually promising moment to seek freedom. An uncertain international situation found the United States in a de facto naval war with France that threatened to escalate. Simultaneously, the vitriolic election of 1800 wracked the Old Dominion at home. Jeffersonian Republicans filled the air with charges of Federalist tyranny, and John Adams's party responded with dire warnings against the anarchy that might result if the radical Jefferson became president. Neither party considered freeing slaves, so the election's outcome was unlikely to make much difference for Richmond Blacks. The slaves of Saint Domingue had, however, exploited splits within the French hierarchy and among European powers to forge a Black revolution, and, as shown earlier,

---

[5] For collection and distribution of arms see *CVSP*, v. 9, pp. 109–112, 114; Executive Communications, 6 (Martin). Egerton, *Gabriel's Rebellion*, chs. 6 and 7 reconstructs the course of the trials.

[6] Executive Communications, 6 (Martin). Also see Mullin, *Flight and Rebellion*, 56 (elite complaint that patrollers rarely rode); Rhys Isaac, *The Transformation of Virginia, 1740–1790* (Chapel Hill, 1982), 110 (militiamen hesitant to patrol).

enslaved Virginians knew much about the Haitian Revolution. The conspirators hoped the French, whom they thought at war with the United States, might aid the rebellion.[7]

Though Gabriel probably realized that the odds against a successful rebellion remained high in 1800, the conspirators also recognized that a fortunate confluence of events provided as good a chance to strike for freedom as they had ever seen. Black Virginians had engaged in numerous discussions of insurrection throughout the 1790s. While it is sometimes difficult to know how often such talk of rebellion represented "real" conspiracies, that talk created assumptions that Gabriel could draw upon in the relatively favorable environment of 1800.[8] Gabriel's Conspiracy grew out of the meeting between traditions of resistance that had been transformed during the second half of the eighteenth century and the relative and temporary weakness of White Virginians during the summer of 1800.

Cultural appropriation and resistance

Despite the temporary waning of White Virginians' overwhelming local military advantage over the enslaved, masters' power continued to shape enslaved peoples' lives, but Richmond Blacks did not blindly accept their masters' values. The process through which Richmond-area Blacks built a conspiracy to overthrow slavery reveals the ways that they worked within social boundaries largely defined by their masters to develop a cultural world related to, but quite different from, that of Whites. Enslaved Virginians had, during the previous forty years, come to see themselves increasingly as Virginians, but in their efforts to overthrow the state's social system they revealed the ways that they had appropriated elements of Virginia's dominant culture to forge a

---

[7] Egerton, *Gabriel's Rebellion*, ch. 3 for the election and Gabriel's Conspiracy; for partisanship in Virginia, see Richard Beeman, *The Old Dominion and the New Nation, 1788–1801* (Lexington, Ky., 1972). Executive Communications, 7.

Egerton, *Gabriel's Rebellion*, 102 calls Woolfolk's report that Gabriel hoped for French aid "a foolish dream" that revealed his lack of "access to the inner sanctum" of the conspiracy, but the Quasi War was a reality and White fears of "French" forces were real enough that Gabriel might well have hoped for French aid. No documentary evidence suggests that Woolfolk was alone in believing it.

[8] See Chapter 1 of this book, and Aptheker, *American Negro Slave Revolts*. Aptheker's argument that enslaved African Americans built a tradition of violent resistance to slavery is famously controversial. The controversy revolves around whether "real" and "imagined" conspiracies are conflated. While Aptheker includes conspiracies that were more rumor than reality in his seminal book, rumors and talk helped to perpetuate traditions of resistance that men like Gabriel could use.

distinctive identity as Black Virginians.[9] This identity that had developed over the course of the previous century was rooted in Black Virginians' distinctive notions regarding the meaning of work, authority, gender, and spirituality. The conspirators, for example, appear from one perspective to have held artisanal slaves in unusually high esteem, something they shared with their masters. Three of the most important leaders of the conspiracy were blacksmiths by trade, and many, perhaps most, of the slaves convicted of participating in the conspiracy by the Henrico County Court had artisanal skills.[10] While masters valued such skills for economic reasons, enslaved Richmonders appear to have valued skills and the skilled for very different reasons. The blacksmiths aside, slaves testifying at the conspiracy trials rarely noted other slaves' skills or occupations. Instead, they mentioned attributes – like literacy and the privilege of self-hire – that other sources indicate were more often acquired by skilled slaves. For example, the records remain silent regarding the occupations of George Smith and Sam Byrd, two important leaders of the conspiracy, but each made a point of displaying his literacy when recruiting followers. Enslaved witnesses also thought it worth noting that Smith and Byrd had gained permission to hire their own time from their owners.[11] Neither literacy nor self-hire was an absolute marker of artisanship, but they

---

[9] For a recent study emphasizing cultural appropriation – a "complex process of 'Euro-Afro-Creolization'" (78) – in building a slave rebellion, see Emilia Viotti da Costa, *Crowns of Glory, Tears of Blood: The Demerara Slave Rebellion of 1823* (New York, 1994), 61–80. My ideas about the role of appropriation in the development of alternative cultures have been influenced by Henry Louis Gates Jr., *The Signifying Monkey: A Theory of African-American Literary Criticism* (New York, 1988); Roger Chartier, *The Cultural Uses of Print in Early Modern France*, Lydia G. Cochrane, transl. (Princeton, 1987), chs. 3, 8, and "Conclusion"; David Warren Sabean, *Power in the Blood: Popular Culture and Village Discourse in Early Modern Germany* (Cambridge, England, 1984) who traces the way "inherited items of culture continually changed shape as they were situated in new contexts" (4).

[10] The courts rarely noted slave defendants' skills, but Virginia law called for masters to be compensated for executed slaves. Of the forty-five men convicted of conspiring with Gabriel, thirty-eight were valued by the magistrates at £100 or more. Virginia county courts condemned thirty-four slaves for crimes other than insurrection between 1799 and 1801, valuing over half of them at less than £100. The average value of slave felons not involved in Gabriel's Conspiracy was £85; the conspirators averaged £105. These figures strongly suggest that skilled slaves dominated the leadership of the conspiracy. Office of the Auditor of Public Accounts, Item 153, Executed and Transported Slaves (hereafter OAI 153), Box 1 (1783–1803) for slaves executed throughout Virginia (LiVa); slaves convicted by the Henrico Court but later pardoned by the executive do not appear in OAI 153, but they can be found in HCCOB #9, 373–400 (LiVa). See Mullin, *Flight and Rebellion* for masters' views of skilled slaves.

[11] Executive Communications, 4–5, 24–5, 28–30.

were the qualities that slave conspirators valued, for they were qualities that permitted enslaved people to exert greater control over their own lives. Masters' values paradoxically helped to shape status among slaves by influencing which Black Virginians could keep Whites at the greatest distance.

This process can be seen more clearly through an analysis of physical mobility. Virginia law prohibited slaves' traveling off their home quarters without passes from their masters. On one level the law was honored mostly in the breach during the summer of 1800: testimony from the conspiracy trials illustrates that many slaves visited among local plantations during their free time – mostly Sundays – with little fear of White interference. The leaders of the insurrection recruited followers at these regular social and religious gatherings of slaves: Prosser's Ben testified that "Meetings were frequently held . . . under pretext of attending preachment, and . . . at a Fish feast and at Barbacues."[12] Whites, however, exerted much firmer control over Black mobility than such testimony suggests. If most slaves could travel within local slave communities on the weekends, far fewer could travel more widely without White supervision.

Some Black Virginians did, however, achieve greater mobility. Literacy provided some latitude for illegal movement – one reason that Sam Byrd opened his attempt to recruit Ben Woolfolk by asking George Smith if he had "any pen and ink." The next Monday night Byrd reinforced the advantages literacy conferred by sending someone with a pass to get Woolfolk.[13] Literate Blacks could write passes for themselves and for others, so the ability to write conferred the power to help others to travel more safely. Forged passes were not, however, legal, so they did not guarantee safe passage. More important, literacy did little to expand the range within which a slave could move, because most slaves with forged passes still had to travel on foot and remained tied to their home neighborhoods.

Certain occupations enhanced Blacks' mobility much more. During the summer of 1800, Blacks who worked transporting goods and information along Virginia's roads and rivers helped to link different centers of the conspiracy, and they surely provided an important medium of communication among enslaved Virginians at all times. Slaves drove wagons filled with produce into Richmond, they manned the stages, and planters often had Black coachmen who drove White families to church or to town. Black batteaumen

[12] Executive Communications, 9.
[13] Ibid., 4–5. A more detailed discussion of the meaning of literacy in Gabriel's world follows in this chapter.

were probably the most numerous and important group of enslaved Virginians whose jobs offered great mobility. Most of Virginia's commerce flowed to and from markets on the rivers that split the Commonwealth into three peninsulas, and Virginia's sloops and batteaus (large plank-built, skiff-like vessels used to transport goods above the fall lines) often had Black crews.[14]

The role allegedly played by Black watermen in the conspiracy illustrates the importance of these men in Virginia's Black communities. It was to the "Batteau Men" that authorities in Cartersville, a small town twenty miles upriver from Richmond, turned when they feared that the slaves' plot had extended to their neighborhood. Stepney, a Black waterman, was detained on suspicion of being one of Gabriel's recruiting officers, and his story illustrates the way that transient boatmen could link Blacks living in different areas. He belonged to a man from Goochland County, was hired to two men in Cartersville (Cumberland County), and was well known in Richmond. Nor was Stepney's case unusual. A Black deckhand named Billy, who would turn Gabriel in to Norfolk authorities, had been jailed in Richmond on suspicion of conspiracy. He and his brother Ned both belonged to Miles King of Hampton, a town near Norfolk. Ned was also jailed – in Hampton – for supporting the conspiracy, again showing how Black boatmen could serve as a medium to communicate ideas and knowledge up and down the rivers. And a Black boat captain named Jacob played a crucial role in passing information from Richmond to the counties downriver.[15]

Governor Monroe realized the threat that Black control of Virginia's rivers posed for Whites during the insurrection scare. Gabriel chose the summer of 1800 for the planned insurrection in part because the Commonwealth was preparing to re-arm the local militias. On September 6, in the face of widespread White anxiety over the fact that Gabriel was still at large, Monroe's fear of rebellious watermen caused him to order his subordinates not to forward the arms allotted to the different counties. Only after twelve days did he order the guns to be distributed without undue delay, and he still remained cautious, ordering the arms put under the care of boatmen of good character

[14] Edward C. Carter II, ed., *The Virginia Journals of Benjamin Henry Latrobe, 1795–1798* (New Haven, 1977), 82, 92–4, 516–17 for entries mentioning black batteaumen (hereafter *Latrobe Journals*). Also see Reginald D. Butler, "The Evolution of a Rural Free Black Community: Goochland County, Virginia, 1728–1832" (Ph.D. dissertation, Johns Hopkins University, 1989), ch. 3 for free Black boatmen upriver from Richmond.

[15] Mayo Carrington to James Monroe, September 17, 1800, Executive Papers, Box 114 (Stepney); Thomas Newton to James Monroe, September 24, 1800, Executive Papers, Box 114 (Billy and Ned); Egerton, *Gabriel's Rebellion*, 61 (Jacob).

and suggesting sending many small loads rather than sending any number of boats at the same time.[16]

The evidence of Black batteaumen's participation, like much else that occurred during the conspiracy, remains murky. Whites suspected much, but they failed to convict a single slave identified in the record as a boatman.[17] Nonetheless, White suspicions reveal a great deal about the roles watermen must have played in the Black community. Billy, the shiphand who would betray Gabriel, and his brother Ned belonged to a man in Hampton, but Billy's wife lived in Richmond. The frequent trips Billy made up and down the James River linked his families in the two places.[18] Similarly, Stepney, the slave suspected of recruiting in Cartersville, was well known in at least three Piedmont counties as well as in Richmond. Black watermen helped slaves to maintain kinship networks despite the forced mobility discussed in the previous chapter, and they could also carry slaves' goods to town markets and bring back commodities from those markets. Such links appeared sinister to Whites during the insurrection scare, but their importance to Black Virginians transcended such moments.

Boatmen were the most numerous but not the only enslaved Virginians whose jobs offered unusual mobility. A smaller group combined the practical advantages of mobility with the symbolic status accorded to men on horseback. They too could serve as conduits for slaves in various parts of the state: one conspirator claimed that "the Black man who carries the Mail to Charlotsville" – probably a man named Tobias – had delivered a message from conspirators at Point of Fork to Sam Byrd.[19] Like batteaumen, the postrider could just as easily (and more routinely) have delivered messages between family members or friends as among insurrectionaries. Unlike the rivermen,

---

[16] Monroe to James Clarke, September 18, 1800, Executive Letter Book (hereafter ELB) 1794–1800. For a complaint about the delay see Benjamin Oliver to Monroe, September 23, 1800, Executive Papers, Box 114. Monroe ties the delay to "the late affair of the Negroes" in Monroe to Miles King, September 30, 1800, ELB 1794–1800 (see Chapter 1, n. 38 for full citation for ELB).

[17] The captain named Jacob, however, was probably murdered before he could be tried (Egerton, *Gabriel's Rebellion*, 113–14), and because most convicted conspirators' occupations remain unknown, others probably worked on boats.

[18] See n. 15.

[19] Gilbert's Confession is in Executive Papers, Box 114. "Tobias a free black man commonly known" as "the Amherst post rider" charged a free Black man with stealing $10 in 1795 (Richmond Hustings Court Order Book [hereafter RHCOB] #3, 340, LiVa). Tobias's involvement may have helped to lead Whites to prohibit Blacks from serving as postriders; see Bruce Levine, *Half Slave and Half Free: The Roots of Civil War* (New York, 1992), 12–13.

he would not have been limited to a single delivery route. Masters routinely used slaves to deliver messages to other Whites, and these unofficial postriders would have enjoyed mobility analogous to Tobias's. Black watermen and messengers traveled around Virginia because it served their masters' economic interests, but by providing slaves with links to friends, family members, and markets they opened up social space within the repressive institution of slavery, and they helped to connect Blacks who lived or worked in Richmond with slave communities in rural Virginia.

Slaves allowed on horseback acquired enhanced symbolic stature that paralleled the practical advantages they gained. William, a slave of William Young, alluded to this when he suggested that the leaders should hire a horse for Ben Woolfolk to ride on a recruiting trip to Caroline County. Woolfolk would have gotten to Caroline much faster on a hired horse than on foot, but he walked that distance regularly.[20] Had ease and convenience been at issue, then presumably Woolfolk himself would have requested the horse, but horses also symbolized power and authority. William presumably thought Woolfolk would impress those he wanted to recruit by arriving on horseback. Other testimony allows fuller analysis of the symbolic meanings of horses for Virginians of African descent.

Blacks and Whites attached overlapping but not identical symbolic meaning to horses. Several historians have noted the cultural importance of horses to the Virginia gentry, explaining that a White Virginian was "only as good as his horse." Horses were, of course, emblems of status throughout Western Europe as well as in many West African societies, and Black Virginians recognized horses' symbolic meaning for Whites.[21] Horses also served a military purpose, and Gabriel's plan included cavalry, so both cultural symbolism and military utility were involved when slaves claimed horses.

According to T. H. Breen, horses were more than simply symbols of authority to White Virginians – "a horse was an extension of its owner." Several conspirators recognized that and symbolically asserted the control they planned to exert over their owners by claiming the right to a special horse. Will, who planned to act as a horseman, needed a mount, but he introduced a revealing

[20] Executive Communications, 26–7.
[21] T. H. Breen, *Puritans and Adventurers: Change and Persistence in Early America* (New York, 1980), 156 (quotation); Isaac, *Transformation of Virginia*, 56; Robin Law, *The Horse in West African History: the Role of the Horse in the Societies of Pre-Colonial West Africa* (Oxford, England, 1980); Herbert M. Cole, *Icons: Ideals and Power in the Art of Africa* (Washington, D.C., 1989), ch. 7. Adiele Afigbo, *Ropes of Sand: Studies in Igbo History and Culture* (Ibadan, Nigeria, 1981), 137–8 ("the horse was brought in [to Igboland] for ritual and ceremonial purposes only.").

degree of specificity when he declared first that he would kill his master, and then that he had reserved "his Masters Sorrel Horse" for himself. Similarly Billey, a slave of Roger Gregory, accepted Gabriel's commission as a captain and announced he "was to have Mr. Gregory's horse." Gilbert regretted that his master "had rode away the horse he intended for himself – but said as it was, he would take the Bald." A conspirator named Lewis most clearly exemplified the symbolic equation between horses and White masculine power by planning to take a horse of his master's named Cumberland as far as Richmond, where he would switch to "Harry Shores Horse."[22] Henry Shore was a prominent Richmond merchant and an important local political figure. By claiming Shore's horse (and by using a diminutive form of Shore's name), Lewis laid claim to a position that had traditionally commanded the respect and deference of White and Black Virginians alike.

Like horses, weapons played crucial practical and symbolic roles in the slaves' conspiracy, and the conspirators' discussions of weapons reveal a similar dynamic of cultural appropriation. White Virginians controlled most of the Commonwealth's firepower, and historians have often and rightly cited that near-monopoly as a chief obstacle to any successful slave insurrection. Whites' monopoly was not, however, complete, for trial testimony reveals that several slaves owned weapons. Moreover, they did not think White Virginians found their possession of firearms troublesome under normal conditions.

Gabriel planned to take advantage of this small cadre of armed followers. Gilbert, for instance, owned a broken pistol. Gabriel fixed it for him, and Gilbert went to Richmond on August 29 to "purchase powder, for the purpose of the insurrection." Natt, a conspirator who guarded a warehouse in Richmond, "purchased a Sword from one Wilchire the property of Benjamin Mosbey." Wilchire admitted that he had sold the sword but explained that Natt "wanted it to Stand guard . . . at the Warehouse," suggesting that Whites would have accepted Wilchire's sale of the sword to Natt if it was done without knowledge of the conspiracy. This appears reasonable given that Wilchire owned the sword in the first place. Other slaves shared the opinion that Whites did not normally mind slaves being armed. Prosser's Ben and a man named Michael were with friends when they heard that "the insurrection had blown." Prior to this news no one much cared that one of these Black men had a gun, but when Michael heard that some of the neighbouring slaves had been apprehended, he became anxious that the gun should be hidden. In the treacherous environment produced by an insurrection scare,

---

[22] Breen, *Puritans and Adventurers*, 156; Executive Communications, 10 (Will), 15 (Billey), 23 (Gilbert); Executive Papers Box 114 (Lewis).

these slaves thought it dangerous for Whites to find them armed, but it is equally clear that they did not think it dangerous in less tense times.[23]

In normal times, owning weapons might have troubled Whites and thus been dangerous for Blacks, except that Whites knew that enslaved Virginians lacked the arms necessary to challenge White supremacy. If the slaves who possessed guns and swords formed a small base for the conspiracy, that base was far from adequate, and Gabriel realized that his plan could not succeed unless he could provide all his followers with the guns Whites normally controlled. Accordingly, Gabriel visited Richmond "every Sunday . . . to find where the military Stores were deposited." When he found that the armory was in the capitol, he recruited Colonel Wilkenson's Jupiter and Peter Tinsley's James, two friends of Robert Cowley, the free Black man who kept the keys to the capitol. Gilbert saw Jupiter and James borrow the keys from Cowley, and he accepted Gabriel's assurance that James and Jupiter would open the capitol on the night of the insurrection.[24] On August 30, Gabriel planned to send a group through Richmond to set fire to the warehouse district in southeastern Richmond called Rocketts, while another group would take possession of some arms that were in a tavern near Prosser's plantation. Then, as Richmond's White male inhabitants charged down to Rocketts to put out the fire, the other conspirators would rendezvous with James and Jupiter who were to "have all the arms in readiness." Only then, when armed with guns, would the insurrectionaries meet concerted opposition and "Slaughter the People on their return from Rocketts."[25] Whether the conspirators could have executed such a plan will never be known, but Gabriel and the other leaders recognized that the success of their insurrection rested largely on acquiring guns before they encountered organized opposition.

[23] Executive Communications, 6 (Gilbert's pistol), 22 (powder in town), 14–15 (Natt), 26 (Michael). Also see Philip D. Morgan, "The Development of Slave Culture in Eighteenth Century Plantation America" (Ph.D. diss., University College, London, 1977), 43; and T. H. Breen and Stephen Innes, *"Myne Owne Ground": Race and Freedom on Virginia's Eastern Shore, 1640–1676* (New York, 1980), 24–28 for the history and historiography of Blacks' access to guns in colonial Virginia.

[24] Executive Communications, 4 (Gabriel's trips to Richmond); Deposition of Young's Gilbert, September 22, 1800, Executive Papers, Box 114 (viewing arms). Egerton believes Cowley was a conspirator (*Gabriel's Rebellion*, 57–8). Authorities investigated and were confident enough of his innocence to allow him to continue to keep the keys to the capitol (Monroe to Storrs and Selden, October [8?], 1800, ELB 1800–3). As Egerton points out, Cowley had much to lose, so I suspect that authorities were right that he stayed out of the conspiracy, but perhaps he joined and fooled them into believing he had not.

[25] There are several slightly different versions of Gabriel's plan. These quotations are from Ben Woolfolk's Confession, Executive Communications, 4–8.

Thus it appears curious that much of the testimony at the trials centered around swords rather than guns. Swords remained effective weapons
in 1800, and Gabriel and his followers intended to use them. In early July
when Gabriel grew anxious to push the insurrection into motion, he asked
his brother Solomon "to make *Scythe Swords.*" Prosser's Ben reported that
Gabriel planned to distribute these swords for use by horsemen, though some
foot soldiers also acquired scythe swords. At least one sword was issued – a
slave named Michael obtained his sword from Gabriel on the evening of
August 30 and later used it to resist arrest – and others remained unissued
in Gabriel's and Solomon's blacksmith shop, where they were found by authorities. The conspirators realized that swords would be insufficient for the insurrection and planned to use them only until they got arms from the capitol,
but swords did play a practical role in the plan.[26]

Swords' practical utility should not overshadow their symbolic meanings.
In traditional Western and West African religious and political thought, the
sword – often the sword of state, a sovereign, or a deity – represented the
ultimate coercive authority. Throughout much of West Africa, symbolic swords
represent authority in art dating from before the era of the slave trade, and
they continue to play that role in modern rituals.[27] Similarly, European notions
of courtiers engaged in swordplay and images of military leaders, sabers held
high, exhorting their men to attack, may have reinforced the association of
swords with gentility and authority. And in Virginia swords indicated their
bearers' status as officers in the militia. By arming themselves with swords,
conspirators appropriated another symbol of authority that had complicated
roots in the state's diverse cultural heritage. Gilbert, who reserved one of
his master's horses for his own use, also planned to take the sword his master left hanging up in the house. Most of the participants armed themselves
through a different process. When Will, a slave of John Mosbey Sr., joined,
he had "to carry two Scythe Blades to Solomon to be made into swords."
Solomon, Thornton, or Gabriel, the three blacksmith leaders, would then
cut the blades in half and attach each piece to a handle, making two swords
out of each scythe. Many other conspirators stole blades and turned them
over to one of the blacksmiths to be made into swords: Prosser's Ben testified
that Woolfolk had six scythe blades in his cabin waiting to be made into

---

[26] Executive Communications, 4 (Solomon), 9 (swords to cavalry), 12 (foot Soldiers), 14
(Michael), 18 (switch to guns); Monroe to the Speakers of the General Assembly,
December 5, 1800, ELB 1800–3 (discovered swords).
[27] Herbert Cole, *Icons*, 36, 106, and figures 17, 36, 43, 48, 55, 120, 128. For swords among
some Igbo people, see Richard N. Henderson, *The King in Every Man: Evolutionary
Trends in Onitsha Ibo Society and Culture* (New Haven, 1972), 275–9.

swords by Gabriel.[28] Woolfolk recruited actively, so these blades were probably given to him by slaves when they signed up.

The leaders' request that recruits supply a scythe blade served several
purposes. It contributed to the conspirators' military readiness. By forcing
new soldiers to commit a minor legal violation for the insurrection and to
supply a physical object emblematic of their participation, it may also have
strengthened their psychological allegiance. Equally important, the swords
that would symbolize the rebels' authority were made out of agricultural implements that represented the slaves' degradation. Each slave probably brought
a tool that he had used beneath a master's or an overseer's gaze when har-
vesting grain for his master's benefit. The blacksmiths' ability to transform
these tools of servility into weapons of liberation probably helps to explain
their prominence in the conspiracy.

The biblical injunction to beat swords into ploughshares is well known.
Less familiar is Joel 3:10: "Beat your plowshares into swords, and your prun-
inghooks into spears: let the weak say, *I am strong*." This command comes
in the context of a lament that "the children of Jerusalem have" been "sold
unto the Grecians," and a warning that God would "return . . . recompense"
upon the oppressor by selling his "sons and . . . daughters into the hand of
the children of Judah." No witness ever cited this passage during the trials,
so there is no evidence that the conspirators thought of it when they moved
to reconstitute the meanings associated with two of the central symbols of
Western culture. But the conspirators knew the Bible, and Joel might have
appealed to slave rebels. Perhaps the symbolic inversion represented by scythe
swords was a conscious effort to follow the path laid out in the Old Testament
for empowering an oppressed people. It was certainly part of the conspirators'
assertion of strength, and, whether biblical or not, it represents another
example of the role of cultural appropriation in building the conspiracy.[29]

Slaves wanted horses and swords because both would enhance their military strength. Given White men's tendency to see their horses as a part of
themselves, slaves were also symbolically asserting the desire to control or
kill their masters. When Gabriel, Solomon, and Thornton used their skills
to transform scythes into swords, they transformed symbols of Black oppression into weapons with which slaves could demand freedom and respect.

---

[28] William Waller Hening, 13 vols. *The Statutes at Large, Being a Collection of All the Laws
of Virginia* (Richmond, 1809–23), v. 7, pp. 94–9 (militia law); Executive Communications,
22 (Gilbert's sword), 10 (Will); Prosser's Ben's testimony against Woolfolk is in Executive Papers, Box 115.
[29] Thomas Cole told me of this passage in the Book of Joel.

Only through insurrection could the enslaved aspire to such power, and the symbolic assertion of slaves' right to that claim was an important step in preparing to take it.

To progress beyond that symbolic assertion of the right to power, Gabriel and his followers organized themselves to fight their masters. When the leaders of the conspiracy sought support from other slaves, they pursued influence in ways reminiscent of the sociopolitical techniques used by their masters. Many travelers in eighteenth-century Virginia commented on Whites' obsession with military titles. The conspirators shared it, and a persistent motif running through the depositions is the request for titles of authority. The trial records are peppered with testimony that a recruit had "wanted the appointment of Captain," or that, "being a Captain," a conspirator planned to go recruiting. Gabriel sometimes used the promise of rank to motivate followers: Charles "wanted to be a Captain," and grew angry, "curs[ing] mightily," when Gabriel told him he was "too trifling a fellow" to be more than a sergeant. This elicited Charles's promise to "raise 30 or 40 arms" if made a captain. Thornton, one of several conspirators who claimed to be Gabriel's chief aide, displayed most clearly the connection between White and Black interest in military titles when he declared himself "a General" who was to go under the "name or title of Colonel Taylor." Thornton, who lived in Caroline County, wanted both the prestige of a general and that associated with local political luminary John Taylor of Caroline.[30]

If these slaves claimed titles in ways reminiscent of their masters, they also followed practices that resembled established Virginia methods of seeking followers, though with an important difference. Charles Sydnor showed long ago how elite White Virginians turned election days into social events, buying liquor to treat the voters and joining their poorer friends for a day of recreation at the courthouse. Finally, when the polls opened, each citizen stood before the community to declare his preference in the election, and the candidates often thanked each supporter for his vote. More recently Sylvia Frey and Mechal Sobel have described the ways that new-light evangelists, many though not all of whom were White, sought to win converts. At these

---

[30] Isaac, *Transformation of Virginia*, 109 (titles and Virginia gentry); Executive Communications, 10 (first quote), 11 (second quote), 16 (Charles), 32. Executive Papers, Box 115 (Colonel Taylor). Henry H. Simms, *Life of John Taylor: The Story of a Brilliant Leader in the Early Virginia States Rights School* (Richmond, 1932), 10–15. This should not, however, be interpreted as a claim that there were no African roots to Virginian interests in titles. See Onwuka Dike and Felicia Ekejiuba, *The Aro of South-eastern Nigeria, 1650–1980: A Study of Socio-Economic Formation and Transformation in Nigeria* (Ibadan, Nigeria, 1990), 111 for title systems among Igbo people.

meetings the standard form of speaker and listeners was complicated, for Black congregants reacted collectively – often collectively within segregated space – to ministerial pleas for individual salvation. As conversion was "reinterpreted and ritualized by participants," it became "both a transformation and a ritual process."[31]

Gabriel fused these models of proselytizing in improvising a ritual for mass recruiting. The planned insurrection had to remain a secret from Whites, so Gabriel could hardly have called all the slaves together on a single day to seek their support. Instead, he traveled to religious meetings where Blacks gathered, and following the service he invited "some of the Negroes to drink grog down at the Spring." After treating them, Gabriel asked whether they wished to join his war against slavery. Realizing that this was a difficult and dangerous step, however, Gabriel encouraged his audience to feel comfortable joining. He asked those willing to fight to rise to their feet, and he planted several followers in the crowd to lead the way. Thus, Sam Byrd, one of the conspirators who recruited Gabriel, "was one who stood up" when Gabriel asked for volunteers. Presumably Gabriel hoped that each meeting would result in all of his listeners finally rising as one to join his movement. Other recruiters also used this technique.

The ritual the insurrectionaries developed to win slaves' allegiance bears unmistakable similarity to those that White Virginians used to choose their political leaders and those that evangelicals used to win converts, but it had been significantly transformed in the act of appropriation.[32] When a White man cast his vote in Virginia elections, he stood before the sheriff and the county as an individual voter, while the Black people who stood to join Gabriel's Conspiracy did so together as a group. Black converts to Christ responded to preachers collectively, but they often did so in a spiritual trance rather than as sober people making a political choice. Gabriel's communal twist on Virginia's individualistic political culture had roots in the slave communities that had developed over the course of the eighteenth century and in the evangelical religious culture that had been so influenced by Black worshippers and African spirituality.

---

[31] Charles S. Sydnor, *American Revolutionaries in the Making: Political Practices in Washington's Virginia* (New York, 1965 [1952]), ch. 4; Sylvia Frey, "Shaking the Dry Bones: The Dialectic of Conversion," in Ted Ownby, ed., *Black and White Cultural Interaction in the Antebellum South* (Jackson, Miss., 1993), 23–44 (p. 35 for quote); Mechal Sobel, *The World They Made Together: Black and White Values in Eighteenth-Century Virginia* (Princeton, 1987), Part 3. Also Chapter 1 of this book.

[32] The trial testimony contains several descriptions of this recruiting ritual. See Executive Communications, 22, 24 for quotations.

That Gabriel worked with various sources, including White forms, to impro-
vise new models of political action should surprise no one. Few slaves in the
Richmond area had been born in Africa, and Black Virginians had been sys-
tematically denied any opportunity to organize politically since they had arrived
in the Americas. Under those circumstances, Blacks had no chance to meld
their various African political traditions into a viable Afro-Virginian one.
Instead, they appropriated the forms of their masters, transformed them to
mirror their own communal ethos, and infused the appropriated forms with
new meanings. Gabriel made these political forms his own when he asked
recruits "to join him to fight for *his* Country" (my emphasis).[33] In the struggle
for their country, the slave conspirators claimed for themselves the symbols
of gentility and authority with which local masters had traditionally legitim-
ized the exercise of power.

The testimony in the conspiracy trials illustrates how pervasive was a
master's power over his slaves in Virginia. The level of independence and
mobility he allowed individual slaves influenced their status within the Black
community. Blacks expressed their notions of power and authority by using
many of the same symbols Whites used, and they organized themselves in
ways that echoed forms common to White political culture. Gabriel and his
followers left no evidence of having used ring shouts or blood oaths – rituals
that historians have placed at the center of some other slaves' cultures of
resistance – to build their movement to overthrow slavery. At the same time
that the conspirators showed evidence of the extent of White power, however, they revealed limits to Whites' influence. Blacks won the privileges with
which they could enhance their status through White favor, but they used
those privileges to link Black communities together. Conspirators worked
with cultural forms they shared with their masters, but they transformed the
meanings associated with those forms, creating symbols of Black liberation
out of bulwarks of White power.

The word, writing, and resistance

The written word and the books that contained it had even greater "symbolic potency" as sources of authority in eighteenth-century Virginia than
did horses and military titles, but the appropriation of the authority of literacy entails a broadening of the analysis to include more detailed attention to
the communal world of slave religion. The laws, both secular and sacred,

---

[33] Executive Communications, 22.

that governed the behavior of White and Black Virginians was enshrined in books, and the common, but far from universal ability to read and write conferred important advantages on those who enjoyed it. Many of those advantages were quotidian. The mercantile economy of Richmond created a demand for clerical workers, and surviving papers from the town's courts indicate that some draymen and wagoners wrote and signed receipts for the goods they transported among wharves, shops, and warehouses.[34] The more important secular advantages, however, had less to do with the daily business of making a living than with the meaning of literacy in Atlantic culture. As Henry Louis Gates Jr. has argued, "reading, and especially writing, in the life of the slave represented a process larger than even 'mere' physical manumission, since mastery of the arts and letters was Enlightenment Europe's sign of that solid line of division between human being and thing."[35]

Reading also provided access to God's word. Christianity lay at the heart of antebellum slaves' worldview. Slaves probably found little appealing in Christian doctrine before the Great Awakening, but great numbers joined evangelical churches during the second half of the eighteenth century. Their religious fervor contributed much to the style and substance of developing new-light practices in Virginia.[36] The Great Awakening was a "period of intensive mass interaction" between White and Black Virginians, during which White new-light divines expressed their opposition to slavery and worked hard to convert slaves. Simultaneously, many lay evangelicals took advantage of the liberalized manumission law of 1782 to free their slaves. During the 1790s, White churchmen began to shy away from condemning slavery, in part because antislavery stances proved a hindrance when trying to convert slaveowning Whites, and this retrenchment weakened some slaves' allegiance to White churches. Black Virginians increasingly attended services led

---

[34] Rhys Isaac, "Books and the Social Authority of Learning: The Case of Mid-Eighteenth-Century Virginia," in W. L. Joyce, D. D. Hall, R. D. Brown, and J. B. Hench, eds., *Printing and Society in Early America* (Worcester, Mass., 1983), 228–49 (230 for quotation). Signed receipts can be found scattered throughout the Richmond Suit Papers (hereafter RSP), a collection of miscellaneous papers relating to cases heard in the Richmond Hustings Court (LiVa). Edmund Berkeley Jr., "Prophet Without Honor: Christopher McPherson, Free Person of Color," *Virginia Magazine of History and Biography* 77 (1969): 180–90 (demand for clerks).

[35] Henry Louis Gates Jr., *Figures in Black: Words, Signs, and the 'Racial' Self* (New York, 1987), 3–28 (p. 25 for quotation).

[36] Eugene D. Genovese, *Roll, Jordan, Roll: The World the Slaves Made* (New York, 1972), 659; Albert J. Raboteau, *Slave Religion: The "Invisible Institution" in the Antebellum South* (New York, 1978), 127; Mechal Sobel, *World They Made Together*, esp. Part 3.

by African Americans who felt called to preach. Black preachers often held
services outdoors, and little documentary evidence about them has survived.
Thus, by the time Gabriel and his followers began organizing the rebellion,
the Black church was becoming a separate and for historians a maddeningly
"invisible" institution. Black worshippers continued to dominate the membership of many evangelical churches, and many other Virginians of African
descent worshipped a Christian God outside of official congregations.[37]
   Nonetheless, institutional ties between Black and White Christians remained important. In Richmond the Baptists – the denomination that won
most area slaves' loyalty – were led by a White preacher named Richard
Courtney, "who assemble[d] a large congregation of Negroes every Sunday."
The Caroline County Baptist church had 150 Black members and only 50
White members in 1800, and many Black Christians surely attended separate religious services presided over by Black preachers.[38] The upheaval surrounding Gabriel's Conspiracy produced suggestive evidence about the role
of Christianity in the Richmond Black community in 1800. It illustrated more
compellingly than church names, membership lists, or attendance figures
the contradictory influences of Christianity on Black Virginians' corporate
identity. Many conspirators worshipped at the integrated Hungary Baptist
Meeting House, and the insurrectionaries often spoke of sparing Methodists
and Quakers during the insurrection. Nonetheless, they withdrew from their
White co-religionists to plan the conspiracy, and when planning they spoke
of Black Virginians as God's chosen people.
   Though some historians have argued that religion played a minor role
in Gabriel's plans, the intended rebellion and the slaves' worldview can best
be understood by taking seriously the conspirators' religious commitment.
Gabriel and other organizers recruited many footsoldiers at Baptist religious meetings. Of course, there were purely pragmatic reasons for potential
leaders of a slave insurrection to gravitate toward religious meetings when
searching for followers. Religious meetings attended primarily by slaves provided one of the few forums in which large numbers of slaves from different plantations could meet with little fear of White interference. Gabriel and
the other leaders also sought followers at secular gatherings like barbecues,
and Gerald Mullin and Douglas Egerton have argued that the leaders of the

---

[37] Sobel, *World They Made Together*, 178–213; Sobel, *Trabelin' On: The Slave Journey to
    an Afro-Baptist Faith* (Westport, Conn., 1979), 291–309 (recognized Black churches);
    Latrobe Journals, 191–2.
[38] *Latrobe Journals*, 191–2 (from a journal entry in 1796); Sobel, *World They Made Together*,
    189 (Caroline Church).

conspiracy lacked the religious zeal of plantation slaves.[39] The conspirators' testimony, however, powerfully suggests that the leaders shared the religious values of most Richmond-area slaves and that they believed themselves to be God's chosen people and were taking action to restore his justice to their world. Reinserting Christianity into historians' understanding of Gabriel's Conspiracy serves simultaneously to underscore the conspiracy's connections to the communal culture that enslaved Virginians had struggled to create during the eighteenth century and to emphasize the important role that religion played in creole slaves' struggles for liberation throughout anglophone America.[40]

The court proceedings that produced most of the surviving evidence of the conspiracy focused, of course, on the guilt or innocence of defendants. Because guilt consisted of joining the conspiracy, the testimony usually centered on recruiting scenes. Aspects of the conspiracy that were peripheral to defendants' immediate commitment to participate in the planned insurrection proved less likely to be in the testimony. Evidence of the Christian core of the conspiracy has survived in only a few snippets of communication that permit glances into the rich intellectual world of the conspirators. Some of the evidence for Christianity's role takes the form of religious language that participants used to discuss their plans. On September 20, 1800, one conspirator wrote a letter to comrades in "gloster" [Gloucester County] warning them to "keep still yet." He promised that "brother X" would "come and prech a sermont" that would allow them to "[k]no[w] more about the bissiness." If conspirators called their leaders' speeches sermons, then Christianity must be considered to have been a potential influence on the conspiracy.[41]

The only prolonged and open reference to religion in the conspirators' testimony occurs in Ben Woolfolk's description of a pivotal meeting among

---

[39] Mullin roots Gabriel's failure in his separation from the evangelical religion of most slaves (*Flight and Rebellion*, 159–60). Egerton largely concurs, asserting that freedom was Gabriel's "only religion" (*Gabriel's Rebellion*, 20, 51–2, 179–81).

[40] Sobel, *World They Made Together*; Michael Craton, *Testing the Chains: Resistance to Slavery in the British West Indies* (Ithaca, 1982), Part 5 (though he warns against overstating Christianity's causal importance); Viotti da Costa, *Crowns of Glory*; Frey, *Water from the Rock*, ch. 9.

[41] A. W. to B. H., September 20, 1800, Executive Papers, Box 115. Egerton says that "Brother X" was "doubtless" (208, n. 20, which refers to p. 74 in the text) Gabriel, but he does not comment on the religious significance of the fact that Gabriel would have been communicating in the form of a sermon (*Gabriel's Rebellion*, 74). Jones to Monroe, September 9, 1800, Executive Papers, Box 114 for a Petersburg White man's claim that a slave preacher told him that other slave preachers were involved.

the leaders that took place in early August. George Smith presided over the discussion at the beginning, but Gabriel had seized control by adjournment. Smith opened by announcing that he "wished the business to be deferred some time longer." Gabriel opposed this suggestion, but, rather than challenging Smith directly, he "proposed that the subject should be refered to Martin his Brother to decide upon."[42] Gabriel did not say why Martin's authority in the matter might be decisive, but a contemporary White attributed Martin's authority to his "acquaint[ance] with the Holy Scriptures." Gabriel and the other conspirators appear to have believed that Martin had felt a call to preach.[43] Martin began by warning that an "expression in the Bible" says that "Delays bring Danger." He then proceeded with purely secular arguments for commencing the insurrection immediately: "the Country was at peace, the Soldiers were discharged, and the Arms all put away – there was no patroling . . . and before he would any longer bear what he had borne he would turn out and fight with a Stick." If one accepts a dichotomy between religious and secular motivation among eighteenth-century Virginia slaves, then the bulk of Martin's speech is secular. As the debate that ensued illustrates, however, such a dichotomy distorts rather than makes sense of the conspirators' view of the world.[44]

After Gilbert, a slave of William Young, seconded Martin's call to action, Ben Woolfolk took the floor to say:

I told them that I had heard that in the days of old, when the Israelites were in Servitude to King Pharoah, they were taken from him by the Power of God, – and

---

[42] Executive Communications, 5–6 (for entire debate). Egerton states that Martin spoke up at this point because he had played "almost no part in the recruiting" and "wanted to play a role at the end" (*Gabriel's Rebellion*, 65). This undocumented projection of Martin's motivation implies that Martin forced his way into the discussion, but Woolfolk's deposition explicitly states that Gabriel called on his brother. One cannot be certain what Martin's role had been prior to this meeting; one can only say that the depositions provide no evidence that he had played an important role. Much that happened in the conspiracy escaped notice at the trials.

[43] *Virginia Argus*, October 14, 1800. Egerton stresses that no "extant primary document supports the contention that Gabriel was a deeply religious slave or that Martin was a slave preacher" (*Gabriel's Rebellion*, 179). Indeed, no one specifically referred to Martin as a preacher, though given the uncertain lines dividing preachers, exhorters, and congregants among Black worshippers, the absence of such a reference is not surprising. I do not believe that Martin was recognized as a preacher by an official Baptist meeting house; but the context within which Gabriel called on him to speak to the conspirators strongly suggests that Gabriel and his followers believed Martin to have been called to preach.

[44] Martin's speech and debate with Ben Woolfolk (as reported in Woolfolk's confession) are in Executive Communication, 5–6.

were carried away by Moses – God had blessed them with an Angel to go with him, But that I could see nothing of that kind in these days.

At first glance Woolfolk's metaphorical response to Martin's exhortation appears odd. There can be little doubt that Woolfolk was siding with George Smith in calling for the insurrection to be postponed, though he never explicitly stated that. When he claimed to see nothing like an angel at the head of the conspiracy, he may have been playing on Gabriel's name while metaphorically rejecting his leadership. More to the point, he made no effort to refute Martin's secular reasons for thinking the rebellion should proceed. To modern ears attuned to a sharp distinction between secular and sacred argument it sounds as if Woolfolk spoke past, rather than to, Martin. Martin's response belies that interpretation. He did not argue that what had happened in King Pharoah's time lacked relevance. He answered Woolfolk's biblical tale by invoking God's promise to his chosen people, as recorded in Leviticus (26:8):

I read in my Bible where God says, if we will worship him, we should have peace in all our Lands, five of you shall conquer an hundred and a hundred, a thousand of our enemies.[45]

When Martin finished, the leaders "went into a Consultation" about when to carry off the insurrection. "Martin Spoke and appointed" August 30.

This discussion makes sense only if Christianity played a central and active role in the insurrectionaries' view of the world, in their conception of resistance, and in the conspiracy. Martin opened the debate with a claim that White Virginians were unusually vulnerable to violent attack because they had demobilized and were not patrolling. Woolfolk answered with a biblical analogy that suggested that Whites were far too powerful to defeat, whether patrolling or not. When he pointed out that God had sent no angel to lead the slaves to freedom, he was surely insisting that they could not reach the promised land without divine aid against their more powerful oppressors. Martin replied with the claim that God had indeed assured them of his help, and of victory, and of "peace in all our Land," if they would only "worship him."

---

[45] The biblical text was compressed and very slightly altered either by Martin himself or by Woolfolk in reporting it. Leviticus 26:6 reads: "And I will give peace in the land, and ye shall lie down, and none shall make you afraid: and I will rid evil beasts out of the land, neither shall the sword go through your land." Verse 7 promises that the chosen will "chase your enemies"; verse 8 reads: "And five of you shall chase an hundred, and an hundred of you shall put ten thousand to flight: and your enemies shall fall before you by the sword."

Martin's ability to call up so apt and accurate a biblical passage suggests
both his deep knowledge of the Scriptures and the care with which he and
Gabriel must have prepared for this pivotal meeting. Lawrence Levine finds
evidence in antebellum spirituals that slaves developed a sense of sacred time
that merged into their present. Thus they "extended the boundaries of their
restrictive universe backward until it fused with the world of the Old Testament."[46] Martin's debate with Woolfolk suggests that enslaved Virginians had
developed that sense of sacred time by 1800 and that under favorable circumstances Black Virginians could use the sacred not to transcend the temporal
limits of their lives but to transform the conditions in which they lived.

One more surviving snippet of communication among conspirators reveals
how central Christianity was to Gabriel and his followers. After the conspiracy had been blown, Gabriel tried to escape from Virginia aboard a boat
that conveniently ran aground just below the city. On board was a man named
Billy, who had been arrested on suspicion of participating in the conspiracy
but released, presumably for lack of evidence.[47] Gabriel threw away a weapon
before climbing on the sloop, so he must have believed himself to be among
friends. Billy and another slave named Isham soon began to question him,
however, and upon realizing that he remained in some danger, Gabriel told
his inquisitors that "he was called Gabriel but [that] his name was Daniel."

One cannot, of course, prove that Gabriel intended a biblical reference,
but given the metaphorical lion's den in which he found himself, the choice
of Daniel was too apt for coincidence to be a likely explanation. Furthermore, Daniel is the first book in the Bible in which God's angel is given the
proper name Gabriel, and it is one of the prophetic books that have traditionally provided "inspiration to those who have had to face the power of
tyrants while remaining confident that God supports the endurance . . . of the
righteous." Not surprisingly, Daniel plays a prominent role in antebellum
slave spirituals.[48] Part of God's support came in preventing the lions from

---

[46] Lawrence Levine, *Black Culture and Black Consciousness: Afro-American Folk Thought From Slavery to Freedom* (New York, 1977), 33.

[47] This account is drawn from Thomas Newton to James Monroe, 24 September 1800, Execut-
ive Papers, Box 114. Quotations from that letter unless otherwise noted. Also see Egerton, *Gabriel's Rebellion*, 104–8. It seems most likely that Billy and Richardson Taylor, the White captain of the ship, cooperated with Gabriel's escape attempt but that Isham was not in on the plan and wanted to cash in on the reward money when he realized that Gabriel was on board. Billy then apparently panicked and decided to turn in Gabriel.

[48] W. Sibley Towner, "Daniel," in James L. Mays, ed., *Harper's Bible Commentary* (New York, 1988), 695–706 (697 for quotation); Levine, *Black Culture and Black Consciousness*, 36–38, 50–51 (spirituals).

killing Daniel, and the scriptural language describing God's protection suggests that Gabriel was issuing a coded warning to Billy to keep quiet: the God of Israel "sent his angel" to "shut the lions' mouths," for Daniel was being punished for worshipping God rather than following human law (Daniel 6: 12–27). Surely Gabriel meant to warn Billy to keep his own mouth shut, a warning he expected Billy to understand. Ultimately Billy ignored the warning but only after eleven days of deliberation.

Gabriel's ability to invoke such an appropriate and resonant biblical analogy, like Martin's invocation of Leviticus, bespeaks a remarkable familiarity with the Bible. Peter Wood has rightly labeled African Americans' conversion to Christianity a "forgotten chapter in eighteenth-century southern intellectual history" and has insisted that historians remember the unrecorded but searching discussions that must have taken place among Black people during periods of large-scale conversion. Gabriel's allusion to Daniel, Martin's facility with scriptural quotation, and the seamless movement from secular to sacred during Martin's debate with Ben Woolfolk attest to the ways that such discussions could foster a sense that enslaved African Americans were God's chosen people and that he would lead them to the promised land.[49]

The slaves' Christianity was not inherently revolutionary. Eugene Genovese is right that it most often functioned as a form of "resistance within accommodation."[50] But Martin's use of scriptural arguments to convince other skilled and acculturated slaves to attack their masters shows that at least in 1800 Black Virginians could use their religion for purposes that were in fact revolutionary. Gabriel and the other leaders of the insurrection, like other Christians throughout history, proved capable of using their religious convictions to justify contradictory actions. Of course, not all actions could have been justified. Ben Woolfolk and Martin agreed that racial slavery violated the precepts of the Bible, and the arguments of both men assumed that enslaved Virginians were God's chosen people. This agreement on basic values left open the question of what strategies God's chosen people might pursue.

---

[49] Peter H. Wood, "'Jesus Christ Has Got Thee at Last': Afro-American Conversion as a Forgotten Chapter in Eighteenth-Century Southern Intellectual History," *The Bulletin of the Center for the Study of Southern Culture and Religion* 3 (1979): 1–7; Theophus H. Smith, *Conjuring Culture: Biblical Formations of Black America* (New York, 1994), chs. 2–5. The documentary record is too fragmentary to be certain, but I suspect the conspirators were engaging in what Smith would call "conjure;" they were at least making "a (hermeneutic) *application* of mythic narrative" (p. 148 for the distinction).

[50] Genovese, *Roll, Jordan, Roll,* 659. Genovese refers to antebellum slave Christianity, but his point holds for this earlier period. My claim here does not contradict his interpretation.

The importance of biblical interpretation in the conspirators' discussion
helps to highlight the cultural meaning of literacy for eighteenth-century Black
Virginians. Slaves' religious beliefs rested on the word of God as transmitted
through a written text. Unlike some southern states, Virginia had no law
prohibiting teaching slaves to read in 1800, but if Blacks encountered no legal
barriers to literacy, the practical ones remained formidable, and only a small
minority of Richmond Blacks could read or write. The Baptists' deemphasis
of hierarchically controlled catechisms and their substitution of personal revelation made the denomination attractive to many slaves, but Baptists remained
Protestant Christians who looked to the Bible for God's word.[51] Those who
could read had more direct access to the text through which God revealed
his plan. In his debate with Ben Woolfolk, Martin responded to Woolfolk's
claim to have "heard in the days of old," by asserting that "I read in my Bible."
He literally claimed possession of God's word. If the slaves' sacred world
impinged directly on their secular world, then direct access to God's word
would have conferred almost supernatural power on those who enjoyed it.[52]

Conspirators' uses of lists reflect this sacred power of writing. Among the
first things that Sam Byrd did to convince Ben Woolfolk to join the conspiracy was to invoke his own ability to write by bringing out "his list of
men" who had joined. Of course, literacy conferred practical advantages, so
Byrd had good reason to let Woolfolk know that he could write, but a few
forged passes could have accomplished that purpose. Keeping lists of men
who had joined the conspiracy, though dangerous, may have been necessary,
but brandishing those lists before men who had not yet joined appears in
retrospect to have been foolish. Nonetheless, the leaders of the planned insurrection kept several lists – Prosser's Ben testified that "Gabriel and Solomon
. . . kept lists of the names of the Conspirators" and a free Black named Matt
Scott also supposedly had a list – and they displayed them openly at recruiting

---

[51] John Thornton, *Africa and Africans in the Making of the Atlantic World, 1400–1680*
(Cambridge, England, 1992), ch. 9 argues that these changes brought Christianity more
in line with both African Christianity and African animism.

[52] Sobel, *World They Made Together*, ch. 14 (for Baptist practices); Executive Communications, 5–6. See Jack Goody, "Restricted Literacy in Northern Ghana," in Jack Goody,
ed., *Literacy in Traditional Societies* (Cambridge, England, 1968), 202; Jack Goody, *The
Interface Between the Written and the Oral* (Cambridge, England, 1987), 137 for the meaning of writing among largely nonliterate groups who live (or lived) on the cultural margins of literate societies; and Jack Goody, "Writing, Religion and Revolt in Bahia," *Visible
Language* 20 (1986): 318–43 for his exploration of writing in Bahia in 1835. Also João
José Reis, *Slave Rebellion in Brazil: The Muslim Uprising of 1835 in Bahia*, Arthur Brakel,
transl. (Baltimore, 1993), 96–104.

meetings. The danger of such lists can be seen in several letters White Virginians wrote to Governor Monroe asking whether specific slaves' names were on the conspirators' lists.[53] Gabriel needed little insight – and he displayed deep insight over the course of the conspiracy – to recognize this potential danger. Why then did he make the lists, and more to the point, why did he make them so public? Such behavior makes sense only if the lists played a public and quasiceremonial role that was at least as important as any bookkeeping function. This ceremonial power grew out of the experiences of a largely nonliterate people who lived in a culture whose sacred and secular laws were contained in official books. The debate between Martin and Woolfolk demonstrates the importance of the sacred words of the Bible in shaping enslaved Virginians' visions of themselves and their society. Because literacy inevitably expanded an individual's access to God's word, the ability to write became associated with sacred power.

Just as the spiritual world of the conspirators merged with their secular world, so the sacred power of writing merged with literacy's secular advantages. To sign an agreement, to make a contract, was a right denied enslaved Virginians. Gabriel and his lieutenants used their mastery of the written word to organize a conspiracy, and they conferred on those who would join them the capacity to tap into the symbolic power of writing. That symbolic power had tremendous practical influence over slaves' lives. By signing up with the conspiracy, Gabriel's followers created an obligation as powerful and enforceable as the obligations created in religious and secular law. They signed contracts to remain loyal to the cause; free men, or men deserving freedom, could make contracts, and they could be held to them. Conspirators in fact pledged to "put to death" all "Negroes who did not join the insurrection."[54] Many who joined did so in ceremonies that contained elements reminiscent

---

[53] Executive Communications, 5 (Sam Byrd), 9 (Prosser's Ben); Young's Gilbert's Confession, Executive Papers, Box 114 (Matt Scott); Information of John Foster, September 9, 1800, Executive Papers, Box 114 (display). Prentis to Monroe, September 6, 1800, Executive Papers, Box 114; unsigned note in Box 115. The lists themselves have not survived, and it is unclear whether Monroe ever actually received them. Egerton, *Gabriel's Rebellion*, 103–4 suggests that Monroe destroyed them because their mention of White Frenchmen was potentially damaging to the Republican Party. I find that unlikely – too many people knew of the reports of Frenchmen, and Monroe made no discernible attempt to repress those reports – but much material reported (or suspected) to exist in various documents is missing from the Executive Papers.

[54] Executive Communications, 11, 13 (for three examples of threats to kill slaves who failed to join). Egerton, *Gabriel's Rebellion*, 205–6, n. 59 does not address these statements when claiming there is "no evidence to support the assertion . . . that all blacks 'were to be forced to join the rebels or die like whites.'"

of Virginia election rituals and of Baptist religious gatherings. After being treated with liquor, men stood before an assembled group to pledge their allegiance, and only then did they sign up "by making their marks."[55] By signing up, these men who could not, after all, write, asserted their rights before the laws of God and Virginia at the very moment that they pledged to overthrow the system those laws created.

Religion, secular law, and the written word played elusive but important and related roles in the mental world of Gabriel and the other insurrectionaries. The slaves' conception of God and of his message created a framework through which they perceived what happened around them. The power of the written word – a power it derived from both the Bible and secular law – commanded their respect. At times the slaves almost appear to have invoked that power as a magical force. These powerful cultural influences did not shape the slaves' responses to slavery in the ways one might expect. Together they might have been expected to exert tremendous hegemonic power. White Virginians certainly hoped that Christianity, at any rate, would blunt enslaved Virginians' concerns about earthly justice. Gabriel's Conspiracy offers an unusually vivid illustration of why those hopes went unrealized. Black Virginians worshipped in integrated churches and acted respectfully in the presence of the state's legal system, but when enslaved people withdrew into segregated spaces they revealed the ease with which they could appropriate the power of Christianity and the law. Gabriel and his followers were Virginians, but they developed a corporate identity as Black Virginians that stood at odds to that of their masters. Because testimony about Gabriel's Conspiracy has survived, the process of appropriation that contributed to building that corporate identity can be traced, but analogous processes went on during more normal times.

Africa, Virginia, and traditions of resistance

The absence of a *distinctively* Afro-Virginian political tradition does not indicate that African cultures lacked influence over the Virginian political culture that Gabriel and his followers appropriated. As Mechal Sobel has shown, eighteenth-century Virginian cultures contained deeply rooted aspects of African and European cultures.[56] The prominent role that blacksmiths played in Gabriel's Conspiracy offers a suggestive perspective on the shadowy

[55] Information from John Foster, Richmond, September 9, 1800, Executive papers, Box 114.
[56] Sobel, *World They Made Together*.

(and ultimately inseparable) Old World roots of the symbolic structures Gabriel appropriated while delegitimating White authority in Virginia. Important recent work stressing African dimensions in slave culture may lead too easily to the assumption that conscious memories of African elements were sustained and articulated among enslaved Virginians. No doubt to some extent they were, but culture often operates at a level below conscious deliberation. Gabriel and his followers unquestionably retained African elements in their worldview, but they exhibited no discernible or conscious interest in those roots. Less concerned with origins than historians or anthropologists are, Gabriel and his followers acted on their cultural inheritance rather than trying to trace it.

Gabriel, Solomon, and Thornton – all blacksmiths – emerge from the trial testimony as among the five or six most important leaders of the conspiracy. Blacksmiths' influence among enslaved Virginians can be explained without recourse to complicated arguments about cultural heritage. They were highly skilled and valued artisans who enjoyed a high level of autonomy while at work, and their shops were often placed on busy thoroughfares – the shop of Gabriel, Solomon, and Prosser's Ben bordered the road that carried wagon traffic into Richmond from western counties – so those shops could serve as communicative nodal points for slave communities. Given the capital investment required to build and outfit a forge, owners of blacksmiths who also owned forges rarely would have hired them out, so smiths probably did not enjoy the lack of constraint that came from working at different sites or from hiring their own time.[57] Nonetheless, their relative autonomy on the job, their ability to sell work done "after hours" and thus gain access to the market, and their position in Black communication networks contributed to their status within slave communities. That status, along with blacksmiths' very practical ability to make and repair weapons, helps to explain their prominence within the conspiracy.

---

[57] Sometimes blacksmiths were hired out – especially when they were part of an unprobated estate – but I found no examples of blacksmiths hauled before the Richmond court for hiring their own time. Thus, I am unconvinced by Egerton's undocumented assertions that "Gabriel, and to a lesser degree, Solomon, spent more than a few days each month smithing in and around Richmond" (*Gabriel's Rebellion*, 24), or that Gabriel probably worked out a hiring out arrangement with Prosser that "allowed Gabriel, in effect, to choose his own master" (25). Given the absence of any documentary evidence that Gabriel was hired out, it seems safer to assume that Gabriel spent his working time in Prosser's blacksmith shop, though he presumably took on jobs beyond those assigned by Prosser, executing them after his normal work hours and pocketing the fee. While this seems a small point, it is important to Egerton's (28) "artisanal republican" reading of the conspiracy. See n. 68 for a discussion of artisanal republicanism and the conspiracy.

These pragmatic sources of status for blacksmiths were, however, only part of the story. Just as literacy afforded those who enjoyed it both practical advantages, like the ability to forge passes, and cultural advantages, like access to God's word, blacksmiths' ability to shape metal afforded dual advantages. Splitting scythes to make weapons provided arms for the rebels, but it also entailed the transformation of powerful symbols of subordination into weapons for liberation. As argued earlier conspirators may have linked this transmutation to the biblical injunction in the book of Joel, but regardless, the blacksmiths' skill allowed them to accomplish a metamorphosis of profound significance within Western culture.

Just as an attempt to privilege either the practical or cultural aspects of blacksmiths' standing within slave communities would be misleading, so a single-minded reliance on Western traditions effaces African sources for the cultural authority of blacksmiths. Africans forced to settle Virginia came from agricultural societies with long-standing metalworking traditions, just as did European settlers, and material evidence indicates that some slave blacksmiths retained identifiably African styles of metalworking into the late eighteenth century.[58] In addition to metal-working skills, people sold to Virginia brought assumptions about the importance of blacksmiths in sacred and secular realms. Some may have known of the Yoruban God Ogun, who lived "in the flames of the blacksmith's forge, on the battlefield, and more particularly on the cutting edge of iron." Yorubans associated Ogun with the knowledge that allowed men to fashion useful implements and weapons out of iron, and victims of the Atlantic slave trade continued to worship him in Cuba and Brazil.[59]

Few Yorubans were sold into Virginia, but blacksmiths also played prominent roles in the cosmology of the neighboring Igbo, the people most frequently sold into the colony. In one Igbo origin myth, the supreme deity sent "an Awka blacksmith with the bellows, fire and charcoal" to dry the land and make it habitable. Smiths were granted special status – including safe

---

[58] John Michael Vlach, *By the Work of Their Hands: Studies in Afro-American Folklife* (Charlottesville, 1991), 26–7.

[59] See Chapter 1 of this book for the ethnic makeup of slaves sold into Virginia. While Igbo blacksmiths did not share the worship of Ogun with Yorubans, they traveled and traded with Yorubans (Elizabeth Isichei, *A History of the Igbo People* [New York, 1976], 29–31), and Igbo people had a concept of Ogun (Robert G. Armstrong, "The Etymology of the Word 'Ogún'," in Sandra T. Barnes, ed., *Africa's Ogun: Old World and New* [Bloomington, Ind., 1989], esp. 31–4). Robert Farris Thompson, *Flash of the Spirit: African and Afro-American Art and Philosophy* (New York, 1983), 52–7 (p. 52 for quotation). The essays in *Africa's Ogun* trace the belief in Ogun in the New World. Cole, *Icons*, 48, 99 for similar traditions among several other West African peoples.

passage throughout Igboland – as the providers of agricultural, military, and spiritual implements.[60] No evidence has survived of the worship of Ogun or of the oracle of the Awka smiths in Gabriel's Virginia. Gabriel and his followers displayed respect for African peoples – one conspirator planned a trip to the "pipeing tree to enlist . . . the *Outlandish* people" who dealt with "witches and wizards" – but the need to travel in search of Africans and the conspirator's use of the term "outlandish" underlines the creole nature of Richmond's slave population and the foreign-ness of Africans.[61]

Nonetheless, the traditional authority of blacksmiths in West African cultures – authority that the worship of Ogun in Cuba and Brazil shows did cross the Atlantic – may have contributed to smiths' status among enslaved Virginians.[62] Africans brought knowledge of metalworking with them to Virginia, and that knowledge was presumably valued by planters who needed blacksmiths to help them produce and market commodities. The cultural authority that some African blacksmiths carried with them across the Atlantic may have been reinforced by the privileges that they won as skilled craftsmen who were valued by their masters. Or, to reverse the formulation, the status that slave blacksmiths acquired by virtue of their skill may have been enhanced by the cultural authority they brought from African societies.[63] It is difficult to understand why two brothers like Gabriel and Solomon, who were roughly the same age, would both have been trained as blacksmiths unless their father had practiced the trade. He would have been of a generation much more likely to be African-born than Gabriel's, and he might have conveyed to his sons the spiritual and military power attributed to blacksmiths in his homeland. There is no way to determine whether this indeed happened, but the ambiguity inherent in that possibility is a powerful reflection of the real but buried influence of African cultures on Virginia's social norms. By 1800, the various pragmatic and cultural roots of the eminence

[60] Dike and Ekejuiba, *Aro of South-eastern Nigeria*, 105–15 (p. 110 for origin myth); Afigbo, *Ropes of Sand*, 137–41.
[61] Executive Communications, 30 (Woolfolk's testimony against George). "Outlandish" was the term White Virginians used for African-born slaves.
[62] Afigbo, *Ropes of Sand*, 9, 137–41. Monday Efiong Noah and Tom Ekpo, "Warfare and Diplomacy in Ibibio," in Toyin Falola and Robin Law, eds., *Warfare and Diplomacy in Precolonial Nigeria: Essays in Honor of Robert Smith* (Madison, 1992), 191; Cole, *Icons*, 48, 99 for examples of blacksmiths' standing in other cultures from which enslaved Virginians originated.
[63] See Sidney Mintz and Richard Price, *The Birth of African-American Culture: An Anthropological Perspective* (Boston, 1992 [1976]), esp. chs. 4 and 5 for the theoretical model behind this specific formulation and behind my general approach.

of slave blacksmiths had become so tangled that it makes no sense to pull them apart.[64]

More important for understanding the mental world of Gabriel's conspirators, there is no evidence that cultural roots mattered to the slaves who sought their freedom in the summer of 1800. The cultural traditions of which Gabriel and his followers appear to have been most conscious were Christian and Virginian. Both traditions had been profoundly influenced by the cultures that Africans brought to America, but the conspirators do not appear to have placed any value on the "African-ness" of those traditions. Of course, that may reflect Whites' determination to keep dangerous (or perhaps to Whites, irrelevant) discussions of African cultures out of the record, but given the degree to which such discussions found their way into evidence of other American slave conspiracies, such an explanation seems unlikely.[65]

Gabriel and his followers sought to overthrow slavery by using living and changing cultural traditions to communicate ideas about freedom and legitimate authority. The genealogy of those cultural traditions does not appear to have mattered much to those who sought to use them. While much in the mental world of Gabriel's conspirators had genealogical lines that reached toward Africa, the conspirators were not engaged in a conscious struggle to establish a distinct cultural identity for Virginians of African descent, so they had little reason to foreground such African genealogies.[66]

[64] John Randolph Barden, "'Flushed With Notions of Freedom': The Growth and Emancipation of a Virginia Slave Community, 1732–1812" (Ph.D. diss., Duke University, 1993), 152 for clear evidence of what must have been a common practice of skilled fathers teaching their crafts to their sons. Coincidentally, this example involves a blacksmith bringing up his two sons in the craft. Cole, *Icons*, 48 (blacksmith descent groups in Africa).

[65] See David Barry Gaspar, "The Antigua Slave Conspiracy of 1737: A Case Study of the Origins of Collective Resistance," *William and Mary Quarterly*, 3rd. Ser. 35 (1978), and Gaspar, *Bondmen and Rebels: A Study of Master-Slave Relations in Antigua With Implications for Colonial British America* (Baltimore, 1985), ch. 11; Michael Mullin, *Africa in America: Slave Acculturation in the American South and the British Caribbean, 1736–1831* (Urbana, 1992), esp. ch. 8 and pp. 228–30; Craton, *Testing the Chains*, esp. Parts 3 and 4; William W. Freehling, "Denmark Vesey's Peculiar Reality," in Robert H. Abzug and Stephen E. Maizlish, eds., *Race and Slavery in America: Essays in Honor of Kenneth M. Stampp* (Lexington, Ky., 1986), esp. page 30 for Gullah Jack; and John Thornton, "African Dimensions of the Stono Rebellion," *American Historical Review* 96 (1991): 1101–13.

[66] Similar possible African genealogies can be traced for other aspects of the conspiracy, including the organization of secret male societies (Isichei, *History of Nigeria*, [London, 1983], 288–9), and the ceremonial use of writing (Isichei, *History of the Igbo People*, 35–9). My purpose here is not to exhaust the exploration of possible African influences but to explore the meaning of such influences for the conspirators.

Masculinity, community, and resistance

The terms in which the conspirators discussed their goals and motivations and the gender dynamics of the organization that they built provide another perspective on the way Virginians of African descent perceived themselves and their world. Gabriel and his followers spoke in idioms associated with the American, French, and Haitian Revolutions, but such intellectual currents are never independent forces. Instead, they mixed with other motivations that arose out of the experience of slavery, motivations like the desire to escape bondage and to avenge oppression. Discussions about freedom and vengeance took place as would-be rebels moved in a predominantly male world, and the association they built bore a strong resemblance to a secret fraternal society. In an odd way, Black men traveling the roads in and out of Richmond found in that most public of spaces an escape from the danger of observation, an escape that permitted the creation of effectively private space. In that space they could forge the community necessary to cooperate in an effort to overthrow slavery. The process of cultural appropriation that lay near the heart of Gabriel's Conspiracy took many of its meanings from this fraternal community of Black men.

The most frequently mentioned reason that slaves gave for joining Gabriel was the desire for freedom, and many of Gabriel's followers expressed that desire in terms that reflected the natural rights philosophy of the Age of Revolution. They planned to conquer the "whole . . . Country where Slavery" existed, unless "the White people agreed to their freedom," and Gabriel planned to write "death or Liberty" on a silk flag. This may have been a somewhat pessimistic inversion of the speech Patrick Henry had delivered at Richmond's St. John's Church at the beginning of the American Revolution, and perhaps it was a play on the cry of western Virginians during the Whiskey Rebellion of the 1790s. If so, it established a claim that the conspirators were fighting for rights in which their oppressors professed belief. An unidentified conspirator made this assertion more explicit by declaring on the gallows that he had nothing more to say in his own defense than "what General Washington would . . . had he been taken by the British and put to trial": he had "adventured [his] life . . . to obtain the liberty of [his] countrymen, and . . . [was] a willing sacrifice in their cause."[67] As unsuccessful revolutionaries,

---

[67] Executive Communications, 4 (Country), 30 (freedom), 32 (flag). All quotes attributed to Gabriel. Aptheker, *American Negro Slave Revolts*, 209 (Whiskey Rebellion). Robert Sutcliffe, *Travels in Some Parts of North America in the Years 1804, 1805, and 1806* (York, England, 1811), 50 ("General Washington").

Gabriel and his followers never fully elaborated their vision of natural rights, but that strain of thought clearly influenced them.[68]

Many conspirators also sought vengeance. Will, a slave of John Mosbey Sr., "was determined to kill his Master," and Billey, who freely joined Gabriel, "remarked that he had been abused by Claiborne Lipscombe and expressed a wish for revenge." Occasionally, according to Ben Woolfolk, conspirators anticipated special joy in killing Whites: Jacob declared "I will kill a white man as free as eat," and Thornton was "damn'd glad to hear" they would soon meet "to Kill the white people."[69]

The would-be rebels also wanted money. Gabriel intended to divide the money in the state treasury among his soldiers. Lewis, who longed to avenge his oppression by cutting "off the heads of his master and Mistress," also "knew where their money was." One recruiter challenged a potential insurrectionary's virility by asking if he was a man and then offered to pay him well. There is no reason to suppose that each slave's entire motivation was recorded in the trial testimony; no doubt conspirators joined for complex

---

[68] This point has been made by Mullin, *Flight and Rebellion*, ch. 5; Frey, *Water From the Rock*, 320–1. See Genovese, *From Rebellion to Revolution*, esp. 44–6 (for Gabriel) for the seminal work on slave revolts and the Age of Revolution, and Craton, *Testing the Chains* for the most important challenge to Genovese's thesis. Egerton, *Gabriel's Conspiracy*, esp. 38–41 goes further, claiming that Gabriel believed in artisanal republicanism and thought "that white mechanics would see in his own struggle for liberty and economic rights grounds for" an alliance (41). He bases much of the case for artisanal republicanism on his claim that Gabriel specified the "merchants" as his enemy. That claim is based on an ambiguous passage in the trial transcripts in which Gabriel was reported saying that "if the White people agreed to their freedom they would then hoist a white flagg, and he would dine and drink with the Merchants of the city" (Executive Communications, 30). It does not seem clear to me that merchants are the enemy in this passage, and conspirators much more frequently identified White people in general as their foe (Executive Communications, 7, 10, 11, 12). Stronger support for a nonracial, though not necessarily an artisanal republican reading comes from Prosser's Ben's claim that Gabriel "expected the poor white people" to join him (Executive Communications, 31), but that must be set against a confusing group of claims about different Whites that ran the gamut from a claim that "whites were to be put to Death indiscriminately" (Executive Communications, 11), to a claim (also by Prosser's Ben) that Gabriel planned to "slay the white males from the Cradle upwards" but spare women (Trial of Woolfolk, Executive Papers, Box 115), to the most frequently expressed perception of divisions among Whites in which Quakers, Methodists, and Frenchmen were to be spared. No extant report said that Gabriel, Solomon, or Thornton – all blacksmiths – expressed a sense of kinship with White blacksmiths or with other White artisans. Thus, I find the artisanal republican reading unconvincing.

[69] Executive Communications, 10–11 (Will). Executive Papers, Box 114 (Billey and Jacob), Box 115 (Thornton).

combinations of reasons, only some of which have survived. The central impulse behind the planned insurrection was straightforward: slaves believed themselves entitled to freedom and sought to win it. Gabriel, at any rate, was willing to forgo money and revenge for liberty: if "the White people agreed" to free the slaves, he planned to "dine and drink with the Merchants of the city."[70]

Joining an association to fight for an end to slavery was dangerous, and the conspirators developed a metaphorical code that allowed them to discuss the planned insurrection while minimizing the fear of being overheard. When a conspirator named Daniel stopped by Prosser's blacksmith shop, Solomon asked about "the boys in town." Daniel replied that they were "well and nearly ready to do the business." Prosser's Ben, who heard this conversation, claimed this was "Solomon's usual way of addressing persons concerned in the plott."[71]

"The business" was by far the most frequent euphemism used in the trials to refer to the insurrection. When George Smith tried to convince other leaders to postpone the rebellion, he asked for "the business to be deferred," and Gabriel responded that he "wished to bring on the business as soon as possible."[72] This mercantile metaphor may reflect the urban nature of the conspiracy. Gabriel and most of his followers lived on plantations and farms in the rural counties surrounding Richmond. Some, like the smiths working in Gabriel's shop, literally did business with those traveling to and from Richmond. Others were undoubtedly affected by temporary fluctuations in the town's labor (and thus slave-hiring) market. And most probably traveled into Richmond on their own time to pursue their own business. While Virginians of African descent who lived in rural Isle of Wight County referred to a revolt planned for 1810 "as an earthquake," slaves living in and around Virginia's towns readily perceived the power of economic markets and thus turned to that language when searching for powerful ways to speak of change.[73]

---

[70] Executive Communications, 30 (treasury; merchants), 16 (Charles's offer). Executive Papers, Box 114 (Lewis).

[71] Executive Communications, 19.

[72] Executive Communications, 5–6. I have counted fifteen different uses of "business" to refer to the conspiracy in the trial records. This count does not include uses outside of the conspiracy trials, like that in the slave letter cited in n. 47 above. An interesting parallel existed in nineteenth-century New Orleans. Ishmael Reed's novel *Last Days of Louisiana Red* (New York, 1974) opens: "*Note:* In order to avoid detection by powerful enemies and industrial spies, 19th-century HooDoo people referred to their Work as 'The Business.'" Reed plays off that metaphor throughout the novel.

[73] Aptheker, *American Negro Slave Revolts*, 246–7 (earthquakes). I am indebted to Cathy Jurca for pointing out the urban quality of this euphemism.

The conspirators also frequently referred to those who joined their plot as "the boys." One told a friend that "the boys on the Brook, were going to fight the White people." A slave from Manchester (the small town across the James River from Richmond) told Prosser's Ben that when "the *Boys*" from Richmond "made a brake the *Boys* from Manchester, would . . . join them."[74] This fraternal language emphasizes the masculine nature of the conspiracy.

The world described during the insurrection trials was overwhelmingly male. Only one Black woman testified at the trials, and she was not present at any event related to the planned rebellion. Gabriel's wife Nanny knew of the conspiracy, and she tried to recruit one man, but hers is the only reported female involvement in the plot of any kind. The conspirators may not have trusted Black women: Ben Woolfolk required one recruit to "keep the business secret, and not divulge to a *woman*" (emphasis in original). That is, however, the only indication of that kind, so the case for such distrust is far from decisive.[75]

The conspirators spent much of their time inhabiting a male world, which may explain why Black men did not include women in their plans for violent rebellion. Many incidents described at the trials took place at barbecues, but not one witness to these events described an incident in which men and women did anything together. When witnesses described Blacks "gaming with quaits," or "engage[d] in the Game of Cards" they mentioned only males. Prosser's Ben, Gabriel, and two brothers went to a barbecue unaccompanied by women. Some women attended that barbecue, but others refused to go. Nutty, the one Black woman who testified at the trials, said that Isham's wife had been unwilling for him to go but that he "was persuaded to it" by George. Similarly, several descriptions of conspirators going to taverns to buy liquor do not mention Black women. Ben Woolfolk and Thornton took their friend Edmund with them to Ellis's Tavern to buy some liquor to treat their men. Shortly after the planned insurrection was discovered, a slave named King "with sundry other negroes" entered the shop of Mrs.

[74] Executive Communications, 17 (Brook), 25–6 (Manchester). Emphases in original. Whites did not begin using "boy" to refer derogatorily to Black men until after the War of 1812 (Mullin, *Africa in America*, 234).

[75] Executive Communications, 21 (testimony of Black woman), 12 (Nanny), 28 (Woolfolk). Such language sheds important light on gender divisions without necessarily providing an accurate gauge to the way people in rebellion would have behaved. See Viotti da Costa, *Crowns of Glory*, 191–3 for a male conspiracy that culminated in a rebellion in which women took part. Secret societies organized along gender lines were common among the Igbo people, so cultural traditions complemented social realities in encouraging such divisions (Dike and Ekejiuba, *The Aro*, 77–8).

Martin and "purchased Spirits." King addressed the other slaves drinking in the shop as "Boys."[76]

King's testimony suggests that the common practice of men and women who belonged to different masters marrying one another may have contributed to the social division between the sexes. King addressed the "boys" because they were going to his wife's neighborhood. Normally he would have accompanied them on that trip, but because of the crackdown in the wake of the Whites' discovery of the conspiracy, he decided that such travel had temporarily become too dangerous. Several other witnesses described the fraternal world that developed among Black men as they engaged in the weekly ritual of taking to the road to visit their wives. Prosser's Ben began walking the six miles home from Richmond when he fell in company with a slave who lived in Manchester and was traveling to visit his wife in Henrico County. When George Smith and Sam Byrd first recruited Ben Woolfolk, they invited him to "come over to their houses on a friday night," but by the time Woolfolk arrived everyone "had . . . dispersed" and gone "to see their Wives."[77]

Witnesses did not say why men left their homes to visit women rather than vice versa, but presumably the fact that children stayed with their mothers explains this. The testimony suggests, however, that by 1800 Black men and women defined the spatial parameters of their lives in different ways. Men took to the road. On the road they visited with other men, stopped to drink in taverns, and went to barbecues. Women whose husbands worked in Richmond but who did not themselves live in town remained at home, presumably working in fields and caring for their children. They were visited by their husbands. That Isham's wife tried to convince her husband to stay at home rather than accompanying George to the barbecue suggests that Black women may have considered themselves in competition with the fraternal world beyond the plantation.[78] The social spheres inhabited by enslaved

[76] Executive Communications, 19–20 (gaming and fishing), 21 (Nutty);. Thomas B. King affidavit, Executive Papers, Box 114 (cards). Perhaps women were present but were not mentioned in trial testimony; Trial of King, Executive Papers, Box 114.

[77] Trial of King, Executive Papers, Box 114; Executive Communication, 25 (Prosser's Ben), 5 (Woolfolk).

[78] Traditions analogous to "abroad marriages" that existed among Igbo traders might have contributed to enslaved Virginians' adjustment to this brutal aspect of slave life (Afigbo, *Ropes of Sand*, 136). For a parallel among twentieth-century Afro-Caribbean people, see Roger D. Abraham's analysis of St. Vincentians' gendered cultures of the "yard" and the "road" (or the "crossroad," or even more extreme, of town) in *The Man-of-Words in the West Indies: Performance and the Emergence of Creole Culture* (Baltimore, 1983),

Black men and women were different, and Gabriel's Conspiracy was organized in the masculine sphere.

On one occasion a recruiter reportedly referred to the organization he was building as a Freemason's society, and more commonly many conspirators acted as if they were joining a secret fraternal order. In addition to calling each other "the boys," at least two recruits pledged their "harts and . . . hands," and promised to wade to their "knees in Blood Sooner than fail." Upon inviting one man "to join his Society," Woolfolk ordered that he "keep, the business, secret." When Black men met on the road, however, secrecy seemed less essential. One day Woolfolk fell in with a man named Solomon (not Gabriel's brother) "on the Road in Company with others." When Solomon grabbed some peaches out of Woolfolk's basket, one in the group asked how he dared to do so, and Solomon answered that Woolfolk was "one of our Society . . . to fight the White people."[79]

The members of this secret society came together, often at a spring, to drink grog, initiate new members, and plan an insurrection. No doubt their knowledge of the danger of their course brought them closer together, and they gained confidence as the numbers attending these meetings grew and as sites for meetings multiplied. The "party" – another term favored by some conspirators – never did prosecute "the business." They failed largely because two of their number – two of the brotherhood – betrayed the cause. The betrayal is important.[80] But more important is the attempt these men made to build a fraternal organization to fight for their liberty. The absence of Black women from the world in which this movement grew suggests that gender division among Black Richmonders played an important role in shaping their social relations. The fraternal aspects of the conspiracy, like the importance of blacksmiths, recalled African traditions (e.g., famous Igbo age cohorts) that contributed in ways that cannot be separated from the contributions of European traditions (e.g., Freemasonry) and those rooted in adjustment to social realities (e.g., separation of spouses).[81]

---

ch. 10 (pp. 151–2, 154–5 for his schematic contrast between the "female respectability" of the yard, and the "male reputation-building" of the road).

[79] Executive Communications, 28–9 ("Freemasons" and "harts"), 19–21 (secret); Executive Papers, Box 114 (Solomon). The Solomon whom Woolfolk met on the road belonged to Joseph Lewis's estate.

[80] See Chapter 3 of this book.

[81] Isichei, *History of the Igbo People*, 22–3; Isichei, *History of Nigeria*, 288–90. Evidence for the importance of African cultural inheritance in this development can be found in the existence of similar male age-cohort groups, called "crewes," in twentieth-century Afro-Caribbean communities (Roger D. Abraham, *Man-of-Words*, ch. 10).

Conclusion

During the eighteenth century, Black and White Virginians built a world together. During the summer of 1800, Gabriel and his fellow conspirators worked within the contours of Virginia's culture, a culture whose roots reached back to Africa and Europe, to appropriate symbols of authority that lay at the heart of their masters' cultural universe. The overlapping worldviews of Black and White Virginians were rooted in creole cultures that had by 1800 grown for more than a century in contact, conflict, and response to one another. Gabriel's Conspiracy reveals how profoundly these two worlds were intertwined by illustrating the degree to which enslaved Virginians struggling to win freedom appropriated symbols of authority that lay at the heart of their masters' cultural universe.

The slaves did not use these symbols uncritically. The assertion of the right to freedom and equality for people of African descent represented a rejection of one core element of White Virginians' culture; by rejecting that element, the slaves necessarily reconstituted the meanings of the elements of the culture that they used. While their recruiting rituals resembled traditional Virginia election rituals, those who responded by joining the conspiracy sought to destroy the racist foundation of the White equality that those election rituals represented. Christianity played a key role in the conspiracy, but when Gabriel's brother Martin spoke of religion, he spoke of slaves as God's chosen people and used the Bible to foment rebellion and disorder, not the obedience that White Virginians hoped slaves would find in Christianity. Gabriel and his followers appropriated the power of the written word to overthrow the social system whose rules were inscribed in powerful law books. They did not want to attend fine horses or to ride them for their masters' glory on the racetracks of Virginia but to sit atop them as they invaded and conquered Richmond. In short, they sought to turn the culture upside down, and a key part of that struggle entailed appropriating and reconstituting the meanings of the central symbols with which White Virginians expressed their notions of legitimate authority.

In their struggle to do that, they revealed how profoundly Virginian they were, while continuing a century-old process of developing a local oppositional culture. Their struggle and the documents that it generated produced an unusual and valuable opportunity to examine this cultural process in action and thus an opportunity to approach the rich contradictions that animated enslaved Virginians' ever changing sense of corporate identity. One conspirator, a leader named Gilbert, highlighted these tensions on an individual level. He expressed his determination that "his master and Mistress should be put to death," but he planned to delegate the task to "the men under him (as he could not do it himself) they having raised him."[82]

In a very different sense Gabriel and his followers also sought to destroy that which had raised them as a people. The brutal institution of eighteenth-century slavery brought disparate African peoples together in Virginia and created the conditions in which they became a people. The culture that enslaved Virginians forged from their diverse backgrounds in Africa, their interactions with Virginians of European descent, and the social realities they confronted in America existed in these precise forms only in Virginia. Gabriel shared his world with White Virginians – they were the product of the same century of history – and his conspiracy represents a peculiarly Virginian attempt to destroy that world in a search for a better one.

[82] Trial of William Young's Gilbert, Executive Papers, Box 114 (Ben Woolfolk's testimony).

3

Individualism, community, and identity in Gabriel's Conspiracy

Gabriel sought to overthrow Virginia's social structure and to free all Virginians of African descent. Instead, only three enslaved individuals – Pharoah Sheppard, Tom Sheppard, and Prosser's Ben – acquired freedom as a result of Gabriel's Conspiracy, two by informing Whites of the approaching insurrection and one by testifying at length during the trials of alleged conspirators. Slave conspiracies and revolts, like other subaltern attempts to overthrow oppressive social structures, were plagued by informers. Scholars have generally analyzed informers through moral categorization, treating them as weaklings who sold out their true allies for the "economic regard and . . . freedom" that Whites offered turncoats.[1]

Such moral categorization creates comfort, neatly classifying those who lived in Gabriel's world according to modern observers' sympathies. This comfort is purchased, however, at a cost that few stop to acknowledge. Ascribing betrayal to simple cowardice and venality – to bad personal qualities – allows historians to sidestep the ways in which Pharoah's betrayal (no less than Gabriel's Conspiracy) grew out of the creole cultures that had developed in Virginia by the end of the Revolutionary War period. Those who decided whether to join Gabriel's Conspiracy faced a range of choices, some of which offered long odds for fundamental change and others of which offered better chances for incremental change. Only rarely, as in the case of Gabriel's Conspiracy, would the various strategies have conflicted with one another. The conspiracy offered the longest odds and, in freedom for all enslaved people, the most fundamental change, and those who unequivocally joined implicitly rejected other strategies. Many potential conspirators hesitated, however, preferring delay or hoping to join "half-way" while holding other options open. Had the conspiracy become an insurrection, half-way covenanters

---

[1] Herbert Aptheker, *American Negro Slave Revolts* (New York, 1987 [1943]), 61.

would have had to choose sides, but instead two of them abandoned collective freedom to pursue narrow self-interest.

Gabriel's Conspiracy represented an oppositional movement built through a communal appropriation of Virginia's individualistic culture. Pharoah and Tom Sheppard rejected Gabriel's vision of collective improvement and sought individual freedom at the cost of their former comrades' lives. Individual and communal impulses existed side by side among the conspirators and within Richmond's slave communities, so placing Pharoah and Tom back into the world of the conspiracy uncovers the dynamics of betrayal within the culture that spawned the conspiracy. In part because the conspirators were so Virginian, pursuing individual interests by making deals with authorities appeared natural, and Pharoah's betrayal, though it was certainly not made inevitable by these patterns, did grow out of similar forces. The act of betrayal, rooted in some of the values shared by the cultures of Black and White Virginians, pushed Pharoah outside the Black community's boundaries. One price for his freedom was to be banished from Black Virginians' oral traditions and thus from the community's history.

Conspiracy and strategies for improvement

The quarter century preceding 1800 brought limited improvements in the life chances of enslaved Virginians, particularly those who lived in and around Virginia's towns. Manumission laws were liberalized, a small urban boom occurred, and religious revivals opened new opportunities for Black Virginians. Complicated choices faced enslaved residents of the Richmond area as they decided how best to improve their lives. A substantial number (though a tiny percentage) acquired freedom during this period by cultivating patrons who manumitted them, either in return for faithful service or for money earned through extra labor. Another substantial but small group fled to the towns or to sea in search of freedom. Many more people improved their lives incrementally by winning the right to hire their own time, by being hired into the city, and by joining the more egalitarian Baptist churches.

Blacks living around Richmond in 1800 did not see their society in purely racial terms. While several conspirators described the rebellion as an "Insurrection against the white people,"[2] other witnesses offered less totalizing pictures of the White community. Perceived differences varied, so no single Black perception of White Virginians existed. Nonetheless, the insurrectionaries'

---

[2] Executive Communications, 27 (quotation), 14, 16, 17. See Chapter 2, n. 3 for a discussion of the nature and location of primary sources regarding Gabriel's Conspiracy.

belief in significant variations among Whites' attitudes toward slavery reveal complications inherent in building a movement against a system that sanctioned a rich and complex range of relationships and interactions among Blacks and Whites but embedded those relationships in a legal and economic system based on crude racial distinctions.

Conspirators spoke most highly of French immigrants among all White Virginians. Black Virginians' belief that the French supported their struggle grew out of the Haitian Revolution and the relatively new but rich traditions of "frenchness" discussed earlier. The tradition of French support for Black freedom struggles was enhanced by the "two white French Men" who, Jack Ditcher claimed, "were the first instigators of the Insurrection." Virginia authorities never found the implicated Frenchmen, but several conspirators echoed the report that "the Whites were to be murdered and killed indiscriminately excepting French men, none of whom were to be touched." Quakers and Methodists were also to be spared because they were "friendly to liberty."[3]

Conspirators spoke of other Whites as potential friends to Black liberty, but the rebels' attitudes toward other groups were less consistent. Prosser's Ben testified once that Gabriel wanted to "slay the white males from the Cradle upwards," but Solomon reported that Gabriel planned to spare those who "beged quarters and agreed to serve as Soldiers" in the rebellion. Others testified that the rebels joined together "for the purpose of Murdering the White Citizens," or that "the whites were to be put to Death indiscriminately." Prosser's Ben claimed, in yet another setting, that Gabriel "expected the poor white people would . . . join" the insurrection. Rebel leaders' various claims about poor Whites reflected the contradictory state of urban poor Whites' relations to enslaved Blacks. The rebels' language regarding poor Whites varied by situation, just as did their relations. Ben Woolfolk testified that Gabriel planned to spare any Whites who "agreed to the freedom of the Blacks," but the rebels "would at least cut off one" arm of each of those

---

[3] Executive Communications, 9 (Ditcher), 10 ("indiscriminately"), 7 (Quakers and Methodists). Douglas R. Egerton, *Gabriel's Rebellion: The Virginia Slave Conspiracies of 1800 and 1802* (Chapel Hill, 1993), 182–5 (the Frenchmen); Chapter 1 of this book for traditions of "frenchness"; Michael Craton, *Testing the Chains: Resistance to Slavery in the British West Indies* (Ithaca, 1982), 213 (French agents in the United States in 1795). Winthrop D. Jordan, *White Over Black: American Attitudes Toward the Negro, 1550–1812* (Chapel Hill, 1968), 349–72; Robert McColley, *Slavery and Jeffersonian Virginia*, 2nd ed. (Urbana, 1973), 150–62; David Brion Davis, *The Problem of Slavery in the Age of Revolution* (Ithaca, 1975), ch. 4 and 5; Sylvia R. Frey, *Water from the Rock: Black Resistance in a Revolutionary Age* (Princeton, 1991), ch. 8; Donald G. Mathews, *Slavery and Methodism: A Chapter in American Morality 1780–1845* (Princeton, 1965), ch. 1 (esp. pp. 15–25).

spared. This bargain would not have appealed to poor White Virginians, and
it does not represent the considered position of leading conspirators, but it
stands as a rich emblem of the ambivalence that characterized the relations
between enslaved Black and nonelite White people who worked, drank, fought,
and competed in Richmond.[4]

Some conspirators also believed White women to be relatively free of
responsibility for slavery. Gabriel once said that "the females of all ages were
to be Spared," and Ben Woolfolk partially corroborated this testimony in his
confession, explaining that the insurrectionaries were "to spare all the poor
white Women who had no Slaves." In contrast to these expressions, however, several slaves expressed the desire to kill their mistresses.[5]

Conspirators' responses to different categories of White people – their
very inclination to categorize White Virginians by nationality, class, religion,
and gender when discussing a war to end slavery – reveal divisions that they
perceived on the other side of Virginia's racial divide. The ambivalence of
their responses to the categories of class and gender underscores the wide
range of relationships among White and Black people around Richmond. Urban
social relations offered Black Virginians many avenues to personal or collective improvement, but none was reliable. The Commonwealth's social system oppressed Virginians of African descent by virtue of their race, and all
White Virginians who advocated enforcing the state's laws were enemies of
enslaved Blacks. On one level, the conspirators realized as much: many targeted all Whites as their enemies and identified freedom as their goal. At the
same time, many Black Virginians (presumably including some conspirators)
cultivated friendly relations with White individuals, hoping to find a patron.
Neither of these positions represented Blacks' "real" worldview; the tension
itself was real and important.

The decisions made by various Black Richmonders upon learning of
Gabriel's Conspiracy make most sense within this context of perceived strategies. Urbanization and the halting but real post-Revolution liberalization in
the law of slavery created small cracks in the system of racial control. Joining
the conspiracy meant taking a huge chance, risking one's life and those of

---

[4] Executive Papers (see ch. 2, n. 3), Box 115 ("Cradle") Executive Communications, 4 ("quarters"), 12 ("Citizens"), 11 ("indiscriminately"), 31 ("join"), 32 ("arm").

[5] Executive Papers, Box 115 ("all ages"); Executive Communications, 8 ("poor white").
Compare Catherine Clinton, *The Plantation Mistress: Woman's World in the Old South*
(New York, 1982), esp. ch. 10, with Elizabeth Fox-Genovese, *Within the Plantation Household: Black and White Women of the Old South* (Chapel Hill, 1988), esp. chs. 6 and 7, to
see how this division among enslaved men about White women's culpability for slavery's
evils anticipated divisions that continue in historians' discussions of plantation mistresses.

many others, in pursuit of collective freedom. Slaves whose daily lives were regularly touched by the broad range of gambles opened up through the development of urban slavery were accustomed to taking chances, but the opportunities for autonomy that urban social relations had opened also meant that Richmond-area slaves had more to lose in an unsuccessful insurrection. The rising expectations created by urbanization, combined with the realization of most area slaves that real change in their status remained highly unlikely, stimulated both a willingness to seek radical change and a tendency to protect limited gains. Rather than divining which response predominated, scholars should explore the potential power of both impulses in order to explain the ambivalence that many enslaved Virginians displayed when facing the conspiracy.

Ambivalence and the decision to join Gabriel

Uncertainty pervades the testimony about the insurrection. Some involves basic facts about how many slaves joined Gabriel. Estimates varied from 500 to 5,000, and no accurate number can be assigned. Some uncertainty centered around the slaves' perceptions of how various White Virginians would react to the insurrection. These tensions often came to the surface when a potential insurrectionary decided whether to commit to the conspiracy. Understanding the ambivalence that lay at the root of so many slaves' responses to Gabriel's attempt to lead a rebellion helps to contextualize the crucial but sometimes neglected role of informers in southern slave rebellions, and it helps to highlight some important tensions in the collective identity that Virginians of African descent had forged over the course of the eighteenth century.

Because the key issue at each alleged conspirator's trial was whether the defendant had joined Gabriel's Conspiracy, the depositions provide fascinating pictures of enslaved Virginians deciding whether to risk rebellion. Testimony from convicted slaves' trials was much more likely to survive than from those of acquitted slaves, so many depositions present fairly straightforward commitments to the insurrection. Some of Gabriel's followers masked the fear they naturally felt in taking such a momentous and dangerous step by declaring with bravado that they longed to "slay" White people "like Sheep," or to "wade to our knees in Blood."[6] But a surprising number of witnesses

---

[6] Trial of King, Executive Papers, Box 114 ("slay"); Executive Communications, 20 ("wade"). See Executive Communications, 17 ("Trial of Martin, the Property of Roger Gregory") for rare surviving testimony in the trial of a slave acquitted of conspiracy. Only

eschewed the boastful claims one might expect from understandably hesitant young men and openly displayed doubts about committing to so hazardous a course.

Many who supported the idea of the conspiracy hesitated to join, because doing so meant committing a capital crime under Virginia's slave law. Thus, Michael declined Gabriel's invitation "to join him on an insurrection," but promised that "should he see the business progress well, he would afterwards join him." And Prosser's Ben, who knew as much about the insurrection as anyone outside the leadership, reported to another conspirator that "he had taken time to consider" and had not yet committed.[7] Other slaves responded to the dangers inherent in rebellion by protecting their ability to deny knowledge of the conspiracy. Thus, Edmund met with his friends Ben Woolfolk and Thornton one Sunday during August. He accompanied them to Ellis's Tavern where they bought liquor and then joined them at a religious meeting. After the meeting, Woolfolk and Thornton used the liquor to recruit rebels, but before that happened, Edmund "step'd to the top of the Hill" and left. Edmund later claimed to know nothing of what went on at the spring where his friends recruited followers. Similarly, Daniel refused an invitation to "a great Barbacue . . . being informed that the purport . . . was to concert measures to raise an insurrection."[8] These slaves surely knew that an insurrection was in the works but sought to act as if they were ignorant of it. They were not enemies to the rebellion, and like Michael they might all have taken part had the "business progress[ed] well," but they remained too aware of the dangers involved to join without taking time to think about it.

Slaves who rejected the insurrectionaries' overtures also displayed ambivalence. At the Caroline County meeting where Woolfolk and Thornton recruited followers, the rebellion began to take on too serious an appearance

---

a fragmentary picture of the conspiracy made its way into trial records. Slaves were tried for joining the conspiracy, so evidence of anything other than recruiting was recorded by chance. Conspirators' confessions were taken in order to understand the conspiracy, so they include more information but are less numerous.

[7] Executive Communications, 14 (Michael's promise), 23 (Prosser's Ben). Apparently Prosser's Ben ultimately joined, because an observer of the trials reported that Ben had "assisted in making cutlasses" and described himself as a "noviciate" in the insurrection (*Virginia Argus*, October 14, 1800). His hesitance may have reflected uncertainty regarding Tom (the slave to whom he was talking), or it may have been a harbinger of his role in the trials.

[8] Executive Papers, Box 115 (Edmund against Thornton); Executive Communications, 11 (Daniel).

for two listeners. Primus and Bristol attended at the spring following the preach-
ing but grew concerned upon hearing the conspirators' plans and threatened
to "inform the white people" if Thornton did not desist. Primus and Bristol
then headed home. The slaves who had joined the insurrection chased down
the potential informers "with an intention . . . of putting them to death."
Once overtaken, Bristol and Primus "denied that they had any . . . intention"
to betray the Conspiracy.[9] The conspirators accepted the word of those who
threatened betrayal, and Bristol and Primus kept their word.

Sources provide scant evidence for sorting the degree to which fear of
Whites led Bristol and Primus to threaten to inform or the degree to which
fear of the rebels led them to remain silent. They opposed the insurrection
and sought to dissuade their acquaintances from taking part, but they refused
to betray and stop it. By the same token, the slaves who joined the insurrection had made a commitment real enough to cause them to threaten to
kill Primus and Bristol, but they allowed the potential traitors to go on their
way with nothing more than a warning. While the rebels invoked violence
by claiming that they were "determined to kill, every black, who should not
aid in . . . the Insurrection,"[10] they balked at killing friends. Later, conspirators who survived the trials also failed to exact revenge on those who did
betray the plan.

Expressions of ambivalence provide no guidance, however, to the way individuals would have reacted had the insurrection taken place. Michael, who
rejected Gabriel's invitation to fight with the promise to join if "the business progress[ed] well," was later captured by two White men only after
resisting with "a Scythe blade made into the form of a Sword."[11] Michael
was the only rebel who left a record of physically resisting arrest, and he did
so despite the failure of the business to progress at all. On the other side,
Martin, who had once advised Billey to join the insurrection "to fight the
White people," reportedly "curse[d] the black people for intending to rise
against the Whites" once he "heard . . . the plott was discovered."[12]

Expressions of ambivalence reveal, instead, the apprehension that potential
rebels felt about the course of action they were choosing, and they provide

---

[9] Sam Graham's Confession, Executive Papers, Box 115 (Primus and Bristol threat);
Executive Communications, 33 (conspirators chasing Bristol and Primus).
[10] Executive Communications, 13. Compare Egerton, *Gabriel's Rebellion*, 205–6, n. 59. Eugene
D. Genovese, *From Rebellion to Revolution: Afro-American Slave Revolts in the Making
of the Modern World* (Baton Rouge, 1979), 9–12.
[11] Executive Communications, 14.
[12] Executive Communications, 17. Martin belonged to Roger Gregory; he was not the Martin
who was Gabriel's brother.

a crucial context for understanding the slaves who moved beyond ambivalence and betrayed Gabriel. The fears shared by many conspirators led several
to turn against the rebellion. The informers' behavior cannot be understood
as the action of people loyal to masters or slavery. They used their knowledge of the impending insurrection to better their own lives within a system
they feared they could not change. In doing so, they turned their backs on
the fraternal organization they had joined, choosing a surer path toward individual advancement, but a path that undermined any chance of collective
liberation and that doomed Gabriel and others who pursued their broader
vision of justice.

Individualism and communalism in context

The betrayal of the conspiracy loses some of its moral clarity but explains a
great deal about the enslaved Virginians' world if it is understood in the context of the many compromises with power and the small, medium, and large
acts of accommodation engaged in by participants in Gabriel's Conspiracy.
The many men who made small compromises should not be understood
as having abandoned – even temporarily – their belief in the ideals of the
conspiracy. Instead they, like all human beings, had complicated and contradictory values. Like other enslaved Virginians, they saw themselves both
as enslaved people of African descent seeking to overthrow structures that
oppressed them collectively and as individuals seeking to pick their way through
a treacherous minefield without being blown to pieces. All enslaved Virginians moved between these two poles, and such movement rarely involved
any change in allegiance or identity. The Conspiracy produced an unusual
moment when movement from one pole to another represented a fundamental
and lifelong choice, regardless of the intent behind the decision.

The least perplexing examples of collaboration involved slaves convicted
of participating in the insurrection who confessed and implicated comrades.
Convicted slave rebels received death sentences, and the state hanged Gabriel
and at least twenty-four of his followers. Little wonder that a frightened
eighteen-year-old like Prosser's Ben chose "to save his life by turning traitor
himself." Turning state's evidence, however, was not reserved for a novi-
tiate like Ben. Ben Woolfolk, an acknowledged leader of the conspiracy who
admitted that "he deserved to die as much as any," offered to make "important discoveries" if the court spared him.[13] Both men testified extensively at

---

[13] *Virginia Argus*, October 14, 1800. Egerton says Woolfolk served as Gabriel's "contact
with Caroline County" and "lacked access to the inner sanctum and its secrets" (*Gabriel's*

the trials, and both escaped the gallows by helping to convict and hang many insurrectionaries.

Once Woolfolk and Prosser's Ben had won their pardons by turning state's evidence, magistrates could convince other slaves to cooperate with the possibility of mercy. Local attorney James Rind took George Smith's confession and "impressed . . . upon him . . . that the fuller his confession" the better his chance for a pardon.[14] No doubt those who took confessions from other slaves – men like Sam Graham and Gilbert – "impressed" the same message upon them, but despite extensive confessions, Gilbert and Smith were both hanged in mid-October. Graham's shorter confession also failed to win a pardon.[15] Each man cooperated after the information he possessed had lost much of its value. Authorities still wanted to learn about the insurrection but no longer felt compelled to deliver on implied promises. Of course, these men might not have cooperated had they believed their confessions could still undermine the insurrection.

The fear and uncertainty that enveloped White Virginians in the wake of the discovery of the insurrection created chances for others to cash in on their knowledge. Gabriel and Jack Ditcher remained at large for most of a month. White Virginians did not feel sure that the insurrection had been thwarted until the two leaders had been arrested and jailed. Presumably for at least part of the time between September 1 and their capture, they hid in the woods and called on relatives and friends for aid just as runaway slaves normally did.[16] Each no doubt tried to limit the number of people who learned of his whereabouts, but each slave who did find out faced a wrenching decision. Monroe offered $300 for information leading to either leader's capture, and though no Black was likely to receive that princely sum, the state did promise a "full PARDON" for up to five "accomplices who shall apprehend

Rebellion, 102). Woolfolk, however, was recruited early in the conspiracy by George Smith and Sam Byrd (Executive Communications, 4–5), and his role in the argument over when the insurrection was to start (Chapter 2 in this book) indicates that he was a leader among the conspirators.

[14] James Rind to Elisha Price, n.d., Executive Papers, Box 114.

[15] All three are listed among slaves executed for participation in Gabriel's Insurrection in Office of the Auditor of Public Accounts, Item 153, Executed and Transported Slaves, Box 1 (hereafter OAI 153), LiVa.

[16] Gerald W. Mullin, *Flight and Rebellion: Slave Resistance in Eighteenth-Century Virginia* (New York, 1972), esp. 55–7; Allan Kulikoff, *Tobacco and Slaves: The Development of Southern Cultures in the Chesapeake, 1680–1800* (Chapel Hill, 1986), esp. pp. 343–5; Rhys Isaac, *The Transformation of Virginia, 1740–1790* (Chapel Hill, 1982), 323–358; and Chapter 1 of this book.

the said GABRIEL."[17] The rewards eventually accomplished what authorities desired, but slowly and in unexpected ways.

Jack Ditcher remained at large until October 9, when he suddenly appeared at the house of magistrate Gervas Storrs, accompanied by "Peter alias Peter Smith a free negroe." Storrs renounced his claim to the reward on condition that the state pay Smith "50 dollars for the service he has rendered, the risk he has run and the odium he may incur from the blacks." Storrs believed that Smith "operated considerably" to convince Ditcher to give himself up and that Smith had given "all the intelligence he could collect" about Ditcher's whereabouts while at large. Nothing indicates that anyone got in trouble from the information Smith provided, and the Executive Council paid him the reward. Perhaps winning a monetary reward for a friend was Ditcher's final small blow against Virginia's social system. Smith could not, after all, have forced Ditcher – "perhaps as strong a man as any in the state" – to surrender. Rather, Smith seems to have helped Ditcher to evade authorities until White Virginians' passions cooled and then to have brought him in to a perhaps trusted magistrate. If that was the case, then the strategy worked. Smith received $50, and Ditcher was transported out of the state rather than hanged.[18]

Gabriel was even less fortunate than Ditcher. He too hid in the area, but rumors emerged from Hanover County that he was "enquiring the route to James town."[19] Two weeks after he had planned to lead an assault on Richmond, he hopped aboard a conveniently grounded sloop sailing to Norfolk. Circumstantial evidence strongly suggests that Richardson Taylor, the White captain, conspired to help Gabriel escape, probably with one of his crew, Billy, who had been jailed on suspicion of having joined the conspiracy. Gabriel almost surely believed the sloop was safe for him, for he threw away "a bayonet fixed on a stick" before boarding.[20]

---

[17] *Virginia Gazette*, September 12, 1800 (pardon offer); *Virginia Argus*, September 23, 1800 (rewards).
[18] Gervas Storrs to James Monroe, October 10, 1800, Executive Papers, Box 114 (Ditcher's surrender); *Virginia Argus*, September 23, 1800 (Ditcher's strength).
[19] James Monroe to Mayor of Williamsburg, September 12, 1800, ELB, 1794–1800 (see chapter 1, n. 38 for Executive Letter Books).
[20] Quotations from Thomas Newton to James Monroe, September 24, 1800, Executive Papers, Box 114 unless otherwise noted. See Egerton, *Gabriel's Rebellion*, 104–8, 177. Taylor disappears from the records, and Egerton reasonably asserts that he escaped the state. However, in March 1803 someone in Henrico County was charged with "venerial communication with a Cow the property of Richardson Taylor" (Henrico County Order Book #10, 527). I cannot determine whether the owner of the cow and the ship captain were the same man.

He had not, however, counted on trouble with a second Black crew member named Isham. Apparently Isham was not in on Gabriel's escape, but he recognized the new passenger as "Gabriel . . . the person the reward was offerd for." This left Billy caught in the middle, balancing his loyalty to and fear of Gabriel against his fear of the consequences should Isham turn in Gabriel and tell authorities that Billy had helped the fugitive. Upon reaching Norfolk, Billy decided the risks had become too great, so he left the vessel, told "Norris, a blacksmith . . . that Gabriel was on board," and two magistrates were summoned to arrest Gabriel. He was taken to Richmond, tried, and hanged. Billy did not escape suspicion – Norfolk authorities advised Monroe to interrogate Billy's "wife at Mr Norris's" in Richmond (a relative of the Norfolk blacksmith?) to discover whether Gabriel had planned the escape with Billy – but Billy was not tried for his role in Gabriel's flight.

Each of these slaves acted in some way to betray the rebellion. They did so knowingly. In each case, an individual faced a frightening dilemma and made an agonizing choice. They did so for a variety of reasons, but they did not choose accommodation out of a completely open universe of options, and choosing accommodation once did not represent a lifelong declaration of allegiance. Enslaved Virginians lived with the stifling influence of the men and women who owned them, and planned insurrections, even if they never occurred, momentarily altered the balance of power between slaves and masters. Suddenly Black people had information that was invaluable to Whites, and they could use that information to win concessions from those under whose power they lived. But the power offered by this knowledge came at a high cost, because exploiting it required the kind of fundamental choice between communal and individual strategies that enslaved Virginians rarely had to make. Each slave who knew something about an insurrection must have faced constant temptation to use that power for personal gain. Only by inscribing clear abstractions about individualism and communalism back into this messy world of power, temptation, and compromise, can one outline the context for the choice made by Pharoah and Tom.

The betrayal

Had Pharoah and Tom not chosen to tell Mosby Sheppard of the impending insurrection on that Saturday afternoon, Virginia's history might have been different. Their choice must be placed within the wider context of eighteenth-century Black Virginians' compromises with power, but not all compromises were equally significant. Acts of accommodation that occurred after authorities learned of the planned rebellion were not benign. Many men paid with their lives for Ben Woolfolk's testimony, and potential rebels must have been discouraged by how quickly the conspiracy unraveled once pressure was brought to bear upon participants. Nonetheless, after contexts have been created and parallels established, the importance of Pharoah and Tom's betrayal remains.

Pharoah and Tom, two Sheppard family slaves, went to Mosby Sheppard on the day of the insurrection to inform him that Blacks in the area planned to rise and take Richmond.[21] Monroe called out the militia after Sheppard's warning, but when the rainstorm on August 30 caused the insurrection to be postponed and patrols discouraged the rebels from meeting the next evening, the governor "was on the point of concluding there was no foundation for the alarm." However, William Mosby, a county militia officer who had patrolled Saturday and Sunday nights, received a warning upon his arrival at home on Monday morning. He had collapsed into bed when a slave woman sneaked into his room and asked if he had heard that the Blacks were going to rise." Her story matched that of Pharoah and Tom, convincing Monroe "of the existence of such a project." He sent militia men to "commit to prison . . . all the slaves . . . they . . . suspect[ed]." Soon Prosser's Ben cracked under interrogation.[22]

Prior to the decision of Pharoah and Tom to betray the conspiracy, neither Gabriel nor other conspirators appear to have thought them untrustworthy.[23]

---

[21] Egerton, *Gabriel's Rebellion*, 69–72 believes that Pharoah and Tom turned in the conspiracy on Sunday, August 31, perhaps after being frightened by the storm that prevented the insurrection from occurring the previous night. A letter to Monroe in which William Mosby recounted his experiences on patrol supports Egerton (Mosby to Monroe, November 10, 1800, *Virginia General Assembly's Journal of the Senate . . . 1st day of December 1800* [Richmond, 1800], 28). But Monroe twice asserted otherwise: he reported to South Carolina Lt. Gov. John Drayton that "the plot was discovered, about two o'clock in the afternoon of the day on which the Stroke was to have been given" (October 21, 1800, ELB, 1800–3); and he told the legislature that "on the 30th of August, about two in the afternoon, Mr. Mosby Shephard . . . informed me he had just received advice . . . that the negroes . . . intended to rise that night." This version is corroborated in the *Virginia Argus*, October 14, 1800, which preceded Monroe's letters and thus could not have been misled by them. The apparent contradiction between the two accounts remains, as does the odd fact that Monroe sent Mosby's letter to the legislature without commenting on the inconsistency.

[22] Mosby Sheppard to James Monroe, August 30, 1800, Executive Communications, 2 (Sheppard's warning); Monroe to the Speakers of the General Assembly, December 5, 1800, ELB, 1800–3 (Monroe's response). *Virginia Argus*, October 14, 1800 (Prosser's Ben).

[23] My analysis focuses on Pharoah (rather than on both Pharoah and Tom), because I have more information about him. Both, however, received full "credit" from Whites for turning in the conspiracy: the state bought and freed both men, and a group of Richmond merchants created a $1,000 trust in each man's name.

Little evidence exists proving that either was recruited, but such evidence was produced only when slaves were tried as rebels. Pharoah and Tom, of course, were never tried. They probably joined the insurrection before informing on it, as suggested by one of the small ironies of the conspiracy. Solomon ran into Pharoah as the latter was returning from Richmond after warning Mosby Sheppard of the impending rebellion. Apparently Solomon had gotten word that something was up, but he showed no suspicion of Pharoah. Instead, he asked "whether the light horse of Richmond were out." Pharoah, having ensured that the cavalry would be out, replied that "he had seen some at colonel Goodall's tavern." Solomon observed that "the business . . . had . . . advanced" too far to turn back.[24] Solomon would have confided this only to someone involved in "the business."

Pharoah was not an artisan. Nonetheless, he had a source of money while still enslaved, perhaps from hiring himself out during harvests as an expert scythesman.[25] In 1797 and 1798 Mosby Sheppard sold Pharoah three hats and several articles of clothing made from luxury cloths like "casimer" and "muslinet." Pharoah made piecemeal payments on the debt with cash while he was still a slave. Only three slaves then had accounts with Sheppard, so Pharoah enjoyed standing beyond that of most bondmen.[26]

Pharoah's status as a modestly privileged slave did not allow him to escape the hardships of bondage. The accounts reveal privilege but also hint at hardship. Among the items Pharoah purchased in 1798 was "1 Boys Hatt" for seven shillings, six pence.[27] Sheppard does not reveal whom the hat was for, but on September 3, 1803, he noted that "Pharoah Sheppard (F[ree] N[egro])" entered into a debt of £70. Mosby Sheppard paid that sum for Pharoah's son, also named Pharoah, and charged an additional £5 for "expences in

[24] Executive Communications, 9–10. Genovese, *From Rebellion to Revolution* points out that "both rebel leaders and supreme accommodationists came from the same ranks, for they were men of wider experience than ordinary field hands and had talents they could turn in either direction" (27). Contrary to my reading of this event, however, Genovese maintains that members of the "privileged strata" of slaves were "least likely to equivocate on the political issues. That is, either they identify with their oppressors and seek individual advancement or they identify with their people and place their sophistication at the disposal of the rebellion" (28).
[25] James Monroe to Mr. Philip Sheppard, March 5, 1801, ELB, 1800–3 (not artisan); Samuel Coleman to James Monroe, February 28, 1801, Executive Papers, Box 116 (scythesman).
[26] Mosby Sheppard Account Book, 1794–1812, 28 in the Sheppard Family Papers, Meadow Farm Museum, Henrico County Department of Parks and Recreation, Henrico County, Virginia. Egerton, *Gabriel's Rebellion*, 70 refers to these items as "gifts" from Sheppard to Pharoah, but the account book indicates that Mosby Sheppard charged £4 8s. 9d.
[27] Mosby Sheppard Account Book, 28.

traveling . . . 100 miles" each way when buying the boy. Mosby Sheppard retained ownership of Pharoah Junior until his former slave repaid £75 "in full with Intrest" five years later.[28]

Pharoah's family may first have been separated when the Sheppards purchased him "at a publick sale," but, regardless of the mechanism, Pharoah paid a monumental price for being born enslaved in Virginia.[29] Installments remained to be paid after he acquired freedom. In 1806 the Virginia legislature passed a law requiring all slaves manumitted after that year to leave the state within twelve months or face reenslavement. Because Pharoah Junior did not officially become free until his father discharged the full debt to Mosby Sheppard in 1808, the boy was subject to the 1806 law. Pharoah Senior had to petition the legislature, reminding them of his earlier service, while pleading that they "suffer" Pharoah Junior "to remain in this Commonwealth."[30] It seems unlikely that Pharoah Sheppard betrayed Gabriel out of conviction that slavery was just.

How, then, can Pharoah's decision to tell Mosby Sheppard of the impending insurrection be understood? A man who attended the trials of the conspirators claimed in a letter to the Richmond *Argus* that "a negro man . . . terrified with the thought of the danger to which he was about to expose himself, informed his master" that an insurrection was planned.[31] Pharoah and Tom's fear may have grown out of conspirators' threats to kill any slaves who failed to support the rebellion, but the White correspondent in the *Argus* suggested that fear of the danger that an insurrection would create prompted Pharoah's decision to inform. No hard evidence of the informers' perceptions exist, but these dangers can be deduced. The first was physical, for Pharoah could easily have anticipated that White Virginians would have responded to Gabriel's rebellion, had it occurred, with brutal and, at least initially, almost indiscriminate violence against Black residents of Richmond and the surrounding countryside. Bloody reprisal certainly characterized White Virginians' response to Nat Turner three decades later.

The likelihood of bloody repression does not, of course, mean that a rebellion would not have accomplished anything. It might have turned some

[28] Mosby Sheppard Account Book, 52, 70.
[29] Samuel Coleman to James Monroe, February 28, 1801, Executive Papers, Box 116.
[30] Pharoah Sheppard petition, December 14, 1810, Legislative Petitions, Richmond City, Box 7 (1810–12), LiVa.
[31] *Virginia Argus*, October 14, 1800. Executive Communications, 2 (Sheppard's account of the betrayal).

White Virginians against "the peculiar institution," and an insurrection in the state where slavery was perceived to be most civilized and benign would have provided a major boost to the fledgling English and northern antislavery movements. The short-term effects were more certain and bloody, and they surely helped to push Pharoah toward Mosby Sheppard's counting room. Perhaps as important as the physical threat posed by the insurrection was the danger that Virginia masters, rather than turning against the peculiar institution, would close some of the cracks that had opened in the slave system. A historical truism holds that rebellions and revolutions often grow out of rising expectations, and Gabriel and many of his followers benefited from the loosening bonds of slavery in the growing city of Richmond.[32] But slow and uncertain improvements might just as logically have led some who had begun to see beneficial changes to protect their limited gains.

Pharoah benefited disproportionately from the new and limited opportunities that Richmond-area slaves enjoyed in late-eighteenth-century Virginia. No doubt he frequently walked into town to visit tippling shops, gambling and disorderly houses, or dances. His ability to buy goods on credit from his master indicates that he was hiring some of his time, selling goods on the open market, or at the very least working overtime to make money. Moreover, Mosby Sheppard placed more elastic limits on his slaves' possibilities than did many Virginia masters. Sheppard left no evidence of thinking slavery wrong: he never manumitted a group of slaves, and he insisted on a hefty price when the legislature voted to buy and free Pharoah and Tom. He did, however, allow one man to buy his own freedom. On October 20, 1796 "Gabriel (Negro)" incurred a £30 debt for the "purchase of self." This was not an act of charity on Sheppard's part. Gabriel (Sheppard)[33] had to pay his former master with interest – much as Pharoah would later have to pay for his son – and Gabriel (Sheppard) did not discharge the debt for more than six years.[34] But for someone like Pharoah, with a proven ability to accumulate cash, Sheppard's willingness to sell freedom to Gabriel (Sheppard) may have constituted an opportunity he feared might disappear. One of Mosby Sheppard's ledgers even refers to "Pharoah Free negro" in an entry dated

[32] See Part II of this book for the development of urban slavery in Richmond.
[33] There is no evidence that this Gabriel ever took his master's surname, but I will put that surname in parentheses after his name to avoid confusion with the Gabriel who led the conspiracy.
[34] Mosby Sheppard Account Book, 32. Gabriel's Deed of Emancipation is in Henrico County Deed Book #5, 624–5, LiVa.

February 1799, strongly suggesting that Pharoah would have been allowed to buy his freedom.[35] Perhaps he surmised that Virginia would not leave such loopholes open if an insurrection occurred.

How, then, would Pharoah's world have appeared as August 30 approached? Once he learned of the Conspiracy, Pharoah faced several alternatives. He could have joined and fought with other area slaves for his and their freedom, or he could have ignored the pending insurrection and lived his life as if nothing unusual were happening. Instead, Pharoah chose a third alternative by informing on his comrades. But just as his decision followed a seemingly contradictory one to join the Conspiracy, the way he informed suggests that he remained cautiously on the fence throughout the ordeal. He gave White Virginians little time to organize to put down the insurrection. Governor Monroe heard about the conspiracy only at about two o'clock in the afternoon of August 30, an hour so far advanced that he could only struggle to make "the best disposition for such an emergency the time would allow."[36] Having started this train of events, Pharoah returned home as if nothing had happened. On the way home he ran into Solomon but made no effort to hide the fact that the cavalry had been called out and were close by.[37]

No one can know how Pharoah would have reacted had the rains not fallen and the rebellion not fizzled. Perhaps he would have sat out the event and hoped to win favor with whoever had won the battle, once bloodshed ended. Pharoah did not inform in a way that would have cut him off from the rebels had the insurrection succeeded, as Primus and Bristol had threatened to do. Nor did he inform early enough to give White Virginians time to be assured of thwarting the Conspiracy.

In some ways Pharoah left a surprisingly full documentary record, but in others the evidence is maddeningly scarce. Account books and court records indicate more than one might expect about what Pharoah consumed and where he worked after he achieved freedom. They provide few clues, however, to what he thought or why he betrayed the Conspiracy.[38] His behavior on August

---

[35] Mosby Sheppard Ledger A, 1798–1817, 1. It is also possible that the entry was copied into the book after Pharoah became free, but there is no indication that the accounts were copied into the book at a later date.

[36] James Monroe to the Speakers of the General Assembly, December 5, 1800, ELB, 1800–3.

[37] Executive Communications, 9 (Pharoah and Solomon).

[38] In a petition asking the Virginia legislature to let his recently-manumitted son remain in the state, he claimed to have acted "from motives truely gratifying to himself and all the good people" of Richmond, but that explanation is both ambiguous and untrustworthy; Pharoah Sheppard petition, December 14, 1810, Legislative Petitions, Richmond City, Box 7 (1810–12).

30, 1800, is consistent with at least two explanations. Perhaps he panicked as the moment of truth approached. Unable to stomach the risk that rebellion entailed, he opted instead for the good chance that White authorities would reward his loyalty and the more certain prospect that his limited but real chances to improve his life under Mosby Sheppard would be protected. Conversely, he may have been a shrewder and more devious man than his contemporaries could see. Perhaps he cagily waited until the last second to tell authorities of the impending insurrection so that the rebels might have a chance. Then, if Gabriel was successful, Pharoah could have joined his triumphant brethren in Richmond as if he had supported them all along. Had the conspirators failed, he could have looked forward to being rewarded for surreptitiously revealing that the rebellion was in the works.

If two such divergent interpretations of Pharoah's motives are consistent with his behavior, then there is limited utility in lingering on different explanations, but several important points should be made. Pharoah and Tom betrayed the rebellion and their probable comrades more fundamentally than did others, but they were not alone in compromising with White power. Slaves' lives consisted of endless compromises with the master class, and it is hardly surprising that such compromises also characterized attempts to build an oppositional movement. Such compromises need not indicate sympathy with the status quo. One survival lesson that members of subordinate groups learn in oppressive societies is how and when to cut their losses and settle for partial victories. Pharoah, Tom, Ben Woolfolk, Prosser's Ben, and others chose to make individual deals with those in authority, and in so doing they thwarted the rebellion and cost many Black Virginians their lives. The reactions of other slaves who survived the conspiracy trials to those who turned on the rebels reveals more of the complexity inherent in the roles that informers played in slave rebellions.

The informers' lives

The slave informers did not live in an area completely free of surviving conspirators. The state never tried to execute or transport all who expressed support for the rebellion. Trial depositions and confessions implicate more than 100 Black Virginians in the planned insurrection, while probably fewer than 70 were tried.[39] At least some of those acquitted appear to have been

---

[39] There is no way to know precisely how many slaves were tried for participating in the conspiracy, because Hanover County's Court Order Books have not survived. A compilation of known slave insurrection trials in Virginia is the appendix of Philip J. Schwarz,

conspirators: Daniel was acquitted despite testimony that Solomon spoke to
him in the "usual way of addressing persons concerned in the plott," and
that Gabriel described him as "one of his party." One White observer of the
trials claimed that "the least doubt . . . will often accuit Negroes who are
really criminals," and Monroe himself noted "that the combination extended"
through the city and surrounding counties, and speculated that it might have
"pervaded . . . the whole of the State."[40] The state's brutal repression was
designed to kill leaders and punish enough others to serve as a warning to
slaves who might have shared the rebellious impulse rather than to kill all
who had joined Gabriel.[41] In this regard (as in many others), White Virginians' response to Gabriel's Conspiracy was characteristic of slave societies'
responses throughout most of plantation America.

With many conspirators remaining around Richmond after the trials ended
and life returned to normal, one would expect the informers' lives to have
been in jeopardy.[42] Eugene Genovese has pointed out how crucial threatened
vengeance was in balancing the constant presence of White terror and in
forcing slaves to choose sides with reference to something other than concern for physical safety.[43] Retribution against informers after the fact must
have been equally important for future resistance. Seeing a few slaves who
cooperated with authorities meeting violent deaths might have gone far to
counteract the example of slave rebels swinging from the gallows. How, then,
did those slaves who compromised with White Virginians fare after the furor
over the insurrection died down? What does their experience reveal about
the world of Gabriel's Conspiracy?

Many who cooperated with White authorities during the insurrection scare
were executed or deported, so there was no opportunity for Richmond-area
blacks to exact their own revenge. Several who survived – Billy and Isham
(the shiphands who turned in Gabriel) and the woman who warned Mosby
of the conspiracy – never reappeared in local records. Prosser's Ben was freed

Twice *Condemned: Slaves and the Criminal Laws of Virginia, 1705–1865* (Baton Rouge, 1988).

[40] Executive Communications, 19; *Virginia Argus*, October 14, 1800 ("accuit"); James Monroe to the Speakers of the General Assembly, December 5, 1800, ELB, 1800–3.

[41] The confession of Gilbert, the slave of William Young, (Executive Papers, Box 114) alone includes accusations against three Black Virginians who appear never to have been tried for any role in the insurrection.

[42] Egerton, *Gabriel's Rebellion*, 173–5 asserts, for example, that "the fear of sudden death at the hands of vengeful slaves . . . haunted . . . those bondmen who had assisted in bring-ing the rebels to the bar of White justice" (173).

[43] Genovese, *From Rebellion to Revolution*, 9–12.

by his master in return for £110 paid by five prominent Richmonders, but he then disappears from the records.[44] By chance, however, documentary evidence survives regarding three of the most important informers who would have topped the surviving conspirators' hit list – Pharoah Sheppard, Tom Sheppard, and Ben Woolfolk.

None of the three appear to have suffered physical retaliation for collaboration. Pharoah and Tom Sheppard continued to do business with Mosby Sheppard until after 1810.[45] Ben Woolfolk bought his life but not his freedom through cooperation. He later reprised his early role by serving as a prosecution witness in a trial of Blacks charged with burglary in 1807, but then he disappeared from the record.[46] Physical retaliation, while probably the most effective form of revenge, was not the only sanction the Black community could have imposed on those who betrayed the insurrection. The sketchy surviving records provide no evidence, but Woolfolk, Pharoah Sheppard, and Tom Sheppard may well have been ostracized by Richmond Blacks.

Pharoah and Tom Sheppard did, however, continue to live, work, and consume in the Richmond area for at least a decade after 1800. During the ten years following the insurrection scare, neither appeared as a witness in court against a Black defendant. Each received freedom from the state, and wealthy white Richmonders joined together to establish a $1,000 trust fund for each informer.[47] These guaranteed incomes made them more secure than most free Blacks in Virginia, and the trust funds encouraged Pharoah and Tom to retain their ties to Mosby Sheppard by making him a trustee. The informers and the man they informed continued to do business with one another for some time.

Soon after Pharoah was freed, he began to acquire trappings of authority, buying a secondhand saddle and a martingale from Mosby Sheppard. The martingale – used to control a horse – suggests that he had acquired a young

[44] Henrico County Deed Book #6, 227. The deed never specifies that the Ben freed was the same as the witness at the slave trials, but it is hard to understand why else Charles Johnston, William Foushee, James Heron, Samuel Myers, and John Adams would have paid Thomas Henry Prosser £110 to free a slave. Egerton, *Gabriel's Rebellion*, 173–4, unaware of this deed, reasonably assumes that the "Prosser's Ben" tried by the Henrico County Court for conspiracy in 1806 was the same man who testified in the earlier conspiracy trials.
[45] Mosby Sheppard Account Book and Ledgers A and B.
[46] Richmond Hustings Court Order Book #7, 199–203 (LiVa). Woolfolk belonged to Wilson Cary Miles in 1807.
[47] Henrico County Deed Book #6, 289–93.

horse, and he also bought a "pair leather breaches," perhaps for riding. Just as important as the goods he bought, Pharaoh moved more fully into the commercial world of free Virginians. Part of the debt he incurred by purchasing riding equipment was paid by "Cash of Gabriel (F[ree]N[egro])" and part by cash "of Tom S (FN)." He also delivered more than £4 "at John Winstons" and paid part of a debt with "5 pecks of Oat."[48] By 1802 Pharoah had created a small commercial circle of Black and White Virginians within which he could move. He commanded credit, extended credit, and paid bills with both cash and goods. That there is nothing exceptional about this behavior in late-eighteenth-century Virginia is precisely the point. In these small economic transactions, Pharoah behaved like the independent farmer that he apparently sought to become.

One attribute of Virginia yeomen engaged in market-oriented production was litigiousness. It took Pharoah Sheppard little time after achieving his freedom to resort to the county court system to protect his liberties. In August 1803 and again in August 1804 "Pharoah a free black man commonly called Pharoah Sheppard" sued Benjamin Mosby for trespass, assault, and battery. In his first civil case, the newly freed plaintiff hired an attorney, summoned John P. Winston to testify against his attacker, and won a $22 judgment from the jury. The disposition of the second case was not recorded, but once again Pharoah appeared and insisted on the protection of the laws.[49]

Not all of Pharoah Sheppard's appearances in court involved assaults, cases that might have grown out of the failure of Whites who knew him as a slave to accept him as a free man. By 1805 he took a member of the White Sheppard family to court for a "Trespass In Case." Suits brought "In Case" involved plaintiffs' asking damages for a defendant's failure to perform a promised service or to deliver promised goods. The county clerk did not record the particulars of *Pharoah Sheppard v. Philip Sheppard*, but he did note that the plaintiff called four witnesses and hired an attorney. The jury assessed the damages suffered "by occasion of the non-performance of those assumptions to $170.20." Pharoah Sheppard then executed an unusual maneuver through which he symbolically turned the tables on at least one member of the family that had formerly owned him by reversing the direction of the patron–client relationship. He declared in open court before the constituted authority of the county that he released "to the defendant $70.20, part of

[48] Mosby Sheppard Account Book, p. 52.
[49] Henrico County Court Order Book #11, 132, 364, 375 (suit against Benjamin Mosby), 438 (second assault suit, presumably settled out of court), LiVa. Order books recorded what the court ordered done (e.g., continuations, dismissals, or outcomes); they normally provide little evidence of the activity that resulted in the suit.

the said damages," and required that Philip Sheppard pay only "$100 . . . and his costs."[50] Rhys Isaac points out that the Virginia gentry displayed its liberality by filling important public offices without pay and treating social inferiors with a generous and patronizing respect.[51] As a Black man, Pharoah Sheppard was socially and legally barred from serving as a justice of the peace or sheriff, but he could assert his liberality and his equality with his former masters by publicly forgiving a debt. That he did so before the assembled justices of Henrico County must have made the moment an even greater symbolic triumph. His insistence on the payment of the bulk of the debt underscored the victory that he won before the jury. Not surprisingly, given his successes, Pharoah Sheppard continued to turn to the courts in disputes with White Virginians.[52]

There is a more obviously unpleasant side to Pharoah's behavior once he ascended to freedom that parallels the unsavory way he got there. If Pharoah Sheppard's early purchase of a horse and riding equipment and his assertions of his liberties within the county court system signaled desire for status and authority, later entries in Mosby Sheppard's account books show that, like other Virginians who aspired to "quality," Pharoah ultimately exercised power over enslaved people. On November 26, 1808, Mosby Sheppard recorded £6 cash "paid the [sic] pharoah the Overseer in part for his part of the crop of wheat."[53] No evidence reveals how harshly Pharoah Sheppard treated the enslaved men and women he supervised, but in a culture in which "a man had to be either a master or a servant,"[54] dominion over servants – even the contingent kind enjoyed by overseers – represented another step toward the world of free and independent Virginians. With the decision to take that step, Pharoah climbed nearly as high as a Black individual could on the ladder he had begun to ascend with his betrayal of Gabriel, and he completed his turn away from the communal world of the conspirators.

Conclusion

An ambiguous conflation of resistance and accommodation characterized Gabriel's Conspiracy. In this regard the conspiracy parallels interpretations

[50] Henrico County Court Order Book #12, 247, 333–4. The court noted Pharoah's release of part of the damages on pp. 333–4. I did not find a similar notation anywhere else in the Richmond or Henrico order books.
[51] Isaac, *Transformation of Virginia*, 130–3.
[52] Henrico County Court Order Book #13, 422–3; Henrico County Court Order Book #14, 425.
[53] Mosby Sheppard Account Book, 60. Tom Sheppard also worked as a supervisor of slave labor after winning freedom (Egerton, *Gabriel's Rebellion*, 175).
[54] Isaac, *Transformation of Virginia*, 132.

of more normal aspects of slave culture during the antebellum period (e.g., religion and folklore).[55] It has long been known that informers plagued slave insurrections, and Gabriel's Conspiracy provides a textbook case illustrating that problem. Examining the informers' lives and behavior for what they shared with the rebels as well as the ways they differed sheds new light on the ways a specific group of late-eighteenth-century Virginia slaves reacted to human bondage and provides new perspectives on the barriers Blacks faced in fighting slavery.

These insights can be summarized by conceptualizing two events that have been central to this chapter. Two men, Primus and Bristol, attended a Sunday recruiting meeting and openly threatened to betray the conspiracy. Two other men, Pharoah and Tom Sheppard, surreptitiously informed Mosby Sheppard that an insurrection was about to occur. All four men found the prospect of rebellion frightening. All four men hoped to protect the lives they had built and perhaps to protect the small gains Blacks had made in late-eighteenth-century Virginia. Evidence suggests that all but the most committed conspirators shared some of these concerns.

Both pairs of men sought to stop the rebellion, but they chose different strategies, strategies that cast them, for all that they shared, into unalterably opposed camps. Primus and Bristol invoked the threat of White intervention, but they did so in front and as part of the conspirators' meeting. They attempted to convince the community of conspirators that it was making a mistake, but then Primus and Bristol withdrew. They refused to participate in the conspiracy, but they never withdrew from the Black community.

Pharoah and Tom Sheppard, on the other hand, left no evidence of having stood openly before the conspirators to argue against the rebellion. Instead, they moved behind the conspirators' backs, seeking individual gain at collective expense. Black Virginians had been pursuing individual self-interest for as long as Blacks had lived in the state, and the creole culture built by Virginians of African descent certainly sanctioned individual striving. By winning freedom at the cost of the rebels' lives, however, they moved beyond the pale of the Black community. In an almost exact reversal of the courageous protest against the rebellion mounted by Primus and Bristol, Pharoah and Tom never openly withdrew from the conspirators' collective, withdrawing instead from the Black community.

---

[55] Eugene Genovese, *Roll, Jordan, Roll: The World the Slaves Made* (New York, 1972), esp. pp. 280–4, 594–8, 658–60; Lawrence Levine, *Black Culture and Black Consciousness: Afro-American Folk Thought from Slavery to Freedom* (New York, 1977), esp. pp. 81–133.

This does not mean that Pharoah and Tom were inherently different — were latently and essentially informers before they spoke to Mosby Sheppard. Surviving conspirators' failure to follow through on explicit threats and to exact vengeance on the two betrayers may in fact reflect an uneasy recognition that they shared more than they might like to admit with the collaborators. But if Black Virginians failed to kill the betrayers, they did not react indifferently. Gabriel's Conspiracy became, as I will show later,[56] an important moment in the collective memory of Virginians of African descent. Pharoah and Tom were expunged from the oral traditions passed down through the generations and thus metaphorically removed from the community and its history.

[56] See Chapter 8 of this book for the oral traditions of Gabriel's conspiracy. Chapter 4 of this book discusses area slaves' attempts to make sense of the act of betrayal before enough time had passed to know whether surviving conspirators would kill Pharoah.

4

Making sense of Gabriel's Conspiracy

Immediate responses to the conspiracy

Making sense of Gabriel's Conspiracy requires more than analyzing the way Gabriel and his lieutenants organized their attempt to overthrow slavery and analyzing the dynamics of the betrayal that undercut their attempt.[1] It also entails studying the ways that those who lived through the conspiracy made sense of it. One (and only one) of the things that the conspiracy represented was an assertion that Virginians of African descent had a rightful claim to the state's revolutionary tradition, a claim their masters failed to recognize. Elite Virginians, then, faced a dual challenge upon discovering Gabriel's plan. First, they had to crush the incipient rebellion. Then, they had to formulate explanations of the conspiracy that undercut Gabriel's implicit claims by placing slavery in a narrative of Virginia's history, society, and culture. Black Virginians also forged understandings of Gabriel's Conspiracy, and at least one enslaved man left a coded trace of his interpretation of Gabriel's and by extension Black Virginians' place in the state's history. In making sense of Gabriel, Black and White Virginians developed conflicting interpretations not only of the conspiracy itself but of the place of race and slavery in the state's history and of what it meant to be a Virginian.

When Pharoah and Tom told Mosby Sheppard of the impending insurrection, they unleashed a reaction that explains much about White Virginians' vision of their world. During the last four months of 1800, White Virginians struggled first to defeat and then to understand their bondmen's attempt to win freedom.[2] Governor James Monroe began by doubting the reality of the

[1] I am indebted to Kevin Kenny for allowing me to borrow the title of his dissertation – "Making Sense of the Molly Maguires" (Ph. D. diss., Columbia University, 1994) – for use as the title of this chapter, as well as for a helpful reading of this chapter.

[2] Some of the best recent historical scholarship has explored the creation of "whiteness" as a racial category in the antebellum United States (David W. Roediger, *The Wages of Whiteness: Race and the Making of the American Working Class* [New York, 1991]). Edmund S. Morgan, *American Slavery, American Freedom: The Ordeal of Colonial Virginia* (New

slave conspiracy. Once convinced, he tried to repress news of the insurrection. When that became impossible, he sought to repress the spirit of rebellion. The measures necessary to crush Black rebellion, however, undercut White notions of fairness and liberality. Soon after authorities began imprisoning, trying, and executing slaves, some Whites started wondering about the proper limits of coercive action. As trials of alleged insurrectionaries progressed, White Virginians published accounts of the conspiracy and its aftermath. By the end of December 1800, James Monroe had declared the insurrection scare over, written its first history, and published the first collection of documents relating to Gabriel's Conspiracy.[3]

While not all White Virginians viewed the insurrection scare in the same way, Monroe sought to forge a White consensus in response to the slaves' challenge. His official report, which shaped legislative discussion of the event, contains no obvious falsehoods, but like all interpretations it highlights some things, downplays others, and is most subjective in its broader framework. Thus his interpretation – the story he told to communicate his understanding of Gabriel's Conspiracy – says much about his conception of the state's social system. Like other White Virginians, Monroe recognized the inherent contradiction of "the existence of slavery in one of the freest republics on earth." Perhaps, like a communicant in the *Virginia Gazette*, he rationalized this contradiction through the belief that "paradoxes" vexed "all human systems of government," but Gabriel's Conspiracy assuredly highlighted Virginia's paradox.[4] If Whites sometimes implied that nothing could resolve it,

York, 1975), 295–387 anticipated much of this literature by outlining cultural mechanisms through which whiteness was created. Rhys Isaac, *The Transformation of Virginia, 1740–1790* (Chapel Hill, 1982), Part III (can be read as a study in the reconstitution of whiteness in post-Revolutionary Virginia); and Allan Kulikoff, *Tobacco and Slaves: The Development of Southern Cultures in the Chesapeake, 1680–1800* (Chapel Hill, 1982), Part II. Theodore W. Allen, *The Invention of the White Race: Racial Oppression and Social Control* (New York, 1994), 15–21 promises an alternative analysis of Morgan's cultural mechanisms in the second volume of his study (which is not yet available), but he too thinks that "whiteness" was created out of the upheaval of Bacon's Rebellion. Thus, although this chapter focuses on elite responses to Gabriel's Conspiracy, I sometimes refer to "White" responses without socioeconomic modifiers.

[3] James Monroe to the Speakers of the General Assembly, December 5, 1800, ELB 1800–3 (see ch. 1, n. 38 for full citation). The documents are in the *Virginia General Assembly's Journal of the Senate . . . begun . . . 1st day of December, 1800* (Richmond, 1800 [actually 1801]), 26–33. This version contains minor errors, so I have used the original copy in Executive Communications (see ch. 2, n. 3 for full citation). Douglas R. Egerton, *Gabriel's Rebellion: The Virginia Slave Conspiracies of 1800 and 1802* (Chapel Hill, 1993), chs. 5–7 covers the repression of the conspiracy.

[4] *Virginia Gazette and General Advertiser*, December 11, 1800 ("paradox").

they sought to reconcile it by restoring the imperfect but workable system that Gabriel and his followers had disrupted.

In that, they largely succeeded.[5] But having restored the status quo, they also had to explain the event to themselves in a way that made that status quo acceptable. Thus the process of repressing Gabriel's Conspiracy led to and was related to the process of representing the conspiracy, and when Monroe and others constructed stories of the insurrection scare, they continued their attempts to control the slaves' rebellious acts. The effort to control and use Gabriel's Conspiracy by telling a story of it is one that has continued into the twentieth century, and each effort says something about the meaning of slavery in American culture.[6] But in the immediate wake of the conspiracy, White Virginians made four notable attempts to embed the story of Gabriel in a largely implicit history of the Old Dominion. In doing so they tacitly attempted to respond to the claims asserted by the conspirators, and they revealed the difficulty inherent in reconciling the best and worst features of Virginia's revolutionary heritage. Black Virginians told their own stories about Gabriel, stories that contested Whites' versions while constructing a different history of race and slavery in the Atlantic world and projecting a different end for the history of Virginia. They conceived of the conspiracy as a lost battle in what would ultimately have been a victorious struggle to claim Virginia for its Black settlers.

A theater of White power

In its broad outlines, the White response to Gabriel's Conspiracy repeated patterns established by masters responding to other slave conspiracies in plantation America. As was so often the case, word of the conspiracy began

---

[5] Egerton, *Gabriel's Rebellion*, ch. 11 (esp. 164–8) argues that White Virginians instituted a severe crackdown on Black autonomy in the wake of the 1800 and 1802 conspiracies and reviews the statutory responses to the conspiracy. I do not think the crackdown persisted past the initial panic that followed the conspiracies, because Richmond's local records suggest that urban life returned to the status quo following the conspiracy. For the role of law in a slave society see Robert A. Olwell, "Authority and Resistance: Social Order in a Colonial Slave Society, the South Carolina Lowcountry 1739–1789" (Ph. D. diss., Johns Hopkins University, 1991), ch. 2.

[6] Ranajit Guha, "The Prose of Counter-Insurgency" in Ranajit Guha and Gayatri Chakravorty Spivak, eds., *Selected Subaltern Studies* (New York, 1988). This book is, of course, among those efforts as are other historical works. Gabriel's Conspiracy has also attracted attention from nonhistorians. See Chapter 8 of this book for some of these. More recently, Gabriel has even found his way into Sunday newspaper comic strips in "Flashbacks" by Patrick M. Reynolds, *Washington Post*, January–March 1992.

to leak out weeks before the insurrection was to occur, but authorities hesitated to take the risk seriously. On August 9, 1800, Petersburg Whites reported hearing "whispers" of a planned insurrection that was to take place some Saturday night. Governor Monroe and Richmond Mayor James McClurg agreed to call out a patrol for the night, but when the evening passed without event both men behaved as if the threat had passed. Three weeks later, when Monroe got wind of Gabriel's planned insurrection, he had to scramble to get a guard out on patrol. Authorities were so unprepared for insurrection that the governor could not properly arm the militia he called up, and despite ample stores of gunpowder in the Richmond magazine, he asked militia Captain William Austin for the loan of a cask of powder. Austin's command patrolled the neighborhood surrounding Thomas Prosser's plantation on August 30 and 31.[7]

Monroe and McClurg approached the first hint of rebellion with the skepticism characteristic of authorities hearing of conspiracies in other American slave societies, especially societies with large numbers of creole slaves.[8] Even after Pharoah and Tom informed Mosby Sheppard of the impending insurrection, the governor remained skeptical. He mobilized patrols on August 30 and 31, but he "endeavored to give the affair as little importance as the measures necessary for defense would permit," and he hoped the suspected conspiracy "would even pass unnoticed by the Community." When no rebellion materialized, Monroe almost "conclud[ed] there was no foundation for the alarm."[9]

Once William Mosby's slave confirmed the story of Pharoah and Tom, Monroe concluded that he faced an authentic insurrection and pushed the investigation. The Virginia Constitution reflected the revolutionary generation's distrust of executive power by limiting his authority. On Monday, September 1, he advised McClurg to arrest "the informers, and the suspected, and extort from them what can be obtained." He further recommended that a magistrate or two from Henrico County, along with one or two town magistrates, be appointed to look into the affair. Recent information necessitated

---

[7] McClurg to the Governor, August 10, 1800, *Calendar of Virginia State Papers and Other Manuscripts, 1652–1869, Preserved in the Capitol at Richmond* (hereafter *CVSP*) 11 vols., ed. by William Price Palmer and Henry W. Flournoy (Richmond, 1875–93), v. 9, p. 128 ("whispers"); Monroe to McClurg, 10 August 1800, ELB 1794–1800 ("guard the city"); Monroe to Austin, 3 September 1800, ELB 1794–1800 (powder).

[8] See, for example, William W. Freehling, *The Reintegration of American History: Slavery and the Civil War* (New York, 1994), ch. 3 (Denmark Vesey's conspiracy).

[9] Monroe to the Speakers of the General Assembly, December 5, 1800, ELB 1800–1803.

immediate action, but because he lacked power to act he could "only suggest
this measure." He also called an emergency meeting of the Council of State
for ten o'clock the next morning (September 2).[10]

Armed with the constitutionally mandated advice and consent of the council, the governor stationed a guard of sixty men in the city and mustered
Goochland County troops to guard the state arsenal upriver at the Point of
Fork.[11] As the week progressed, he also stationed fifty men at Watson's Tavern
for the defense of the neighborhood surrounding Prosser's plantation and
issued a circular order mobilizing the militia to "apprehend all Slaves, servants or other disorderly persons unlawfully assembled, or strolling from one
place to another without due authority." Monroe then placed guards over
United States army guns in Manchester and suspended the distribution of
arms to county militias, a distribution that the legislature had mandated prior
to the insurrection scare.[12] Failure to deliver these guns left many counties'
militias poorly armed, but Monroe thought that was less risky than sending
guns throughout the state in boats manned by slaves.

Monroe's escalating response reflects his gradual realization of the scope
of Gabriel's Conspiracy. After Prosser's Ben's revelations, the governor
became convinced that Gabriel had recruited a dangerous army. Recognizing
the state's lack of readiness – James Thomson Callendar, in a characteristic
but revealing overstatement, said that Gabriel could hardly have failed had
the rainstorm not foiled his plans, because the government could muster only
400 to 500 men and only thirty had muskets[13] – Monroe saw no reason to
believe that these insurrectionaries had abandoned their plot even after the
trials had begun. Gabriel and Jack Ditcher remained at large, and the governor feared that they were hiding around Richmond and rallying their troops.
Regardless of whether Monroe was correct, the mobilization of the state's
militia reflects his growing apprehension about the conspiracy. He believed

[10] Monroe to the Mayor of Richmond, September 1, 1800; Monroe to the members of the
Council of State, September 1, 1800, ELB 1794–1800.
[11] Constitution of Virginia of 1776 for the need for Council's advice; Monroe to Lambert,
September 2, 1800 (Richmond guard); Monroe to Miller, September 2, 1800 (Goochland
guard), ELB 1794–1800. Point of Fork was roughly forty-five miles up the James River
from Richmond.
[12] Monroe to Mayo, September 3, 1800 (Watson's Tavern); Circular Orders to Commandants of Regiments, September 3, 1800; Monroe to Baugh, September 4, 1800 (Manchester); Monroe to Clarke, September 6, 1800 (suspension of arms shipments), ELB
1794–1800.
[13] Callendar to Thomas Jefferson, September 13, 1800, Thomas Jefferson Papers (microfilm).
Callendar was in jail in Richmond for violating the Sedition Act.

that his show of force "inspired the Citizens with confidence" and "depressed the spirits of the slaves."[14]

While protecting and reassuring his constituents, Monroe investigated the conspiracy. On September 3 he asked Gervas Storrs and Joseph Selden, Henrico County's investigating magistrates, to apprehend and confine the slave informers, "as well from a regard to their own safety as to prevent their running away." He sought to prepare the unfinished state penitentiary for the twenty prisoners who would be sent "in the course of a few weeks." The penitentiary became a busy place. By September 9 about thirty were in prison awaiting trial, and others were being "daily discovered and apprehended."[15] The first trials took place on the eleventh, and the first executions followed by a day.

As often happened in cases of slave conspiracies, Virginia authorities took a two-pronged approach to the planned insurrection. They sought simultaneously to crush the conspiracy and to contain the threat of Whites panicking. In both roles Monroe staged a theater of public power in which he magnified both the strength of the state and the impotence of the captured conspirators. He hoped to discourage conspirators who remained at large, while assuring frightened Whites that authorities could handle the insurrection. Simultaneously, if unintentionally, he reasserted the traditional White supremacist meanings of many of the symbols of authority that Gabriel and his followers had appropriated while building their conspiracy.

White Virginians needed reassurance. In the chaotic environment following the discovery of Gabriel's Conspiracy, the movement to repress the insurrection threatened to spin out of control. With the militia mobilized in several counties and patrols constantly looking for slaves suspiciously "strolling from one place to another," almost all area Blacks must have been subject to arrest.[16] Some Whites sought conspirators among any distrusted Blacks. Petersburg magistrates asked Monroe for reliable information out of fear that a similar conspiracy might be "in contemplation among the Negroes" of that nearby town. On the basis of a rumored insurrection alone, they suspected "Jacob [,?] Brandeen [,] J[ ] Bartlett – Marlin Bartlett – and John Pidgeon." Perhaps

---

[14] Monroe to the Speakers of the General Assembly, December 5, 1800, ELB 1800-3.

[15] Monroe to Storrs and Selden, September 3, 1800 ("own safety"); Monroe to Clarke, September 3, 1800; Monroe to Thomas Jefferson, September 9, 1800 ("discovered"), ELB 1794–1800.

[16] Circular to Commandants of Regiments, September 3, 1800, ELB 1794–1800. Philip N. Nicholas's slave King provided a glimpse of this crackdown from a Black perspective: "if the poor negroes were just caught out after night they were taken up and hanged" (Executive Papers, Box 114. See ch. 2, n. 3 for full citation.).

these men were among the six Blacks reportedly "taken up" in Petersburg, but none of them was ever tried.[17] Presumably they were seized by frantic Whites and jailed without evidence until the panic subsided.

After advising Monroe that six slaves were incarcerated in Petersburg, Joseph Jones, a resident of the town, recommended that the governor proclaim martial law. Jones warned of being "too Scrupulous" about suspects' legal rights. Authorities, he said, should "Slay them all where there is any reason to believe they" knew of the conspiracy, "let them be Whites, Mulattoes or negroes." Only by acting "violently and very severely" could the government stamp out the insurrectionary movement, and prevent having "at last to kill and destroy a great many more." Jones was, of course, more concerned that if Blacks were treated leniently, they might kill Whites. In this situation, authorities must be willing to "do wrong or right that good may come of it."[18] Few other Whites committed to paper their willingness to flout the law in suppressing the conspiracy, but local authorities' actions revealed similar proclivities. Throughout the James River region magistrates imprisoned Blacks on flimsy evidence. Billy, the crew member of Richardson Taylor's sloop who turned in Gabriel, had been jailed on suspicion of involvement in the conspiracy but was released for lack of evidence. His brother Ned, who lived far downriver in Hampton, had been thrown in jail there for "some words . . . he had dropped approv'g" of Gabriel's plan. The magistrates in charge of the investigation in Henrico County could not keep up with the arrests. As early as September 13 – just two days after the first trials – Storrs and Selden were reduced to sending Monroe a list of six slaves confined for trial by the executive; they wanted to know the grounds upon which the slaves were detained and "where testimony against them" could be "procured." Apparently no evidence was found, for the men were never tried.[19]

---

[17] Prentis to Monroe, September 6, 1800 ("Magistracy"), Jones to Monroe, September 9, 1800 ("taken up"), Executive Papers, Box 114. Similar concerns were presumably expressed to Monroe by Richmond authorities in face-to-face meetings that left no written records. On September 9, 1800, the Common Hall Council of Richmond appointed a "committee to wait upon and confer with the Governor on the present alarming state of danger" and convey the Common Hall Council's sentiments to Monroe. No evidence of the committee's advice survives (Richmond City Common Council Minutes, 1796–1807, LiVa).

[18] Jones to Monroe, September 9, 1800, Executive Papers, Box 114.

[19] Newton to Monroe, September 24, 1800 (Billy and Ned); Storrs and Selden to Monroe, September 13, 1800, Executive Papers, Box 114. Most slaves jailed without trial during the scare would not have shown up in the records. Presumably some of these men were actually conspirators, just as some who were convicted and hanged probably were not.

The frenzied reaction to Gabriel's Conspiracy proved to be short-lived. One alleged conspirator was probably lynched, but with this horrific exception extralegal sanctions against Black Virginians appear to have been limited to oppressive but relatively short stays in jail.[20] Monroe's staging of official power crushed what was left of the conspiracy, at least for the short term, and convinced White Virginians to leave the reimposition of order to state and local governments. The visual display of military power, combined with public executions of convicted conspirators, were the most important scenes in this theater of power.

Executions are designed to emphasize the state's power to enforce community standards, a goal they sometimes accomplished in early Richmond. In 1796 architect Benjamin Henry Latrobe witnessed the hanging of "a negro, a notorious thief" in Richmond. Though William Harris, the hangman's victim, had committed (according to Latrobe) "many . . . villanies," he became a convert to Christianity when confronted with the gallows. He confessed and faced death with "cheerfulness" at "the certainty of *being soon with God in glory* [original emphasis]." Such executions removed "incorrigible criminals" from the community and warned others who might follow that path that they flirted with violent death. Harris's late conversion and acceptance of the community's verdict underscored for contemporaries the "justice" of the proceedings and legitimated Virginia's social system.[21]

Authorities made a bigger spectacle of hanging Gabriel's conspirators than they did of more routine executions of individual offenders. On September 15, Monroe ordered a detachment of fifty soldiers to follow a group of condemned conspirators from the jail to the place of execution and then to surround them "till execution is performed." Simultaneously, a cavalry corps was to "patrole on the exterior of the Guard . . . to keep the people from approaching the troops." After the hangings, the troops, with cavalry in front, were to "return in order to the Capitol Square."[22]

Monroe choreographed this performance to accomplish several ends. Any conspirators remaining at large who contemplated rescuing their condemned comrades surely reconsidered upon seeing the troops. In addition, Monroe may have hoped to elicit the contrition that William Harris had displayed on the gallows. At least one convicted conspirator, while he waited for the

---

[20] For Jacob's death see Egerton, *Gabriel's Rebellion*, 113–14.
[21] Edward C. Carter II, ed., *The Virginia Journals of Benjamin Henry Latrobe, 1795–1798* (New Haven, 1977), 191–2 (emphasis in original). Harris's trial and execution did not, of course, meet modern standards of justice.
[22] General Orders, September 15, 1800, ELB 1794–1800.

hangman to drive away the cart, underwent a final interrogation about any White men involved in the plan, but White Virginians were disappointed in their hopes that slave rebels would renounce their conspiracy when faced with death. A correspondent to the *Virginia Argus* observed that not one of the executed slaves had betrayed the cause, remarking that the rebels had "uniformly met death with fortitude."[23]

The elaborate ceremony surrounding the execution was not, however, designed primarily to encourage confessions. The public executions of the conspirators offered the governor a stage on which to present the might of the state. Many of Richmond's slaves and free Blacks attended. Fifty well-armed men marching in file behind the wagon carrying the now-powerless conspirators to their fate created an intimidating contrast for Black spectators.[24] The orderly procession of the troops returning to Capitol Square to protect the symbol of the Commonwealth reinforced the futility of insurrection and reassured White Virginians of their safety.

Public executions were the most powerful scenes in this drama, but there were others. Almost as important were the parades of militia units on Capitol Square and on Church Hill in Richmond and through nearby Chesterfield County.[25] Monroe hoped this gaudy show of force would conceal the real weakness of the state's forces: he paired the order for this military display with a secret order for "discreet, capable" militia men to report to the new penitentiary to make cartridges so that the mustered militia could be armed.[26] By September 10, ten days after the intended rebellion, Monroe finally formulated an organized plan to defend Richmond against attacking slaves. He stationed groups of twenty-five or fifty men at strategic points throughout the city, ordered patrols throughout the region, and placed an artillery unit near the capitol to fire warning shots as an alarm. To reinforce this rather

---

[23] The story of the gallows interrogation has survived because the slave implicated William Young, a wealthy neighbor of Prosser's, in response to the question. Young felt compelled to clear his name and recounted the incident in the *Virginia Gazette*, September 30, 1800 and the *Virginia Argus*, October 3, 1800. Presumably other slaves were interrogated at the gallows, but their responses have not survived. *Virginia Argus*, October 14, 1800 ("met death").

[24] See Greg Dening, *Captain Bligh's Bad Language: Passion, Power and Theatre on the Bounty* (Cambridge, England, 1992), 39–48 for a similar analysis of rituals of execution. The need for such security surely conveyed another message about the potential of Black power, but Monroe left no evidence that he recognized this paradox.

[25] Monroe to Austin, September 6, 1800 (Capitol Square); Monroe to Cheatham, September 6, 1800 (Chesterfield), September 9, 1800 (Church Hill), ELB 1794–1800.

[26] Monroe to Lambert, September 10, 1800, ELB 1794–1800.

clear message of White power, the whole regiment was to parade each morning at Capitol Square. The congratulatory tone of Monroe's general orders of September 12 reflects his confidence that the Commonwealth was now fully prepared to rebuff the insurrection that no longer threatened.[27] On September 13 he began to demobilize by dismissing part of Chesterfield County's militia. Two days later he "announce[d] that the late combination of slaves . . . for the purpose of an insurrection" had been "completely broken," and he asked Thomas Jefferson when "to arrest the hand of the Executioner."[28]

Jefferson answered that there "had been hanging enough," though he displayed his characteristic timidity with regard to slavery by asking that his opinion be kept secret. Monroe may have shared Jefferson's sentiment, but many White Virginians did not. During the next two weeks, the governor received numerous reports from different parts of the state evincing Whites' continued fear of Gabriel's Conspiracy, and he slowed the pace of demobilization in order to conserve White consensus.[29] Though the system of defense was reduced, the troops remained a visible presence in Richmond into October. Popular concern dissipated only after authorities captured Gabriel in Norfolk and Jack Ditcher surrendered to Gervas Storrs in Richmond. The incarceration of the two leading conspirators ended the "anxiety and perturbation" that had "convulsed the public."[30] Gabriel's public execution on October 10 relieved many White Richmonders' remaining immediate fears.

This public and visual reimposition of order helped to defuse the danger of a panicked reaction to Gabriel's Conspiracy and to place primary responsibility for dealing with the conspiracy in the courts, the Executive Council, and, later, the state legislature. Virginia law mandated that slave trials follow standard procedures. These trials, though hardly "fair," included safeguards

---

[27] General Orders, September 11, 1800; General Orders, September 12, 1800, ELB 1794–1800.

[28] Monroe to Cheatham, September 13, 1800 (Chesterfield militia); General Orders, September 15, 1800 ("broken"), ELB 1794–1800; Monroe to Jefferson, September 15, 1800, Thomas Jefferson Papers (microfilm).

[29] Thomas Jefferson to Monroe, September 20, 1800. Jefferson offered his thoughts for private "consideration only." Egerton surmises that Monroe would have made Jefferson's opinion regarding the hangings "clear to the [Henrico County] court" (*Gabriel's Rebellion*, 101), but if Monroe did that he acted against Jefferson's express request. For a sample of evidence of continuing White fear, see Mayor Amos Alexander of Alexandria to Monroe, September 15, 1800; Oliver to Monroe, September 23, 1800 (Oliver from Hanover County); Prentis to Monroe, September 24, 1800 (Petersburg); Hudson to Monroe, September 24, 1800 (Albemarle County), Executive Papers, Box 114; and September 19, 1800 Meeting, Journal of the Council of State of Virginia, 1799–1801, LiVa.

[30] *Virginia Argus*, September 30, 1800.

against some abuses. Courts appointed attorneys to represent accused slaves. Though juries did not sit on slave trials, the five-magistrate panels that passed judgment could convict only by unanimous vote. Accused conspirators were represented by prominent local attorneys, and a single magistrate's dissenting vote acquitted and freed several accused plotters. The Executive Council reviewed the trial record of each convicted slave, pardoned some, and commuted eight capital sentences to banishment from the state. No record survives that a slave who escaped official punishment suffered vigilante action afterward.[31] Having successfully taken the first step to answer the slaves' challenge by crushing the conspiracy, Monroe and the legislature turned from defusing the insurrection to forging a unified official understanding of the chronic long-term threat to White Virginians that Gabriel's struggle against slavery had revealed.

Narrating conspiracy in a progressive mode

Reports that unknown White Virginians had participated in Gabriel's Conspiracy posed the most serious challenge to a unified White response. Soon after authorities imprisoned the first Black suspects, someone dropped a worn and open letter addressed to Charles Purcell on Capitol Square. The letter, signed "X," lamented the downpour that had hindered the intended insurrection but promised that it would "not prevent the cause of liberty, for those we espoused, being carried into effect" and promised "the earliest information" on the new date for the insurrection. Purcell responded to this threat to his "reputation as a citizen" by publishing the letter in the newspaper and offering $200 for the identity of its author. Presumably, the original letter was a fake,[32] but as the trials progressed, potential political and religious fault lines were revealed in the unified White front that authorities sought to construct.

Gabriel planned for the insurrection to occur during the buildup to the election of 1800. That contest centered in part on differing perceptions of

---

[31] Because many private reactions to the conspiracy surely escaped the public record, there may have been some vigilante action, but it was not analogous to that which followed Nat Turner's Rebellion in 1831 (see Alison Goodyear Freehling, *Drift Toward Dissolution: The Virginia Slavery Debate of 1831–1832* [Baton Rouge, 1982], ch. 1). I am not arguing that accused conspirators were treated fairly; instead, I want to specify the nature of the treatment – clearly unfair – to which they were subjected.

[32] *Virginia Argus*, September 16, 1800. It seems unlikely that a conspirator who signed with an "X" would have written out the addressee's full name. It is, however, worth noting that Charles Purcell was among those on the periphery of Jacob Valentine's alleged conspiracy in 1797 (see Chapter 5 of this book).

the French Revolution – a question considerably complicated within Virginia by the Haitian Revolution. Potentially powerful divisions were invoked when Prosser's Ben testified in Solomon's trial that "two white French Men were the first instigators of the Insurrection." Solomon confirmed White participation when he confessed. Some Federalists jumped on the revelation of French participation to tar Jeffersonians with Black insurrection: the *Virginia Gazette* attributed the conspiracy to the infusion of "the French principle of Liberty and Equality . . . into the minds of the negroes." A self-styled gentleman asserted in a Fredericksburg paper that the "dreadful conspiracy" originated with "some vile French Jacobins, aided and abetted by some of our own profligate and abandoned democrats." While "liberty and equality" might be fine doctrines in "a land of freemen," he thought them "dangerous and extremely wicked . . . where every white man is a master and every black man is a slave."[33] It was, perhaps, an even more dangerous doctrine in a slave society that included many White men who were not masters and many Black men who were not slaves.

Jeffersonian lovers of French doctrine were not the only internal enemies feared by nervous elites. Religious dissenters also supposedly threatened to rip the Commonwealth's social fabric. This threat also had some basis, for the Great Awakening in Virginia was in part a challenge to the traditional social order.[34] On a more immediate level, the leaders of the insurrection were Baptists who thought "their cause was similar to that of the Israelites who had escaped from the Egyptians." A Baptist magistrate's sympathy for a fellow confessioner may have contributed to one conspirator's acquittal, raising concerns among some White Virginians about White Baptists' loyalties. Alleged conspirators' testimony that Methodists' lives were to be spared during the rebellion also contributed to elite suspicion of evangelicals. The "gentleman" who wrote to the Fredericksburg paper was convinced that doctrines "preached by Methodists, Baptists, and others" encouraged Blacks to fight for their liberty.[35]

Neither evangelicals nor Republicans paid a dear price for these accusations. When the Richmond *Examiner* reported the acquittal of the Baptist conspirator in what its publisher considered "civil, but . . . plain terms, . . .

---

[33] Executive Communications, 3 and 9 (Ben's testimony and Solomon's confession); *Virginia Gazette*, September 16, 1800; Fredericksburg *Virginia Herald*, September 23, 1800.

[34] Isaac, *Transformation of Virginia*, esp. ch. 8.

[35] *Virginia Argus*, October 14, 1800 ("Israelites;" for trial depositions on the same subject see Executive Communications, 6–7); Callender to Jefferson, September 13, 1800 (Baptist magistrate's acquittal), Thomas Jefferson Papers (microfilm); *Virginia Herald*, September 23, 1800 ("preached").

A prodigious racket was raised against the Editor, as if he had designed to insult" all Baptists. Similarly the *Virginia Gazette's* initial report regarding White Frenchmen elicited an immediate response from *"An American citizen from the heart, though born of France."* This correspondent insisted that "other principles, openly avowed on this continent" could have operated just as powerfully upon slaves' minds as French doctrines did and expressed little confidence that French residents of Richmond would have survived the rebellion.[36] Most White Virginians appear to have agreed, for the Commonwealth voted Republican in 1800.

The General Assembly's response to Gabriel's Conspiracy also attests to many White Virginians' refusal to believe that the plot revealed fundamental flaws in their social system. On December 1, 1800, the legislature met in annual session. On December 5, Governor Monroe reviewed the conspiracy and the executive's response to it in an address to both houses of the legislature. He asked the General Assembly to "weigh with profound attention this unpleasant incident," and to adopt a system to save Virginia from possible calamitous consequences of future conspiracies. During that session the legislature passed six laws and a resolution related to the insurrection scare that ranged from a law authorizing Monroe to purchase and free Pharoah and Tom Sheppard to laws mandating greater security for the state's armaments and closer supervision of urban slaves. Provisions of several laws targeted free Black people, perhaps because White Virginians thought several free Black conspirators escaped prosecution on legal technicalities. Cumulatively, these laws made only minor adjustments in the supervisory regimen faced by Black Virginians. Long-standing attempts to end private manumission continued to come up short in the legislature – the law was not changed until 1806. Instead, the state requested that the federal government look into acquiring a site to which "persons obnoxious . . . or dangerous to the peace of society may be removed." Most White Virginians preferred to treat Gabriel's Conspiracy as a frightening aberration rather than a warning of fundamental danger.[37] The legislature at any rate failed, according to Virginia jurist

---

[36] Callender to Jefferson, September 13, 1800 ("racket"); *Virginia Gazette*, September 19, 1800 (emphasis in original). John Randolph of Roanoke disdainfully reported Federalist attempts to "make an electioneering engine of" the conspiracy (quoted in William Cabell Bruce, *John Randolph of Roanoke, 1773–1833* [New York, 1922], v. II, p. 251).

[37] Executive Papers, Box 115 ("persons obnoxious"); *Acts Passed at the General Assembly of the Commonwealth. . . . Begun and Held . . . on Monday the 1st Day of December, 1800* (Richmond, 1801), 19, 21, 24, 34–5, 37–9. Specific provisions of these laws included the creation of a public guard to protect public property in Richmond; authorization for the governor to sell out of the country slaves convicted of insurrection or other crimes;

St. George Tucker, to enact any conclusive measures in response to the conspiracy.[38] Instead, it sought to return Virginia to the status quo.

For White Virginians to accept a return to the status quo that existed prior to Gabriel's Conspiracy, however, they needed to believe in the stability of the state's slave society. Such belief depended in part on the ways White Virginians chose to structure their accounts of the conspiracy. Of the many ways to categorize the stories that contemporary White Virginians told about Gabriel's Conspiracy, one of the most interesting is the degree to which the texts reflect confidence in the stability of Virginia's slave society. The division between White Virginians comfortable with slavery and those uncomfortable with the state's defining social and political institutions prefigured divisions that animated the antebellum politics of slavery in Virginia.[39] Gabriel's Conspiracy did not fundamentally alter White perceptions of the place of slavery, but the contemporary texts that it inspired reveal White Virginians' evolving notions of republicanism and slavery.

the provision of arms to several town militias and grants of greater local control over urban militias in times of emergency; prohibition on slaves hiring their own time; requirements that free Blacks register with court clerks in their resident localities; the authorization of slave testimony against free Blacks in criminal cases. See Egerton, *Gabriel's Rebellion*, 158–62 for a discussion of Jefferson's response to the petition for the federal government to find a place where Black Virginians could be colonized. While I do not agree that in 1802 "conditions were auspicious" (162) for an elite-led movement to rid Virginia of slavery, Egerton contributes to continuing reevaluations of Jefferson's actions regarding slavery.

[38] St. George Tucker to Thomas Jefferson, January 23, 1801, Thomas Jefferson Papers (microfilm). Egerton, *Gabriel's Rebellion*, ch. 11 argues that Gabriel's Conspiracy, when combined with the 1802 conspiracy, elicited a strong, concerted reaction that created "new and tighter shackles" (172) for Black Virginians. He points out that between 1801 and 1806 the General Assembly passed many laws calling for stricter regulation of slaves and free Blacks, but they seem to me part of a movement to tighten up restrictions that can be traced back to the 1790s. The conspiracies accelerated that movement, but the fact that it took until 1806 to pass an effective limitation on the manumission law suggests that the conspiracies themselves were not the mainsprings. The social patterns that characterized life in Richmond during the first decade of the new century suggest that these restrictive codes reflected elite uneasiness over the continuing vitality of urban life. See Part II of this book for life in Richmond.

[39] This is not a division between those "for" and "against" slavery. Some who thought slavery at odds with what we might now call Jeffersonian republicanism argued for the gradual elimination of slavery (e.g., George Tucker); others who shared this view might opt for a vastly more authoritarian version of republicanism (e.g., the gentleman essayist in the Fredericksburg *Virginia Herald*). Similarly, belief in Virginia's fundamental stability could coincide with basic comfort with and support of slavery or with Jeffersonian distaste for the peculiar institution.

Four critical texts – a speech to the legislature, a pamphlet, and two long letters to newspapers – revealed that contrast, but they also shared a striking element: an almost complete lack of interest in Gabriel's personality.[40] None of the texts denied his leadership or denigrated his efforts, but just as significantly none sought to uncover the key to his charismatic leadership. Nor did those who sought to represent the meaning of Gabriel's Conspiracy turn, for example, to the influence of "Frenchmen" on Gabriel to explain the problem. In all these texts Virginia was portrayed as far too central a part of the Western world for outside agitators or a "dreamer of dreams, and would be prophet," as Nat Turner was later called,[41] to be necessary to explain the slaves' decision to revolt. Instead, White Virginians' analyses of the conspiracy focused on the compatibility of slavery and republicanism.[42]

James Monroe, though no fan of slavery in the abstract, was ultimately comfortable with the place of slavery in Virginia. As governor of the state, he coordinated efforts to repress Gabriel's Conspiracy; by December 1800, he probably knew more about the slaves' plot than any other White person in the state. He used that knowledge to compose a report to the legislature on the course of the insurrection and the measures needed to discourage possible future conspiracies. His report – in some ways the first history of the conspiracy – is a curious document.

Monroe's essentially conservative approach to the conspiracy did not grow out of a belief that the conspiracy was small or unimportant.[43] While

---

[40] The four texts are James Monroe to the Speakers of the General Assembly, December 5, 1800; [George Tucker], *Letter*; a letter in the *Virginia Gazette*, December 11, 1800; and a letter in the *Virginia Herald*, September 23, 1800.

[41] *Richmond Enquirer*, December 30, 1831 as quoted by Joseph C. Carroll, *Slave Insurrections in the United States, 1800–1865* (New York, 1969 [1938]), 132. Turner's confession contributed to the interest in his personality, but see *The Southampton Slave Revolt of 1831*, Henry Irving Tragle, ed. (Amherst, Mass., 1971), 52–3, 59–62, 90–9 (esp. 92–3), 99–101 for articles written before Turner's apprehension that devoted significant attention to his personality. Michael Mullin sees the confession as central to Turner's revolt in *Africa in America: Slave Acculturation in the American South and the British Caribbean, 1736–1831* (Urbana, 1992), 265–7. A fascinating reading of this is in Eric J. Sundquist, *To Wake the Nations: Race in the Making of American Literature* (Cambridge, Mass., 1993), esp. pp. 36–56.

[42] Compare the view of Gabriel's soldiers as "poor things" who were "deceived and tempted and led on by designing men" in a post–Civil War novel by a White Virginia woman. Marion Harland, *Judith: A Chronicle of Old Virginia* (New York and Philadelphia, 1883), 29 (see chapter 8 of this book for Harland's presentation of Gabriel).

[43] By "conservative approach," I mean that Monroe did not consider the conspiracy reason to reevaluate any of the bases of Virginia society. I am *not* referring to his level of hostility to the idea of slavery or to the French Revolution or to Federalism.

he responded to the earliest hints of a slave conspiracy with skepticism, he soon came to believe that the slaves in Richmond and its environs probably enjoyed support from the slaves in other parts of the state, and he ultimately came to suspect that knowledge of Gabriel's Conspiracy may well have pervaded the slave population of the whole state.[44] But if Governor Monroe was inclined to believe that Gabriel had recruited a vast following, he did not believe that the slaves' conspiracy constituted a fundamental challenge to the state's survival. He never saw Toussaint Louverture's spirit lurking dangerously in Gabriel's body.

Monroe did not deny the very real danger that Gabriel's Conspiracy posed for the people of Richmond. He noted the large number of slaves near Richmond and the relative unpreparedness of the state or city to raise the respectable force needed to answer an attack. Had the city been surprised, then the slaves' first effort might well have succeeded with horrific results: "the town in flames, its inhabitants butchered, and a scene of horror extending through the country." But Monroe insisted that this sight would have been only momentary. The militia would soon have been mustered to confront the rebels, and Whites' superiority in "Numbers, in the knowledge and use of arms, and indeed in every other species of knowledge," would have prevented slaves from "sustaining themselves for [more than] a moment in rebellion." Thus, while Gabriel's Conspiracy and the threat of future conspiracies constituted a "crisis to be avoided *so far as prudent precautions could accomplish*," (my emphasis) Monroe did not ask for basic revisions of the state's slave code. While slavery existed Whites could never "count with certainty on [slaves'] tranquil Submission." Monroe insisted, however, that while Whites could not prevent the recurrence of "the like in future," they could fairly easily "secure the Country from any calamatous consequences."[45]

Ultimately, Monroe's text strikes a remarkably optimistic tone. Despite his admission that the militia was ill prepared for a slave rebellion, he found its performance, once mustered, encouragingly efficient. Rather than calling for greater military strength, he insisted that if a crisis had occurred, the militia would have been as firm and decisive in action as necessary. Thus, he argued, one outcome of Gabriel's Conspiracy was enhanced confidence in a citizen militia's "competence to every purpose of publick safety."[46] The

---

[44] Monroe to the Speakers of the General Assembly, December 5, 1800, ELB 1800–3.
[45] Ibid.
[46] Republicans believed militias to be far safer for liberty than standing armies. Monroe's endorsement of the militia constitutes a more important reaffirmation of republican faith than might be readily apparent today.

Commonwealth's success in meeting Gabriel's challenge emphasized the strength and stability of its republican system.

Monroe structured his story of Gabriel's Conspiracy so as to reassure his audience. The seemingly terrifying tale of slave rebellion culminated with the triumph of White Virginians over the contradictory social forces at play in the world, turning the narrative of Gabriel's Conspiracy into an archetypally comic story of reconciliation. In such comic narratives, the resolution of conflict allows the condition of society to be "represented as being purer, saner, and healthier as a result of the conflict among seemingly inalterably opposed elements." Monroe offered no plan for ultimate reconciliation: a true Jeffersonian, he devoutly hoped slavery and Blacks would disappear, but he shrank from taking specific action to further that cause. His narrative did, however, include a partial reconciliation: as he structured the tale of the conspiracy, it ended with the legislature meeting to culminate the process of change and transformation that lies at the heart of the comic plot line.[47] Monroe's vision of Virginia was not static, but it was profoundly conservative. Minor changes might be necessary, but the legislature could be counted on to take "suitable measures . . . to prevent" any serious danger, and Virginia would remain safe.[48]

Not all White Virginians shared the confidence in the Commonwealth's social system embedded in James Monroe's interpretation of Gabriel's Conspiracy, but enough Virginians claimed that Gabriel's Conspiracy represented "nothing formidable" to stimulate a blistering newspaper attack on the "infatuation and blindness" of such belief.[49] And the legislature's failure

---

[47] Hayden White, *Metahistory: The Historical Imagination in Nineteenth-Century Europe* (Baltimore, 1973), "Introduction" (p. 9 for quotations). White's discussion of emplotment relies on Northrup Frye, *Anatomy of Criticism* (Princeton, 1957). Had Monroe's history promised ultimate reconciliation of slavery and freedom, then its mode of emplotment would have been romantic, not comic; comic emplotment presumes the failure of men to transcend social forces and thus involves temporary, not permanent, reconciliation.

[48] Monroe to the Speakers of the General Assembly, December 5, 1800, ELB 1800–3. Monroe, as sitting governor and supporter of Jefferson, had state and national political motivations for downplaying the conspiracy's importance, but I am less interested in Monroe's true beliefs than in the interpretations of the conspiracy that were current at the time. See Egerton, "'As Much Right to Fight for our Liberty as any Men': Gabriel's Conspiracy and the Election of 1800," *Journal of Southern History*, 56 (1990): 209–12 and *Gabriel's Rebellion*, chs. 7, 11 for arguments that Monroe deliberately downplayed politically threatening aspects of the conspiracy.

[49] *Virginia Gazette*, December 11, 1800. The authors of these texts may not have perceived the same differences in interpretation that I do. This article, which I argue directly contradicted Monroe's interpretation, expressed gratitude for the "essential services" Monroe

to enact any sweeping changes in the state's slave code suggests broad support for Monroe's position within the General Assembly. But if those who
thought the conspiracy represented a "great and imminent . . . danger" failed
to carry the legislature, they did not lack voices.[50] They could and did tell
alternative stories of the conspiracy that were based on very different visions
of Virginia.

White Virginians who lacked James Monroe's confidence in the social
order believed that slavery was ultimately incompatible with Virginia's republican society. George Tucker, a recent immigrant from Bermuda, insisted
that every one recognized the "danger arising from domestic slavery." He
rejected the council of those, presumably including Monroe, who opted for
"palliating what they think admits not of radical cure," because he considered the peculiar institution an "eating sore" that "endanger[ed] the life
of the state."[51] Similarly, "A PRIVATE CITIZEN" insisted in the *Virginia Gazette*
that the causes of Gabriel's Conspiracy were "level to the conceptions of any
man," and rested "in the very spirit of our government."[52] And the gentleman who analyzed the conspiracy in the Fredericksburg *Virginia Herald* thought
only a "fool" could believe there to be "any compromise between liberty and
slavery." He spoke for Tucker and the CITIZEN when he contended that White
Virginians faced a straightforward choice in the wake of Gabriel's Conspiracy: "Shall we abolish slavery, or shall we continue it?" Whites, he claimed,
must confront the absence of any middle course and choose "one thing or
t'other."[53] Virginia faced this stark choice because the contradictions that lay
at the heart of Gabriel's Conspiracy were rooted in "the existence of slavery
in one of the freest republics on earth."[54]

Each of these texts considered and rejected straightforward abolition as a
reasonable answer to the fundamental challenge that slavery posed for Virginia.

rendered to the state during the "perilous crisis." Perhaps the author was softening his
attack on Monroe's recently delivered report to the legislature, or perhaps he interpreted
Monroe's report differently than I do.

[50] *Virginia Gazette*, December 11, 1800.   [51] Tucker, *Letter*, 3, 5.

[52] *Virginia Gazette*, December 11, 1800.

[53] *Virginia Herald*, September 23, 1800. Tucker, *Letter*, 8–11 and 14–22 poses the same
problem less succinctly. The CITIZEN in the *Gazette* claimed to have found a middle
ground, but I argue later that his proposed solutions to the problem reflect a rejection
of the democratic tendencies of Virginia's republican society even if the CITIZEN did not
recognize that.

[54] *Virginia Gazette*, December 11, 1800 (quotation); Tucker, *Letter* focuses on the spirit of
enlightenment then sweeping the Western world; the gentleman from Fredericksburg
expressed a similar sentiment (with a different value judgment) when he stated that "liberty and equality have brought evil upon us" (*Virginia Herald*, September 23, 1800).

Each author professed to find the apparent blessing of "a general emancipation of this class of people" to be impractical unless the freed slaves could be removed from Virginia. Either Black Virginians were supposedly not ready for freedom, or White Virginians' prejudices were too entrenched to treat free Blacks fairly. The gentleman from Fredericksburg summed up the problem by observing that abolition entailed millions of difficulties, that citizens of Virginia were "not prepared to discuss" and lacked the "courage, . . . virtue, . . . [and] power to surmount."[55] Solutions would have to be found elsewhere.

Tucker found the answer in colonization. He would rid the state of enslaved and free Blacks and protect Virginia's place among the enlightened polities of the world. He advocated buying land beyond the Mississippi, creating a colony for free people of color and using tax policy to encourage Virginia masters to free their slaves and send them west. As good Black citizens developed their new society, the value of the unclaimed land would climb. Virginia would retain ownership of that land and sell it to newly arriving free people or increasingly prosperous older settlers, using the profits to fund further emancipation and transportation. White philanthropy and Black virtue would create a prosperous, safe, and White Virginia and a free and economically dynamic Black colony west of the Mississippi. White Virginians – soon to be the only Virginians – could then rest assured that the Commonwealth's status as "one of the fairest portions of the globe" would be protected.[56]

Two other writers, the CITIZEN and the gentleman from Fredericksburg, rejected colonization and opted instead for firmer controls on Virginia's enslaved people. Each alluded to the "dreadful scenes . . . of St. Domingo" when explaining the danger Virginia faced.[57] Both suggested that White Virginians must turn away from the "enlightened" world to survive. The gentleman did this openly, declaring that "slavery is a monster – the most horrible of monsters" and that Virginians must keep that monster in chains. The state would be safe, he argued, only if the legislature "re-enact[ed] all those rigorous laws which experience . . . proved necessary." The slaveholder, he insisted, "can never be a Democrat."[58]

The CITIZEN preferred not to admit the incompatibility of slavery and freedom, but the remedies he proposed to secure the state from potential

[55] *Virginia Gazette*, December 11, 1800 ("emancipation" and unprepared for freedom); Tucker, *Letter*, 16 (White prejudices); *Virginia Herald*, September 23, 1800 ("difficulties").
[56] Tucker, *Letter*, 16–21 (quotation on 21).
[57] *Virginia Gazette*, December 11, 1800 (quotation).
[58] *Virginia Herald*, September 23, 1800. The gentleman amended his claim that slavery was the "most horrible" by adding "*tyranny excepted*" (emphasis in original).

rebels – strengthening the executive branch of the government, increasing the discretionary power of local militia lieutenants, monitoring the inhabitants of each urban household, closing access to manumission, and creating a standing army to guard the state from its internal enemies – would have overturned much of the libertarian heritage of the American Revolution. The CITIZEN's "only object[s]" were "the public good, and the general safety" of White Virginians.[59] Such ends could be accomplished, he argued, only by creating the vigorous and potentially tyrannical government that White Virginians feared above all else but emancipation. Like Tucker, these authors believed slavery incompatible with Virginia's increasingly democratic republic.[60] Unlike Tucker, they thought White Virginians should reject the democratic trends rather than rejecting slavery.

Nonetheless, a shared metaphor reinforces an underlying compatibility between these embryonic proslavery arguments and Tucker's antislavery analysis of Virginia's slave society. By 1800 "enlightenment" had come to stand for the march of progress through the Western world. The growth of knowledge, economic development, and "democratic" notions of natural equality all contributed to progress and enlightenment. Both Tucker and the gentleman from Fredericksburg suggested that the institution of slavery subverted the process of enlightenment in ways that made progress dangerous. For the gentleman, the doctrine of liberty and equality might be "intelligible and admissible, in a land of freemen." But the "love of liberty in the breast of a slaveholder," was "like a diminutive, distant, and hardly visible star in the center of a black cloud in a dark night, serving only to render the scene more dismal, and, as Milton says, 'to make darkness visible.' "[61]

Tucker also reversed the conventional trope of enlightenment. Having begun his essay within the conventions of the late eighteenth century by positing a "progress in human affairs which . . . nothing can arrest," he described the "advancement of knowledge among the negroes of" Virginia as an example. But the increase of knowledge was the "principal agent in evolving the spirit" of insurrection. Knowledge "kindle[d] . . . into flame" the "celestial

---

[59] *Virginia Gazette*, December 11, 1800.
[60] Virginia's government was not becoming more democratic in form – there would be no new constitution until the 1830s – but these texts reveal wide agreement that the spirit of republicanism in the state was growing more democratic. Because of this agreement, I have conflated "republicanism" and "democracy" in this discussion. They were not the same thing, and a history of political thought in this era must distinguish between them. This is not, however, a history of political thought. Separating republicanism and democracy would confuse rather than clarify the texts' arguments.
[61] *Virginia Herald*, September 23, 1800.

spark" of the "love of freedom."[62] As slaves moved from "the darkest ignorance" into the "dawn of knowledge," the ambiguous conflation of light as
progress with the destructive force of fire became complete. The dawn, rather
than hopeful, "warns . . . of an approaching day." Enlightenment and progress remained inevitable: "of the multitude of causes which tend to enlighten
the blacks," Tucker knew of none "whose operation" could be "materially
check[ed]."[63] But unless White Virginians could free themselves of slavery,
progress threatened rather than promised, and the brightening future looked
dark indeed. The ironic twist on the trope of enlightenment reinforced the
fear that White Virginians were becoming dangerously subject to historical
forces beyond the control of virtuous citizens.

These texts, then, rejected the comic plot line of Monroe's letter to the
General Assembly, emplotting the history of slavery in Virginia along tragic
lines instead.[64] If each proposed a program in response to Gabriel's Conspiracy, each offered that program in pessimistic terms that promised little
hope for any reconciliation of slavery and progress in Virginia. One or the
other must come to an end. Tucker offered a prophetic romance of ultimate
reconciliation if White Virginians would turn away from slavery, but such
action required sacrifices that Tucker suspected most Whites would reject.
The CITIZEN and the gentleman offered White Virginians the continued enjoy-
ment of their slave property but at the cost of the Commonwealth's self-
perceived position at the forefront of the struggle for human liberty. It is
hardly surprising that Monroe's comedy of partial reconciliation, which spared
White Virginians that unwelcome choice, appears to have carried the day.

Who won the argument is less interesting than what the terms of the argument reveal. Though Gabriel's Conspiracy never turned into an insurrection, it challenged White Virginians on several fronts. It provoked a judicial
response unprecedented in Virginia history since Bacon's Rebellion. It dared
White Virginians to repress the conspiracy without destroying the liberality that lay at the heart of their self-image. And it mocked elite Whites' belief
that their society lay at the vanguard of the advancing tide of liberty. Authorities surmounted the first challenge most easily, and they answered the second through the careful and, in their eyes, liberal use of pardons. But White
Virginians could respond to the third only by constructing stories of the
conspiracy that placed it within the process of the state's historical development. In doing so they revealed the degree to which the factional divisions

---

[62] Tucker, *Letter*, 5–6.   [63] Ibid., 7.
[64] This paragraph is heavily influenced by White, *Metahistory*, and by the first and third
essays in Frye, *Anatomy of Criticism*.

regarding slavery that would periodically split antebellum Virginia existed in latent form as early as 1800.

In the wake of Gabriel's Conspiracy

The state's repression of Gabriel's Conspiracy did not, of course, end resistance to slavery in the Richmond area. Slaves' grinding daily struggle over the terms of labor and their perpetual battle for increased personal and familial autonomy continued apace, and neither the existence of the conspiracy nor its repression fundamentally altered the terms of that struggle.[65] If, however, as I have argued, the roots of Gabriel's Conspiracy stretched back to the Great Awakening and the American and Haitian Revolutions, and if the large-scale planned insurrection of 1800 represents in some ways a culmination of an accelerating sense among some Black Virginians that slavery could be overthrown at home as it was being overthrown on Hispaniola, then the events of the summer and fall of 1800 did influence the nature of slave resistance in Virginia. The changing patterns that characterized Richmond-area slaves' discussions of insurrection in the wake of Gabriel's Conspiracy provide a valuable perspective on the dynamics of physical coercion – up to and including judicial and extrajudicial terror – and cultural hegemony in affecting one group's struggle against an oppressive social system. Those patterns can also be understood as representing Black Virginians' continuing attempt to forge an interpretation of their relationship to the history of resistance to slavery, an interpretation central to their sense of themselves as a people.

The official repression of the planned insurrection left many conspirators – the number is unknowable – living and working in and around Richmond.[66] Following the trials and executions, even those people of African descent who had not known of the conspiracy before its repression heard much about Gabriel's ideas of freedom and his plan for achieving it. Of course, authorities made sure that Blacks also witnessed the cost that White Virginians would try to exact on slaves who pursued such ideas, but while the high cost could discourage people from pursuing the ideas, it could not erase the ideas'

[65] See Chapters 5 to 7 of this book.
[66] Because, as noted in Chapters 2 and 3, historians can never know the number of slaves who joined the conspiracy or the number who "halfway" joined, one cannot know how many conspirators remained alive in Richmond in 1801. A probable minimum estimate would include over sixty people, for depositions and transcripts mentioned over 100 alleged participants by name, and fewer than forty were killed or transported. Far more than sixty people of African descent who knew of the conspiracy and had some sympathy with it probably continued to live and work in and around Richmond.

appeal. In the years immediately following the repression of the conspiracy, enslaved Richmonders continued to discuss possible attempts to overthrow slavery, but they did not again reach a point at which a large-scale rebellion became a near possibility. The frequent talk, however, even in the mediated versions that have survived in records recorded by White Richmonders, reveals the centrality of Gabriel's Conspiracy to Black Richmonders' understandings of their struggle against slavery.

Following the repression of Gabriel's Conspiracy, Blacks in and around Richmond, as well as in much of the rest of Virginia, continued to discuss the possibility of overthrowing slavery. Herbert Aptheker counted about eight insurrection scares in the state of Virginia between 1801 and 1806.[67] Scares do not equal conspiracies, but they do indicate that Virginians of African descent often spoke to one another in terms that frightened Whites into believing that rebellion was in the offing. Close examination of what Whites reported hearing Blacks say and of what Blacks said when testifying before Virginia courts shows the influence of Gabriel's movement on many Black Virginians' attempts to envision a rebellion against slavery. It also reveals a period of flux during which the lesson that Black Virginians would learn from the conspiracy – that is to say, Blacks' interpretation of the place of the conspiracy in Virginia's history – was rapidly taking shape.

From the time the conspiracy was defeated, Black "insolence" made White authorities nervous that enslaved Virginians would again organize to rebel. Though Governor Monroe announced to the General Assembly on December 5 that the crisis had passed, he also noted that a similar challenge might occur again at any time. The slaves' traditional Christmas holidays brought the season when, Monroe claimed, Whites had the "most to apprehend from the Negroes," so he requested that the militia patrol the city of Richmond. The governor was especially concerned about the "many negroes . . . from the Country, perhaps from the Coal pits," who were spending time in the city, because miners who had to coordinate work in the pits might be "more capable of" executing a conspiracy than were slaves who were "dispersed on estates." He asked the mayor to expel all country Blacks from the city as soon as they had completed their legitimate "business . . . at Market."[68] Perhaps because

<hr>

[67] Herbert Aptheker, *American Negro Slave Revolts* (New York, 1987 [1943]), ch. 9. Different readers will no doubt reach different totals, depending on how many of reports of they believe to have been true and how many of plots they believe to have been independent of one another.

[68] Monroe to the Speakers of the General Assembly, Dec. 5, 1800; Monroe to Captain William Austin, Dec. 27, 1800; Monroe to The Mayor of the City of Richmond, Dec. 27, 1800, ELB 1800–3; Austin to Monroe, Dec. 27, 1800, Executive Papers, Box 115 (for one report).

of the constant patrols, Richmond-area slaves appear to have avoided open challenges to White authority over the holidays, but enslaved Virginians resumed discussions of resistance shortly thereafter.

White residents of Nottoway County, a Southside county that formed part of Petersburg's agricultural hinterland, reported unrest during the first week of the new year. Authorities rounded up at least eight enslaved men whom they thought they could prove guilty of leading a conspiracy to attack and take over Petersburg. Six weeks later Monroe received warning that "a Number of Negroe Men" planned "to do Mischief to the Whites," and in August of that year a former resident of the Norfolk–Portsmouth region who had been sold to the West Indies returned and was reportedly "attempting by some underhand practices, to excite the Slaves . . . to insurrection."[69] Black Richmonders were not reported engaging in any specific conspiratorial acts, but enslaved people in and around the city kept authorities fearful that they had "not relinquished [Gabriel's] project." Around the first anniversary of the discovery of the conspiracy, Monroe asked the militia of Hanover County to take care to guard the county's guns; he also asked the mayor of Richmond to ensure that the "most vigilant police be observed in the city."[70]

In each of these cases, as in most other contemporary instances in which slaves were reported discussing insurrection, the evidence is spotty and un-reliable, rendering it impossible to judge with assurance what precisely lay behind any individual report. The abundance of reports during the first five years of the new century and their geographical dispersion throughout the southeastern quarter of Virginia strongly argues that enslaved Virginians continued to discuss the possibility of overthrowing slavery during the years immediately following the repression of Gabriel's Conspiracy.[71] As numer-ous historians have pointed out, however, discussing insurrection is not the same as planning it, something that at least some White Virginians under-stood. In May 1802 more than twenty citizens of Hanover County signed a petition asking Monroe to pardon two men convicted of conspiring to rebel

[69] James Fletcher to B. Edwards or N. Friend, January 1, 1801, Executive Papers, Box 116. The role of slaves in communication among Whites in Virginia is emphasized by the notation on this letter that it was sent "by Anthony." W. Claiborne to Monroe, Feb. 15, 1801, Executive Papers, Box 116; Monroe to Colonel Thomas Newton, Aug. 30, 1801, ELB 1800–3.

[70] Monroe to Major John Thompson, Sept. 13, 1801; Monroe to The Mayor of Richmond, Sept. 13, 1801, ELB 1800–3.

[71] There is a remarkable but thus far unexplained absence of reported conspiratorial activ-ity in Northern Virginia during this time. The key loci of conspiratorial activity among enslaved Virginians at least from 1780 to 1810 lay in Richmond, Petersburg, and Norfolk, and in their agricultural hinterlands.

against slavery; the petitioners did not deny that the two prisoners had held
"a conversation . . . relating to something about an insurrection" but asserted
that slaves often engaged in "conversation relative to what hath not only
already happened, but what may hereafter come to pass, without having a
real intention of puting the same into Execution."[72] Only by examining specific
cases of talk and organization, however, can one begin to untangle the different meanings of such actions.

During the spring of 1802, the intermittent flow of rumors of rebellion
was punctuated by a complicated series of reported conspiracies in the agricultural hinterlands of Richmond, Petersburg, and Norfolk.[73] Some Whites
in all three areas came to believe that a unified conspiracy connected an incipient attempt by slaves from each region to rebel and conquer southern
Virginia's three biggest towns on Easter Monday. This belief was no doubt
partially rooted in the talk of rebellious activity that reached White ears in
all three locales during the first few months of 1802.[74] White Virginians
uncovered convincing evidence that enslaved residents of several Southside
counties had indeed taken concrete steps to organize a movement to attack
and conquer Petersburg, but the evidence uncovered in the Richmond and
Norfolk areas – in each case a single witness either tortured or pressured into
"revealing" a conspiracy – cannot withstand scrutiny.[75] The coerced confession

[72] Petition on behalf of two Slaves belonging to Capt. Paul Thilman, May 24, 1802, Executive Papers, Box 123, Pardon Papers. The petitioners noted that a similar case of talk
without immediately intended action had "lately been" discovered in King William County,
though records of that scare have not survived.
[73] Egerton, *Gabriel's Rebellion*, chs. 8, 9; Bertram Wyatt-Brown, *Southern Honor: Ethics and
Behavior in the Old South* (New York, 1982), ch. 15.
[74] Richard Jones to Monroe, Jan. 2, 1802, Executive Papers, Box 120; G. Green to William
Prentis or James Durell, Jan. 2, 1802, Executive Communications with the Legislature,
Dec. 19, 1799–Dec. 29, 1802, LiVa; and numerous letters in Executive Papers, Box 119
for early indications of conspiracy against Petersburg; Frank Goode to Roling Pointer,
Jan. 18, 1802, and Horatio Turpin to Monroe, Jan. 22, 1802, Executive Papers, Box 119;
and Monroe to John Harris, Jan. 23, 1802, and Monroe to Colonel Littleberry Mosby, Jan.
23, 1803, ELB 1800–3 for scare in Powhatan County, which was in Richmond's hinterland; General Matthews to Monroe, Mar. 10, 1802, and John Cowper to Monroe, Mar. 22,
1802, Executive Papers, Box 120; Monroe to The Mayor of Norfolk, Mar. 17, 1802, and
Monroe to Brigadier General Matthews, Mar. 17, 1802, ELB 1800–3 for unrest in Norfolk.
[75] Wyatt-Brown, *Southern Honor*, ch. 15 argues that the Norfolk scare was primarily a White
communal ritual that had little to do with slaves' struggle for freedom; Egerton, *Gabriel's
Rebellion*, ch. 8 sees the Southside as the center of the Easter Conspiracy, discounts the
reports of an active conspiracy in Richmond, but believes that it did reach into Norfolk
and that the testimony of Will in Norfolk was accurate. One of the corroborating pieces
of evidence that he accepts – the discovery of "messages from the Petersburg rebels [kept]

of Lewis, the slave who testified that Arthur Farrar headed a conspiracy to conquer Richmond, reveals instead the way that Black residents of Richmond's hinterland spoke of insurrection in the immediate wake of Gabriel.

Not surprisingly, Lewis described insurrection in terms shaped by his understanding of Gabriel's Conspiracy. In fact, as Douglas Egerton points out, one of the obvious indications that Lewis made up the stories about Arthur Farrar is the much-too-close resemblance to the insurrection plans of 1800.[76] The conspirators were to come from Richmond as well as from Henrico and Hanover Counties. They were to meet one night near Prosser's plantation at the Brook Bridge, set fire to Richmond, get arms from the magazine, and take the town. The recruiting was to take place at "every [religious] meeting [and] every drinking frolick," and anyone who betrayed the plan was to "loose his life." The supposed 1802 conspirators shared the ambiguous relationship to nonelite Whites that Gabriel's followers had expressed, asserting both that "poor white people" had joined the conspiracy and that the rebels would not leave "one young man from 18 to 8 and from 18 to 80 years old to live, nor a white woman upon earth." Their goal, however, was unambiguously to "set the whole Country free of the White people" and create a "free Virginia."[77] In short, Lewis, caught running away and "whipped . . . one whole day" while being "repeatedly threatened with immediate death if he did not disclose his partizans in conspiracy," cobbled together a thinly disguised retelling of the story of Gabriel's Conspiracy, changing the names to endanger the innocent. As such, his tale is useless as a guide to the conspiratorial activity of enslaved Richmonders in 1802.

If understood as a story about Gabriel, however, Lewis's testimony provides an invaluable picture of how one enslaved man made sense of Gabriel's

'as a stopper of a jug'" on a free Black man's boat (128) – was identified by William Prentis, the mayor of Petersburg as a sheet of paper with a list of "names of those [slaves] . . . employed" at tobacco stemming in a Petersburg tobacco factory, with the "quantity of tobacco stemmed by each in the course of the day." Prentis reported that "the mighty army of [Petersburg] blacks" that Norfolk authorities thought the list represented was "no more than as many pounds of Stemmed Tobacco" (Prentis to Monroe, May 27, 1802, Executive Papers, Box 120). The probability that authorities unintentionally manufactured false evidence means not that no "real" conspiracy existed but that reliable evidence for it has not survived.

[76] Egerton, *Gabriel's Rebellion*, 141–2; Arthur Farrar to the Honorable the Governor and Council, June 12, 1802, Executive Papers, Box 123. This is Farrar's petition for a pardon in which he tells the story of Lewis's confession.

[77] Several complementary versions of Lewis's confession and testimony are in Executive Papers, Box 120 and Box 123. Quotes are from the second of his two confessions to Peter Randolph, and are in Box 120.

struggle for freedom and of White Virginians' repression of that struggle.[78] Lewis's tale cannot, of course, shed reliable light on what happened in 1800: while he left a remarkable number of parallels to the earlier plan in his story, he was not foolish, and he certainly altered many factual details. His story illustrates beyond doubt, however, that black Virginians as far away as Goochland County did indeed understand that Gabriel had wanted to lead Black people in "tak[ing] the Country of Virginia," because "the white people ha[d] had the Country long enough."[79] Gabriel was understood, then, to have staked a claim to Virginia for its Black residents.

Lewis's confession also sheds light on his understanding of the place of betrayal in Gabriel's Conspiracy. As noted earlier, Gabriel and his followers had threatened with death Blacks who did not join the insurrection, and Lewis reported that Arthur Farrar had extended the threat, warning Lewis that if he betrayed the conspiracy his "words [would] make against" him "at the day of [his] death." The fact that Pharoah Sheppard, Tom Sheppard, and Ben Woolfolk remained alive in 1802 might have weakened the effect of threatened physical revenge and contributed to the invocation of divine judgment. When, however, Peter Randolph asked Lewis why he expected that his "words [would] kill" him, the witness suggested that, as late as 1802, some Richmond-area blacks still expected the betrayers of Gabriel to suffer in this world for their actions. Lewis made an explicit contrast between White people, who "whip[ped] openly," and "the Blacks [who] kill[ed] slily [slyly]." Lewis said that he preferred to be "hanged [rather] than poizoned." If members of greater Richmond's Black community believed that the betrayal of Gabriel was still to be avenged in 1802, then they maintained a very different sense of the end of the conspiracy than that expressed by authorities.

Lewis provided even clearer evidence of the alternative understanding of Gabriel's place in Virginia's history that animated the slaves' struggle against

[78] Lewis was from Goochland County, which was on the outskirts of the areas from which Gabriel drew support, and he made clear that he had not spent much time in Richmond. Lewis's tale probably represents the understanding of Gabriel's Conspiracy of the majority of Black Virginians who were relatively or completely ignorant of the planned insurrection. Lewis, then, provides an unexceptional enslaved person's perceptions of the conspiracy in the wake of its repression. It should be noted that in the unlikely case that Lewis's testimony was a factually accurate representation of his conversations with Arthur Farrar – and we cannot prove that it was not – then this line of analysis can remain largely intact with the added significance that memories of Gabriel shaped a more immediate blueprint for another advanced movement for freedom in 1802.

[79] This and future quotes from Lewis's story are from the two confessions he gave to Peter Randolph in Executive Papers, Box 120 and Box 123.

slavery. When Peter Randolph asked whether the Blacks would ever stop trying and when, Lewis replied simply that "they will never cease." Enslaved Virginians, he warned, would "Continually plan in secret," and their secret plans would be put into action whenever "White people [were] off gard." Upon winning freedom, Lewis said, they planned to "take possession of the Country and divide it amongst themselves as the whites now possessed it." Whites certainly recognized that Gabriel's Conspiracy revealed dangerous fault lines in Virginia society, but they preferred to conceive of it as an isolated event that had to be repressed and that was over once repressed. Lewis's confessions suggest that, in the almost immediate wake of the elaborate theater of power that had been staged to intimidate them, enslaved Virginians – even when providing coerced testimony before White authorities – situated Gabriel's struggle in a very different history of the struggle of Virginians of African descent to claim Virginia as their own. The defeat of Gabriel apparently was seen as a lost battle rather than the defeat of a movement, and Black Virginians continued to enunciate a belief that they were the rightful owners of the state.[80] Gabriel's Conspiracy formed a part of a larger story that they implicitly structured along a romantic plot line that would culminate in the end of slavery and the creation of justice on Earth.[81]

Resistance, conspiracies, and identities

Gabriel's Conspiracy was not originally about claiming Virginia, it was about taking it. But, as is so often true in human affairs, the intentions of the participants were not met, and the conspiracy took on new meanings in the wake of the White repression, as it has continued to take on new meanings over the past two centuries. In this analysis the conspiracy provides a window on the ways that Black Virginians perceived themselves, their oppressors, and their world in 1800 – that is, on the complicated senses of corporate identity that Virginians of African descent had developed over the course of the eighteenth century – and it stands as an important moment in the process of identity formation that continued, as such processes always do, after 1800.

Conceiving of the conspiracy as a "moment" involves moving from an analysis of the conspiracy itself to an analysis of the various ways that the

---

[80] See the final chapter of this book for enslaved Virginians' restructuring of the history of Gabriel and of betrayal when they could no longer plausibly believe that Pharoah and Tom would (or did) suffer earthly vengeance, and when their struggle against slavery moved beyond Virginia's boundaries.

[81] See White, *Metahistory*; and Frye, *Anatomy of Criticism*.

conspiracy has been understood through time. I return to this question in the final chapter of this book when I trace some of the narratives of the conspiracy that have been told by Blacks and Whites at different times during the past 200 years. It is important to realize, however, how quickly the conspiracy became a part of Virginia's history and the degree to which Black Virginians constructed a folk history of Gabriel's attempt to win freedom that implicitly contested Whites' versions of the event. Access to the two versions is unequal, because slaves rarely managed to insert their stories of such events into the written record. The version embodied in Lewis's confessions shows that in 1802 Black Virginians placed Gabriel's Conspiracy in a historical narrative that envisioned a very different culmination to the history of the people of Virginia. It was a vision that could and did change while informing a struggle for freedom and equality.

As a window on the way Virginians of African descent perceived their world, Gabriel's Conspiracy reveals a complex matrix of racial and provincial, communal and individualistic, and religious and secular identities. There is, of course, nothing peculiar or even unusual in the fact that Virginians of African descent had developed crosscutting and on occasion apparently contradictory senses of corporate identity. The conspiracy does, however, allow analysis to move beyond merely identifying the different languages that Black Virginians used to describe themselves (e.g., religious and secular) and to explore the ways these different strands of social identity affected enslaved Virginians' perceptions of their world and thus their attempts to shape it.

Like creole slave rebels throughout plantation America, Gabriel and his followers built their conspiracy within a distinctly American – in this case a distinctly Virginian – context. That context had been forged through two centuries of cultural contact among settlers of African, European, and mixed descent, contact that had been influenced by patterns of commerce, politics, and revolution that had shaped the Atlantic World of which Virginia was a part. Gabriel and his followers built a conspiracy in part by appropriating and reconstituting the meanings of the most powerful elements of Virginia's culture while making a claim that Virginia more properly belonged to its Black than to its White people. In doing this they illustrated the way that tensions between the rich traditions of racial and provincial identity could produce a potentially radical cultural dynamism. The same dynamic, however, appears to have contributed to the strain of cooperation and accommodation that characterized some of the behavior of many individual conspirators and that contributed to the betrayal of the conspiracy. To understand more fully the social basis for the complex sense of identity revealed in the conspiracy, however, requires a movement to a different type of historical analysis. Only by reconstructing the patterns of day-to-day life that Virginians of African descent experienced in and around Richmond during the decades surrounding the conspiracy can the ideas revealed in the exceptional events of 1800 be placed in a fuller and less extraordinary context.

PART II

Social practice

*Urbanization, commercialization, and identity
in the daily life of Gabriel's Richmond*

THE CULTURAL PROCESSES through which Virginians of African
descent expressed and created crosscutting senses of collective
identity emerge with unusual clarity from an examination of
Gabriel's Conspiracy, but the clarity is achieved at the cost of
understanding the day-to-day practices that constituted the social
world in which the conspiracy was built. Gabriel and his followers
grew up in and around Richmond during and after the American
Revolution, a period during which Virginia's General Assembly
moved the state capital from Williamsburg to Richmond. Becoming
the new state's capital turned the town into the political center of
Virginia, and the rapid development of Richmond's hinterland
helped to turn it into a commercial and manufacturing center.
Black and White residents of this new urban area, most of whom
had grown up in rural Virginia, adapted themselves to the urban
conditions that they found and created. Richmond's density of
settlement, the transience of the Black and White workers who
carried goods into and out of town, the influence of free people
of color who moved into town, and the recreational possibilities
created by the city combined to produce patterns of interaction
among people of different races and statuses that were qualitatively
different from those that had prevailed on Virginia's plantations.
Ascribed racial identity remained the most important determinant
of individuals' lives, but relations among Black and White working
people became less predictable and more flexible, a situation that
offered new opportunities for Black Richmonders and that
sometimes troubled elite Whites. Those elites did not, however,
make concerted efforts to eliminate the social and cultural spaces
created by urbanization, in part because those spaces grew out of
the labor requirements of an urban economy and thus out of the

very economic processes that produced the elite's wealth. Black
Richmonders understood their own economic value and used
several sometimes conflicting strategies to enhance their influence
over their individual and collective lives. Close attention to the
ways that gender differences were built, challenged, and rebuilt on
the streets and in the homes of early Richmond provides a valuable
perspective on the processes of negotiation, cooperation, and
conflict through which Black and White, enslaved and free, female
and male Richmonders shared their different but profoundly
overlapping cultural worlds in the age of Gabriel's Conspiracy.

5

The growth of early Richmond

The recorded history of what became Richmond can be traced back to the earliest period of English colonization when the leader of the powerful indigenous Powhatan Confederacy that dominated eastern Virginia held court there. It might also embrace Nathaniel Bacon, who began his 1676 rebellion in Henrico County, and William Byrd I, who lived near and traveled through the area to trade with Native Americans. But the history of Richmond itself begins with Byrd's son and heir, William Byrd II, who inherited the land that came to comprise Richmond and who founded the town in 1737.

Byrd built a small settlement on Shockoe Creek at the falls of the James River well before he made formal plans for the town. During the 1720s and 30s he built a tobacco warehouse that brought him "at least £50 per annum" and a mill to grind the grain grown on his and other area plantations. In 1730 the House of Burgesses increased the value of Byrd's investment by designating his warehouse an official site for the inspection and storage of tobacco destined to be shipped to European markets. No doubt Byrd used his extensive political connections to encourage the legislature to seat a public warehouse on his land, but the falls of the James represented an obvious choice: it was indeed, as Byrd claimed, a place "naturally intended" for a market "where the traffic of the outer inhabitants" of Virginia "must center."[1] To encourage development he had a neighbor survey the land and lay out lots, which he offered to sell to anyone who would build a "House in Three Years Time." Eventually people bought lots and turned Richmond into the market that Byrd imagined. It also became the most significant industrial city of

[1] William Byrd II to Micajah Perry, 27 May 17[29], Marion Tinling, ed. and comp., *The Correspondence of the Three William Byrds of Westover Virginia, 1684–1776* (Charlottesville, 1977), 398–9 (warehouse); Louis B. Wright, ed., *The Prose Works of William Byrd of Westover: Narratives of a Colonial Virginian* (Cambridge, Mass., 1966), 339–40 (mill), 388 ("traffic").

the Old South. But these developments took time, and for Byrd's life his town-projecting spirit resulted only in a city built "in air."[2]

In fact, prior to 1780, Richmond remained so insignificant that few descriptions of the early village have survived. During that time it was a small marketing center for surrounding plantations, and the social and race relations that characterized life there resembled, and were subordinate to, rural Virginia norms. When in 1780 Virginia's General Assembly made Richmond the capital of the new state, it greatly accelerated the town's growth into a true urban center with social relations qualitatively different from those of the countryside. Gabriel and most of his followers grew up within this urbanizing environment, and the complicated senses of collective identity that they displayed during the conspiracy were rooted in both the general history of race and slavery in Virginia that is discussed in Chapter 1, and in the patterns of urban and social development specific to Richmond and its immediate hinterland.

A tobacco town

Although Richmond did not become a city immediately upon being founded, it did develop into one of Virginia's modest tobacco towns. During the second and third quarters of the eighteenth century, large plantations run by men historian Aubrey Land has dubbed "planter-merchants" began to be replaced by small towns as central nodes in Virginia's tobacco economy. These towns grew around public warehouses where tobacco was inspected, but they were also home to a rising breed of small traders tied to mercantile houses in Great Britain.[3] Such towns often were, or became, county seats and thus home to monthly county court meetings, so they served as centers for local politics as well as commerce.

The two functions became inextricably intertwined. These villages typically remained largely empty for most of the month, but men from throughout the county flowed in on court day. While in town, planters took care of any

[2] *Virginia Gazette*, April 15–22, 1737, quoted in Maude H. Woodfin and Marion Tinling, eds., *Another Secret Diary of William Byrd of Westover, 1739–1741, With Letters and Literary Exercises 1696–1741* (Richmond, 1942), 55n.; *Prose Works of William Byrd*, 388.
[3] Aubrey C. Land, "Economic Base and Social Structure: The Northern Chesapeake in the Eighteenth Century," *Journal of Economic History* 25 (1965): 639–54; Carville Earle, *Geographical Inquiry and American Historical Problems* (Stanford, 1992), ch. 3 (esp. 99–106); Darrett B. Rutman and Anita H. Rutman, *A Place in Time: Middlesex County, Virginia, 1650–1750* (New York, 1984), ch. 7 (esp. 226–31). Allan Kulikoff, *Tobacco and Slaves: The Development of Southern Cultures in the Chesapeake, 1680–1800* (Chapel Hill, 1986), 104–16; Alan L. Karras, *Sojourners in the Sun: Scottish Migrants in Jamaica and the Chesapeake, 1740–1800* (Ithaca, 1992).

business they had with the justices of the peace. They also visited stores kept by town merchants, relaxed and drank in the ordinaries that were always close to courthouses, and perhaps placed a few bets at horse races or cockfights. And it was to these same towns that small planters and the slaves of great planters brought hogsheads of cured and packed tobacco to be inspected and sold into the economy of the Atlantic World.[4] Tobacco towns alternated long stretches when they resembled sleepy rural hamlets with periodic outbursts of social, economic, and political activity.

Richmond lies too far inland to have developed during Virginia's initial urban boomlet. Henrico County remained a "frontier" region during the first three decades of the eighteenth century when towns like Urbanna, Yorktown, and Portsmouth were growing in the eastern Tidewater. As White planters and Black slaves pushed westward, another ultimately more successful urban boom occurred around the middle of the eighteenth century, when significant towns were seated at the fall lines of each of Virginia's major rivers. Petersburg, Fredericksburg, and Alexandria, along with Richmond, eventually became larger and more important urban centers than the tobacco towns of the east, but until the revolutionary era they resembled eastern towns.[5]

From the 1730s to the 1760s, Richmond grew gradually while remaining a quiet rural place. In 1742 the House of Burgesses granted the settlement legal status as a town, and in 1752 Richmond became the Henrico County seat. Sometime during the 1750s William Byrd III built what Andrew Burnaby, a Scottish visitor, called a small but elegant place named Belvidere on the falls of the James. In 1760 Byrd's home afforded him a view of two or three villages surrounded by "a prodigious extent of wilderness" that was divided by the James River "winding majestically along through the midst."[6]

---

[4] Rhys Isaac, *The Transformation of Virginia, 1740–1790* (Chapel Hill, 1982), 88–104; Carville Earle, *Geographical Inquiry*, ch. 3 (marketing of tobacco).

[5] I ignore Norfolk, an eastern town that grew earlier than these fall-line towns and whose economic and demographic history is unusual (see Earle, *Geographical Inquiry*, ch. 3; and Jacob Price, "Economic Function and the Growth of American Port Towns in the Eighteenth Century," *Perspectives in American History* 8 [1974]: 123–86; Thomas C. Parramore with Peter C. Stewart and Tommy L. Bogger, *Norfolk: The First Four Centuries* [Charlottesville, 1994], chs. 6–8). John W. Reps, *Tidewater Towns: City Planning in Colonial Virginia and Maryland* (Williamsburg, 1972), esp. chs. 4, 9, 11, 12, is the standard work on town planning in the colonial Chesapeake.

[6] Harry M. Ward and Harold E. Greer Jr., *Richmond During the Revolution, 1775–1783* (Charlottesville, 1977), 3–8; Louis H. Manarin and Clifford Dowdey, *The History of Henrico County* (Charlottesville, 1984), 102; M. Tinling, *Correspondence of the Three William Byrds*, 603 (Belvedere); Andrew Burnaby, *Travels through the Middle Settlements in North-America in the years 1759 and 1760 with observations upon the state of the Colonies* (Ithaca, 1960 [1775]), 9 (quotation).

These villages, which eventually grew together to form Richmond, included Shockoe, named after a creek that emptied into the north side of the James, and Rocky Ridge (later Manchester) on the opposite bank. In a different context, Burnaby reported that the forty-four towns designated by Virginia's House of Burgesses were "little better than inconsiderable villages," so Richmond in 1760 must have remained little more than a crossroads.[7]

Small as it was, however, Richmond played an important role as a place for planters from Henrico County to meet, do business, and socialize, and for slaves to travel through – usually involuntarily – and occasionally to visit. Planters gathered first at the court house, which faced the James River, to sue and be sued in order to register, and sometimes even collect, the small debts they contracted with one another in operating the area's tobacco economy. They also bought and sold slaves – in 1769 one town resident reported selling eighty slaves on consignment for a London firm – thus contributing to the demographic shift through which the Piedmont supplanted the Tidewater as the center of Virginia's Black population.[8] Many newly arrived Africans, struggling to comprehend their new surroundings, found themselves hauled before these courts so that justices could pass judgment on their age and thus their status as taxable property.

The Black people sold into early Henrico County and the surrounding Piedmont encountered conditions akin but not identical to the Tidewater experiences discussed in Chapter 1.[9] A sizable minority of the enslaved settlers came directly from Africa, and they began their lives in Virginia with the dehumanizing experience of being bought by foreigners and transported to new quarters in a strange land. On those quarters, most found some African-

<hr />

[7] Burnaby, *Travels,* 14. Burnaby never used "Richmond," though the colonial legislature and the father of Burnaby's host had both adopted the new name. William Hugh Grove described the "delicat village" of Yorktown in 1732 in terms that might have applied to Richmond twenty-five years later: "A Stranger [would] Conclude there were at Least 100 houses whereas there are really not 30 – for Their Kitchins, Warehouses etc are . . . Seperate from their Dwelling houses and make them appear different habitations[.] there are about 10 good houses not above 4 of Brick the rest of Timber. . . . They are not Contiguous but Seperat[e]d 40, 50, or 100 Yards from Each other." William Hugh Grove, Diary, Selections, 1732, 1 (typescript); U. Va.
[8] Richard S. Dunn, "Black Society in the Chesapeake 1776–1810," in Ira Berlin and Ronald Hoffman, eds., *Slavery and Freedom in the Age of the American Revolution* (Charlottesville, 1983), 54–61 (esp. Map 1, p. 55 and Map 2, p. 57). Also Chapter 1 of this book.
[9] Much of Henrico County is in the Tidewater, and the county is labeled a Tidewater county. Richmond, however, is on the border between the Tidewater and the Piedmont, and its commercial connections to the west make the Piedmont the appropriate context within which to discuss the development of the town.

born people living among a majority of Virginia-born Blacks who had been moved west from the Tidewater. The average size of Piedmont slave quarters grew quickly, meaning that most enslaved people living in the Richmond area encountered conditions – even sex ratios and relatively high densities of slave populations – reasonably favorable for family and community formation shortly after arriving. Thus, many presumably became enmeshed in the growing kin-based communities discussed earlier, and creolization probably proceeded rapidly.[10] Most enslaved residents of the Piedmont participated in tobacco cultivation, and some accompanied their masters into Richmond to help transport goods to market on court day.

With many people present for court day, planters could trade information about prospective prices for their crops: during the summer of 1769, they learned that the surrounding countryside held "one of the largest . . . Crops [of] Wheat" in memory but that tobacco would "turn out Short again." No doubt they also discussed the prices that commodities were bringing in British ports. And through all their commercial and legal maneuverings, the men would gather at Cowley's Tavern, which was immediately adjacent to the courthouse, to drink and socialize.[11]

Occasional glimpses of life in various Virginia towns provide a sense of other activities that sometimes accompanied court day in early Richmond. Virginia planters loved horse racing, and tobacco towns often hosted match and quarter races. Shortly after arriving in the Northern Neck as a tutor for the children of Councilor Robert Carter of Nomini Hall, New Jersey native Philip Fithian "rode . . . to Richmond [County] Court-house" to watch a race

---

[10] This paragraph is based on Philip D. Morgan and Michael L. Nicholls, "Slaves in Piedmont Virginia, 1720–1790," *WMQ*, 3rd ser., 46 (1989): 211–51; Dunn, "Black Society in the Chesapeake"; and Kulikoff, *Tobacco and Slaves*, 336–45. To understand how creole the Richmond-area Black population was by the end of the eighteenth century, note that census-takers from Richmond and Petersburg alone reported more people of African descent in 1790 (3,319) than the total number of Africans (2,266) estimated by Morgan and Nicholls to have been brought into Virginia's Central Piedmont counties between 1725 and 1774 (p. 248).

[11] Quotes from Richard Adams to Thomas Adams, 5 July 1769, Adams Family Papers, Section 6, Virginia Historical Society, Richmond (hereafter VHS). Richard Adams lived in Richmond, and his brother Thomas worked in London; this letter passed along useful information about crops, illustrating the networks connecting Richmond to the metropolis, but the details about social life on court day were included only because Richard reported a fire in which he lost his lumber house and in which many of the gentlemen "at Cowley's Door" were almost killed. Though Landon Carter had a contemptuous attitude toward such activity on court days, he left little doubt that it was the norm in Tidewater Virginia (Jack P. Greene, ed., *The Diary of Colonel Landon Carter of Sabine Hall, 1752–1778* [Richmond, 1987 (1965)], v. II, p. 1073).

for "a purse of 500 Pounds; besides small Betts almost enumerable." And almost as soon as tutor John Harrower walked down the gangplank of the ship that brought him from Scotland to Fredericksburg, he witnessed a race between a "Bay Mare [with] a white boy ridder" and a "gray Mare . . . with . . . a black boy ridder."[12]

Such races did not offer the only chances White Virginians had to socialize in these small towns. Among the many faults that planter Landon Carter found in his sons was their fondness for going to various towns to gamble at cards and dice. Several diarists mentioned incidents in which small groups of Virginians converged from different directions on a store or an ordinary, where they met, dined, and drank in places that suddenly "thronged with company."[13] Entertainment and business frequently came together in these small urban enclaves.

Philip Fithian participated in an unusually grand and elaborate gathering that took place in a prerevolutionary Virginia town. In August 1774, he was invited by the Tayloes from nearby Mount Airy plantation to watch a boat race at the small Rappahannock River port of Hobb's Hole (now Tappahannock). The Tayloe's guests were ferried out to an anchored and shaded ship where "45 Ladies, and . . . 60 Gentlemen . . . dined . . . twice" while watching two (unshaded) boats rowed by slaves race around a two-mile course. Captain Benson, who received credit for his enslaved rowers' victory, was then challenged by another white captain, and the two surely exhausted crews had to row the course again. The White spectators then descended upon the small village of Hobb's Hole, where "25 Ladies" and "40 Gentlemen" danced to the music of "two [presumably enslaved] Fidlers" while consuming "an unusual Quantity of Liquor."[14]

This boat race was an unusual event, but Fithian's description calls attention to the ways elite Virginians presented themselves during these public events and to the nature of the small towns in which the events took place. Fithian frequently criticized slavery and other aspects of life in Virginia. Nonetheless, in his description of the luxurious boats, the elegant ladies, and the

[12] Hunter Dickinson Farish, ed., *Journal and Letters of Philip Vickers Fithian, 1773–1774: A Plantation Tutor of the Old Dominion* (Williamsburg, 1957), 32. (Richmond County is in Virginia's Northern Neck, so Richmond Court House was not in Richmond, Virginia.) Edward Miles Riley, ed., *The Journal of John Harrower: An Indentured Servant in the Colony of Virginia, 1773–1776* (Williamsburg, 1963), 40.
[13] Greene, *Diary of Landon Carter*, v. I, p. 522, v. II, pp. 640–1, 830, 859 (sons' gambling), v. I, p. 539 (socializing in store); Farish, *Journal of Fithian*, 68–9, 74 ("thronged"); Harrower visited Fredericksburg at least twenty-seven times in two years (Riley, *Journal of Harrower*).
[14] Farish, *Journal of Fithian*, 200–4.

sumptuous treatment he received, Fithian inadvertently revealed the seduct-
ive quality of the gentry's competitive world of display and luxury. He described
a small town in which six to ten ships normally rested at wharf loading
tobacco and unloading manufactured goods. He portrayed a culture in which
great planters remained at the pinnacle of society but in which merchants
were growing increasingly prominent.[15]

Fithian's lack of interest in the slaves who participated in this event and
in town life best reveals the power this display of gentry values had upon
him. Throughout his journal he showed great interest in his employer's (Robert
Carter) enslaved laborers, and he frequently commented on the injustice of
slavery. Under the sway of this event, however, he almost erased the Black
presence. Servants, rowers, and fiddlers – all certainly slaves – played crucial
roles in the festivities. The small village life was enlivened by the no doubt
largely Black crews of the ships docked in the river, but in mentioning all
these groups, Fithian makes passing mention of only the rowers' race. In short,
Fithian presented the gentry's perception of life in Hobb's Hole, but he inevitably left traces of the slaves' different world in these small urban places.[16]

Presumably, a second party took place that night in or around Hobb's
Hole, a gathering those at the "big" party knew about but ignored. The Black
oarsmen, perhaps rewarded for their efforts with some liquor or money, the
Black sailors who helped man the six ships then riding in the harbor, the
Black pilots and watermen who surely worked the schooners and smaller vessels at Hobb's Hole probably met with personal servants who accompanied
their masters and mistresses to the town ball and with slaves from surrounding
plantations. The oarsmen, having worked so hard for the amusement of White
gamblers, may have sought diversion in some gambling of their own. Perhaps
they organized and bet on cockfights as slaves at Robert Carter's nearby
plantation often did. These partygoers may also have barbecued a stolen pig
or enjoyed a communal fish feast, as Gabriel and his conspirators frequently
did before their planned rebellion during the summer of 1800. Their evening
surely included the playing of fiddles and "bangers" (banjoes), perhaps while
singing "*Guinea* Love-song[s]," or the "legendary ballads, [and] narratives
of alternate dialogue and singing" that other Black Virginians reportedly performed.[17] Such singing would perhaps have been accompanied by dancing

---

[15] Ibid.   [16] Ibid.

[17] Ibid., 82, 83, 121, 128; John Davis, *Travels of Four Years and a Half in the United States
of America During 1798, 1799, 1800, 1801, and 1802*, A. J. Morrison, ed. (New York, 1909
[1803]), 416 (Guinea love songs and bangers); George Tucker quoted in Willie Lee Rose,
ed., *A Documentary History of Slavery in North America* (New York, 1976), 79 (ballads).

in the style a European visitor thought "without any method or regularity," and that he believed their masters had borrowed for their famous Virginia "jiggs." With all these activities the people of African descent who were brought together by White Virginians' recreational activities would have expressed the aesthetic sensibilities and the social values of their developing creole communities just as powerfully as the White Virginians about whom Fithian wrote expressed their own. And similar, though no doubt less elaborate gatherings of Blacks and Whites surely occurred in the other urban centers of colonial Virginia, including the small Piedmont town of Richmond.[18] But as long as these towns remained small places that only occasionally hosted such events, the customary patterns of social relations that characterized "urban" Virginia differed little from those of the countryside: similar "big" and "shadow" parties frequently took place at great plantations.[19] It was the growth of Virginia's fall-line towns during the Revolutionary era that created a distinctive urban Chesapeake world.

Richmond's transformation began prior to the Revolution when the town became an important node in the commercial network connecting the rapidly developing Shenandoah Valley to the Atlantic market. As early as the 1740s seven or eight settlers in the Shenandoah county of Augusta "had accounts with Andrew Berkeley, a merchant in Henrico County," but it was not until the 1760s that Richmond became an important center for the valley's trade. By that time, western settlers were growing hemp and sending it to Richmond in return for goods like cloth, nails, sugar and salt.[20] The hemp trade probably helps to explain why the state built a ropewalk in Richmond during the Revolutionary War. Richmond merchants also trafficked in indentured

[18] Burnaby, Travels, 26 (jiggs); Thad W. Tate, The Negro in Eighteenth-Century Williamsburg (Williamsburg, 1965), and Gerald W. Mullin, Flight and Rebellion: Slave Resistance in Eighteenth-Century Virginia (New York, 1972) for Black Virginians in eighteenth-century Virginia towns. Riley, Journal of Harrower, 105, 139, 153 (slave messengers to Fredericksburg).
[19] Farish, Journal of Fithian, 82, 83, 180–1; John Randolph Barden, " 'Flushed with Notions of Freedom': The Growth and Emancipation of a Virginia Slave Community, 1732–1812" (Ph.D. diss., Duke University, 1993), 215–16, n. 17 for examples of slave recreational activity on area plantations. Roger D. Abrahams, Singing the Master: The Emergence of African American Culture in the Plantation South (New York, 1992), chs. 1 and 4 for fuller evidence of slaves' parties during the 1850s.
[20] Robert D. Mitchell, Commercialism and Frontier: Perspectives on the Early Shenandoah Valley (Charlottesville, 1977), 152–60 (155 for quote; 162–72 (hemp in Shenandoah).); Albert H. Tillson Jr., Gentry and Common Folk: Political Culture on a Virginia Frontier (Lexington, Ky., 1991), 26–30; Colonel William Preston's Account with Edward Johnson and Company, October 1769, Preston Family of Virginia Papers, microfilm, Library of Congress (hereafter LC). Johnson was from Manchester, which remained politically separate from Richmond until the nineteenth century, but I will use evidence from Manchester as if it were officially part of Richmond.

servants and slaves for the Shenandoah gentry. And Richmond became a center for the growing trade in James River Valley wheat.[21] Atlantic merchants also began to perceive of the town as a place of future importance. By 1769 the London mercantile house of John Morton Jordan entered into a partnership with Thomas Adams, partially on condition that Adams would "use his best indeavours to establish" the trading house's interests "on James River and to engage the good offices of" Thomas's brother Richard. Two years later, despite a devastating flood that destroyed property in the town, the legislature authorized Rocketts, the third tobacco inspection warehouse in the Richmond area.[22] In 1772 the House of Burgesses voted to move the colonial capital to Richmond, an act that Richard Adams realized might greatly enhance his wealth. He enlisted brother Thomas to lobby for the Crown's approval, and he reported on efforts to raise money for a canal around the falls of the James River that would have provided Richmond with easier access to the produce of the developing Piedmont and western portions of Virginia. His optimism proved premature when the governor's council blocked the move in 1772, but most of his hopes were realized before the end of the century.[23]

Nonetheless, if Richmond began to diversify and grow, it continued to look much like a tobacco town until after the Revolution. On the eve of the Revolution it had only 600 inhabitants, and in 1779 there were only ten to twelve town merchants "in the habit of entrusting Goods in credit to Planters." This scarcely differed from the eight to ten merchants who could be supported by the tobacco produced in the hinterland of a typical tobacco town.[24] A 1781 map sketched by a British cavalry officer who led a raid on the town suggests that Richmond consisted of several warehouses and two clusters of smaller buildings. All were grouped around a single road that crossed Shockoe

---

[21] Edward Johnson to William Preston, April 8, 1774 (indentured servants sent to valley); Frank Preston to John Preston, December 22, 1798 (planned to buy slaves in Richmond), Preston Family of Virginia Papers; Richard Adams to Thomas Adams, July 5, 1769, Adams Family Papers (wheat's importance). Earle, *Geographical Inquiry*, ch. 3.

[22] Articles of Agreement between Thomas Adams and John Morton Jordan, August 10, 1769; Richard Adams to Thomas Adams, August 11, 1771, Adams Family Papers.

[23] James O'Mara, *An Historical Geography of Urban System Development: Tidewater Virginia in the Eighteenth Century* (Downsview, Ontario, 1983), 210–11; Richard Adams to Thomas Adams, March 24, 1772, Adams Family Papers.

[24] Ward and Greer, *Richmond During the Revolution*, 8; Richmond Suit Papers (hereafter RSP), Box 45, Nov. 1807 Bundle, *Hunter, Banks, and Company v. Wilson Miles Cary*, deposition of W. Hay. The Richmond Suit Papers include miscellaneous loose court papers (summons, depositions, warrants, writs, etc.) from the Richmond City Hustings Court organized and bundled by individual case, Library of Virginia, Richmond (hereafter LiVa); Earle, *Geographical Inquiry*, 102.

Creek just before the creek emptied into the James River. Including Manchester would add another warehouse and one group of perhaps ten houses. In 1780 the new state's General Assembly moved the capital to Richmond. The rough, frontier quality of the new capital can be discerned in the response of Eliza Ambler, daughter of State Treasurer Jacquelin Ambler, to her new home: she sarcastically labeled Richmond a "famous Metropolis," and complained that it could not house half the people who had to move there. At the time she considered the move from the relative sophistication of Williamsburg to Richmond "one of the calamities of" her life.[25]

A political and commercial center

If moving the capital was a calamity for young Eliza Ambler, it initiated an immediate boom in Richmond. The combined effects of the arrival of the state government and the continuing extension of settlement and commercial agriculture into the Piedmont helped to transform the sleepy tobacco village of the 1770s into an important town. The intensification of commerce and manufacturing, the development of the construction trades, and the annual influx of men associated with the legislature created in Richmond an urban center with clearly discernible and changing neighborhoods, transient populations that elites found difficult to control, and changing patterns of relations among nonelite people of African and European descent. The growing town became a magnet for Virginia's rapidly growing free Black population and attracted numerous runaway slaves who sought the relative anonymity and autonomy created even in this modest town.[26] As Richmond grew, it developed patterns of social and race relations that were qualitatively different from those that prevailed in rural Virginia.

Beginning in 1780, the new state capital grew rapidly into Virginia's largest and most important urban center. By 1782 the town had about 1,000 inhab-

[25] Reps, *Tidewater Towns*, 272 (Simcoe's map). Simcoe's map served military purposes, so he did not delineate the number of structures, but he presumably provided an accurate picture of where structures were grouped; Eliza Ambler to Mrs. Dudley, 1781, *Virginia Magazine of History and Biography* 38 (1930): 167–9; and Ambler, quoted by Ward and Greer, *Richmond During the Revolution*, 41.

[26] Mullin, *Flight and Rebellion*, 115–21. Enslaved Virginians sought the autonomy of towns, but one should not overestimate the anonymity available in these places. Pre-Revolutionary Philadelphia had 13,000 residents – twice as many as Richmond in 1800 – but it retained an intimate enough ambiance for a "prominent Philadelphian" to claim to know "every person white and black, men, women and children by name." Quoted in Gary Nash, *The Urban Crucible: Social Change, Political Consciousness, and the Origins of the American Revolution* (Cambridge, Mass., 1979), 4–5.

itants. Its designation as state capital certainly spurred this growth, but Virginia's government remained small, so the direct effects of the arrival of the executive branch mattered less than the indirect effects. In 1782 the households of government members accounted for only sixty people in the first city census; of these persons nearly two of every three (39 people) were Black and enslaved. People whose Williamsburg businesses had catered to government – men like innkeeper Serafino Formicola and printer William Prentis – also moved upriver to Richmond. The annual meeting of the General Assembly brought a seasonal flood of Black and White temporary residents.

Others with less obvious connections to the government moved to town once it became the state capital. In 1782 more than two out of every five Richmond households had been established less than two years. Working people, not government officials, dominated the new town demographically. They included people like Elijah Bowles, his young wife Mary, and their infant son Claiborne, all of whom moved to Richmond in 1781. Bowles, a wagoner, may have hoped to cash in on the wartime demand for transporting military supplies, or he may have hoped for work transporting goods to and from the town's warehouses. Others, like carpenter John Hawkins, who brought fifteen enslaved people as well as his White wife and daughter to Richmond, probably sought steady and reliable work building houses and public buildings in the growing town.

Urban growth did not slow down after the initial spurt fueled by the arrival of the state government. Just two years after the 1782 census, the town had over 1,300 residents. Like other contemporary American towns, Richmond continued to be a very unsettled place: of 123 identifiable household heads listed in 1782, only 64 continued to head households two years later. A town whose population had grown by 30 percent had simultaneously lost almost half of its heads of households. Richmond was also a slave town: Blacks (92% of whom were enslaved) comprised half of the population in 1784. In addition 60 percent of the population was male.[27]

Richmond during the 1780s had three distinct neighborhoods (see Map 5). The heart of the city lay in its oldest district, a small area east of Capitol Square and west of Shockoe Creek. Both Byrd's warehouses and the two Shockoe warehouses had been built in this district, so I have labeled it the Warehouse Area. This land had been settled before William Byrd II commissioned a plan for the town, so it did not consist of the neatly laid out

[27] 1782 census, Richmond Common Hall Council Minute Book, 295–311 (LiVa). The 1784 census is also in the Common Hall Council Minute Book, but I have used a computer printout kindly given to me by Michael Lee Nicholls.

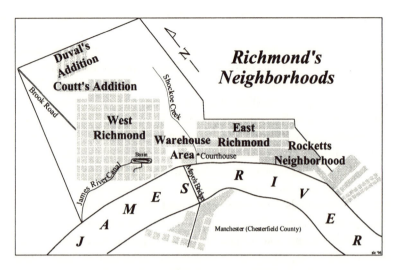

Map 5. The neighborhoods of Richmond before the extension of the James River canal into town. DuVal's Addition and Coutt's Addition were later extensions of the town.

quarter-acre lots characteristic of the rest of Richmond. Downriver (and east-southeast) from the Warehouse Area was East Richmond, the area Byrd had projected as a town. Upriver (and west-northwest) was the newest and least settled neighborhood – West Richmond – incorporated into Richmond when it became the state capital.

The three neighborhoods differed demographically (see Appendix). In 1784 the long-settled Warehouse Area accommodated 50 households and almost 390 people on its 70 to 75 irregular lots. Residents subdivided those lots that were relatively safe from spring flooding, paying "a very enormous price" for "Small quantit[ies] of land," because of the commercial value of property close to the warehouses. As the eighteenth century progressed, residents continued to subdivide these valuable lots in order to fit as many people as possible into this commercial district.[28] This business district, then, was the most crowded and urban portion of the early town.

[28] Henrico County Legislative Petitions, Box A, LiVa ("enormous price"). Census-takers rarely recorded lot numbers of Warehouse Area residents, but the neighborhood's density is indicated by the fact that of the 19 households whose lot numbers were recorded, four composed of 22 enslaved blacks and 15 whites shared lot 336. By 1800 over 40 different listings of improved property on this lot are recorded in the land tax book. There were two plots of land listed as lot 336, but one bordered the river and probably flooded too easily to hold improvements.

The Warehouse Area was also characterized by greater extremes of wealth than were other neighborhoods. It contained few households centered on traditional conjugal families and an unusually high number of households headed by either members of the town elite or unskilled day laborers. The area had the lowest rate of slave ownership in the town (still, a quite high 64 percent of listed householders owned at least one slave), but it had a Black majority, and slaveholding households in the neighborhood included an average of over six slaves – easily the highest in the town. Enslaved residents of the area, unlike their masters, enjoyed a balanced sex ratio. During the day this commercial center was filled with Black and White visitors doing business in warehouses and stores, but it was demographically dominated by Blacks. Many merchants in the Warehouse Area, like their counterparts in other early American towns, probably owned estates outside of town where they lived much of the year with their families. As a result, the Warehouse Area probably had an even larger Black majority than early censuses indicate, and it probably served as the first social and cultural center of Black Richmond.[29]

East Richmond was the next region of the town to be settled and was the area that William Byrd II had laid out in town lots when he first envisioned a city at the falls of the James River.[30] When Richmond became Henrico County's seat, the courthouse, jail, and market were built in the east, as were taverns that catered to the courthouse trade. Church Hill (sometimes called Richmond Hill), the site of St. John's Church (and thus of Patrick Henry's "Liberty or Death" speech), dominated East Richmond and provided an elevated site for Richard Adams's home, but most residents of the area were less wealthy than Adams and lived down closer to the river. By 1784 the neighborhood had become home to small-scale craftsmen and merchants (Table 3, Appendix). Slaves lived in most (28 of 40) of the White working people's households, but fewer than half of those slaveholding households (11 of 28) included adult male slaves, and only two artisanal households in East Richmond included more than two adult male slaves. Free White workers predominated in the skilled labor force of East Richmond in 1784, and many

---

[29] Eric Foner, *Tom Paine and Revolutionary America* (New York, 1976), 23 (similar situation in Philadelphia); figures from 1784 census. Fewer than 40 percent of households included a married White couple; elites headed twenty-six of fifty households; skilled and semiskilled laborers headed only nine. Of fifteen households listed as "others" in Table 3 (Appendix), almost half were headed by slaves who hired their time and lived separately from their masters, or by free Blacks. Three White women without listed occupations headed households. Two householders were listed as laborers.

[30] Reps, *Tidewater Towns*, 266.

lived in households centered on married White couples. The neighborhood linked the Warehouse Area to the wharves and to the other warehouses that had developed just south of the town limits (and downriver from the falls) in Rockett's Neighborhood.

West Richmond, the town's largest and newest neighborhood, was annexed when Richmond became the capital, and it was here that the state acquired land for the capitol building and the governor's mansion. Like East Richmond, the newer neighborhood was dominated by a hill – Shockoe Hill – on which wealthy settlers like Jacquelin Ambler and John Marshall built fine houses. Much more than the rest of town, however, in 1784 West Richmond remained an uncleared, wooded expanse. Its 29 households were scattered among more than 380 quarter-acre lots. West Richmond was also relatively prosperous and stable: households were large – they averaged more than ten members, almost five of whom were enslaved – and over two-thirds of its households centered on conjugal families.[31] The artisans who dominated the area's free population were more prosperous than their eastern neighbors: sixteen of the twenty laboring households included slaves, and ten of those included adult male slaves, many of whom presumably possessed the same skills as their masters.[32] West Richmond in 1784 was the town's least urban neighborhood and the neighborhood whose demography suggests the greatest stability and highest rate of family formation for White settlers and perhaps the least for slaves.

During the three decades following 1784, Richmond continued to grow. Its population reached 3,700 people by 1790, 5,700 by 1800, and almost 10,000 by 1810.[33] As the population multiplied, Richmond developed into an increasingly important marketing center and the biggest manufacturing

---

[31] Reps, *Tidewater Towns*, 269–71. Western Richmond's average household included 4.7 slaves; its average slaveholding household included 5.7 slaves. The neighborhood included 28 White women and 72 White children (2.6 White children per White woman) compared with 1 White child per White woman in eastern Richmond and 1.5 White children per (much rarer) White woman in the Warehouse Area.

[32] For example, Dabney Minor, a joiner, headed a household of fourteen adults, including three White women, two White apprentices, and eight adult male slaves. Presumably he led a substantial eleven-man gang to construction sites in the growing town. Only 35 percent of adult slaves owned by artisans in western Richmond were women, suggesting that the anomalous sexual imbalance among western Richmond slaves reflected the tendency of prosperous artisans to acquire artisanal slaves in order to enhance productivity.

[33] Figures from decennial federal censuses. The raw returns from 1790 and 1800 (for Virginia) have been lost, so I cannot use them for household reconstruction. Returns for 1810 have survived and allow limited household reconstruction.

center in Virginia. As a result, the heavily commercial district of Richmond
expanded beyond the confines of the Warehouse Area, and the entire urban
riverfront developed stores, landings, and patterns of social relations that
offered Black Virginians unusual levels of autonomy. The lines dividing
the town shifted from east-west to a more amorphous line separating those
who lived on the hills looking down on Richmond from those who lived
nearer to the buying, selling, and manufacturing that took place along the
river.[34]

The James River Canal was the most important factor fueling this change
in Richmond neighborhoods. In 1784 the General Assembly fulfilled Richard
Adams's early hopes by chartering the James River Navigation Company (soon
to become the James River Canal Company) to build a canal around the falls
of the James River. By allowing boatmen to bypass the rocks and falls above
the town, this canal greatly eased the passage of the twenty-yard-long batteaus
that carried tobacco and coal to market. By 1795 the canal had been dug to
the outskirts of the city, and in 1800 the company channeled water into the
canal basin, a three-acre rectangular reservoir halfway between Capitol Square
and the river. Boats used the basin to unload goods before returning up the
canal. During the nineteenth century, the company extended the canal westward, but the basin remained the eastern endpoint as long as the canal remained
in operation.[35]

Building canals in preindustrial America required an enormous amount
of labor. In 1787 the James River Canal Company paid personal property
taxes in Henrico County alone on one free Black and 116 slave tithables. The
company hired 129 slaves for that year, spending roughly $60 per slave. Because
many of the Whites whose slaves the company hired were Richmonders,
building the canal injected capital into the town's economy. More important
for social relations within the town, by the 1790s workers were digging the
basin, and many of the laborers involved in this project lived and worked in
West Richmond.[36] Neither company nor local records reveal much about the
lives of these canallers, but presumably they lived in shanties, drank to excess,
and forged a competitive, masculine world of work and (limited) leisure like

---

[34] For a similar process in a city of about the same size at a slightly later period, see Paul
E. Johnson, *A Shopkeeper's Millennium: Society and Revivals in Rochester, New York, 1815–
1837* (New York, 1978), ch. 2.

[35] Samuel Mordecai, *Richmond in By-Gone Days, Being Reminiscences of an Old Citizen*
(Richmond, 1856), 233–5; Edward C. Carter II, ed., *The Virginia Journals of Benjamin
Henry Latrobe, 1795–1798* (New Haven, 1977), v. II, pp. 516–17.

[36] In 1800 the company paid city taxes on thirty-three slaves, more than twice as many as
any other single taxpayer that year. James River Company Ledger (VHS); 1800 Richmond
City Personal Property Tax Book (LiVa).

navvies in nineteenth-century North America.[37] During the digging of the basin, their "rough culture" may have dominated West Richmond, but the basin's long-term influence on the neighborhood was even greater.

Because goods destined for the Atlantic market had to be brought into the basin and unloaded before being carried to docks farther downstream in Richmond, businesses sprouted on the shores of the basin. Draymen and carters found steady employment carrying goods down to Rocketts or the Warehouse Area, and storekeepers set up shop along the basin to cater to western planters whose goods were transported on the canal. This immediately affected settlement patterns. In 1784 no one had improved a single lot surrounding what would become the canal basin, but by 1800 fifteen improvements surrounded the basin and the traces connecting it to the canal. In 1809 Richmonders listed twenty-six improved parcels on these lots, and the declared value of the land and improvements had more than doubled since 1800.[38]

The canal was not alone in spurring development in West Richmond between 1784 and 1800. The state initiated several large-scale construction projects, including the capitol building, an armory, and the state penitentiary. During those same years, David Ross, Thomas Rutherfoord, and Joseph Gallego all had large merchant mills built to grind the wheat and corn that farmers from Virginia's western counties sent into Richmond. Slaves did much of the heavy labor on all these projects – at least one "valuable negroe man slave" lost his life building the state armory when "an immense mass of . . . earth" crushed him[39] – bringing new workers into the neighborhood. These diverse but related factors caused West Richmond to fill up and become more urban during the final two decades of the eighteenth century.

The rest of the town grew at the same time, but the process of change experienced in East Richmond and the Warehouse Area is better understood as an elaboration on previous patterns of settlement rather than the kind of transformation experienced in West Richmond. In 1789 Henrico County residents petitioned the legislature to enlarge the warehouse at Rocketts, an indication that the economic development experienced in West Richmond also

[37] Peter Way, "Evil Humors and Ardent Spirits: The Rough Culture of Canal Construction Laborers," *Journal of American History* 74 (1993): 1397–1428; Way, *Common Labour: Workers and the Digging of North American Canals, 1780–1860* (Cambridge, England, 1993), ch. 1.

[38] William Austin claimed his property on the basin was "adjacent to where all the produce of the upper country is landed" (*Virginia Argus*, February 9, 1805); Richmond City Land Tax Books for 1784, 1800, 1809, LiVa.

[39] Moses Bates Petition, December 14, 1799, Richmond City Legislative Petitions, Box 5, LiVa. Bates sought (but was denied) restitution for the dead man.

extended downriver.[40] This growth created a strip of commercially developed property that stretched unevenly along the riverfront from Rutherfoord's mill and the armory, on the upriver edge of town, down to Rocketts. Wealthy Richmonders who owned the mills and warehouses along the river increasingly withdrew their families from the complications of life along the waterfront. Thomas Rutherfoord, for example, moved into the Warehouse Area when he immigrated to Richmond in 1784, but a decade later he left the "lower part of the city," where his family had experienced a "free and easy intercourse with . . . neighbors," to build a house on a hill on the outskirts of the city. His desire to escape led him to contemplate building his house "in the center of Franklin Street" to "prevent the extension of the city." Rutherfoord did not lose interest in the commercial area of Richmond; he retained his mercantile house in the Warehouse Area and his mill along the river. Similarly, merchant James Brown owned several pieces of commercial property in the Warehouse Area, but he and his family probably lived slightly removed from it on his improved lot atop Shockoe Hill near the Capitol Square. Wealthy Richmonders increasingly withdrew their families from the riverfront and settled on the hills immediately surrounding the growing town.[41] It was down along the James River and the canal that residents and visitors developed new urban norms to govern interaction between people of different status and racial background.

Workers' culture in a growing town

Evidence that working people in Richmond were developing an alternative culture that left elites uneasy about urban social relations had already begun to surface in the 1780s. Grand juries, which met quarterly, began to cite numerous free Blacks and Whites for interacting with slaves in ways prohibited by law, and wealthy Richmonders began to grow uneasy in response to temporary alliances that developed among poor whites, free Blacks, and slaves. All this occurred in the commercial areas that were increasingly transformed by the town's economic development. Richmond's elite did not find these trends troubling enough to institute a full-scale crackdown on the cultural practices that emerged among working Richmonders in the tippling

[40] Henrico County Legislative Petitions, Nov. 12, 1789, Box A.
[41] Thomas Rutherfoord Memoirs (typescript), 52–5, VHS. Policies #67, 68, 69 (Brown), and 74, 523 (Rutherfoord) of the Mutual Assurance Company of Virginia, LiVa. Also see the 1800 Richmond City Land Tax Books. This separation, while real, should not be overstated. Richmond remained a walking city, so these "removed" sites remained in the heart of the town by twentieth-century standards.

shops and disorderly houses that lined the river – the Hustings Court made only sporadic and halfhearted efforts to suppress these activities. The occasional efforts to enforce "order" revealed elites' fears that working people in Richmond were evading their control; more important, Black and White Virginians who lived and worked near the river began to carve out relatively autonomous physical and cultural spaces. They could not use those spaces to escape those who exercised formal power in Virginia, but they could work within those spaces to alter some of the rules that had traditionally governed the state's race relations.

As early as 1782, thirty-three residents of Henrico County, including at least seven who owned property in or near the Warehouse Area in Richmond, petitioned the state legislature to take action against the many persons who allowed their slaves to hire themselves out. They complained that such slaves led "Idle and disorderly" lives, and stole frequently "in order to pay their Masters their . . . hire." This early petition underscores connections between Richmond and the surrounding farms and plantations. Most of the petitioners lived outside the city, but they asserted that slaves who "frequently" stole in the "Neighbourhood[s] in which they reside[d]," also "encourage[d] the Neighbouring Slaves to steal from their Masters." Rather than working in the fields, as the petitioners thought bondpeople should, self-hired slaves could pursue their own interests by becoming "receivers and Traders of . . . Goods" and spreading "discontent to other Slaves . . . [who were] not allow'd such Indulgencies."[42] That enslaved Virginians began to establish so much autonomy while Richmond remained a small town of 1,000 people foreshadowed the more complicated relations among people and between the city and countryside that would evolve as Richmond grew into a more significant town.

Elite Richmonders registered their discomfort regarding working people's "unauthorized" activities with increasing frequency as the eighteenth century drew to a close. By 1787 the reputedly vagrant "negroes and Mulattoes" who traded and socialized in Richmond so unsettled authorities that they ordered town constables to patrol on Sundays and detain Blacks who neither "belong[ed] to . . . [a] Citizen" of the city nor provided "a good account of their business."[43] Such patrols, if and when they occurred, apparently did little to discourage slaves from taking advantage of the active social life and nascent commercial possibilities that Richmond offered. People of African

---

[42] Henrico County Legislative Petitions, June 8, 1782, Box A. The city and county were administratively separate, but Richmonders signed the petition addressed from citizens of Henrico County. Perhaps some simultaneously maintained plantations in the county.

[43] Common Hall Council Minute Books, January 24, 1787.

descent continued to visit the disorderly house kept by Aggy Meade, a free Black woman and the one kept by George, a slave who "live[d] as a free person" with the consent of James Currie, his master. Both disorderly houses were probably in the Warehouse Area, and Aggy Meade remained in business at least through 1795.[44] Meade and George faced increasing competition as the decade progressed. "Negro Slaves and white persons" patronized Thomas Poindexter's disorderly house in the Warehouse Area at "unreasonable hours of the night." At the same time, "George Lucas or Locust a free blackman" kept a "very disorderly House" on the outskirts of the neighborhood in which people enjoyed "fighting drinking, and making improper noises at all hours . . . of the night." No doubt some of the fights arose over the illegal gambling that Lucas permitted; others may have been fueled by the "Spiritous Liquors such as Rum and Whiskey" that he sold "without License." Visiting slaves did not have to go to these establishments to find social activities in Richmond: "negro dances where people of all colours . . . assembled" in the streets offered chances for meetings and relaxation for the enslaved, free Black, and White working people who did most of the physical labor in Richmond but lacked the money or inclination to patronize disorderly houses.[45]

As the eighteenth century drew to a close, the "disorderly" region of Richmond grew, as reflected in the increasing frequency with which White and Free black Richmonders who lived outside the Warehouse Area were cited by the grand jury for "illicit" commerce. In 1798 Lewis Degogue, a White man, ran into trouble for "entertaining negro Slaves and white persons at the same time" in his East Richmond ordinary just across Shockoe Creek from the Warehouse Area. Jacob Abrahams and Hannah Burgess both lived on the other edge of East Richmond, near Rockett's, and they received citations for keeping disorderly houses and entertaining Blacks at night in 1796. A near neighbor, the free mulatto man Larken Key, ran into trouble for selling liquor in his disorderly house in 1800 and 1801. Several other Richmonders ran similar businesses in East Richmond and Rocketts.[46] Such activity also spread

---

[44] Richmond Hustings Court Order Book (hereafter RHCOB) #2, 689 (Meade and Currie). Currie owned four lots in the Warehouse Area in 1800, and Meade was listed as his tenant on one of them (1800 Richmond City Land Tax Book 2). Meade was presented twice more (RHCOB #3, 105, 295–6).

[45] RHCOB #4, 119 (Poindexter who was White); 371–2 (Lucas); RHCOB #3, 315–16 ("negro dances"). Poindexter was reported to the grand jury by a resident of the Warehouse Area (William Austin), and Lucas lived on a lot #357 in the Warehouse Area.

[46] RHCOB #4, 152–3 (Degogue); RHCOB #3, 493 (Abrahams, who was White, and Burgess); RHCOB #4, 454, 630 (Larkey and Larken Key, probably the same man). See RHCOB #5, 229; RHCOB #6, 58, 203, 212–13, 367–8 for similar presentments involving residents of either East Richmond or Rocketts.

to West Richmond with the arrival of the canal. In 1799 a grand jury reported that "numerous collections of negroes and other persons" gathered "(almost) every Sunday in the Street near . . . Houses" that sold "Spirits." The jurors singled out James Boulton's house "on the margin of the Canal" as a place where Blacks enjoyed "Gaming, fighting and other disorderly Conduct." These jurors found the resulting disorder troubling enough to merit the posting of a constable "near the Canal . . . particularly on Sundays and Hollidays" – slaves' days off. Boulton, a White man, was not alone in operating a business that catered to the slaves and free Blacks who entered the city on the canal. In fact, by 1806 one witness at a trial claimed that "all the shops in Richmond" served liquor to Blacks.[47]

One should not, however, envision the waterfront of early Richmond as a late-eighteenth-century Storyville, with well-established bars, gambling houses, and brothels. Grand jury presentments provide snapshots of a constantly changing scene and thus risk creating the impression of a static, or settled, neighborhood. Selling liquor to slaves or buying goods from them without a master's written permission was illegal. Many of the free Blacks and Whites who engaged in these activities lacked the financial resources to own their houses, so they moved from rented houses in one neighborhood to rented houses in others, in part perhaps to escape town authorities' occasional crackdowns. "Abra Taborn a free mulatto man" kept a "Faro Table" and sold "spiritous liquors" near Rocketts in 1805 and 1806, but by 1808 he had moved his operation across town to the house he then occupied on Shockoe Hill on the border between the Warehouse Area and West Richmond.[48] Similarly, Winney Gabriel (or Gabe), a free Black woman, ran a Warehouse Area disorderly house owned by Daniel Couch in 1803, but she had moved to Archelaus Hughes's house on the basin of the canal" by 1806.[49]

A Storyville analogy would also create a false impression of cultural separation parallel to that of physical distance – an impression that a world of "vice" was distinct from the "regular" world of Richmond residents. Such is the impression created by the elite representations of the "illicit" activity among Blacks that appear in court records. There is little evidence that Black or White working Richmonders perceived the same dichotomy. Many Black Richmonders attended the town's Baptist church, developed stable family

---

[47] RHCOB #4, 273 (Boulton); RHCOB #5, 43; RHCOB #7, 44–5 for other examples. RSP, Box 54, May 1810 Bundle, *Hurt v. Tyree* ("all shops").
[48] RHCOB #6, 203, 212–13; RHCOB #8, 127. Faro (sometimes "Pharo") Bank was a popular card game among Richmond gamblers.
[49] RHCOB #5, 307; RHCOB #7, 44–5.

relationships, acquired trades, and sought freedom. There is no evidence, however, that this "good" side of Richmond life – good in the eyes of the elite that controlled the grand jury and perhaps of some historians – was separated from the underside of Black life in the town. Enslaved and free Black Richmonders had good reason, after all, to attend to the most hypocritical aspects of elite condemnations of gambling, drinking, and extramarital sex.[50] One might reasonably guess that because almost all Blacks, whether free or slave, were forced to work in occupations that served White Richmonders' needs, they rejected efforts to stigmatize some of those occupations as immoral. Black townspeople left few indications, at any rate, that they accepted the court's negative characterization of keepers of disorderly and tippling houses.[51]

Richmond grand jurors' concerns suggest in fact their fear that Blacks were blind to the supposed dangers of vice. Jurors did not complain that one sector of the growing town was becoming a den of degeneracy. They warned instead that much of the town was falling prey to a level of chaos that threatened the elite's sense of proper social relations. On four occasions during the 1790s, grand juries that were dissatisfied with the apparently ineffectual process of presenting individuals for violating city ordinances, made general complaints to the courts, constables, and Common Hall about undesirable activity taking place in the town. Many "vagrants, beggars, free negroes and runaway slaves" who "daily infest[ed] the streets" robbed inhabitants, caused "the increasing corruption of morals," and created the need for "a well regulated police."[52] Two years later, jurors recommended an ordinance regulating "the great number of tipling Shops" in order to help "prevent the corruption of our Servants" and end the frequent robberies in the city. Later

---

[50] "Autobiography of George Tucker," *Bermuda Historical Quarterly* 28 (1961): 107–19 (elite gambling); William J. Rorabaugh, *The Alcoholic Republic: An American Tradition* (New York, 1979); among the many works that deal with White male sexual exploitation of enslaved women, see Deborah Gray White, *Ar'n't I a Woman: Female Slaves in the Plantation South* (New York, 1985) and bell hooks, *Ain't I a Woman: Black Women and Feminism* (Boston, 1981), ch. 1.

[51] The only indication I found was Joseph Dailey's 1801 petition to the Richmond court to have his grandson removed from the custody of "William Cowper a Blackman" who was teaching the boy only horse racing and gambling. Dailey wanted his grandson apprenticed to "some Good Mechanic." RSP Box 26, January–February 1801 Bundle, Dailey Petition. The court bound the boy to "Alexander Mc[Kim] (House Carpenter)," a White man (RHCOB #4, 526).

[52] RHCOB #3, 315–16 (1795). Perhaps better-off free Blacks tried to inculcate "respectability" among Black working people as did some in Philadelphia; Julie Winch, *Philadelphia's Black Elite: Activism, Accommodation, and the Struggle for Autonomy, 1787–1848* (Philadelphia, 1988), 20–25; see my discussion of Christopher McPherson in Chapter 6 of this book.

that same year a jury instructed the constables to be vigilant to stop the many "negroes . . . allowed to go at large" from behaving in a "riotous manner . . . on the Sabbath day." In 1799 they asked the constables to "suppress all collections of disorderly people assembled for . . . dancing at night," a practice that had "become very common throughout the City."[53] In short, they expressed a variation on the fear, quite common among elites in rapidly urbanizing areas throughout the early modern Western world, that common people were getting out of control.[54]

If, however, elites throughout much of the West reacted anxiously to popular urban culture, the particular form the fear took in a locality says much about that place. Richmond elites focused on two particular problems that reflected the nature of urbanization in slave societies. First, masters in and around Richmond expressed fear that developing urban norms would corrupt their slaves. Urban masters, represented by the grand jurors, feared that the opportunities available to drink, gamble, dance, and participate in the market would increase enslaved workers' ability to resist their masters. Slaveowners from the surrounding countryside expressed a corollary concern that urban social relations failed to respect the town's boundaries and that the dangerous corruption of urban life was seeping into the countryside. In part, this fear was tied to the well-known tendency of runaway slaves to head for Virginia's towns to pass as free people.[55] But more was involved. The newspaper essayist PATERNUS was not, in 1807, simply troubled by runaways or the general disorder in the city. He maintained that there were at least 1,000 Black men regularly employed either in bringing produce to the city on the canal or in transporting goods from the basin to Rocketts on drays. PATERNUS maintained that at least every other boat that entered the city carried stolen articles and that every inhabitant of Richmond knew of many retail shops whose entire trade was with draymen and boatmen. PATERNUS perceived danger in slaves being "the common carriers of the lower country" who controlled horses, drays, and boats, and he sought legislative action to sever the connections between urban and rural slaves, for those connections greatly increased slaves' "chances to commit depredations and engage in conspiracies."[56]

---

[53] RHCOB #3, 581 (1797, "robberies"); RHCOB #4, 16 (1797; "Sabbath"), 273 (1799; "City").

[54] For examples, see Nash, *Urban Crucible*; Foner, *Tom Paine*, ch. 2; Philip D. Morgan, "Black Life in Eighteenth-Century Charleston," *Perspectives in American History*, New Ser., 1 (1984): 187–232; Shane White, *Somewhat More Independent: The End of Slavery in New York City, 1770–1810* (Athens, Ga.,1991), chs. 6, 7; Shane White, "'It Was a Proud Day': African Americans, Festivals, and Parades in the North, 1741–1834" *Journal of American History* 81 (1994): 13–50.

[55] Mullin, *Flight and Rebellion*, ch. 3.   [56] *Virginia Argus*, April 24, 1807.

Rural masters especially decried the degree to which the canal extended the corruption of urban slavery into the countryside. They complained that boatmen committed "almost innumerable" thefts in order to sell to their urban fences and also "indus[ed] the others to commit depredations" throughout the surrounding countryside. A Goochland County planter claimed that robberies stimulated by the market in Richmond and the ready access to it provided by the canal cost area planters around "1000 barrels of corn and 2–3000 bushels of wheat plus fowls, livestock" and other things.[57] Perhaps he and PATERNUS both exaggerated, but their fear that urbanization increased Richmond-area Blacks' sphere for autonomous activity was firmly rooted in reality. The frequent interchanges between urban and rural slaves during the planning of Gabriel's Conspiracy underscores the opportunities that access to Richmond opened for slaves living outside the town.

For Richmond did create new opportunities for Black Virginians to gain access to markets, to build communication networks, and to work together toward common ends. Enslaved workers hired into the city, whether for large projects like digging the canal or to work for small artisans, forged relationships within the town. Especially if those hired slaves lived along the James River, Black boatmen could help keep distant acquaintances in contact after hired workers returned to their rural homes. In addition, the enhanced chances to buy and sell goods offered enslaved Virginians limited but real opportunities to engage in a range of social and economic activity beyond the purview of their masters. Within these cultural spaces enslaved Virginians could struggle to build satisfactory private lives, and as Gabriel's Conspiracy illustrates, they could occasionally organize to seek collective goals. This exhilarating increase in Black autonomy troubled many Whites.

If the first major fear of elite Virginians was that urban slaves were gaining too much autonomy, their second fear was, ironically enough, that town slaves were not segregated enough. Grand jurors did not just complain that slaves held dances but that "persons of all colours . . . too often" attended them. The city was not only "infested" by "runaway slaves" but by "vagrants, beggars, [and] free negroes." Disorderly houses that allowed Blacks to behave "in a riotous manner" were bad enough, but others permitted "disorderly Company of all complexions" to come together "fiddling, dancing, cursing, swearing, quarrelling and fighting both night and day." And on a Saturday night in 1796, Archelaus Hughes, a White landlord of several disorderly houses

---

[57] *Virginia Argus*, Dec. 29, 1809, Jan. 19, 1810. Alex Lichtenstein, "'That disposition to theft, with which they have been branded': moral economy, slave management, and the law" *Journal of Social History* 21 (1988): 413–40.

run by free Black women, displayed "Riotous and disorderly" behavior in concert with "divers other persons unknown" in rescuing "several Negroes which the . . . patrol h[a]d taken into Custody."[58] The "corruption" represented by this interracial cooperation also leached into the countryside, in part because so many rural slaves traveled to the city while transporting produce or for recreation on the weekends, and in part because "white [men] who follow[ed] boating for a business" were "generally . . . worse," in the eyes of the elite, than slave boatmen. No doubt these White sailors participated in the underground biracial world of the Richmond waterfront and carried that experience back to the countryside. By 1810 the social relations of the town began to penetrate the countryside enough that the Henrico County grand jury presented Nathaniel Selden for allowing his "negro woman . . . Aggy to keep a riotous and disorderly house on his plantation."[59] Slaves in and around Richmond grew increasingly (and uncomfortably for their masters) autonomous, and they and the nonelite Whites with whom they worked, played, fought, and bargained developed more flexible norms to govern race relations than those that prevailed in rural Virginia.

Much of the evidence of this urban world has survived in court records and thus centers on illegal activity, but the opportunities for relative economic advancement and cultural autonomy were not limited to slaves and free Blacks operating beyond the bounds of legal authority. Richmond's need for labor created economic niches for many Black Virginians, especially those with artisanal skills.[60] In addition, evangelical Christianity, especially in the guise of the Baptist Church, provided a legal setting where race relations mirrored the contradictory dialectic of autonomy and integration that characterized the underworld of Richmond.[61] By the end of the eighteenth century, the Baptist Church had become the most popular of the new-light

---

[58] RHCOB #3, 315–16 ("colours" and "vagrants"), 52 ("suffer[ed]"); RHCOB #6, 212–13 ("complexions"); RSP, Box 20, Sept., Oct., Dec. 1796 Bundle, *Commonwealth v. Hughes.*

[59] *Virginia Argus*, Dec. 29, 1809 (sailors); Henrico County Court Order Book (hereafter HCCOB) #15, 224 (Aggy), LiVa.

[60] James Sidbury, "Slave Artisans in Richmond, Virginia, 1780–1810," in Howard B. Rock, Paul A. Gilje, and Robert Asher, eds. *American Artisans: Crafting Social Identity, 1750–1850* (Baltimore, 1995), 48–62; and Chapter 6 of this book.

[61] Mechal Sobel, *The World They Made Together: Black and White Values in Eighteenth-Century Virginia* (Princeton, 1987), chs. 14,15; Sylvia R. Frey, *Water From the Rock: Black Resistance in a Revolutionary Age* (Princeton, 1991), chs. 7–9; Sylvia R. Frey, "Shaking the Dry Bones: The Dialectic of Conversion," in Ted Ownby, ed., *Black and White Cultural Interaction in the Antebellum South* (Jackson, Miss., 1993), 23–44; Luther P. Jackson, "Religious Development of the Negro in Virginia From 1760–1860," *Journal of Negro History* 16 (1931): esp. 170–203; Chapter 1 of this book.

churches among Richmond-area Blacks. Richard Courtney, a White man, took charge of the First Baptist Church of Richmond in 1788. While Courtney's congregation certainly included Whites, elite Richmonders probably shared a wealthy visitor's belief that the church consisted of a "large congregation of Negroes" who gathered each Sunday in a "miserable meeting house."[62] Evangelical churches were the most racially egalitarian institutions in post-Revolutionary Virginia.

During the 1790s, however, the Baptist Church became more established within Virginia and began to move away from its most radically egalitarian doctrines – including its flirtation with open antislavery doctrine. As a result, Black Baptists began to pull away and develop a more autonomous position within the church. This trend included substantial movement toward institutional autonomy – Black preachers founded all-Black or predominantly Black congregations in Williamsburg, Norfolk, Petersburg, and several counties.[63] The divisions between Whites and Blacks in integrated churches also widened during this period. The increasingly hierarchical nature of the church and the presumption that Black and White religious experiences may not have been the same were illustrated in 1802 when the Dover Baptist Association, which included the churches of Henrico County and Richmond, advised that "none but free male members" could "properly exercise authority" in true Christian churches. The association suggested, however, that other members ought to play a role in "Church discipline." Women, slaves, and children should retain the right to "admonish, reprove or rebuke" wayward members; furthermore, a disciplinary case involving a "servant" (meaning a slave) should be "confided to the hands of the most considerable and experienced" slaves in the church.[64] Implicitly, the association recognized the growing gulf separating the meaning of religious experience for church members of different social and legal status.

---

[62] Robert B. Semple, *A History of the Rise and Progress of the Baptists in Virginia* (Richmond, 1810), 111; *The Virginia Journals of Benjamin Henry Latrobe*, 191–2 (quotations). The church had White members, but elites perceived it to be a Black institution.

[63] Jackson, "Religious Development of the Negro," 186–90; Mechal Sobel, *Trabelin' On: The Slave Journey to an Afro-Baptist Faith* (Westport, Conn., 1979), 291–311.

[64] Dover Association Circular Letter, 1802, printed in J. D. McGill, *Sketches of History of the Baptist Churches Within the Limits of the Rappahannock Association in Virginia* (Richmond, 1850), Virginia Baptist Historical Society (hereafter VBHS), Richmond. In June 1809 the Antioch, or Boar Swamp, Baptist Meeting House (in Henrico) appointed "Bro. Frank belonging to Sister Trueman and Bro. Tom Easter belonging to Daniel Hilton" to "have the oversight of . . . Black members" and to "admonish" them should they "walk disorderly." Antioch or Boar Swamp, Baptist Meeting Minute Book, 1787–1828, VBHS.

Baptist churches, not unlike boats and shops, also became important nodal points in local communication networks connecting rural and urban Virginians. Richard Courtney, for example, while pastor of the Richmond church, had regularly traveled into Henrico County around 1798 to revive the moribund Hungary Meeting House. No doubt some Black members of the Hungary church traveled to town to worship at Courtney's church while their congregation was in the process of being revived. It may not be coincidental that the Hungary church served as a central meeting point when Gabriel built a conspiracy among urban and rural slaves in 1800.[65] The Hungary church also had a biracial congregation, but, as Gabriel showed in 1800, Black members could easily separate themselves from their White brethren to pursue their own goals.

Urban growth combined with the cultural changes associated with new-light Christianity transformed Richmond and the rural areas surrounding it. Black Baptists, while they usually remained within integrated churches, drew away from their White co-confessioners. Towndwellers witnessed the development of a waterfront neighborhood visited daily by Black and White strangers. Elite Richmonders profited enormously from the business transacted in that area, but they also distrusted the apparent autonomy that Black and poorer White people enjoyed there. While the Richmond waterfront did not spawn a persistent biracial alliance against the town's elite, it became home to a world that was exhilaratingly autonomous for Black and White working people and uncomfortably – occasionally even dangerously – disordered from the perspective of the elite.

Subversive possibilities in early Richmond

Perhaps the clearest way to represent the complicated and ambiguous possibilities that could develop in this world is to explore the shadowy activities of two people who lived within it. Angela (sometimes Angelica) Barnett was a freeborn Black woman who first appeared in the Richmond-area records during the early 1790s, and she lived in the area until her death in 1810.[66] During the 1790s, she became sexually involved with a White man named Jacob Valentine, who had served as a captain in the Revolutionary War. Valentine speculated in Warehouse Area land in the 1780s, and from 1812 to

---

[65] Semple, 110–11. Semple refers to the "Hungry" Meeting House, but I have changed the spelling to be consistent with other sources. See also Chapter 2 of this book, for conspirators meeting there.

[66] HCCOB #4, 428. HCCOB #15, 279 (Barnett's will recorded in 1810).

1815 he served as high constable of the city of Richmond.[67] During the 1790s, these two challenged town authorities and the rules governing "proper" behavior in ways that illustrate the shadowy potential for subversion in Richmond's developing urban culture.

Barnett participated actively in the contentious world of the early city. In 1791 she and two men were hauled before the county court for an unspecified breach of the peace. Unable to find anyone willing to sign a bond guaranteeing her good behavior, she spent time in jail. Nineteen months later she returned to jail on a more serious charge. Two White men, Peter Franklin and Jesse Carpenter, had suspected that Barnett and William Anthony were offering runaway slaves sanctuary in their house. Free blacks in and near Virginia's towns often offered temporary refuge to escaping slaves, and Franklin and Carpenter apprehended a small boy in Barnett's house who matched the description of a slave for whom a reward had been offered in the *Virginia Gazette*. Encouraged by their initial success, the two slavecatchers returned "the following evening about eleven O'Clock at night to apprehend two other runaways." Neither Anthony nor Barnett was thrilled by the appearance of these late-night intruders, and when Franklin and Carpenter forced their way into the house, a dispute arose. Franklin threatened Barnett with a whip, and she defended herself by knocking him down with an adze, inflicting a wound that killed him. Angela Barnett was tried, convicted, and sentenced to hang for murder.[68]

About the first of November 1792, while Barnett was in jail awaiting execution, Jacob Valentine was arrested and jailed for a debt. Valentine remained in jail for three weeks, during which he found a way to spend time with Barnett, "over persuaded" her, and she "yeilded to" his "desires . . . in repeated acts of coition." Valentine returned to jail in February 1793, and he and Barnett resumed their sexual relationship. During one of those two stays he impregnated Barnett, and she petitioned the governor to postpone her execution to preserve "the Guiltless infant" from being "murdered by her execution."[69] The execution was temporarily stayed, and during the interim

---

[67] *Report of the State Librarian, Revolutionary Soldiers of Virginia* (Richmond, 1912), 407; RSP, Box 12, Nov. 1789 Bundle, *Lyle v. Valentine* (Warehouse Area); Edward P. Valentine Papers, v. 4, p. 2328, Valentine Museum Archives, Richmond.

[68] HCCOB #5, 277–8. This incident is recreated from Carpenter's deposition, the only testimony recorded by the court clerk. In 1810 a "Sally Anthony alias Barnet" was tried for a felony, and Angela Barnett registered a child named Sally Barnett as freeborn, so Angela Barnett and William Anthony were almost surely spouses (HCCOB #13, 299; HCCOB #15, 140).

[69] *CVSP*, v. 6, pp. 363–4 (see ch. 2, n. 3 for full citation).

a number of prominent Richmonders (including future Supreme Court Chief Justice John Marshall) who had been at, or heard about her trial petitioned the governor for her release. They argued that she should be pardoned because Peter Franklin had infringed upon "the great right of personal immunity" that she should have enjoyed in her "own home." She was pardoned and lived in Richmond for seventeen more years.[70] Her story illustrates the complicated personal antagonisms and alliances that could develop among Blacks and nonelite Whites as urbanization altered patterns of race relations in the town and the surrounding countryside.

It is her connection to Jacob Valentine, however, that leads to the most potentially "subversive" quality of these shadowy connections. In the texts produced by Angela Barnett's run-ins with the court system, Valentine appears as a debtor, seducer (more likely a savior), and a presumably absent father. During the 1790s, he had other encounters with town authorities, often involving unpaid debts and other disputes common in Richmond during the 1780s and 1790s.[71] On December 3, 1797, Valentine was charged with an offense that creates a radically different context within which his earlier involvement with Angela Barnett can be interpreted: on that day he posted bond to appear before the Hustings Court to answer for "committing and encouraging an Insurrection among the Slaves of the City of Richmond."[72] Town authorities lacked the evidence needed to convict him of this crime, so they did not try him before a jury. Instead, in a clear abuse of their offices and an open violation of the spirit of Virginia's constitutional guarantees of jury trials and protection of liberty, he was required to post a $10,000 bond for two years of good behavior. He failed to find four people willing to post $2,500 to secure his bond, as the magistrates knew he would, so he spent more than six months in the town jail.[73]

As is so often true with reported insurrectionary conspiracies, the surviving record of the Valentine conspiracy is anything but clear, and there is no way to determine what really happened. Rumors regarding Valentine's relationships with slaves and his attitude toward slavery began to circulate

[70] Executive Papers, (see ch. 2, n. 3 for full citation), Box 81 (petition); HCCOB #15, 279 (Barnett's will ordered recorded in 1810).

[71] For examples beyond those cited above, see RSP, Box 7, May 1787 Bundle, *Southall v. Valentine*; Box 8, July 1787, *Currie v. Valentine*; Box 12, 1789, *Valentine v. Lyle*; Box 16, Nov. 1793, *Oram v. Valentine*; HCCOB #5, 592.

[72] Unless otherwise noted, all the quotations relating to this incident are from papers found in RSP, Box 22, Dec. 1797 Bundle, *Commonwealth v. Valentine*; or Box 23, Apr., Jn., Jl. 1798 Bundle, *Commonwealth v. Valentine*.

[73] RHCOB #4, 67.

at least as early as October 1797. On October 30, he wrote Mayor James McClurg to deny the charge that he "was about to raise a Rebellion in America," but he showed little discretion in the language he used to dispel these rumors. He had "figured out . . . and pictured" in his mind "the horrid situation that America" would face in case of invasion. "Blacks," he said, "were a hardy race of People" who would fight valiantly to "defend this Country" if emancipated, but if they remained enslaved he "fear[ed] the consequences." Not surprisingly, his letter failed to reassure Richmond's leadership of his benign influence on the town's slaves, so authorities continued to keep an eye on him.

During the first week of December, an anonymous informer apparently warned Alderman William DuVal that Valentine was inciting rebellion.[74] DuVal responded by issuing a warrant to search Valentine's quarters, where authorities found a number of cryptic and ambiguous documents that strongly suggested the possibility of a conspiracy. Among Valentine's papers was a sheet of questions and answers; among the questions were: "Who was the cruel inventor of Slavery?" and "Will you Americans . . . continue . . . to suppose that a White Man shall . . . slash a poor Black Man?" Later in this dialogue, "Cudjo" spoke "boldly," declaring that "Your Bill of Wrights declares that all men are by nature born free." Another scrap of paper said, "I will let all your Blacks free and will you Speak to the Greatest Men of the nation." The same scrap also included scribblings about a gold mine in Botetourt County and iron mines in Chesterfield and Buckingham. And there was a self-proclaimed "foolish Memorandum" that declared:

If you want a Man of close attention and high invention take Valentine If you Want Men after this for [execution?] take Stockdell and Valentine – If you want a Man for Language – quickness and dispatch in Writing take William J. Vereker – If you want a man to Copy for fairness take John V. Kautzman.

Richmond authorities found this unsettling enough to stretch the state's laws in incarcerating Valentine, but it is impossible to say with certainty what Valentine was about or who was allied with him.

That need not be a problem in unraveling the importance of Valentine's conspiracy. It was, after all, the uncertainty about what went on along Richmond's waterfront that contributed to elite discomfort. Accepting that uncertainty and exploring the many (and sometimes conflicting) possibilities in

---

[74] In a Feb. 12, 1798 letter petitioning for release, Valentine complained that his "accusers did not confront" him. His response to the charges altered slightly over time. In February he defiantly denied wrongdoing; by June he suggested that he had atoned sufficiently for "unguarded expressions" made in a state of "Intoxication," and in July he "resign[ed]" himself to his "fate," while insisting "(I remain an American)."

Valentine's conspiracy provides a valuable, if quirky, angle on some of the
possibilities for radical activity in Richmond during the 1790s.

First, it may be true that Valentine was involved with others in some kind
of conspiracy. The sheet of paper with questions and answers includes two
references to "your Bill of Wrights," suggesting a writer with a relatively
informal education. When Valentine was in jail, however, he showed an impressively detailed knowledge of Virginia's Constitution, by calling "the attention
of the [Hustings] Court" to the "1st, 8th, 9th and 10th Sec[tion]s of the Bill
of Rights."[75] Surely, then, at least two different people wrote these texts. Or
perhaps not. Both times the "Bill of Wrights" was invoked, it was done in
"Cudjo's" name whereas when Valentine wrote using his own name, he referred
to the "Bill of Rights." Perhaps the misspelling reflected Valentine's condes-
cending conception of the way a Black man might spell. It is certainly striking that "Cudjo's" discussion of "Wrights" includes the assertion that "we
are a Haredy race of people," a misspelled version of the claim Valentine made
in his October 30 letter to the mayor of Richmond. Was Valentine imagining
a Black man's claims, or might he have borrowed the phrase in his letter from
a Black conspirator? The other White men mentioned in the "foolish Memorandum" – Stockdell, Kautzman, and Vereker – made little mark on the town's
records. Kautzman and Vereker both lived in Richmond and were charged
with a poll tax in 1796, but neither owned any slaves, horses, or wagons.[76] No
doubt they, like Valentine, struggled to make their way in the growing city, but
there is no way to know whether they were privy to Valentine's plan (fantasy?).

As ambiguous and interesting as the question of Valentine's accomplices
is the question of French influence on the conspiracy. By 1797 the slaves in
the French island colony of Saint Domingue had gained the upper hand in
the Revolution that still raged there. The French government had by then
abolished slavery in its colonies, and the government's representative in Saint
Domingue – Leger Sonthonax – had allied himself with Toussaint Louverture
before being expelled from the island.[77] Events in Saint Domingue were famil-

[75] These sections include a guarantee of natural liberty, of a jury trial, of protection against
    excessive bail, and of protection against "general warrants," all clearly relevant to Valen-
    tine's case.
[76] 1796 Richmond City Personal Property Tax Book, LiVa. Vereker was listed as having failed
    to pay his taxes for the year (RSP, Box 24, June–Aug. 1799 Bundle, City Insolvents Returned
    for 1796). Kautzman and Vereker both lived in Richmond as early as 1791 (RSP, Box
    13, May 1791 Bundle, A List of Fees Due the Clerk of Henrico in the City of Richmond).
[77] Carolyn Fick, The Making of Haiti: The Saint Domingue Revolution from Below (Knoxville,
    Tenn., 1990), chs. 7, 8; David Geggus, "Racial Equality, Slavery, and Colonial Secession
    during the Constituent Assembly," American Historical Review, 94 (1989): 1290–1308.

iar to Virginians through newspaper accounts and reports from the numerous refugees from the island who came to the state.[78] Though none of Valentine's papers made explicit mention of Saint Domingue, one scrap did speak of "Toombs" of "Monarchs," and probably (the writing is barely legible) referred to "Louis in the Dust." An even more cryptic note read as follows:

It has been said that the son of Duke of Orleans is come to Town – If a man[,] shew himself – If a Beast[,] let the creature be kept for the benefit of the Owner by way of Shew.

The connections to France become even more elusive and perhaps more interesting upon consideration of another text discovered among Valentine's papers. In an apparently undelivered letter to[79] Charles Purcell that was dated May 9, 1797, Valentine referred to someone "tak[ing] possession" of something in order to "compleat what has been sacredly mentioned," and assured Purcell that the possessor would "stand ready to perform his promise." This obviously coded letter may have had nothing to do with slave conspiracies, but just three years later Purcell would be anonymously accused of participating in Gabriel's Conspiracy. Might Purcell represent a link between Valentine's conspiracy and Gabriel's? And might the term "Frenchmen," when used in the depositions produced in the trials of Gabriel's conspirators have been a coded way of referring to allies with roots in Valentine's conspiracy? Might the Frenchmen have been "Dukes of Orleans," like Valentine or Purcell?[80]

Answers to these questions are unknowable. More important, answers to questions about the extent of Valentine's conspiracy and its connections to Richmond's waterfront life were unknown to the magistrates who set excessive bond for Jacob Valentine in 1797. The level of uncertainty that an event like Valentine's conspiracy must have created, combined with the clear sense manifested in contemporary grand jury presentments that social and race

---

[78] Frey, *Water from the Rock*, 230–2; James Sidbury, "Saint Domingue in Virginia: Ideology, Local Meanings, and Resistance to Slavery,1790–1800," *Journal of Southern History* (forthcoming). See also Chapter 1 of this book.

[79] I believe the letter to be an original rather than a copy of a delivered letter, because it was sealed with wax, some of which remains on the paper.

[80] *Virginia Argus*, Sept. 16, 1800. Purcell offered a reward for the identity of his accuser; see Chapter 4 of this book. Names reputedly belonging to the two Frenchmen were printed in a Richmond newspaper after Gabriel's Conspiracy, and Douglas Egerton ("Gabriel's Conspiracy and the Election of 1800," *Journal of Southern History*, 56 [1990]: 205–7; and *Gabriel's Rebellion*, 182–5) has traced probable identities for the Frenchmen, but this connection is also possible.

relations in Richmond were spinning out of authorities' control, must have hovered behind the Hustings Court's willingness to run roughshod over Valentine's constitutional rights. The Common Hall Council also responded to the immediate threat of Valentine's conspiracy by ordering the mayor to appoint "a Captain of a Watch" to patrol the city streets "for 10 days," and by asking for a committee report on the establishment of "a permanent Watch to patroll the Streets, Lanes and Alleys of this City."[81]

One interesting aspect of the official response to the upheaval surrounding urban growth in general and the Valentine conspiracy in particular is the modesty of elite efforts to reassert control over life in Richmond. For if it is true that Jacob Valentine spent over six months in jail in 1798, it is equally true that only a decade later he became high constable of the city of Richmond. No doubt his incarceration was tough, but the conspiracy does not appear to have cast a terribly long shadow over Valentine's later prospects in life. A similar point might be made about the Hustings Court's attempts to control what it considered illicit activity on the part of poor Whites and free Blacks along the Richmond waterfront. Though the Common Hall passed numerous ordinances against tippling shops, gambling, and selling liquor to slaves, and though grand juries periodically presented many townspeople for violating these ordinances, the treatment was noticeably gentle. In one sample of presentments, the attorney for the Commonwealth dismissed half of the shopkeepers accused of violating the Sabbath and dealing with slaves, and even those who were convicted suffered fines of only $1.67. Enterprising slaves selling goods and buying liquor surely comprised too lucrative a market for such meager fines to serve as much of a deterrent.[82] In short, though town authorities harassed those who participated in life on the waterfront, they made far less effort to exert real control over what went on there.

This seeming paradox of authorities expressing fear of Black autonomy and of potential subversion but shying away from a serious crackdown disappears if the cultural world of the Richmond waterfront is seen within the context of the growing town's labor relations. Between 1780 and 1810, Richmond grew into a small but vibrant urban center. The nonelite people

---

[81] Richmond City Common Hall Council Minutes, 1796–1807, 32–3, 34 (LiVa). A watch was established in 1801 after Gabriel's Conspiracy.

[82] Richmond City Common Hall Council Minutes, 117, 121, 161, 265, 297 (for ordinances relating to these issues); RHCOB #7, 455–7. Of nineteen people whose presentments for Sabbath breaking and dealing with Blacks were disposed of that day, eight were dismissed. The eleven who were convicted compounded their violation of the law by failing to respond to the court's summons and were probably being punished for disrespect to the court as well as for Sabbath breaking.

of the town carved out space in which to live their own lives, but they were able to do so because the world they built benefited Richmond merchants and area planters. The complex social practices and the rich and contradictory relations among Black and White working people that prevailed in Richmond grew directly out of a system of labor from which elite Richmonders and slaveholders in the surrounding counties benefited.

6

Labor, race, and identity in early Richmond

Disorderly houses, tippling shops, and gambling houses helped to create an urban environment that troubled many White Virginians, and strict attention to White Virginians' complaints about Richmond can create the impression that the activities that took place in such establishments constituted the heart of the Black experience in the town. Nothing could be further from the truth. Had illicit activities comprised the main occupations of Black Richmonders, then authorities could easily have cracked down on the liberties of the city. Urban centers did not develop in postrevolutionary Virginia in order to provide a safety valve for pent-up Black frustration. Towns grew in response to economic development and the need for more centralized and sophisticated urban services than the planter–merchants who dominated Virginia's commerce during the first half of the eighteenth century could provide. Towns like Richmond required large and flexible labor forces, and Richmond's labor force was largely composed of slaves. Work lay at the core of the Black experience in early Richmond, just as it lay at the core of the Black experience in rural Virginia, but the nature and conditions of urban labor differed from plantation labor in ways that helped to shape Gabriel's world.

Through the first half of the eighteenth century, planter–merchants had presided over great plantations with artisanal workshops manned by skilled slaves, tobacco wharves that served their regions, and stores where neighbors could buy manufactured goods imported from Europe. Planter–merchants also served as community bankers, building up sizable networks of nearby smaller farmers who owed substantial sums and who granted them social and political predominance in return for gentle treatment. In the words of one visitor to prerevolutionary Virginia, the family seat of a great planter was much "like a Town" in which "most of the inhabitants . . . [were] black." As Virginia grew and as the economy developed, real towns ultimately took over most urban functions that had once been filled by planter–merchants operating out of their great houses.[1]

In some ways, towns like Richmond were extensions of Virginia's biggest plantations, but even the small cities of Virginia dwarfed the biggest tobacco plantations. Robert Carter of Nomini Hall may have been the single largest slaveowner in revolutionary Virginia before he manumitted his approximately 500 slaves in 1791, but those 500 people lived among eighteen quarters in five counties. Carter's seat at Nomini Hall had the largest single concentration of slaves among his quarters, but only 114 Blacks lived there. By contrast, over 1,700 Black people lived in Richmond, though it covered less than two square miles in 1790. Just as important as the concentration of people of African descent in Virginia's towns – which was central to the urban subculture discussed in the previous chapter – was the alteration in master–slave relationships and the labor process. Artisanal slaves worked at Nomini Hall, but they belonged to Robert Carter and worked under his personal authority. While complicated negotiations could and did occur involving things like an overseer's power to punish slaves or a slave's ability to attend religious services, those negotiations always and necessarily took place within a context that recognized a known master's authority over his bonded laborers.[2]

Towns differed. In 1790 over 250 Black Richmonders belonged only to themselves, and the 1,400 enslaved town residents belonged to many different masters. In addition, Blacks entered and left Richmond on a daily basis, transporting goods to and from the market; many of these people were slaves, but no one in the city owned them. White Richmonders often dealt with Black men and women without knowing whether they were enslaved or who owned them if they were. Lines of authority inevitably blurred.

The nature of urban labor further complicated slavery in Richmond. Most of Robert Carter's slaves worked his fields, cultivating tobacco, corn, and

[1] Hunter Dickinson Farish, ed., *Journal and Letters of Philip Vickers Fithian, 1773–1774: A Plantation Tutor of the Old Dominion* (Williamsburg, 1943), 98 (quotation). Aubrey C. Land, "Economic Base and Social Structure: The Northern Chesapeake in the Eighteenth Century," *Journal of Economic History* 25 (1965): 639–54; Louis Morton, *Robert Carter of Nomini Hall: A Virginia Tobacco Planter in the Eighteenth Century* (Williamsburg, 1945), chs. 4, 7, and 8; Lois Green Carr and Lorena S. Walsh, "Economic Diversification and Labor Organization in the Chesapeake, 1650–1820," in Stephen Innes, ed., *Work and Labor in Early America* (Chapel Hill, 1988), 144–88. See also Chapter 5 in this book.

[2] Morton, *Robert Carter of Nomini Hall*, Table 9 (tables in unpaginated section at the end); Rhys Isaac, *The Transformation of Virginia, 1740–1790* (Chapel Hill, 1982), 75; and Chapter 1 of this book.

wheat. Those lucky enough to have learned artisanal skills experienced less careful supervision, but they spent most of their time working in Nomini Hall's workshops, and they generally reported to and took orders from the same people.[3] The demand for artisanal work in Virginia's growing towns was greater than on a plantation like Carter's, but towns had few single operations that rivaled those of Nomini Hall. Skilled Richmond slaves often worked for many people, and sometimes they belonged to masters who lived in the countryside but leased their slaves to towndwellers. Many slaves convinced their rural masters to allow them to hire their own time; these men and women often moved to Richmond on their own and sold their labor for what they could get. Other skilled slaves belonged to and worked in the shops of White artisans, but they too often worked in other craftsmen's shops when it benefited their masters.

Towns like Richmond required more fluid labor supplies than did rural areas. Slaves did not always benefit. Whites who hired slaves had less economic incentive to worry about their workers' health, so some hired slaves were abused even by the lax contemporary standards Whites used to judge the abuse of slaves. A scarcity of labor combined with a fluid supply should, on average, force employers to treat laborers less harshly. Between 1780 and 1810, enslaved workers in Richmond struggled to make that the case.

As Richmond grew, its White residents sought to adapt the rural institution of slavery to their evolving urban needs. Free towndwellers lacked a master plan to guide this process, so they developed norms to regulate urban slavery through a gradual accretion of custom and case law.[4] Leasors and hirers of slaves – generally White men – reached agreements about what each

---

[3] Rural artisanal slaves were, however, often hired out. Gerald W. Mullin, *Flight and Rebellion: Slave Resistance in Eighteenth-Century Virginia* (New York, 1972), ch. 3. Sarah S. Hughes, "Slaves for Hire: The Allocation of Black Labor in Elizabeth City County, Virginia, 1782–1810," *William and Mary Quarterly* 3d ser., 35 (1978): 260–86.

[4] The point is not that Richmond was unique; urban slavery existed in different forms in anglophone America, ranging from the large slave cities and towns of the Caribbean, to Charleston, South Carolina, to the important role of slavery in northern seaports. For examples, see Franklin W. Knight and Peggy K. Liss, eds., *Atlantic Port Cities: Economy, Culture, and Society in the Atlantic World, 1650–1850* (Knoxville, Tenn., 1990); Philip D. Morgan, "Black Life in Eighteenth-Century Charleston," *Perspectives in American History*, New Series, 1 (1984): 187–232; Shane White, *Somewhat More Independent: The End of Slavery in New York City, 1770–1810* (Athens, Ga., 1991); Eric Foner, *Tom Paine and Revolutionary America* (New York, 1976), ch. 2; Gary Nash, *Forging Freedom: The Formation of Philadelphia's Black Community, 1720–1840* (Cambridge, Mass., 1988), chs. 1–3. Nonetheless, given the decentralized nature of anglophone America, the rural Virginians who moved to Richmond could not – or did not – consciously copy the norms of urban slavery in other places.

could expect from the other, and they resorted to Richmond's Hustings Court to adjudicate the disputes that arose when the two sides discovered that they interpreted those agreements differently. By the beginning of the nineteenth century, established customs generally dictated the hirers' responsibility for slaves' medical care and taxes, and when an owner could expect to be paid.

This process was not one that masters worked out among themselves above the heads of passive slaves. The concentration of Black people in Richmond, the level of transience among them, and the town's demand for skilled labor created conditions that allowed enslaved Richmonders to influence the norms that came to regulate urban slavery. Richmond slaves used the tools at their disposal to enhance their small but real chances to win freedom, to increase their leisure time, to earn spending money, and above all to protect and carve out protected space for their families. Urban life at the turn of the nine-teenth century offered Virginia slaves more autonomy and, at least for some, a greater chance for satisfying and secure family lives than they would have had on plantations. But that happened only because Blacks used White urban-ites' need for a flexible and skilled labor force to create autonomy. George Tucker explained Gabriel's Conspiracy by noting that "towns tend[ed] . . . to enlighten and inform" slaves, thus making them less contented with their lot.[5] Much of that education occurred as they learned to take advantage of new labor conditions in Virginia's burgeoning towns.

The business of slave hiring

Early Richmond's labor market cannot be accurately measured, but the demand for workers increased during the three decades following the Amer-ican Revolution, a period during which the population increased almost ten times. New residents needed houses, and someone had to build them. Between 1800 and 1809 the declared value of the houses, other buildings, and land in Richmond grew by almost 40 percent.[6] Few new urbanites were wealthy

[5] [George Tucker], *Letter to a Member of the General Assembly of Virginia, on the Subject of the Late Conspiracy of the Slaves* (Baltimore, 1801), 7.
[6] Richmond City Land Tax and Personal Property Tax Books, 1800 and 1809, Library of Virginia (hereafter LiVa), Richmond. The total value of listed property in 1800 was $456,345; in 1809 it was $638,675. All the increase reflects new building (rather than a rise in prop-erty values), because individuals continued to list improved parcels of land with the same value throughout the period. Michael Lee Nicholls kindly gave me the data base he con-structed from the 1800 tax lists. I use this relatively late period (rather than comparing 1784 to 1800) to avoid the exaggeration that would result from the low baseline of the earlier period.

professionals or governmental officials, so most White households probably continued to be headed by skilled and semiskilled workers throughout the town's early history.[7] Many free people who moved to Richmond presumably arrived in search of better work than they could find in the countryside. Their migration to the city was both a response and a stimulus to the town's demand for labor.

An active and diverse market in hired slaves developed. Some White urbanites sought "hearty" women to "do the drugery of a small Family." Others dipped into this market in search of highly skilled men who could contribute to artisanal work forces.[8] Nicholas Seabrooke sought to hire two carpenters who understood "sawing and inside work," and Michael Grantland advertised in search of "six or eight Negro Coopers" to work beside "four or five Journeymen" in his shop "near the Mason's Hall." Two years later, Grantland advertised for "ten negro coopers." Other employers sought a few slave apprentices for a nail manufactory, or a number of men to work in some coal mines outside of and to bring coal into Richmond. Occasionally slaves were leased with the sites at which they worked.[9] Hiring slaves became a common and accepted part of commercial life for craftsmen and small businesses in Richmond well before 1800.

Large contractors and companies also had recourse to slave hiring to assemble gangs of slaves for extended but temporary jobs. When the James River Company, for example, was chartered to build a canal into Richmond, it obviously required many workers, but once the canal was completed the company would have had little use for the slave gangs needed during construction. Rather than responding to temporary demand by buying slaves who would later have to be sold, the company leased many of the slaves it

---

[7] Records do not permit household reconstitution between 1784 and 1810, so an accurate occupational profile of the city cannot be drawn. The first Richmond City directory was published after 1810.

[8] *Virginia Gazette*, February 11, 1787 ("hearty woman"). I have retained the contemporary distinction between "skilled" artisanal labor and the "unskilled" work of most rural men and almost all women slaves. "Housewifery," however, required skills, as did farm labor. For an illustration of an urban artisan's struggle to master farm skills see Frederick Douglass's recollections of his helplessness as a rural laborer on Edward Covey's farm in his *Narrative of the Life of Frederick Douglass, An American Slave*, in Henry Louis Gates Jr., ed. *The Classic Slave Narratives* (New York, 1987), 289–90.

[9] *Virginia Gazette*, October 2, 1784 (Seabrooke), August 2, 1797 (coal), August 13, 1789 (slaves offered with lease for tavern), December 18, 1793 (slaves offered with the wagons they drove); *Virginia Argus*, November 27, 1798 and December 20, 1800 (Grantland); December 23, 1800 (nails).

needed. In 1787 it hired over 120 slaves.[10] Other large concerns followed a similar strategy. The Dismal Swamp Company, which sought to dig a canal through the enormous bog in southeastern Virginia, advertised for an indefinite number of laborers in 1792. Twelve years later John P. Shields, a builder of roads and houses, sought seventeen slaves to work in his brickyard, and Shields was also among a group of men who sought gangs of laborers to work on the Manchester Turnpike Road between 1802 and 1805.[11]

A varied lot of slaveowners responded to this market. The executor for carpenter William Lewis's estate offered several slaves for hire in 1801, thus using a common ploy through which Whites could continue to enjoy the benefits of slaves' work while wills were probated and minor children matured.[12] Some town professionals appear to have invested in slaves to cater to the hiring market.[13] The hiring market also afforded options to slaveowners who lived outside of town. Some, like William Mayo Jr. of Powhatan County, decided they could make more or easier money by leasing their slaves than by working them on the land; Mayo offered "30 Negroes of different sexes and ages" for lease in 1790 and requested that those who had hired slaves from him for the previous year "return them with the hire by that day."[14] The hiring market provided slaveowners in and around Richmond important additional options to consider when determining the optimal way to employ their bound labor.

These options were not limited to a simple decision about whether to hire out a slave. The labor market became increasingly complex and offered masters and employers a growing number of options during the decades before and after 1800. The standard agreement called for an owner to lease a slave to

---

[10] James River Company Ledger, Virginia Historical Society (hereafter VHS), Richmond. See J. Harvie and W. Foushee to Beverley Randolph, March 11, 1791, Executive Papers, (see ch. 2, n. 3 for full citation), Box 69, for evidence that the James River Company also bought slaves.

[11] *Virginia Gazette*, October 2, 1792 (Dismal Swamp); *Virginia Argus*, December 12, 1804 (brickyard), June 23, 1802 (50 slaves for turnpike), September 22, 1802 (75 for turnpike), December 31, 1805 (25 for turnpike). Shields was listed only in the last turnpike advertisement.

[12] *Virginia Argus*, December 23, 1800.

[13] Attorney George William Smith offered ten slaves for hire, including a carpenter, a house servant, a stone mason and road paver, and a boy with experience in a tobacco factory. The diversity of skills among his slaves suggests that he leased them frequently (ibid., January 3, 1806). High numbers of adult slaves listed by professionals in the 1800 Personal Property Tax Book include: Dr. William Foushee (8), lawyer Charles Copland (7), merchant James Brown (15), merchant John Hopkins (10).

[14] *Virginia Argus*, December 29, 1790. He ran a similar ad on December 21, 1791.

someone else for a year. The hired slave began working for the new employer on the first day of the year and continued "until the 25th December." The employer paid taxes on the slave and gave "him Cloaths suff[icient] for a working Neg[r]o."[15] Perhaps three in five slaves hired by the year in Richmond between 1782 and 1810 were males.[16] As time went on, a growing number of slaves were hired for shorter periods ranging from eleven months to a single day.

Rates of hire depended on the slave's age, sex, and skills. Enslaved women were hired out for between £2 and £15 for a year (average approximately £7).[17] None of these women's work skills were listed in the agreements, and age does not appear strongly to have influenced what hirers would pay for enslaved women's work. In 1786 Giles Carter and John Smith hired Pettis Ragland's "negroe Girl Darcass" for £6, but the next year Moses Cardoza hired Anthony Singleton's "Woman Hannah" for £3. In 1797 a "Negro Girl named Cate" and "a Negroe Woman named Lucy" were both hired for the year for £8.[18]

Rates paid to hire male slaves varied much more. A year of an enslaved man's labor cost an average of £16 to £17. Terms ranged, however, from jailer William Rose's agreement to pay the city of Richmond 6s. per year for the hire of two runaways confined in his jail, to the agreement of a carriage-making partnership to pay merchant John Adams £50 for "one years hire of Billy (Blacksmith)." Different factors influenced rates. Presumably Isaac Younghusband charged house carpenter Alexander Montgomery only £1 10s. to hire "Negro Boy Ben" in 1784 because Ben was a novice who would learn the rudiments of the trade while working for Montgomery. Exceptionally skillful workers, on the other hand, brought much more money. Obviously, the blacksmith Billy was an exceptionally skilled artisan, and a few other

---

[15] RSP (see ch. 5, n. 24 for full citation), Box 1, April 1783 Bundle, *Sprightly v. Park* (quotations).

[16] This figure (and all figures on hiring unless otherwise noted) are drawn from accounts for slave hiring that found their way into court records because one party sued the other. They represent a small portion of the slave hiring in Richmond, and they contain biases: since most were suits over debts, they are probably skewed toward long-term agreements and toward agreements in which males were hired (since in both cases the amount of hire would have been higher, raising chances of a default and resulting suit). All these figures are soft, and should be considered estimates.

[17] Figures based on the average amount paid for 34 women hired by the year between 1782 and 1810.

[18] RSP Box 10, May 1788 Bundle, *Raglan v. Carter and Smith*; RSP Box 22, March–November 1789 Bundle, *Singleton v. Cardozo*; RSP Box 22, March–November 1797 Bundle, *Barret v. Dove* (woman) and *Walton v. Powers* (girl). When RSP is cited, the year noted in the text often differs from the year of the citation. I refer to the year in which the event took place; the papers were filed under the year in which the suit was settled.

enslaved tradesmen were comparably valued, bringing their masters £30 or
£40 per year. One can gain perspective on the meaning of these rates by
noting that between 1780 and 1810 the highest value any local Virginia court
placed on the life of an executed slave was £150.[19] Richmond employers paid
a dear price for very skilled workers, underscoring how vital skilled slaves'
labor was to the town's economy. Moderately skilled slave craftsmen's labor
power cost less. Carpenter Moses Bates paid Dr. Andrew Leiper only £15
a piece for "the hire of 3 Coopers" in 1797, and William Giles hired a sawyer
to work in his brickyard for nine consecutive years during the 1780s and 1790s,
generally paying £18 to the estate of Josiah Bullington.[20] The young and
unskilled commanded the least money among males on the market: annual
hire for workers specifically listed as "boys" ranged between £6 and £12.[21]

The practice of hiring slaves for periods ranging from one to eleven months
probably developed out of the annual hiring market. Many agreements of this
sort involved slaves hired for nine, ten, or eleven months. Slaves began working for their new employers in February, March, or April and returned to
their masters at Christmas just as if they had been hired for the full year, and
the agreements often specified that the employer clothe and pay taxes on the
hired slave. Such intermediate hires represented a mild adaptation of annual
hire for employers who discovered unanticipated labor needs after the beginning of the calendar year. The adaptation allowed employers greater flexibility, but the frequent insistence that hired slaves return at Christmas suggests
that the intermediate hiring market remained subordinate to the market for
year-long hiring.[22] Annual and intermediate markets were not identical. Slaves

[19] RSP Box 24, March 1798 Bundle (Rose); RSP Box 28, November–December 1801 Bundle,
Adams v. Fox and Wren; RSP Box 2, July–August 1785, *Younghusband v. Montgomery*; RSP
Box 29, August 1802 Bundle, *Brown v. Young* (£40); RSP Box 44, May 1807 Bundle, *Foster
v. Smith* (£30). For average valuations of condemned slaves, see Chapter 2 of this book.
[20] RSP Box 23, March 1798 Bundle, *Leiper v. Bates*; RSP Box 33, January–April 1804
Bundle, *Bullington v. Giles's Estate*. One deposition states that "Will, was a Sawyer, and
worth more on that account."
[21] Later in southern history "boy" became a derogatory term Whites applied to all African
American men, but that was not the general practice during this period. Winthrop D.
Jordan, *Tumult and Silence at Second Creek: an Inquiry into a Civil War Slave Conspiracy*
(Baton Rouge, 1993), 15; Michael Mullin, *Africa in America: Slave Acculturation in the
American South and the British Caribbean, 1736–1831* (Urbana, Ill., 1992), 234.
[22] Not all agreements for intermediate hire fell into this category. Augustine Davis wrote
Isaiah Isaac a note on Dec. 6, 1796 demanding payment for the "hire of Negro James to
the 1st of October last" (RSP Box 21, January–February 1797 Bundle). Agreements for
intermediate hire that were less subordinate to the annual hire market appear to have
become more common after 1800, but my sample is too small to be more than suggestive.

hired for intermediate periods were more predominantly male than slaves hired for a year (82% compared to 68%), and rates varied more.[23] Employers paid more for skilled slaves, and they paid higher rates when hiring slaves for shorter periods, but the evidence remains too sketchy to go beyond these generalizations.

Slaves' labor – or enslaved men's labor – was also sold by the day.[24] Day labor brought an average of 3s. 6d. a day, with the rate ranging from 1s. per day for a boy in 1787 to the 8s. per day ship captain John Cowan paid for "11 Days hire of York" in September 1801. The price for the daily hire of slave labor appears to have risen between 1784 and 1810. It is difficult to determine average wages for daily hire with any reliability, because most accounts in which employers listed the skills of the slaves they hired listed the rate paid in piecework.[25]

In addition to slaves leased by their masters to other employers for various lengths of time, a smaller group bought their own labor time from their masters. The Virginia General Assembly declared slave self-hire illegal in 1781, but the legislature's almost ritual tinkering with the law and numerous grand jury presentments indicate that the practice was far from rare and for reasons that are easy to discern.[26] Many skilled slaves who lived in the

---

[23] Average paid for the fourteen enslaved women hired for intermediate periods: 12s. per month (range: 2s. 8d. a month that Marsden Duke paid for ten months' "Hire of a negro Woman nam'd Milley with her Child" in 1789, to the 20s. per month that William Dyer paid Samuel Everitt for seven months' "Hire of a Negro Girle Rosey." RSP Box 13, May 1790 Bundle, *Thomas v. Duke*; RSP Box 54, May 1810 Bundle, *Evertt v. Dyer*). Average paid for men: 39s. per month (range: 4s. 5d. per month paid by James Bilberry, a free Black man, "For hire of anegro [sic] Boy Wilford" for ten months in 1788, to 120s. per month Peter Moseley paid William Price for the "Hire of Nathan" for two months and twenty-three days in 1807. RSP Box 11, September–October 1789 Bundle, *White v. Bilberry*; RSP Box 48, August 1808 Bundle, *Price v. Moseley*).

[24] Only one of the fifty-two slaves known to have been hired by the day (or by the job) was female. William Giles paid Richard Adams 1s. per day for a "Girl to cook 6 Days." RSP Box 7, May 1787 Bundle, *Adams v. Giles*.

[25] RSP Box 7, May 1787 Bundle, *Adams v. Giles* (boys bringing 1s. per day). RSP Box 37, June–July 1805 Bundle, *Lester's Estate v. Cowan* (York); two skilled slaves received 3s. a day for work in 1785 and 1791 (RSP Box 3, October 1785 Bundle, *Griffin v. Agnew and Thompson*; RSP Box 13, August 1791 Bundle, *Hawkins v. Mayo*). No record of slaves receiving less than 3s. per day has survived from the later period, and the average rate (n = 8) from after 1795 is over 5s. The rates changed depending on the work done, and the sample is small, so it would be misleading to quantify changing rates.

[26] One in four (13 of 52) slaves cited for self-hire between 1782 and 1810 in Richmond's courts was a woman. The fifty-two cases represent only a fraction of the slaves who engaged in this practice, as illustrated by the case in which Jacob was arrested for hiring

countryside surrounding Richmond probably spent part of each year working in the fields, because their home plantations lacked sufficient work to keep
craftsmen optimally employed. In addition, White men often bequeathed skilled
slaves to widows and orphans as an important means of support. Towns
contained the primary market for skilled labor in Virginia at the turn of the
nineteenth century. Enslaved craftsmen who longed to escape to the relative
freedom of towns sometimes convinced widows, executors of estates, and
rural planters to permit them to find work on their own in return for the
wages. For example Bob, a slave of Thomas Woodson of Goochland County,
was "as good a wagoner as any in richmond," and an "honest and cerfull
felow." Apparently Bob hauled things to Richmond for Woodson and came
back reporting that he could get "6 or 7 Dolers per month" working in the
capital. On March 25, 1800, Woodson asked Samuel Pinter to stand as master for Bob to protect the slave "from being interupted when at his bisiness."
Bob would find his own work in town, collect his own accounts, and turn
over his hire to Pinter, who would "cepe[accept]" a bit as compensation for
his trouble. This arrangement saved Woodson the trouble of finding work
for his slave, and it may have produced a surer flow of income, because Bob
had greater incentive to pay Woodson on time than would a White who hired
Bob directly from Woodson. Masters could always revoke the highly valued
privilege if a slave failed to deliver his wages, while they had to go to court
to force recalcitrant employers to pay the agreed upon rate of slave hire.[27]

   This barely underground system also benefited employers. They gained
some advantages of a free labor system – they did not have to house or clothe
the slaves, and they could hire and discharge them at will – while retaining
many advantages rooted in slavery. Even the illegality of the practice must
have benefited employers: slaves could hardly have complained to the courts
about employers who failed to pay illegal wages. When Moses Howlett was
hauled before the court in 1806 for hiring his own time, his papers included
two accounts – both for working on boats – that had remained unpaid for
more than a year.[28] Most important, though, slaves themselves preferred the
relative autonomy of self-hire. The Goochland County wagoner named Bob,

his own time and showed up in the court records because Wilson Allen refused to
help. Allen explained that he had "spent between 50 and 100 $ releiving Jacob at vari-
ous times" from similar difficulties (RSP Box 48, August 1808 Bundle, *Commonwealth
v. Jacob*).
[27] RSP Box 25, June–July 1800 Bundle, *Commonwealth v. Bob*. For a Maryland master
    threatening to revoke Frederick Douglass's privilege of self-hire, see Gates, *Classic Slave
    Narratives*, 318.
[28] RSP Box 42, October 1806 Bundle, *Commonwealth v. Howlett*.

for instance, was able to live with his wife in Richmond, so his arrangement with Woodson reunited a family divided by slavery. In short, self-hire benefited all those directly involved in the process. White society at large may have feared the disorder created by towns seemingly filled with Blacks of uncertain status, but it could do little to stop the practice.

The various forms that free Richmonders used to hire slave labor (rather than buying enslaved people) developed into a key component in the evolving system of urban slavery. Urbanites lacked the large tobacco fields whose need for constant labor kept gangs of slaves steadily employed in the countryside. The work done in Richmond required skills different from those needed in field work, and the demand for labor was less reliable. A contractor building a house might need a group of carpenters while putting up the frame but would need masons and plasterers at other times. Very large contractors often chose to purchase enough skilled slaves to fill most of their labor needs, and hired labor only for special contingencies and specific jobs. Craftsmen working on a small scale did most of the work by themselves; they too probably resorted to the open labor market rarely and only for day labor. Some large contractors and the many free artisans between these extremes used the flexibility slave hiring allowed to adjust their production in response to market forces. Employers could make adjustments without having to face the daunting initial investment needed to buy skilled slaves or to match the higher wages demanded by free artisans.

Such flexibility came at a price. A free Richmonder who hired a male slave for a year paid an average of almost £17. At that rate the employer could have bought a skilled slave in six or seven years. The more flexibility sought, the greater the cost. The average amount paid for slaves hired by the month worked out to an annual rate of more than £23. And those who hired slaves by the day paid an average annual rate of £40 to £50 (assuming a 240- to 300-day work year).[29] Those figures are somewhat misleading. People did not, after all, hire slaves at a daily rate for an entire year, so real (as opposed to hypothetical) employers did not actually pay £50 for a man-year of labor. On the other side of the equation, masters who leased slaves could not always count on finding employers for slaves on the daily market, so masters could not earn £50 annually by hiring out a single slave either. In addition, employers did not have to pay masters until the end of the term of hire, which greatly increased free artisans' ability to respond to changes in the market. A cooper,

[29] Robert William Fogel and Stanley L. Engerman, *Time on the Cross: The Economics of American Negro Slavery* (New York, 1974), 208, report an average work year of 265 to 275 days for plantation slaves in the antebellum United States.

for example, could hire a skilled slave to work in his shop when the price of barrels rose (or a big order came in), and he could pay the hire price with the money he made selling the barrels. The frequency with which Richmonders hired slaves indicates that this flexibility benefited the free people of the town.

Slave hiring also provided a stepping-stone that free townspeople could use to improve their economic standing. As a result, it spread the benefits of slavery among some who could not afford slaves, but it simultaneously hurt other free people by depressing the value of labor. In the late eighteenth century, the Journeymen Cordwainers of the City of Richmond pledged under the "solemnity of an Oath" to work together for standard wages, to pay set prices to their employers for board, and to refuse to work "for any person who had negro workmen in their employ." Jedediah Allen and David Logan were journeymen when the society's charter was signed, but by 1802 they had accumulated wealth, become employers, and, according to their former comrades, lost interest "in the welfare of Journeymen." The associated journeymen informed Allen and Logan that they were "not very solicitous to be imployed in future by men who have no Object beyond the accumulation of money." Apparently Allen and Logan lost their embryonic free-labor ideology along with their concern for journeymen. In 1800 Allen paid taxes on two adult slaves and Logan on one. There is no way to know whether Allen and Logan owned or hired those slaves, but they probably made use of hired slave labor during their climb from journeymen to employers.[30] If so, their case illustrates the way slave hiring could spread the benefits of slavery to some free people who normally did not benefit from the peculiar institution, but by doing so it exacerbated tensions between winners and losers in the struggle for economic advancement.

The prevalence of slave hiring indicates that many free people must have benefited from the practice. The slave-hiring system did not, however, spring into existence without problems. Some tensions were inherent in the arrangement, and free Richmonders had to learn how to resolve disputes arising out of these tensions. Examining the conflicts that arose between lessors and

[30] RSP Box 32, November 1803 Bundle, *Harrison v. Tyree, Bowers, Asley, Mountcastle, Merryman, Shriner, Fellows, Brown, Thompson, Barret, and Hazlewood.* 1800 Richmond City Personal Property Tax Book (for slaves of Allen and Logan). Logan eventually bought slaves to work in his shop: in 1806 he advertised that "a mulatto . . . shoemaker" had forged a pass and run away from him (*Virginia Argus*, August 13, 1806). See Morgan, "Black Life in Eighteenth-Century Charleston," 204 for White Charlestonians complaining that Blacks were taking their jobs. Ironically, given the way racism has retarded unionization in the industrializing South, slavery and racism may have spurred White workers to organize in this earlier period.

hirers of slaves provides a picture of early Richmonders adapting slavery to their needs and constructing the hybrid institution of urban slavery. The tensions between lessors and hirers also produced fissures in the wall of White power through which those whose labor was bought and sold could influence the evolving meanings of labor, freedom, and bondage within the city.

Hirers of slaves could punish their workers as they chose. This presented a problem, because employers of other people's slaves lacked the economic incentive to protect property that partially restrained masters' brutality. In late February 1784, the *Virginia Gazette* reported that "a negro man was found dead in the road" near Richmond, the victim of "inhuman treatment which had been exercised on him by the person to whom he was hired." The newspaper mentioned no names, but the next Henrico County court acquitted Morris Blakey of "the Murder of a Negroe man Slave the property of Henry Stoneham." If this was the same case, it suggests that hired slaves could expect little legal protection from an employer's brutality. It may be more than coincidence that two years later a slave sawyer hired to Blakey "at the [annual] rate of Twenty five Pounds" survived only seven months of the year.[31]

Surprisingly little evidence of unusual brutality committed by hirers of slaves has survived in the Richmond records. No case similar to that reported by the *Gazette* in 1784 was reported during the next fifteen years. Slavery was a brutal system, and the absence of newspaper articles and complaints by masters does not indicate that hired slaves were treated benevolently. It suggests, however, that something in Richmond worked to mitigate the forces that logically might have caused temporary employers to treat slaves unusually harshly. Hired slaves themselves sought to raise the price of brutal treatment to unacceptable levels. In 1786 two pair of sawyers owned by Nelson Anderson went to work for housejoiner Dabney Miller, who promised "good Accomedations, [such] As aplenty of bred and meat, fish, or milk" as well as clothing. Anderson was to make good any labor time lost to Miller from the slaves' "sickness over and above two or three days At a time," or from "Runing away," unless "the Negroes [were] abused."[32]

[31] *Virginia Gazette*, February 28, 1784; Henrico County Court Order Book (hereafter HCCOB) #1, 501, LiVa; RSP Box 6, February 1786 Bundle, *McQuilkey v. Blakey*. Mark Tushnet, *The American Law of Slavery, 1810–1860: Considerations of Humanity and Interest* (Princeton, 1981), 170–88 for southern states' laws regarding slave hiring; and Eugene D. Genovese, *Roll, Jordan, Roll: The World the Slaves Made* (New York, 1972), 391 for a succinct summary of antebellum masters' concerns about the treatment of hired slaves. Thomas D. Morris, *Southern Slavery and the Law, 1619–1860* (Chapel Hill, 1996), ch. 6.
[32] RSP Box 3, February 1786 Bundle, *Anderson v. Miller*. The suit arose because Miller was delinquent in paying the debt, not from a dispute over the time missed.

Miller's insistence on protection against the sawyers' running away made good business sense. He spent £90 for ten months' labor from these four men, and his construction gang probably depended on the hired slaves' ability to produce lumber. Enslaved artisans easily disappeared into Richmond's Black population for a few days or weeks, in part because they had little trouble finding work. Miller sought to ensure that he would get sufficient labor for his money, and he would probably have been tempted to overwork the slaves if he could have gotten away with it. Anderson – perhaps at the sawyers' prompting – realized that he could use the ease with which skilled slaves could absent themselves from work to protect his own investment. Miller would have had to moderate his demands on Anderson's slaves lest the sawyers run off and leave their employer short of expensive labor. At the end of the year, Miller and Anderson "setled the loss time" of the slaves at £9. The sawyers apparently failed to work 10 percent of the time they were hired to Miller. There is no way to know how much of that time the men were sick rather than absent, but that each missed more than a day of work every two weeks suggests that they kept constant pressure on Miller to moderate his demands.[33] None of the other rare surviving contracts for slave hire include this specific proviso, but other skilled slaves hired into Richmond presumably used the threat and reality of running away to pressure their employers and to influence the terms under which they worked.

Some responsibilities of slave hirers remained fuzzy and unclear. Medical care caused several disputes between masters and those who hired slaves, and those disputes reveal more tensions inherent in the system. Some masters, like gambler George Stras, insisted that those hiring their slaves agree to pay for the attendance of a physician if necessary, and some employers took that responsibility to heart: Curtis Carter, a bricklayer, incurred a $25 debt "in consequence of Medical Attendance on a boy" whom he had "hired of Phillip Southerland." Other times, however, the contracting parties failed to spell out such responsibilities explicitly, and problems arose. In December 1803, Peter Hawkins, a free Black doctor and dentist, initiated a civil suit charging that William Winston owed him £4 16s. for "2 months board for John," and £5 for "curing John's leg." Winston did not dispute the charges. Instead, he asked a Mr. Burras, presumably John's master, to "let peter Hawkins Have a [sic] some money as He informs me that John is fit for business aGain and it must be deducted from the Hire." Burras apparently denied

---

[33] RSP Box 3, February 1786 Bundle, *Anderson v. Miller*. The slaves missed more than 10 percent of their required workdays because the agreement covered only the amount of time that Anderson agreed was excessive.

responsibility for the slave's medical care, because slightly less than a month later Winston pleaded with Ambrose Knight to "let peter Hawkins have a little Money as He Has Call'd on me for some."[34] In this case John did not suffer from the unclear lines of responsibility for his medical care; the dispute over payment arose after treatment. Another case illustrates the potential danger such a situation posed for hired slaves.

In 1793, a "slave boy named George" was apprenticed by William Allen to Michael Grantland for six years to learn "the Trade and Mystery of a Cooper." By August 1795 George had progressed as a cooper and was producing "great advantage and emolument." Unfortunately, George injured his leg; Dr. James Wray "examined hit" at Grantland's request, "and found a good deal of fungus flesh in it." Before the injury, George apparently had been sold by William Allen to John Graham, a coalyard operator, and George began living with Graham. George, unhappy with the treatment Grantland provided, complained to Graham, who, upon examining the injury, refused to return the young apprentice. Instead, he sought consultations from two new physicians, John Cringan and James Drew McCaw, who found George's leg severely injured and noted that the young man had a fever. They treated George's leg for a month, but despite improvement "the appearance of the sore was such" that the doctors suspected "the bone of his leg was rotten." Cringan and McCaw "cut down to the bone to examine it," found it rotten, and judged it absolutely necessary to amputate the leg. They operated as "soon as the weather was cool enough."

This infuriated Grantland. He brought suit against Graham for detaining his apprentice and also asked for £150 in damages for the lost labor caused by the amputation. In addition, he sued McCaw and Cringan for cutting off George's leg, demanding £100 damages. When Dr. Cringan gave his deposition for the trial, Grantland exercised his right to cross-examine, and in doing so he dramatized a danger to hired slaves. Cringan asserted that had George "continued . . . without medical aid" and "an exemption from hard labor he must have died in a few Months." Grantland revealed his priorities when he responded by asking whether the doctor had ever known people to suffer bad sores yet remain "capable of working a long time," and asked whether George "might . . . not have lived several years *without*" the amputation. Cringan countered that "to make the boys life comfortable and to make him usefull either to Graham or Grantland it was necessary to amputate his leg," conceding only that Grantland "did . . . forbid to have [George's] . . . leg cut off."

---

[34] RSP Box 23, April–July 1798 Bundle, *Stras v. Cocke*; RSP Box 50, March 1809 Bundle, *Upshaw v. Carter*; RSP Box 33, May 1804 Bundle, *Hawkins v. Winston*.

Similar tensions must often have arisen between slave owners' concern to protect their human property and slave hirers' impulse to maximize returns on their short-term investments, tensions others besides George could use to win greater access to basic human necessities. Grantland retained the right to only three more years of George's service when the amputation took place. No doubt a substantial period of recuperation deprived Grantland of much of the benefit he felt he had earned by teaching George cooperage. The cooper insisted that George remained capable of labor despite his injury: James Wray, the doctor he hired to examine George before the amputation, reported that he found the boy at Graham's stable "with a very large turn of Hay on his shoulder going up a looft." Grantland had specifically asked Wray to take notice of that.

The juries charged with deciding these cases faced an important issue for Richmond's urbanizing economy, because employers increasingly relied on slave hiring to enhance the flexibility of the labor market. In March 1796, a Richmond jury upheld Grantland's property right in George's time by ordering Graham to pay Grantland £3 for detaining the apprentice, but when Grantland sought damages for the amputation, the court apparently lost all sympathy. A jury recognized his right to his apprentice by finding Graham guilty of cutting off the boy's leg "without . . . being legally authorized to do so," but they awarded Grantland only a penny in damages. Another jury further expressed disapproval by finding for Graham in his countersuit for George's medical bills, but the magistrates granted Grantland's motion for a new trial and then dismissed the case. A Richmond jury also rejected Grantland's suit against doctors McCaw and Cringan.[35]

The dispute between Grantland and Graham shows White Richmonders struggling to develop norms to regulate the hybrid form of slavery that evolved in Virginia's towns, and it shows one Black Richmonder's efforts to influence those norms. Some of the jurors who decided these cases no doubt hired slave labor, and others may have leased slaves. Their decisions probably represented an emerging community consensus about the responsibility of hirers of slaves. They recognized Grantland's right to George's time, for to have done otherwise would have denied the sanctity of apprenticeship contracts, but Richmond jurors refused to let Grantland's temporary right to George's labor interfere with Graham's longer-term interests. And though George lacked the legal standing to appear in court as other than the object of White

---

[35] RSP Box 20, March 1796 Bundle, and November 1796 Bundle, *Grantland v. Graham*; RSP Box 20, November 1796 Bundle, *Grantland v. McCaw and Cringan*; RSP Box 21, March 1797 Bundle, *Graham v. Grantland*.

men's economic interests, the case left discernible traces of his perceptions
of the bargaining space created by the divided authority inherent in slave
hiring and of his ability to maneuver within that space in pursuit of his own
interests.

Chattel slavery evolved in the rural Chesapeake during the late seventeenth and early eighteenth centuries. Large planters faced chronic labor short-
ages as they tried to produce tobacco, a labor-intensive crop, for the world
market. The norms regulating the institution developed in these rural settings
where most bondpeople could expect to spend their entire lives working for
a single master on whom they would remain dependent for sustenance, shelter, medical care, and what passed for justice. Rural reality never approached
William Byrd's famous vision of his plantation as a Newtonian machine dependent only on Providence, and slave hiring was on the rise in rural Virginia
during this very period.[36] Nor did owners and employers of slaves in the
town William Byrd founded become some simplified version of Economic
Man responding without hesitation to Adam Smith's invisible hand. The
Richmond juries that rejected Michael Grantland's attempts to recover damages caused by the amputation of his apprentice's leg were horrified by his
inhumanity. How else explain their willingness to ignore the law and order
the cooper to pay Graham more than £18 for illegally incurred medical bills?
Individual masters accepted economic sacrifices to manumit their bondpeople because they thought slavery morally wrong. Others sometimes hired
out a slave in deference to the slave's desire to live near a spouse, rather than
in response to the market. Human motivation is rarely simple, and social
change seldom involves pure and complete transformations from one order
to another.

The institution of slavery did change when it moved from rural to urban
Virginia, and the growth and elaboration of slave hiring played an important
role in that change. The urban labor market differed from its rural counterpart. The demand for skilled labor was greater, but so was the premium
on flexibility and responsiveness to demand. Slave hiring allowed owners of
slaves to maximize the benefits they gained from their bondpeople, and it
allowed employers to minimize the cost of adjusting their labor forces. Many
free town dwellers grew uneasy over the social space created by Blacks as
a result of the decreased supervision of town slaves. Nervous grand juries
periodically called the constables' attention to Black dances, disorderly houses

---

[36] Byrd to Charles Boyle, Earl of Orrery, 5 July 1726, Marion Tinling, ed., *The Correspondence
of the Three William Byrds of Westover, Virginia, 1684–1786* (Charlottesville, 1977), v. 1,
pp. 354–6. See Hughes, "Slaves for Hire," 260–86 for slave hiring elsewhere in Virginia.

serving liquor to slaves, and shops remaining open on Sunday to do business with Blacks. Nonetheless, Richmond continued to grow and develop
economically. Slavery remained a vital institution within the town, in part
because free urbanites adapted it to their changing needs in a process that
enslaved urbanites actively influenced.

Black and White Richmonders at work

Slave hiring involved far more than abstract decisions by employers and
slaveowners aimed at maximizing returns on their investments in human
property. Real people – free and slave, Black and White – did real work in
Richmond. They built houses, roads, and bridges; they constructed barrels,
shoed horses, and made clothes; they unloaded agricultural produce, pro-
cessed it, and shipped it out; they washed clothes, fed boarders, and tended
gardens. Most adult Richmonders spent most of their waking hours at work,
and Whites and Blacks of varying statuses had to deal with one another on
a daily basis at the workplace.

From the early 1780s, when it first began to develop into a substantial town,
through the first decade of the nineteenth century, Richmond developed an
increasingly diverse and complex work force. Hired slaves, free Blacks, and
Whites worked together in varying combinations at work sites that ran the
gamut from small shops or construction projects to major public projects like
building the capitol or the state penitentiary. Slaves constituted the foundation of the town's labor force, but they worked with and competed against
free laborers in all but the most elite occupations. By examining the intric-
ate webs of alliance and contention that developed among working people in
early Richmond, one can begin to understand the nature of the ties that connected White and Black workers, and the powerful constraints on those ties.
Only then can one begin to see the way in which Richmonders of African
descent were simultaneously an integral part of the developing urban social
world and the builders of a world apart.

Richmond women – White and Black – generally worked in or around a
household. The most basic components of women's daily labor were listed
in advertisements placed by Whites seeking to hire slave women: "Wanted
to hire, A trusty, honest Negro Woman who understands Cooking, Washing,
etc." A few people also ran advertisements seeking wetnurses, emphasizing
the importance of women's reproductive labor.[37] White women who presided

---

[37] *Virginia Argus*, January 12, 1798 ("Cooking, Washing"); June 30, 1804, August 15, 1804
(wetnurses). Some Whites thought urban life corrupted slave women: on May 1, 1805

over households that owned or hired Black domestic workers probably spent most of their time overseeing Black subordinates. The Black women who worked for these mistresses cooked meals, did laundry, and cleaned the house. Many worked at spinning and sewing. Of course, many White women in Richmond neither owned nor hired slave women to work in their houses, and they did much of the same kind of work that enslaved women did in elite households.

Newspaper advertisements and occasional court cases reveal that women's labor had recognized market value in early Richmond, but the market for male labor was far more public. Even for men, however, surviving evidence of the labor market provides a distorted reflection. For example, only occasional indications of unskilled day labor survive, but Richmond clearly was filled with Black men available for temporary heavy work. When Samuel Hart and Michael Grantland got into a dispute over back rent, Grantland threatened to seize Hart's goods; a friend reassured Hart "that he might get several negroes and move out his things before" Grantland could summon a constable.[38] Little other evidence of the floating work force upon which Hart could have called survives, but presumably many Black Richmonders – some desperate for day labor to stay alive, others looking for extra spending money – accepted temporary jobs on the town's streets.

Slaves also worked in a wide array of artisanal jobs. Already by 1784 White tradesmen practicing thirteen different crafts headed households that included adult male slaves, many of whom must have shared their masters' skills.[39] As Richmond developed, the number of crafts practiced in the city increased. From 1780 to 1810 183 male slaves were specified in newspapers and court records as practicing one or more of 34 different occupations that ranged from the specialized – sail making, hat making, carriage painting – to the basic (blacksmithing, carpentry, driving wagons). Slaves and free Blacks also worked as personal servants and barbers in all American slave societies, including Richmond. Some Whites, like Anthony Geohegan, John Darrous, and Alexander Wylie were barbers, but as time passed free Black men like John Kennedy, Charles Sablong, Richard Sabb, Henry Carter, and James Smith came to predominate. Yard and garden work also probably fell to

an advertisement in the *Argus* sought a woman to wash and cook, but specified that "one from the country would be preferred." Chapter 7 of this book discusses women's work in Richmond.
[38] RSP Box 39, February 1806 Bundle, *Hart v. Grantland*. RSP Box 42, December 1806 Bundle, *Commonwealth v. Isaac*, and the Richmond Hustings Court Order Book (hereafter RHCOB) #7, 67 for an example of short-term labor for Blacks in the city.
[39] 1784 Richmond City Census, Richmond City Common Hall Council Book.

enslaved and free Black men. Peter Wood accepted a job that probably fell between day labor and landscaping when he agreed to accept £10 as well as "board an lodging for Levelling" George Fleming's garden. At least one free man, Toby Sampson, remained a personal servant after he achieved freedom, charging Dr. James Greenhow three shillings a day for "labor and services . . . as Gardener, Hostler, Cook, etc."[40] Other former slaves probably took similar positions. The vast majority of slave artisans in early Richmond, however, like the majority of free artisans, worked in basic construction, transportation, and clothing trades.[41]

Many people also worked in shops in the mercantile town of Richmond. While most store owners were White, shopkeepers were a varied lot. Many White men worked behind the counter, occasionally with a young slave to help, but White women and free Black people also ran shops. Of the twenty-seven people a grand jury presented for "sabbath breaking, by dealing with negroes . . . and opening . . . [their] shop[s]" in November 1806, five were White women and four were free Black men.[42] Enslaved men, women, and children worked in some of the shops of each of these different groups of proprietors.

Slaves who worked in these divergent occupations interacted on the job with Whites and free Blacks who did the same kind of work. Blacksmiths

[40] Occupations are derived from newspapers, court records, and early city censuses. RSP Box 12, November 1789 Bundle, *Wood v. Fleming*; RSP Box 42, October 1806 Bundle, *Sampson v. Greenhow*. See my "Slave Artisans in Richmond, Virginia, 1780–1810," in Howard B. Rock, Paul A. Gilje, and Robert Asher, eds., *American Artisans: Crafting Social Identity, 1750–1850* (Baltimore, 1995), 48–62.

[41] In the *Virginia Gazette*, 1782–1800, the *Virginia Argus*, 1793–1810, and the Richmond City Hustings Court records I found evidence of male slaves in the following occupations: 3 bakers, 5 barbers, 13 blacksmiths, 3 brickmakers, 2 brickmasons, 2 butchers, 22 carpenters, 1 carriage painter, 1 caulker, 1 coach maker, 2 coalminers, 1 cook, 29 coopers, 3 ditchers, 9 draymen or wagoners, 5 gardeners, 1 hatter, 2 hostlers, 5 house carpenters, 2 nailers, 2 plasterers, 1 planer, 2 postillions, 1 racehorse keeper, 2 ropemakers, 1 sailmaker, 23 mariners, 14 sawyers, 3 ship carpenters, 11 shoemakers, 3 spinners, 1 stone mason and paver, 2 tailors, and 5 tanners. This list does not include all slaves who held specific occupations in Richmond, but it probably includes most occupations commonly held by male slaves and provides a rough indication of the distribution of male slaves among occupations.

[42] RHCOB #7, 24–5, 43–7. Slave economic activity on Sundays may well have spawned the disputes with sabbatarianism that Betty Wood found in Georgia during the second decade of the nineteenth century, but, other than citations for the violation of the blue laws (and the rhetoric surrounding these citations is not infused with militant sabbatarianism), I have found little evidence for this in Richmond up to 1810. Betty Wood, *Women's Work, Men's Work: The Informal Slave Economies of Lowcountry Georgia* (Athens, Ga., 1995), ch. 7 (esp. pp. 144–59).

provide a useful example of the possibilities for contact among men who shared a craft that crossed racial and status lines. Many Richmond-area slaves, like Gabriel, Solomon, and Thornton, who gained fame as leading conspirators in 1800, were blacksmiths. Several free Blacks who lived in Richmond – Nathaniel Anderson, Samuel Redd, and Claiborne Evans – worked as blacksmiths, and many White men like John Burton, William Gaddy, and Richard Crouch worked at the same trade. A similar situation existed among coopers, shoemakers, carpenters, and bricklayers.

Generalizations about how artisans in Richmond reacted to this situation are difficult. As the journeyman shoemakers' society indicates, competition from Black artisans could lead to hostility, but working in close proximity may also have helped to break down racial barriers.[43] Both seemingly contradictory things may often have happened simultaneously, but whatever the effect, Blacks and Whites worked effectively together in a wide range of settings. Relations among people of African and European descent who worked together could not follow clear lines of racial hierarchy, because levels of skill and responsibility did not run reliably along racial lines.[44]

John Sabb was a free man of African descent and a bricklayer who filled different niches in Richmond's busy construction industry at different times, illustrating the range of work experiences a single Black artisan might encounter in the normal course of working life. On several occasions Sabb went to work for large contractors like Ninian Wyse and Anderson Barrett, filling what might appear to have been a "racially appropriate" subordinate position on the job. Even when Sabb worked for large White contractors, however,

---

[43] Perhaps hostility among shoemakers developed early because shoemakers were among the first craftsmen to be pressured by protoindustrial intensification of labor and the centralization of production. In addition to boycotting employers of Black labor, the journeyman's association also boycotted masters who imported shoes "of an inferior quality, manufactured in New York." Alan Dawley, *Class and Community: the Industrial Revolution in Lynn* (Cambridge, Mass., 1976); and Paul Faler, *Mechanics and Manufacturers in the Early Industrial Revolution: Lynn, Massachusetts, 1760–1860* (Albany, 1981). Morgan, "Black Life in Eighteenth-Century Charleston," for tension between Charleston's Black and White artisans.

[44] For biracial work gangs see: RSP Box 40, May 1806 Bundle, *Sheppard v. Moore* ("Matt the blacksmith" sharing a workshop with four White smiths); RSP Box 15, March 1793 Bundle, *McEnery v. Austin* (one White and three Black men working for McEnery in "sheeting the Capitol"); RSP Box 38, November 1805 Bundle, *Gordon v. Means* (Gordon built a house with eight workers, at least three of whom were Black). Not all artisanal shops were integrated: see RSP Box 55, August 1810 Bundle, *Currie's Estate v. Anderson* for Nathaniel Anderson, a free Black man, leasing land in order to build his own "Black-Smith's shop."

he sometimes played the role of an independent subcontractor who hired and supervised his own laborers. And on at least one occasion John Sabb worked as an independent builder, signing a contract to build a house for George Webb and hiring at least three men to complete the job. In Richmond's bustling construction industry, John Sabb sometimes worked for White craftsmen, sometimes worked for himself, and sometimes supervised other laborers, some of whom may have been White.[45]

A fuller picture of Black and White workers with different skills interacting on the job in early Richmond emerges from an examination of a single large construction project. The Mayo family supervised the building of the first bridge across the James River at Richmond in 1788. It was an insubstantial pontoon bridge that the frozen river demolished during the first winter. John Mayo, who had overseen the original construction, had the bridge rebuilt, but it remained a rickety link between Richmond and Manchester. Upon first seeing Mayo's bridge in 1796, architect Benjamin Latrobe thought it a "wretched bridge," whose construction was so haphazard that describing it was "more unpleasant if possible than . . . [crossing] it." The bridge rested on large "enclosures of timber filled with loose peices of Granite" that rested on the bottom of the James. Between each of these "piers," Mayo had run "four or five long timbers, across which planks" were "laid traversely, without being in any manner fixed." The bridge included two islands, on one of which was the toll house. From one end to the other the bridge was nearly a mile long."[46] Not surprisingly, this less than sturdy structure was washed away by the spring floods three years after Latrobe saw it.

John Mayo was a persistent man, and he immediately set about rebuilding.[47] On May 8, 1800, he contracted with John Williamson to supervise "the remainder of the work except battening of the little new bridge" for £149.

[45] RSP Box 28, March–April 1802 Bundle, *Sabb v. Wyse*; RSP Box 34, August 1804 Bundle, *Sabb v. Barret*; RSP Box 6, March 1787 Bundle, *Sabb v. Webb*. Sabb billed Wyse for his own labor and that of five other men. Accounts do not specify the race of those who worked for Sabb. Evidence of Sabb's work history is incomplete: I rely on accounts that were brought into court to adjudicate disputes and happen to have survived in the loose court papers.

[46] Samuel Mordecai, *Richmond in By-Gone Days, Being Reminiscences of An Old Citizen* (Richmond, 1856), ch. 28 (first bridge); Edward C. Carter II, ed., *The Virginia Journals of Benjamin Henry Latrobe, 1795–1798* (New Haven, 1977, v. 1, pp. 96–8 (second bridge). Latrobe sketched Mayo's bridge. See Edward C. Carter II, ed., *Latrobe's View of America, 1795–1820: Selections from the Watercolors and Sketches* (New Haven, 1985), 145.

[47] The analysis of labor on the bridge that follows is based on the John Mayo Cash Book, 1800–1, Valentine Museum Archives, Richmond. All quotations from that source unless otherwise noted.

Williamson had much to supervise. During the next sixteen months, Mayo also contracted with John P. Shields to fill "up . . . the abutments and pens of the large bridge" for £180, and he hired Ninian Wyse "and his masons . . . to raise . . . [a] stone wall" and do other masonry for £150. Austin Talman agreed "to make . . . 6 large Toll Gates." Mayo also spent a great deal of money hiring individual laborers to work on the bridge during the same period. On July 27, 1801, he reported seventy hands at work on the bridge. By August 1801, the building of this bridge had "expos'd" him to such "inconveniences" that he "was oblig'd *to go to markett without one farthing in*" his pocket.

The many workers who rebuilt Mayo's bridge came to the job from a variety of backgrounds. Although most of them presumably lived in Richmond or one of the nearby counties, many traveled from Williamsburg. Large projects of this sort must have helped to make Richmond a center of Virginia's extensive Black communication networks, as enslaved workers from distant parts of the state moved temporarily to the capital. Perhaps relationships that developed on a large work site of this sort explain how Gabriel, who appears to have lived all his life in Henrico County, was "probably acquainted" with slaves from Jamestown.[48] Large work sites also fostered local communication links, as illustrated by several enslaved and free Blacks whom Mayo employed to work on his bridge in Richmond and on the Hermitage, his Henrico County plantation.[49] Large building projects helped to make the capital a center of the state's evolving and racially defined Black community as workers from throughout the James River valley were temporarily drawn in to work, live, and forge relationships in the growing town.

Projects like Mayo's bridge did not, however, rely on segregated work forces; the enslaved workers who came from diverse geographical areas found themselves working beside Black and White men with a variety of skills

---

[48] James Monroe to the Mayor of Williamsburg, September 12, 1800, ELB (see ch. 1, n. 38 for full citation), 1794–1800. The slaves Gabriel reportedly knew belonged to State Treasurer Jacquelin Ambler, so Gabriel may have met them when they worked on a large construction project, when they worked in Ambler's Richmond household, or perhaps he met some Ambler slaves in both settings.

[49] Free Black blacksmiths Samuel Redd and Claiborne Evans made "lightening rods" and did other "iron work for the bridge," but were also hired to fix "plow hoes etc.," and for "horseshoing, mending a rake, putting a handle on branding iron, etc." Similarly a carpenter, "Jerry a black man," put a lock on the bridge's toll house and did "sundry little repairs" at Mayo's home; and Peter Martin, Jacob Martin, Handy, Jack, and Ned put up a "log kitchen in front of the new toll House," and did labor "at the Hermitage." Most revealingly, Jonathan Moore was hired to "superintend . . . plantation business" but spent a week with "a number of hands engag'd in clearing off trash and righting the bridge."

and legal statuses. Highly skilled free Black artisans, like blacksmiths Samuel Redd and Claiborne Evans, supplied metalwork at the same time that "Frank Sheppard the yellow man" was tarring timbers, Frederick Ayton, a White craftsman, was plastering the toll house, and the "2 Masons, Sam and Harry," hired by Mayo from a Mrs. Lyne, were doing brickwork. And all these craftsmen, slave or free, Black, White, or mulatto, had to coordinate their labor with the gangs of enslaved workers supervised by Shields, Williamson, and Wyse. Presumably the burden of rebuilding Mayo's bridge fell most heavily on gangs of enslaved workers whose names Mayo never recorded in his account book, but, while building the bridge, those men worked with Black and White working people of different statuses.

Understanding the relations among these diverse men requires speculation. Many among the wealthy White contractors, middling White and free Black artisans, skilled slaves, unskilled day laborers, and substantial gangs of unskilled slaves who worked on the project surely did more than work. Working people received the meal that Mayo bought "for the use of [the] bridge" as well as the "casks of whiskey . . . for the laborers on the bridge," and presumably they often consumed these together. If Mayo followed practices current among canalbuilders, then the daily alcohol ration that he paid would have kept workers in a state of perpetual intoxication.[50] It would also have provided periodic chances for working people to discuss common grievances and perhaps to conspire to moderate Mayo's demands on their labor. Perhaps it was during such discussions in June 1801 that people planned what Mayo described as a "most villainous attempt to set fire to the old middle bridge." At any rate, the interactions among those working on the bridge can be presumed to have reflected the conflicting impulses arising from shared daily experiences on the job and the distrust and competition engendered by differences of race and status.

The building of Mayo's bridge was not a typical example of the work done in early Richmond, but neither was it unique. Richmonders undertook many large construction projects, including the James River Canal, several large merchant mills, many public buildings, and several turnpikes. While each involved its own particular mix of laborers, they all required labor forces that included Blacks and Whites of various skills and statuses. Nor were such mixes limited to large projects. The sketchier evidence from smaller work sites, which was discussed earlier, indicates that Whites, slaves, and free Blacks also worked together at smaller building sites and in workshops and stores

[50] Peter Way, "Evil Humors and Ardent Spirits: The Rough Culture of Canal Construction Laborers," *Journal of American History* 79 (1993): 1413–14.

throughout the town. Working people also engaged in other market transactions with one another, building up commercial networks that crossed racial and class lines in unpredictable and unreliable ways.[51]

Richmond's many small grocery or grog shops catered to Black and White working people and housed many of these ambiguous interactions. Some storekeepers, like Francis Tyree, who looked after Mrs. Lucy Sydnor's grocery store, not only served liquor to Black customers – Tyree claimed that Blacks "drank in all the shops in Richmond" – but also "play[ed] at *Five Corns*" with slaves "at two Cents per Game." Tyree's loud behavior so angered James Hurt, a White tenant whose family lived above the shop, that he ordered all the blacks to leave the shop immediately. Hurt was unappeased by Tyree's defense that there "were white people" in the store as well as people "of colour," and he subjected the shopkeeper to several humiliating "wrings of the nose."[52] Occasional self-righteous indignation like Hurt's did not, however, interfere with the buying and selling of stolen goods, drinking, and gambling that went on in simple grocery stores, behavior that sometimes led to crossracial interaction that challenged the law in more fundamental ways.

On July 10, 1809, Ned Smith, a slave whom Rachel McClurg hired to her son-in-law James Smith, entered "Mr. Wynegardeners Shop" in the early evening. Inside he found shopkeeper William Day, Benjamin, the cook at the Eagle Tavern, and David Allen, a White carpenter. Smith hired David Allen to forge a pass to facilitate his escape from Virginia, agreeing to pay $6. Armed with a note that permitted "the Barer Ned Smith" to "pass and Repass" between Richmond and Norfolk during the following "fore weakses," Smith boarded the stage to Norfolk. Unfortunately, the driver recognized him, grew suspicious, and sent word to James Smith that Ned was traveling on an apparently forged pass. James Smith chased down the stage, captured Ned Smith, and had David Allen arrested.[53]

Ned Smith's aborted escape suggests that alliances of convenience could easily develop when Black and White workers gathered together to drink, gamble, and relax in Richmond's shops at the end of a day of work. There is no reason to believe the alliance ran any deeper. Allen was the only person

[51] RSP Box 30, June–October 1802 Bundle, *Crouch v. Norton* (for debt). Another example – RSP Box 33, January–April 1804 Bundle, *Taylor v. Easley* ("for work Dun in the Shop by Sam") – illustrates the commercial networks that developed out of these relationships.

[52] RSP Box 54, May 1810 Bundle, *Tyree v. Hurt*. Kenneth S. Greenberg, *Honor and Slavery* (Princeton, 1996), ch. 1 for a provocative interpretation of nose-pulling. This incident supports a Freudian reading that hinges on Hurt's unmanning Tyree in contrast to the reading that Greenberg gives to similar incidents among elites.

[53] RSP Box 51, August 1809 Bundle, *Commonwealth v. Allen*.

in the shop whose name Ned Smith professed not to know, and Smith with-held 50¢ of the agreed price until he received the pass, so it seems unlikely that personal affection played much of a role in the transaction. Allen received good money for little work. But the ease and openness with which Ned Smith solicited and Allen forged an illegal pass indicate that such transactions were far from rare; perhaps Allen sold forged passes out of Wynegardener's shop on a regular basis. Such incidents do not constitute a biracial alliance against slavery, but they suggest that working Richmonders shared a common dis-dain for laws designed to benefit others and that they could count on each other to ignore petty violations.[54]

These relationships were not limited to Richmond's workshops and gro-ceries. As shown in the previous chapter, the waterfront was notorious among elites as a home for often-illegal encounters between Whites and Blacks. Early Richmond was a slave town, but labor was not neatly distributed according to race or legal status. A highly skilled but enslaved cooper might spend part of his day teaching his trade to free White or free Black apprentices. Any member of the shop might work temporarily for Joseph Gallego's merchant mill at harvest time when the mills were busy. Lines of status and author-ity blurred, and Blacks and Whites, slaves and free people, sometimes crossed the lines that separated them. More frequently, however, Richmond slaves used the autonomy they won with their labor to pursue objectives particu-lar to them.

Black workers, families, and communities

Soon after Christmas 1806, a Black man named John – a thirty-five-year-old carpenter – ran away from Armistead Russell's New Kent County planta-tion. For the previous two years John had lived with Anderson Barrett, a building contractor in Richmond. John was "generally known" in town, where he had "a wife." A year later John – now "called by the Negroes John Russell" – fled again. This time Armistead Russell explained that his slave's Rich-mond wife was a free mulatto woman, and he noted that John Russell had lived with Anderson Barrett for three years.[55]

Anderson Barrett had hired John from Armistead Russell in 1805. Barrett, happy with John's labor, hired him again for the following year. Armistead Russell chose not to hire out his slave for 1807, so John was sent back to

---

[54] Ned Smith paid the final 50¢ "in the presence of William Day," the shopkeeper. Perhaps Day received a cut of the take, but regardless, he turned a blind eye to the transaction.
[55] *Virginia Argus*, January 27, 1807 and February 26, 1808.

New Kent County. By this time, however, John had married a free woman in Richmond and built a life there. As a slave, he had no control over his fate; his master could uproot him and force him to live apart from his wife. As a highly valued carpenter, however, John had greater bargaining power than his slave status might suggest. Upon returning to New Kent County, John escaped home to Richmond. Perhaps using Barrett as an intermediary, he informed his master that he would not willingly leave the city. Armistead Russell gave in and hired John to Barrett for another year.

One should not overestimate the power that slave artisans could exert in situations like John Russell's. His master gave in once, but there is no indication of how he reacted the next year. John took a big risk by trying to force his master to hire him into Richmond, and he faced brutal physical punishment if he was captured and returned. He also faced a more horrible possibility: the Lower South was opening up by 1807, and Armistead Russell could easily have chosen to sell his troublesome property to a slavetrader. Had that happened (and it may have happened in 1808), John would never have seen his wife again. John Russell accepted these risks, won a power struggle with his master, and exerted a level of control over his life that slaves were not "supposed" to enjoy. His success illustrates the power that skilled slaves gained from the growth of an urban labor market. It hints at the way White patrons – often for their own interests – could help slaves to pursue autonomy. Yet it also reinforces recognition of the limits to the influence even highly skilled slaves in a labor-poor market could exert over their fate: John Russell remained a slave and a fugitive in 1808 despite the daring victory he had won over his master the previous year. Many skilled Black Richmonders battled against the constraints they faced as African Americans in a slave town, and their struggles reveal some of the aspirations of Black artisans in early Richmond, as well as the strategies they thought most effective for achieving their aspirations. Freedom for themselves and for their families was an overriding goal for Black Richmonders. Experience with slavery had taught them, however, that they would often have to settle for something less than complete freedom. Those who escaped slavery but stayed in Richmond learned that there were severe limits to the freedom any Black could enjoy in nineteenth-century Virginia.

Many Richmond-area Blacks did escape chattel slavery. Masters executed deeds of manumission for over 400 slaves in the Richmond Hustings Court and Henrico County Court between 1782 and 1806. About 35 percent of these people received their freedom from masters who manumitted five or more slaves at once. These emancipators probably rejected slavery. Most who were manumitted, however, were freed individually or in small groups.

Many emancipators felt no need to explain their actions in their deeds. The White emancipators who did explain their motives can be broken down into three broad groups. Some were small slaveholders who found the institution abhorrent and felt that freedom was "the natural right of all mankind." Others acted out of gratitude for an individual's faithful services. Others made deals: in 1782 Thomas Johnson sold his "Mulattoe Wench . . . Rebecca Jackson" her freedom for £80.[56]

Once free, many Blacks began working to free their families or friends. By 1786 Rebecca Jackson acquired ownership of her husband "Toby commonly Toby Jackson" and her son David Jackson, and immediately set them "as free as the Laws of Virginia [would] admit." Similarly Peter Hawkins, a free Black man and Richmond's only dentist, emancipated his "wife Rose . . . and . . . child called Mary" as a token of his "love and regard."[57] Jackson and Hawkins were obviously remarkable people, but they were not alone among Richmond-area Blacks. At least twenty-eight slaves – over 10 percent of those freed individually or in small groups – were freed by Richmond and Henrico County free Blacks. Black emancipators often paid a heavy price for the freedom of their kin. On October 5, 1803, Milley Johnston paid William Fulcher £160 for her nineteen-year-old daughter Milley; two months later she granted the young girl the "rights . . . of a free born Citizen."[58] Only a very highly skilled slave artisan would have cost £160 on Richmond's slave market, so Fulcher clearly exploited Milley Johnston's maternal devotion to reap an ugly financial windfall.

Most Richmond Blacks did not escape slavery. To do so required varying combinations of luck, patrons, and hard work. Many who lacked luck or a patron worked hard to maximize their autonomy within slavery. Often, free Blacks helped by hiring enslaved friends or family members. Blacksmith Samuel Redd, shoemaker Toby Jackson, and clerk Christopher McPherson, all free Black men, hired one or more slaves between 1799 and 1806.[59] One can rarely determine the mix of emotion and economics that stimulated such decisions: these men may only have been seeking labor, and they may have treated their hired workers poorly.

[56] Figures compiled from RHCOB and HCCOB, the Richmond City Deed Books, and the Henrico County Deed Books for 1782–1810. Michael Lee Nicholls kindly gave me abstracts of the Richmond City Deed Books. Quotations are from HCCOB #3, 378 ("natural right"), HCCOB #1, 178 ("faithful services"), 41 (Rebecca Jackson).

[57] Hentico County Deed Book #2, 312–13 (Jackson); HCCOB #6, 78–9 (Hawkins).

[58] Henrico County Court Deed Book #7, 35–6 (Johnston).

[59] RSP Box 20, August 1796 Bundle, *Redd v. Wilson*; RSP Box 42, November 1806 Bundle, *Cringan v. McPherson*; RSP Box 24, February and April 1799 Bundle, *Mosby v. Jackson*.

In other cases, free Black people hired slaves for reasons that transcended economics. In 1806 James Plummer, a free Black man, sued two constables for breaking into his house and taking away a slave "against her will or consent." He had hired this woman "for the term of 12 months" and told the court that he had expected "great profit . . . in his affairs by means of . . . [her] service." The slave's name, however, was Sally Plummer, James's wife, and he surely had hired her hoping to enjoy a year during which they could live together in relative freedom. James Plummer was not the only free Black man who had to fight Richmond authorities to protect his family. Billy Buck "had a wife a negro woman belonging to" Edward Hallam. When Hallam "correct[ed] . . . [her] for some misbehavior . . . she ran away, leaving behind her wearing apparel." She ran to her husband, and that evening Buck took a cart to Hallam's and retrieved his wife's "gowns, petticoats . . . [and] two silver tea spoons." The Hustings Court found Billy Buck guilty of grand larceny and bound him for trial before the District Court.[60] Obviously Richmond Blacks valued their families. Many Black women and men made economic sacrifices to bring families together. Others risked their freedom and well-being. The fluid social relations that characterized Virginia's growing towns provided some – especially those with valued job skills – a better chance to protect kin than slaves in rural Virginia enjoyed, but protecting the family remained a constant and precarious struggle.

Black Richmonders also used the relative fluidity of the city for ends not directly related to the family. As shown earlier, many enslaved people were hired out or allowed to hire their own time and thus enjoyed some autonomy on the job. Blacks probably appreciated the freedom from supervision whether or not they chose, as did many, to exploit it for financial gain. Sometimes they earned extra money with their masters' consent. Caesar, a skilled slave who belonged to building contractor William Griffin, won Griffin's permission to do ninety yards of "Lathing and Plaistering" for the firm of Agnew and Thompson. This afforded Caesar at least nine days of work away from Griffin's supervision, nine days during which he probably enjoyed greater control of his work and leisure time than he normally did. He probably gained more. Agnew and Thompson promised Griffin that they would "see him

---

[60] RSP Box 42, November 1806 Bundle, *Plummer v. Gay and Wood*; RHCOB #6, 225–6 (Buck). The emotional ties involved in free Blacks' hiring slaves could backfire. On March 31, 1807, William Gauldin, a free Black man, returned Haner, a slave woman he had hired from Joseph Myers. He explained that "my woman and hur doant agrea," and asked Myers to "get hur a place" elsewhere. Gauldin admitted his obligation to pay "the balance of the hier" if Myers could not find her another place.

[Caesar] Paid" upon finishing the work.[61] All the principals lived in Richmond, so Agnew and Thompson could just as conveniently have paid Griffin as Caesar. Caesar probably solicited work for himself and kept some of the proceeds when no lathing or plastering was needed at the main work site.

On other occasions, urban Black workers took less "legitimate" advantage of the autonomy their jobs afforded them. Robert Turner drove a dray for his master Martin Turner. On November 19, 1810, Robert Turner saw the sloop *Diligent* unloading cargo and pulled up to the docks to claim a box marked "W. H. C.," which belonged to William H. Craven. The box contained $19.17 worth of cloth that Craven later reported had "been pilfred by" Martin Turner's "Drayman Robbin." The cloth was never recovered; presumably it had been sold to one of the shops that fenced goods for slaves. The drayman was caught only because two bystanders recognized him and saw him receive the chest.[62] Richmond's waterfront provided many such opportunities for Black working people to reappropriate some of the slave-produced wealth that passed through the town.

The autonomy that allowed slaves and free Blacks to do odd jobs and participate in Richmond's underground economy could be dangerous. Daniel Nicolson hired a slave (whose name was not included in the record) from John Spotswood Moore to drive a dray. The drayman solicited work and collected the fees, which he was then to turn over to Nicolson. On Christmas day 1794, probably the final day of the hire to Nicolson, the slave was in Peter Hart's counting house getting paid for "the carriage of tobacco." Nicolson barged into the room and charged the drayman with failing to turn over some of the money he had made, a charge the drayman denied. Nicolson then "took up a large round rule and struck" a blow that broke both the rule and the man's skull.[63] The requirements of an urban labor market afforded slaves the opportunity to exert more control over their lives than most rural slaves could, but they remained enmeshed in the basic power relations of slavery.

Richmond area Blacks attempted to take advantage of the opportunities the town offered them. Several rural slaves who had been hired into town used their knowledge of and contacts in the city to run away from masters. Some who lived in the city left their masters to work for other Whites who treated them more favorably. Slaves with skills were best able to take advantage of

[61] RSP Box 3, October 1785 Bundle, *Agnew and Thompson v. Griffin*. Caesar was paid £4 10s., so he would have worked nine days if he earned the high wage of 10 s. per day.
[62] RSP Box 56, December 1810–February 1811 Bundle, *Craven v. Turner*.
[63] HCCOB #6, 217–18. Nicolson was bound for trial in District Court for murdering the drayman.

opportunities in Virginia's growing towns. Artisanal skills helped, but the skill to cultivate free patrons proved at least as important.[64] Slaves who possessed both skills could build lives that were far more satisfying than one might expect possible in a slave society, but as Christopher McPherson's career illustrates, even those who combined exceptional skill with unusual luck could not escape the bonds of race.

Christopher McPherson was a most unusual man. Born in Louisa County to a slave mother and a white storekeeper, he attended school for nearly two years beginning in 1770 and was working behind the counter in a Petersburg store by 1772.[65] He taught school and worked "for the Commercial Agent" of the state during the lull in commerce caused by the Revolution, and he later served as principal storekeeper for Richmond-area merchant David Ross, where "8 to 10 White Gentlemen" worked "under [his] directions." Freed in 1792, McPherson did clerical work in Richmond until 1799 and then went up to Philadelphia to serve as a clerk to Congress. Soon he returned to Richmond and worked in the court clerk's office where "he received the enormous wages of . . . four dollars per diem," which all thought "judiciously paid," because McPherson "accomplished in about three days a piece of work" expected to take "two weeks labor." Nor was speed his only virtue. While an assistant clerk for the superior court of chancery, he developed a new method for indexing the court docket that saved much time and contributed "to the public" welfare.

McPherson's skills extended beyond the work place. William Hening, Edmund Randolph, John D. Blair, William Wirt, and John Marshall – all prominent men – joined numerous other Richmonders in signing a petition attesting to his "Integrity Industry and general good conduct." While clerking for Congress, McPherson had met Thomas Jefferson, who introduced him to James Madison. Later, McPherson reported sitting "at Table . . . with Mr. Maddison, his Lady and Company and enjoy[ing] a full share of the Conversation." In 1802 his word "was taken by the Jury in the District Court, in preference to the opposite Oaths of two white Witnesses," further evidence that "throughout the whole course of" his life White acquaintances considered him "one of their number." In short, McPherson was born into

[64] *Virginia Argus*, July 16, 1799, July 26, 1799, January 14, 1806, February 11, 1806, February 27, 1807, January 30, 1810 for runaways previously hired in Richmond.
[65] Edmund Berkeley Jr., "Prophet Without Honor: Christopher McPherson, Free Person of Color," *Virginia Magazine of History and Biography* 77 (1969), 180–90. All quotations used here are from Christopher McPherson's 1810 petition to the General Assembly, which included testimonials from Whites as well as a one-page autobiography (Richmond City Legislative Petitions, 1810–12, LiVa).

exceptionally fortunate circumstances for a slave. He worked very hard and
mastered a valued skill completely. He proved amazingly adept at winning
White patrons. Nonetheless, despite the services he "had rendered . . . [his]
Native Country," and the substantial estate he had acquired through the exercise of his talents, he remained subject to disabilities that all Blacks suffered
in early Richmond.

In 1810 the Richmond Common Hall Council decided that the "abuses"
committed by black draymen and wagoners outweighed the convenience that
Whites gained from their work. The Common Hall Council passed an ordinance prohibiting Blacks from driving a wagon, dray, or cart in town. It also
apparently worried that some Black Richmonders were aspiring beyond their
"proper" stations, because it extended the ordinance's reach beyond work
vehicles. Blacks were also prohibited from driving carriages "except in the
capacity of maid or servant to some lady or gentleman." McPherson learned
of this ordinance to his "great astonishment," and immediately petitioned
the Common Hall to ask if he might be excepted from its provisions. The
Hall ignored his request, so McPherson petitioned the General Assembly
for relief. He and his wife, "both advanced in life and occasionally subject
to disease," required "the occasional use of a carriage when . . . unable to
walk." McPherson conceded that the law might properly apply to some Black
Richmonders, but he insisted that it "deprive[d] him of rights to which" he
was "intitled under the laws and Constitution of" Virginia. The legislature
also ignored him.

Christopher McPherson was not typical of any group in Richmond at the
turn of the century.[66] He was far luckier than most Blacks. He was more in-
telligent and industrious than most people. By its very extremes, however,
his story illustrates some fundamental truths about Blacks' opportunities in
early Richmond. Urbanization offered very real chances for social advancement, chances that McPherson had taken advantage of. He made himself
valuable to White employers and worked hard while living a spotless life:
one testimonial mentioned that McPherson never tasted "any thing Stronger
than Water." Exceptionally upright deportment was for him a necessity: many
Whites who testified to his qualities hinted at their surprise in finding them
in a Black man. Throughout his life he carefully cultivated relationships with
powerful White men who could help him overcome barriers created by White
racism. He did not reject other Black Richmonders. Blacksmith Nathaniel

---

[66] There were, however, other well-off free Black people. Mordecai, *Richmond in By-Gone
Days*, ch. 39 contains a White Richmonder's biographical sketches of what Mordecai
labeled "The Colored Aristocracy."

Anderson chose McPherson to write and witness the deed with which he emancipated his son.[67] But he decided that his personal advancement rested on the trust and patronage of Whites.

His advancement was real. Born a slave, he grew old as a free and prosperous man able to care and provide for his family. Relatively few Richmonders of any color were wealthy enough to be affected by laws regulating who could command a carriage. That, of course, is what made that provision in the ordinance so offensive to McPherson. It was not aimed at draymen who exploited their autonomy to steal from ships and sell goods on the Black market. It was aimed instead at members of the free Black elite who had forgotten their status as clients and who had begun to think White patrons thought of them as "one of their number." Blacks could improve their lives substantially through skill and industry in Virginia's growing towns, because Whites needed skilled workers and made social and economic concessions to acquire their labor. Some Blacks won their freedom, others managed to protect their families, others succeeded in making some money, acquiring some property or enjoying the tippling shops and gambling houses of Richmond. Equality was not, however, a concession urban Whites would make.

Most Blacks recognized that and cultivated White patrons for more limited goals. Caesar Hope, a free Black barber, asked Edmund Randolph "and his heirs" to hold Hope's property in trust for his widow and to use the rest of the estate "to purchase . . . and set free" his two children.[68] The common use of patron–client relations for limited goals and McPherson's failure to win recognition of his claim to special equality underscore the way in which people of African descent living in early Richmond forged their identities in spaces produced through their simultaneous inclusion in and exclusion from the state's and the city's dominant culture.

Conclusion

How, then, did conditions created by Richmond's fluid labor market affect race relations in the growing town? Lines of authority became blurred. The standard form used to identify slaves when they appeared before Virginia courts was the slave's name, followed by "negro man [or 'woman'] slave the property of [his or her owner]." Increasingly, the Richmond Hustings Court referred to slaves as "in the service" of someone, or, even more ambiguously, "living with" someone, and sometimes the court floundered in its effort to

---

[67] RSP Box 56, December 1810–February 1811 Bundle, Anderson to Charles.
[68] Will of Caesar Hope, May 1807, Richmond City Hustings Court Will Book #1, 163.

determine the legal status of Black offenders. In April 1807 the Hustings
Court examined "Barnice, a free black man" for stealing a watch. It found
him guilty and bound him for trial at the District Court. Five months later
the District Court of Richmond remanded to the Hustings Court "for trial
and punishment as a slave, Barnice a black man." But it still appeared "to
the satisfaction of the [Hustings] Court that . . . Barnice" was not a slave, so,
judging him "intitled to the privilege of being tried as a free man," it discharged him. The problem did not, however, go away. Before the month
was out "Bernice a Negro Man Slave or Servant of Doct. D. Wilson" was
arrested again, this time for stealing clothes. The court finally decided Bernice
was the property of Daniel Wilson, convicted him as a slave, whipped him,
and confined him to jail for a month.

The courts were not alone in their occasional confusion regarding the
status of Black individuals in Richmond. In 1807 Solomon Marks sued Charles
Parks for failing to pay for a horse. The suit abated, however, when the city
sergeant reported that the Black man pointed out as the defendant was a
slave and thus could neither buy the horse legally nor be sued for failing to
pay for it.[69] The uncertainty regarding status afforded Black Richmonders
some latitude in dealing with Whites. But how did the close proximity in
which slave, free Black, and white artisans worked affect the tenor of race
relations in the growing city?

Unfortunately, much of the surviving evidence is negative. Shared work
space, for example, did not spur manumission. White men who can clearly
be identified as artisans manumitted nineteen slaves in Henrico County and
Richmond between 1782 and 1806. Eleven of those freed were women, and at
least two of the men purchased their freedom. Several other emancipators
gave no reason. Among artisans who emancipated male slaves, only the deeds
signed by Thomas Ladd, who cited "natural rights" when he freed Tom
Johnson, and Alexander Montgomery, who mentioned his slave's "faithful
services," might suggest a sense of kinship growing out of shared work, but
even these two cases are far from clear.[70]

Nor is there much evidence that Blacks and Whites who shared a craft
spent much time with one another when off the job. The Hustings Court disposed of a constant stream of assault and breach of the peace cases involving

[69] RSP Box 45, October 1807 Bundle, *Commonwealth v. Barnice*, and RHCOB #7, 149–50,
317, 341, 373 (Barnice); RSP Box 45, April 1807 Bundle, *Marks v. Parks*.
[70] Henrico County Deed Book #1, 178–9 (Montgomery to Cudjoe); Book #7, 453 (Ladd
to Johnson). An Alexander Montgomery was also listed as a merchant in the 1784 city
census. I have been unable to determine whether he and the carpenter were the same man.

free Blacks, but antagonisms and alliances appear to have been based more firmly on kinship networks than on craft. The journeyman shoemakers who formed an association to boycott employers of Black labor left no record of conflict with free Black shoemakers like Tobias Jackson and Pharis Ducking-field. Nor is there any evidence of rivalry or friendship between Jackson and Duckingfield, or among Nathaniel Anderson, Samuel Redd, and Claiborne Evans, three prominent free Black blacksmiths. That evidence of alliance or antagonism has not survived does not mean that they did not exist, but it suggests that Richmond artisans, especially Black artisans, did not develop a guild-like identification with their trade. Gabriel and two other leaders of the 1800 conspiracy were blacksmiths, but blacksmiths were not among the Whites whose lives they spoke of sparing.

From a different perspective, however, an interracial world of working people did evolve in Richmond. Nonelite Whites danced with slaves and free Blacks; they drank and gambled together; they visited the same disorderly houses. They often fought one another. On rare occasions they rose together to express contempt for town authorities. One Saturday night in September 1796 Archelaus Hughes – a landlord for several disorderly houses run by free Black women – "with divers other persons unknown did . . . Rescue and take away from the Patroll of this City . . . several Negroes." In 1797 Jacob Valentine, a White man, was jailed for "encouraging an insurrection among the Slaves of the City of Richmond."[71] These incidents troubled Richmond authorities, but the presence of a few Whites sympathetic to Blacks' struggle contributed only a small fraction to the benefits urban life offered to free and enslaved people of African descent.

The liberties that Blacks took in Richmond were not dependent on Whites' belief in racial equality but on enhanced bargaining power that was rooted in the urban economy. Whites with legal authority over slaves often granted their bondpeople the privilege to find their own work, their own lodging, and their own food. Christopher McPherson even taught school and super-vised Whites while still enslaved. Slaves had only to convince their masters that they were using these privileges to further the masters' interests. Great danger could result, however, if a master began to see his slave's actions in a different context. A White man who willingly allowed his drayman to cruise the waterfront searching for jobs could choose to beat that slave to death if he thought wages were being withheld. Context was everything.

---

[71] RSP Box 20, September–December 1796 Bundle, *Commonwealth v. Hughes*. RSP Box 23, December 1797 Bundle, *Commonwealth v. Valentine*. Chapter 5 in this book has a longer discussion of Valentine's conspiracy.

Most Richmond slaves had little choice but to work within these boundaries.[72] No doubt more than one slave who self-hired experienced Frederick
Douglass's anger when forced to "pour the reward of" his or her "toil into
the purse of" a master. Some, like Douglass, were driven to escape slavery
entirely. Richard James's "Mulatto Man" Jim Stovall, "a rough carpenter and
coarse shoemaker" apparently made his escape from Richmond by water, and
Robert Gamble's "BLACK MAN named Jackson, a House Carpenter" planned
to use "false papers of freedom" to travel to "the eastern states."[73] Most,
however, stayed in Richmond and carried on a constant struggle to increase
their autonomy. They produced profits for their masters so that they could
find the time and social space to build relatively independent lives. Many
sought to save enough money and cultivate enough friends to buy their freedom; a few succeeded. Most struggled in the face of slavery and racism to
protect the limited but hard-won liberty they enjoyed in Virginia's growing
towns. Their struggles entailed a perpetual balancing act, requiring constant
engagement with and expertise in the ways of White Richmonders in order
to create and defend the space necessary to develop autonomous cultural
practices and to build a more independent urban Black community.

[72] Except, of course, during unusual moments like that created by Gabriel's Conspiracy.
[73] Douglass, *Classic Slave Narratives*, 318. *Virginia Argus*, October 12, 1798 (Stovall);
December 25, 1807 (Jackson). Douglass ran away in 1838, when the abolitionist movement made running to the North a more viable alternative than in 1810.

7

Race and constructions of gender in early Richmond

In January 1806, the Virginia House of Delegates convened at the capitol in Richmond to consider a bill outlawing the emancipation of slaves "by [last] *Will* and testament, and . . . prevent[ing] emancipations" that would "take effect at a distant day." One delegate who debated this antimanumission bill asked his fellow legislators to consider, when deciding how to vote, the "preponderance of the blacks in numbers, over the whites, in the eastern parts of the state" and the threat of insurrection that such a situation entailed. He thought the simple majority of Blacks east of the Appalachians distressing, but he argued that the situation was really much worse than the raw numbers indicated. "To ascertain the force" of each race, he claimed, one should "deduct from the number of whites the females, who would be a weight on them destructive to their energy." Black women, on the other hand, "would be as ferocious and formidable as the males." Virginia had a "peculiar necessity" for precaution, because east of the Blue Ridge Mountains the true "force of the blacks" was "to the whites as 2 to 1."[1] The legislator believed that gender distinctions among Blacks would mean little in a slave rebellion.

In many ways this argument was eminently logical. Enslaved women shared the heavy fieldwork of Virginia plantations with their enslaved male kin, and Black women frequently proved themselves impressively "ferocious and formidable" in their relations with their owners and employers. Just four months after the legislative debate, an incident illustrating this occurred across the James River from Richmond. Martha Morriset left her house and went out to the field "to correct her" slave woman Creese who was ploughing. When Morriset grabbed Creese, the slave "push[ed] her off." Creese and Sall, another slave, then "knocked . . . down [Morriset] with an axe" and killed her. Sall and Jim, a male slave on the Morriset farm, then chopped up Morriset's

---

[1] *Virginia Argus*, January 17, 1806. Michael Lee Nicholls gave me printouts from Richmond newspapers.

body and threw "the peices in the river."[2] Sall and Creese were convicted of murder and hanged, but their response to correction illustrates the willingness of some slave women to respond violently to their oppressors. Women who ploughed fields, wielded axes to cut wood, and shared with slave men the bitterness and hatred that bondage produced might understandably have been expected to play prominent roles in slave rebellions.

From another perspective, however, fears of female slave rebels appear to have been mostly unfounded. When Gabriel organized a conspiracy to overthrow slavery in 1800, Black women played little visible role. Only one woman – Gabriel's wife Nanny – even played a supporting role in the conspiracy if the testimony produced in the conspirators' trials is to be trusted.[3] One recruit had to pledge to "keep the business secret, and not to divulge to a *woman*" when he joined Gabriel.[4] This does not mean that enslaved women would not have fought beside the conspirators had the rebellion occurred; perhaps they would have joined had shots been fired.[5] Nor does it mean that Black women in and around Richmond remained ignorant of the plot; no doubt many knew of it and sought to influence their sons and husbands to join or avoid Gabriel. It does, though, suggest that gender created divisions within the Black community of the Richmond area and that the interaction between gender and race influenced the cultural world of Gabriel and his followers.

As shown in the previous chapter, the growth and elaboration of an urban labor market forced White and Black Richmonders to develop new norms to govern race relations between 1780 and 1810. The town's growth and

---

[2] Trial record of Sall, Chesterfield County Court, Executive Papers (see ch. 2, n. 3 for full citation), Box 139. Women were less likely than men to be convicted of violent crimes: Philip J. Schwarz, *Twice Condemned: Slaves and the Criminal Laws of Virginia, 1705–1865* (Baton Rouge, 1988), esp. 101, 116. Also, though, see 136–9 for a slave man and woman cooperating in an attack on a White man.

[3] Trial Record of Isaac (William Burton), Executive Communications (see ch. 2, n. 3 for full citation), 12. A slave named Daniel testified that Isaac "had been informed by Nanny, Wife to Gabriel" that the insurrection was to occur. Women's minor role in Gabriel's Conspiracy was not an aberration; of 236 slaves tried for insurrection in Virginia between 1785 and 1865, at least 234 were men (Schwarz, *Twice Condemned*, 323–35).

[4] Executive Communications. Emphasis in original.

[5] Emilia Viotti da Costa, *Crowns of Glory, Tears of Blood: The Demerara Slave Rebellion of 1823* (New York, 1994), 192 (for a male conspiracy in Demerara that culminated in a rebellion in which "women enthusiastically joined in"). See Elizabeth Fox-Genovese, *Within the Plantation Household: Black and White Women of the Old South* (Chapel Hill, 1988), esp. 305–32; Barbara Bush, "Towards Emancipation: Slave Women and Resistance to Coercive Labour Regimes in the British West Indian Colonies, 1790–1838," in David Richardson, ed., *Abolition and Its Aftermath: The Historical Context* (London, 1985), 27–54.

economic development also altered the meaning of gender, especially the complex relationships between race and gender. That these two cultural categories affected each other is clear in the distinction between the "femininity" of Black and White women made by the legislator during the antimanumission debate. Examining the texture of interactions among White, free Black, and slave men and women in early Richmond adds a level of specificity that moves beyond the important general work that has been done on the intersection of race and gender under slavery.[6] Such an approach uncovers disparate constructions of gender difference among the different groups – Black and White, elite and common, slave and free – who lived in and around Richmond. The different and sometimes conflicting patterns that characterized the politics of gender in Richmond's households helped to shape Richmond's homes, shops, bars, and brothels, and the roads, farms, and plantation quarters of the town's hinterland. These patterns both illustrate and helped to create the shared world rent by racial divisions out of which Virginians of African descent developed crosscutting senses of racial identity.

Politics and economy of gender in Richmond households

Throughout the early modern world, urbanization contributed to local redefinitions of the proper relations between men and women. Such redefinitions influenced and were influenced by changing class structures in the wake of intensified commercialization.[7] In a slave town like Richmond, this process

[6] Kathleen M. Brown, *Good Wives, Nasty Wenches, and Anxious Patriarchs: Gender, Race, and Power in Colonial Virginia* (Chapel Hill, 1996); Deborah Gray White, *Ar'n't I a Woman? Female Slaves in the Plantation South* (New York, 1985); Jacqueline Jones, *Labor of Love, Labor of Sorrow: Black Women, Work, and the Family from Slavery to the Present* (New York, 1985), 3–43, and Jacqueline Jones, "Race, Sex, and Self-Evident Truths: The Status of Slave Women during the Era of the American Revolution," in Ronald Hoffman and Peter J. Albert, eds., *Women in the Age of the American Revolution* (Charlottesville, 1989); Fox-Genovese, *Within the Plantation Household* are general works addressing issues of slavery and gender in the United States. Also see Victoria E. Bynum, *Unruly Women: The Politics of Social and Sexual Control in the Old South* (Chapel Hill, 1992), esp. chs. 1–4; Jan Lewis, *The Pursuit of Happiness: Family and Values in Jefferson's Virginia* (Cambridge, England, 1983); Daniel Blake Smith, *Inside the Great House: Planter Life in Eighteenth-Century Chesapeake Society* (Ithaca, 1980). Suzanne Lebsock, *The Free Women of Petersburg: Status and Culture in a Southern Town, 1784–1860* (New York, 1984) examines gender in a town near Richmond. Evelyn Brooks Higginbotham, "African American Women's History and the Metalanguage of Race," *Signs* 17 (1992): 251–74 is an important theoretical essay.
[7] For European comparisons, see Natalie Zemon Davis, *Society and Culture in Early Modern France* (Stanford, 1975), 65–95; and James R. Farr, "Consumers, Commerce, and the Craftsmen of Dijon: The Changing Social and Economic Structure of a Provincial Capital,

became more complicated as racial difference affected class and gender relations. These differing definitions of gender were negotiated when Black and
White women and men interacted with one another on streets, in shops, and
in houses.[8]
Demography is one important influence on gender relations in towns and
cities. Unfortunately, although a crude picture of early Richmond demography can be reconstructed, the records hamper attempts to analyze changes
in the relationships among status, race, and gender between 1780 and 1810.
A quite detailed early city census permits a breakdown by sex of Whites and
Blacks living in Richmond in 1784. At that point, the sex ratio among White
adults was quite skewed (2 men to 1 woman), whereas that among adult
slaves was virtually even (see Appendix, Table 2). The small free Black population of Richmond in 1784 included twice as many women as men.[9] The
first three federal censuses failed to record data on the sex and age of Black
Virginians; between 1784 and 1810 the town's Black population multiplied
more than seven times, but little evidence of sex ratios has survived. During
the same period, the sex imbalance among the town's White population gradually changed from about two men for each woman to three men for every
two women.[10] This persistent if shrinking imbalance probably increased the

1450–1750," in Philip Benedict, ed., *Cities and Social Change in Early Modern France*
(London, 1989), esp. 158–62; for a theoretical discussion, see Joan Wallach Scott, *Gender
and the Politics of History* (New York, 1988), esp. 83–90. For the United States, see Mary
Ryan, *Cradle of the Middle Class: the Family in Oneida County, New York, 1790–1865* (Cam-
bridge, England, 1981); Linda K. Kerber, "Separate Spheres, Female Worlds, Woman's
Place: the Rhetoric of Women's History," *Journal of American History* 75 (1988), 9–39;
Carroll Smith-Rosenberg, "Dis-Covering the Subject of the 'Great Constitutional Discussion,' 1786–1789," *Journal of American History* 79 (1992): 841–73.

[8] Christine Stansell, *City of Women: Sex and Class in New York, 1789–1860* (Urbana, 1987
[1986]) provides a partial model for my analysis.

[9] The small imbalance in favor of men among the larger slave population more than
covered the higher number of free Black women, so the sex ratio among adult Black
Richmonders remained slightly skewed toward men.

[10] Richmond's adult White population was 67 percent male in 1784, 68 percent male in
1790 (878 men to 433 women), 61 percent male in 1800 (1,102 men to 719 women), and
60 percent male in 1810 (1,842 men to 1,213 women). The 1790 census included no division between White girls and White women; I calculated the adult sex ratio for that year
by subtracting the number of White boys under age sixteen from the total number of
White females (assuming the sex ratio among children was 1:1) to derive the number of
White women. Richmond Whites' unequal sex ratio may have been partially offset by a
slight excess of adult women that developed between 1790 and 1810 in Henrico County.
In 1790 the county had more men (1,823) than women (1,437); that changed by 1800
(986 men to 1,105 women) and 1810 (1,055 men to 1,274 women). Male migration South
and West probably explains this.

frequency with which White men had sex with Black women and may help to explain the prominence of disorderly houses run by free Black women (discussed earlier and in greater detail below).

Even if the data necessary for the reconstruction of slave and free Black households and kinship networks is absent from the decennial counts, the 1810 census – the first for which raw returns from Richmond survive – points to an interesting anomaly in the world of Black Richmonders. Although people throughout the Western world assumed that men should head households – men headed almost 85 percent of Richmond's White households – women headed more than 64 percent of the town's free Black households.[11] Part of the explanation may lie in Richmond-area masters' preference for manumitting women, but only a very small part. Just under 54 percent of the slaves manumitted between 1782 and 1810 in Richmond and Henrico County were women.[12] Presumably natural increase would have rapidly evened this small imbalance.[13] In short, the extraordinarily high percentage of free Black households headed by women suggests an important difference in the meaning of gender among the town's free Black and White populations. Presumably, a variation in so fundamental an aspect of Virginia's family politics influenced and was influenced by changes in other spheres of life. Those processes can be recaptured and the effects of economic status and racial difference traced by analyzing surviving fragments from the everyday lives of Richmond families.

It is easiest to reconstruct household relations within the town's White elite, and the conventions governing these relations inevitably created norms that influenced gender relations among less privileged groups.[14] During the three decades following the Revolution, the planter elite of the Richmond area was supplemented – nearly supplanted within the town itself – by a mercantile elite. This almost certainly changed gender relations within elite

---

[11] Men headed 812 White households; White women headed 166. Men headed 93 free Black households; women headed 171. This meshes with Lebsock's findings for Petersburg, although the percentage of female-headed free Black households was higher in Richmond in 1810 than it ever was in antebellum Petersburg (Lebsock, *Free Women of Petersburg*, 99–100).

[12] Slaveowners registered the manumission of 500 slaves in the two jurisdictions during this period. Of the 166 slaves manumitted in the Richmond Hustings Court, 93 were female; 176 of the 334 manumitted in the Henrico County Court were female.

[13] This falsely assumes that Richmond's free Black population grew primarily from natural increase. Rural slaves often moved to the city when manumitted, but it remains unclear why freed women would have been more likely to move to towns than freed men.

[14] Easiest in part because Lebsock, *Free Women of Petersburg* does such a thorough job. My discussion of elite households is indebted to Lebsock.

households. While the "wives of planters attend[ed] to dairy and to house-hold manufactures," a contemporary claimed that one rarely saw a woman shopkeeper. White women did work in shops – grand juries occasionally presented them for doing business on the Sabbath[15] – but the wives of very well-to-do merchants apparently remained relatively uninvolved in their husbands' businesses. Like those in the middle classes of other American towns, very successful male Richmonders moved their families away from their shops and created physical and cultural distance between home and business. This did not mean that elite women in Richmond ceased all economic activity: Suzanne Lebsock has shown that in nearby Petersburg "no doctrine of proper spheres prevented women – even upper-middle-class women – from turning their domestic pursuits into profit-making pursuits in the local market."[16] But a growing focus in elite households lay on the affective relationships among members of the conjugal family. Creating a loving environment increasingly defined the activities of adult women in elite homes.

Lebsock traces the development of the companionate ideal of marriage among Petersburg Whites, and her basic argument surely holds for elite Richmonders.[17] In fact, Thomas Rutherfoord's memories of his beginnings as a Richmond merchant provide a male's perspective on these developments that complements the picture that Lebsock draws from primarily female sources. Eliza Selden, who traveled to Richmond to go "husband hunting" in 1791, interpreted men's greater interest in "paper money certificates" as evidence that speculating was "more profitable than wives." Selden's comparison informs Lebsock's belief that male residents of Petersburg thought "marriage an honorable means of making money." Rutherfoord's recollection of courting casts a different light on male conceptions of the connection between money and love.[18]

[15] Harry Toulmin, *The Western Country in 1793: Reports on Kentucky and Virginia,* Marion Tinling and Godfrey Davies, eds. (San Marino, Cal., 1948), 39–40. Richmond Hustings Court Order Book (hereafter RHCOB) #7, 455–7. See later in this chapter for a fuller discussion.

[16] See Chapters 5 and 6 in this book for Richmond. Paul Johnson, *A Shopkeepers' Millennium: Society and Revivals in Rochester, New York, 1815–1837* (New York, 1978), esp. ch. 2; Ryan, *Cradle of the Middle Class,* esp. ch. 2 (northern cities). Lebsock, *Free Women of Petersburg,* 151. Carole Shammas distinguishes this "housewifery work" from domestic work in "Black Women's Work and the Evolution of Plantation Society in Virginia," *Labor History* 26 (1985): 5–28.

[17] Lebsock, *Free Women of Petersburg,* ch. 2 (esp. p. 32). Lewis, *Pursuit of Happiness,* and Smith, *Inside the Great House,* discuss similar processes among Virginia planters.

[18] Lebsock, *Free Women of Petersburg,* 19. "Husband hunting" and "honorable means" are Lebsock's phrases; others are Selden quoted by Lebsock.

Thomas Rutherfoord was born in Scotland in 1766, and after moving to Dublin, he immigrated to Richmond in 1784. He arrived as a supercargo to sell goods consigned by his brother's trading firm and stayed to become a prominent Richmond citizen. He diversified by building a substantial flour mill on the James River and became wealthy – his household, which included twenty-eight slaves, one free Black, and twenty-four Whites in 1810, was large enough to be counted a plantation by historians of the rural South. Rutherfoord's memoirs recount his 1787 courtship of "Miss Sallie" Winston.[19]

He met Sallie Winston in her eighteenth year and immediately admired her "delicate" appearance and sweet manners. Their courtship was interrupted, however, by a visit to Scotland, and, upon Rutherfoord's return to Richmond, he avoided Winston for several months. His silence awakened Sallie Winston's suspicions, and when Rutherfoord finally approached her, she called him deceitful and extracted an explanation for his tardiness. He assured her that he had only "wish[ed] to see that [his] prospects would justify . . . a tender of [his] hand," and, encouraged by her response, Rutherfoord sought her parents' approval.[20]

These recollections suggest that, while Petersburg women correctly perceived that men tied marriage to money, elite men perceived the connection differently than did women. Rutherfoord claimed to have preferred to "marry no lady who was rich," no matter her other virtues, lest others impute to him "sordid views." For companionate marriage to work, husbands had to support a family, and they may have wanted their wives dependent on that ability. This requirement, satisfied in rural areas by access to sufficient land, became more complicated in an urban world in which Rutherfoord's security and thus the security he offered Sallie Winston rested upon the vagaries of the Atlantic market.[21] Merchants played an evolving role of breadwinner, and gender roles in elite families changed in response as men and

---

[19] Thomas Rutherfoord Memoirs, typescript, Virginia Historical Society, Richmond (hereafter VHS), 1–11 (early life), 27 (Sallie). Twelve of the whites were males less than twenty-two years old, many of whom presumably clerked or apprenticed. Alan L. Karras, *Sojourners in the Sun: Scottish Migrants in Jamaica and the Chesapeake, 1740–1800* (Ithaca, 1992), esp. p. 83 for supercargo and consignment system.

[20] Thomas Rutherfoord Memoirs, 27–9, 40–2.

[21] Thomas Rutherfoord Memoirs, 41 ("views"); Lebsock, *Free Women of Petersburg*, 58–9 (male desire for female dependence). Planters also depended on markets, but merchants were more obviously dependent on invisible forces. Toby L. Ditz, "Shipwrecked; or, Masculinity Imperiled: Mercantile Representations of Failure and the Gendered Self in Eighteenth-Century Philadelphia," *Journal of American History* 81 (1994): 51–80.

women sought to create the emotional sustenance expected of home and family.[22]

Thomas and Sallie Winston Rutherfoord built a household based on mercantile activity and manufacturing. The economic and business acumen that he presented to his children as exemplary established his position as a prominent citizen in the new republic. Her care for the household made his outside activities possible, and the development of rooted, stable mercantile families contributed to the town's reputation as a reliable place to do business. She helped to establish Rutherfoord's firm in other ways, first with connections to the local Winston family and then through caring for the generation that would succeed Thomas Rutherfoord when he died. The evolving notions of gender that characterized such households helped to create the mercantile and manufacturing elite that increasingly dominated Richmond.[23] Poor Richmonders never mindlessly adopted these notions, but they built their sense of gender in a world influenced by people like the Rutherfoords.

Ideals of romantic love and companionate marriage helped to shape relations among elite Richmonders, but they may have had less impact among poorer Whites. No doubt poor White Richmonders were as inclined to love one another as were their wealthy neighbors, but life remained hard for those without much money in early Richmond, and the economic functions of marriage and the household retained primacy. At any rate, in the absence of extensive diaries or memoirs from poorer White Richmonders, a fuller picture of economic than emotional relations within these households has survived.

Men conventionally headed nonelite White households in Richmond. These men participated in the market economy as artisans, transportation workers, tavern keepers, or clerical workers, while their wives and daughters remained

---

[22] Thomas Rutherfoord Memoirs, 45 (story of caring for sick child that reinforces Thomas's secondary caregiving). Richmond remained in the same Atlantic culture as New York, so the "cooperative image" of marriage that Rutherfoord chose to relate co-existed with "another view of the family as a place for disciplining women, a means of cloistering them" (Stansell, *City of Women*, 30). Rutherfoord never admitted this tradition in explaining the move, but moving to a hill outside Richmond served in part to cloister Sallie Rutherfoord. Thomas continued to enjoy the town's sociability.

[23] Leonore Davidoff and Catherine Hall, *Family Fortunes: Men and Women of the English Middle Class, 1780–1850* (Chicago, 1987), 279–81 (role of women in peopling mercantile enterprises). This development of Richmond's elite was analogous (though not identical) to the development of a rural creole elite at the turn of the previous century. See Carole Shammas, "English-Born and Creole Elites in Turn-of-the-Century Virginia," in Thad W. Tate and David L. Ammerman, eds., *The Chesapeake in the Seventeenth Century: Essays on Anglo-American Society* (New York, 1979).

responsible for both the heavy, grinding work and the household managerial responsibilities that traditionally fell to women. Occasional glimpses into this world of backbreaking labor survive. First, there was an active demand for enslaved cooks and housekeepers. The willingness of wealthy women to pay others to do this work reinforces the difficult and onerous nature of washing, cooking, gardening, and clothes production in this preindustrial age.[24] In families without domestic slaves, that work fell to White women.

In fact, a woman's membership in a poor White household was established through her labor. During the early 1790s, a fourteen- or fifteen-year-old girl named Mary was orphaned and taken into the home of Alexander Lacy. A wealthy neighbor claimed that the Lacys treated Mary "as people in that rank of life generally do their Children" and described her as "a remarkable Industrious hard working Girl," indicating that labor around the house was a key sign of a girl's membership in a family. A woman's obligations to her father did not necessarily end when she moved out of his household. After Alexander Lacy's wife died, he applied to become "Door Keeper to the Executive." He coveted this job in part because he would get "a House on the Hill, Convenient to *his Daughter* who wou'd wash for him." She would assume this burden in addition to all those she carried as Charles Burnett's wife.[25] While wealthy women may have found value in their supervision of this work, for White "women who had little or no slave help, the benefits of productive labor were probably outweighed by the burdens." Despite this work, or perhaps because of it, wives remained subordinate to husbands, as emphasized by complaints that men physically abused women in these households.[26]

---

[24] Lebsock, *Free Women of Petersburg*, ch. 6 (esp. pp. 148–64). For example of market for "female" work: "Wanted to hire, A trusty, honest Negro Woman who understands Cooking, Washing, etc." *Virginia Argus*, January 12, 1798. The market was not limited to slaves: in 1806 "John Alley and Effey his wife" brought suit against the estate of William Jones for a debt contracted to "Effey Boyd then a single woman for her services as house keeper and manager of his domestic affairs." Henrico County Court Judgments, Box 88–21, March 1806 Bundle, LiVa.

[25] Richmond Suit Papers (hereafter RSP), Box 40, May 1796 Bundle, *Charles and Mary Burnett v. Alexander Lacy's Executors*, LiVa. The Burnetts sued for Mary's right to Lacy's estate and lost, but the neighbor's deposition describes the labor expected of daughters in nonelite households.

[26] Lebsock, *Free Women of Petersburg*, ch. 6 (esp. pp. 149, 158–9). RSP Box 38, October 1805 Bundle, *Commonwealth v. John Scott*; and RHCOB #6, 283. In this case Janet Scott complained that "John Scott her Husband had beat and very ill treated her so that she [was] in Danger of her life." On April 23, 1810, James Young was arraigned for beating his wife to death when she tried "to prevent his beating a servant boy" (RHCOB #8, 494).

In addition to those burdens, however, some White women engaged in market activity less related to household responsibilities. This included women recognized as artisans in their own right: the 1782 census included three mantua makers and four seamstresses – all women. An indeterminate number also took in boarders, thus integrating traditional domestic jobs into the urban market. Other poor White women received public funds for the board, washing, and lodging of even poorer people. Some made money by hiring out slaves who might have helped them at home: in 1786 Zachariah Rowland hired "a negro Girl" from shirtmaker Milly Thomas.[27] These activities occurred frequently and were ways that White women found remunerative niches in the town's economy.

Nonelite White women also remained closely integrated into their households' primary market activities during this period. Unlike the mercantile elite, artisans and shopkeepers maintained the traditionally close physical and cultural connection between workshop and household. Women played key roles in these economic enterprises. Their traditional productive roles kept artisanal households running,[28] and they often participated in other ways. In 1801 Fleming Russell's wife was working behind the counter of his shop, but we know she worked as a shopkeeper only because a thief took stockings and a waistcoat pattern while Mrs. Russell was getting flour for a customer. Similarly, Sarah Boulton apparently kept her husband's store. In 1804 she and her daughter went to a play. Before leaving, they locked the house and gave the key to a neighbor to give to her husband when he returned, but when they got back from the play, James Boulton was still out and $50 had been stolen from a drawer in the shop. Women commonly participated in households' primary market activities before homes were separated from places of business. While such separation had begun in Richmond during the last decade of the eighteenth century, it had not progressed beyond the town's mercantile elite by 1810.[29]

Women's accepted participation in their households' market activities could easily cross the line that separated "respectable" and "illicit" activity. Doing so often – though not always – involved crossing a racial line as well.

---

[27] RSP Box 51, June–July 1809 Bundle, *Cornelius Johnston v. James Smith* (Smith owed "Johnsons wife . . . $15 in part of room"; RHCOB #7, 245; RHCOB #8, 365 (court paid for care of poor); RSP Box 6, March 1787 Bundle, *Thomas v. Rowland*.

[28] James Sidbury, "Gabriel's World: Race Relations in Richmond, Virginia, 1750–1810" (Ph.D. diss., Johns Hopkins University, 1991), 65–8 for evidence supporting this obvious point.

[29] RHCOB #5, 25 (Russell). A female slave of Fleming Russell named Salley also worked in the store at the time. RHCOB #7, 444–5 (Boulton). Chapter 6 this book; and Lebsock, *Free Women of Petersburg*, 149 (gradual separation of work and home).

Shopkeeping was one of the most common ways women participated in Richmond's mercantile economy, and shopkeeping often shaded into less than reputable work. When John Parker and Drury Burch headed home after work in 1807, they decided to stop in the house of Sarah Bristoe for refreshments; Bristoe's was a public house only a few steps from Burch's residence. A dispute arose in which Burch perceived Parker to be bothering Sarah Bristoe. Rising to Bristoe's defense, Burch used language that emphasized the extent to which Bristoe's feminine respectability was endangered by her work in a public house. Why, he asked, was "the lady . . . interrupted at that time of night?" Ultimately, Burch shot Parker in defense of Bristoe's honor.[30] Perhaps in doing so he defended the respectability of his neighborhood by insisting that a barmaid who worked there could not legitimately be harassed by visitors, but the incident also illustrates the degree to which nonelite White women's work could pull them to the edges of sanctioned gender roles. For if Sarah Bristoe was worthy of Burch's chivalrous defense, she was close enough to unworthy to elicit Parker's insult.

In other cases, especially cases involving slaves or free Blacks, work could push White women across those boundaries. The clearest and most common cases involved women shopkeepers violating rules about dealing with slaves. Among the twenty-nine people presented by an 1806 grand jury for "sabbath breaking by dealing with negroes . . . and opening [their] Shop[s]" were at least five women. This number does not include Sarah Boulton, though James Boulton was presented on this count, and his wife sometimes kept shop in his stead.[31] Other male shopkeepers presented for Sabbath breaking may have shared oversight of their shops with their wives. Such activity could expose White women to sides of urban life about which "ladies" should have known little. In September 1800, shortly after Gabriel's Conspiracy had been uncovered, King, an alleged conspirator, entered the shop of a Mrs. Martin and purchased spirits. She later testified that, while there, King made a veiled reference to continuing plans to overthrow slavery.[32]

This world of petty commercial interaction was not one in which proper "ladies" thrived. Women working in household businesses could be provoked to behave publicly in ways that illustrated the differences between the

---

[30] RHCOB #7, 366.
[31] RSP Box 42, November 1806 Bundle. See n. 29 for Sarah Boulton. At least three free Black male shopkeepers were also presented for Sabbath breaking by this grand jury. In another case, Joseph and Sarah Camba were sued by John Laypold because of "the sd Sarah's (late Sarah Miller) dealing with a Slave in [Laypold's] employment." RSP Box 15, August 1792 Bundle.
[32] Executive Papers, Box 114 (trial of P. N. Nicholas's King).

meanings of gender in elite and nonelite households. When William Swain entered "the House of Louis Degougue on Bussiness of Mrs. Mackay," an actress, he met a rude reception. DeGogue, as the name was more frequently spelled, was a baker and ordinary keeper whose wife greeted Swain with "Opprobrius Language." She chased him outside, and "pursued him with a large stick . . . which she threw at him . . . and hit him under the left Eye."[33] Not surprisingly, Swain's complaint failed to mention the interaction(s) that precipitated Mrs. DeGogue's attack, but the incident nicely highlights differences among the lives of Richmond's White women. It is difficult to imagine young Sallie Winston or the slightly older Mrs. Sallie Rutherfoord chasing people out of her house and throwing sticks at them. Mrs. Rutherfoord's was not a house in which business was regularly conducted, and she was not routinely involved in contentious business relations. Wealthy women directed their violent outbursts at the slaves who worked under them, and such violence took place within space denominated private by Virginia's dominant culture.[34] As late as 1810, Mrs. Rutherfoord's experience was rare for White women in Richmond. Most lived and worked in the commercial districts of the town and engaged in market activities. In doing so they lived on and helped to create the margins of gender boundaries that were perpetually being defined and modified.

Richmond Blacks lived on a more complex set of boundaries. No significant number could realistically aspire to the genteel way of life enjoyed by Richmond's elite. Legal, cultural, and economic forces affected gender roles within Black households and within the Black community in ways that White townspeople never experienced. Labor in the household played an important role in shaping Black gender roles just as it did for Whites. The first key to the meanings of masculinity and femininity within the Black world lies in the legal parameters within which these people lived.

Slavery comprised the most important of those legal parameters. Most but by no means all Richmonders of acknowledged African descent were enslaved.[35] The Black community of Richmond does not appear to have been

---

[33] RSP 24, February–April 1789 Bundle, *Commonwealth v. DeGorgue.*
[34] Mechal Sobel, *The World They Made Together: Black and White Values in Eighteenth-Century Virginia* (Princeton, 1987), 148 for a violent outburst against a domestic slave by Lucy Parke Byrd, the wife of Richmond's founder. I have found no specific incidents of such outbursts in Richmond from 1780 to 1810, but because such outburst did not lead to court cases and because relatively few diaries from that time and place have survived, the absence of evidence should not be interpreted as evidence of the absence of such behavior.
[35] In 1790 15 percent of Richmond's Black population was free; in 1810 almost 25 percent was free.

deeply divided along lines determined by legal status, as illustrated by the
abundant if unquantifiable evidence that free and enslaved Blacks married
one another. They worked together on Richmond's docks and boats, in the
town's shops and warehouses, at construction sites, and in workshops.[36] Free
Blacks owned slaves and sometimes clearly exploited them for economic purposes; more frequently free Black slaveowners appear to have owned family
members whom they sought to free.[37] The distinction between family relationships and productive economic relationships was not always clear in households in which all members were expected to contribute labor, but the ties
between free and enslaved Blacks in Richmond meant that the customs and
law of slavery influenced the meaning of gender difference among all town Blacks.

Inheritance was a central prop for patriarchal systems of authority throughout the early modern Western world. Husbands and fathers controlled property – even, to a large degree, property brought into households by their wives
– and wives and children received their wealth, social status, and communal
identities primarily from their husbands and fathers. The law of slavery in
Virginia profoundly undermined this patriarchal system among Blacks. African
American men played no legal role in passing on to their children the single
most valuable characteristic that a Black child in Richmond could inherit –
freedom.[38] From the seventeenth century until the Civil War, all children of
recognized African descent born in Virginia inherited their legal condition
– slave or free – from their mothers. And masters' property rights in slaves
also ran through those slaves' maternal rather than paternal lines.

[36] *Virginia Argus*, February 26, 1808 (Armistead Russell's advertisement for John Russell,
a runaway slave married to a free Black woman); and RHCOB #6, 225–6 (free Black
man "stealing" his runaway slave wife's clothes from her master). Such evidence is scattered throughout Richmond records. See Chapter 6 of this book for abundant evidence
that free Black men and enslaved men worked together. Little evidence shows free Black
and enslaved women working together, but this may reflect a bias in the records.
[37] RHCOB #2, 708–9 for free Black household mortgaging a slave; Henrico County Court
Order Book (hereafter HCCOB) #2, 509, 568 LiVa; HCCOB #6, 169, 184, 586, 596 for
examples of free Black men and women emancipating slaves. The extent of this practice
is unrecoverable, because in addition to these clear cases, sometimes free Blacks gave
money to Whites who bought and freed slaves (Richmond Hustings Court Deed Book
#3, 153 [for Benjamin DuVal's deed freeing "a negro girl Mary Ann the daughter of
said Anthony"; DuVal recorded that Anthony Shelton paid him $100 for this, but he
was under no obligation to record that fact]).
[38] Free Black fathers who bought and freed their children overcame this legal disability.
See, for example, Charles's deed of emancipation executed by his father Nathaniel
Anderson, a Richmond blacksmith. RSP Box 56, December 1810 to February 1811 Bundle,
Anderson to Charles.

This seemingly straightforward and limited legal issue had powerful rami-
fications for basic norms regulating naming practices and the memory of
family relationships. During the 1790s and early 1800s, Virginia law allowed
Blacks who believed themselves legally entitled to freedom to sue their masters *in forma pauperis* if they could convince a lawyer to take the case. Enslaved
Virginians suing for freedom either produced or elicited narrative accounts
of their maternal line of descent.[39] Thus Sally Lewis, "a person of colour,"
petitioned the Richmond Hustings Court as the "daughter of one Letitia
Lewis," claiming "unquestionable evidence, that, Meggy, the mother of the
said Letitia and grandmother of your petitioner was a free Indian." Delpha,
another enslaved Richmonder, demanded freedom for herself and for her
son and daughter. She claimed that her grandmother, "Sucky Nighten, a
White, and free Born Woman" had been brought to Virginia "as a convict
Servant." Sucky Nighten had lived on a plantation in King William County
where she and a "Negro Man Slave named George" had a "Female Child
named Jenny Nighten," who was Delpha's mother. Joseph Parkinson, a New
Kent County planter, bought Jenny Nighten and held her as a slave. During
her life, she had several children by a slave of Parkinson's, and subsequently
she had other children by a Black shoemaker named Nat. Delpha did not
specify which of these men was her father, because her free status rested on
her relationship to Jenny Nighten.[40]

A deep memory of maternal descent developed. In 1806 a group of
Richmond slaves petitioned the court for their freedom. They claimed their
freedom as "descendants by the female line of aboriginal Indians" on Virginia's Eastern Shore. Some claimed to be the children of Agnes, "the daughter of Betty, who was said to be the daughter of Pleasants who was said to
be an Indian." Others said they had descended from an Indian woman named
Rosi Arrow. Still others were children of Leah, a woman "some . . . neigh-
bours supposed" to be a descendant of an Indian named Moll Cook, who
had "been reduced to Slavery about . . . 1699." These people may have been
inventing relationships to these Indian women, but that hardly matters. The
communities in which they grew up – and these people moved in various patterns from the Eastern Shore of Virginia, to Maryland, to Richmond – retained

[39] Quote from Thomas Bailey deposition in RSP Box 39, "Papers relative to sundry negroes
taken from Thomas Moore upon supposition of their being free and detained until evidence can be obtained to asscertain [*sic*] their right to freedom" Bundle (hereafter "freedom suit Bundle"). See Jean B. Lee, *The Price of Nationhood: The American Revolution
in Charles County* (New York, 1994), 211–15 for freedom suits in a Maryland county.
[40] RSP 45, November 1807 Bundle, *Lewis v. Fulcher*; RSP Box 55, August 1810 Bundle,
Delpha v. Berry.

a detailed enough social memory of kinship for members to make plausible claims about their maternal inheritance over at least four generations – a century.[41]

Virginia law provided powerful incentives for such memories, and free-dom suits highlighted them. Testimony from such suits does not, however, shed much light on the roles such memories played in Black Richmonders' sense of personal and familial identity. Naming practices and choices about inheritance open other perspectives on these questions and suggest that free Blacks responded to Richmond's legal structures by trying to maximize flex-ibility in the face of an often hostile system. Richard Bowler, a free mulatto man, and Mary Bee built a stable family in Richmond during the 1790s and early 1800s. They had at least three children whom they named William Bee, Miller Bee, and Elizabeth (Betsey) Bee. The Bee surname did not indicate that Bowler lacked concern or responsibility for the children. In 1804 he conveyed a life estate in a town lot to Mary Bee and specified that the lot should go to her children when she died. Three years later Bowler died and left much of his estate to the three children, whom he now identified for the first time in the legal records as his own. Richard Bowler and Mary Bee may have decided to give their children Mary's surname because it was through Mary that the children could assert their right to freedom, but it seems unlikely that the children thought themselves Bees rather than Bowlers. Just one year after Richard Bowler died, a "Man of Colour" named "William Bowler alias Richard Bowler" was arrested for burglary. Was this William Bee, the son of Richard Bowler and Mary Bee?[42] If so, his chosen identity

---

[41] RSP Box 39, freedom suit Bundle, Thomas Bailey deposition. Bailey's description of their movements emphasizes the different nature of Black and White inheritance. He focuses on the plaintiffs' mothers' movements but explains those movements by describing the various masters' inheritance through male lines. This deposition hints at the way legal conditions could lead Black and White Virginians to develop similar cultural structures – in this case, maternal lines of descent as keys to Black identity – without sharing the values informing those structures. Whites, after all, remembered Black families through maternity for reasons tied to their property rights; Blacks did the same because of the value of freedom. Eric Robert Papenfuse, "From Redcompense [sic] to Revolution: *Mahoney v. Ashton* and the Transfiguration of Maryland Culture, 1791–1802," *Slavery and Abolition* 15 (1994): 38–62 includes evidence of similar communal memories and strong hints that such communal memories were preserved by slave women.

[42] Richmond Hustings Court Deed Book (hereafter RHCDB) #4, 71–2 (for life estate); RHCDB #5, 23–4 (for Bowler's will); RHCOB #7,412–13 and RSP 45, March 1807 [1808] Bundle, *Commonwealth v. Bowler* (for "William Bowler alias Richard Bowler"). I have been unable to untangle reliable rules governing which parent's surname free Black children would take. John Sabb, who worked in construction trades, identified all his

represents the flexibility with which free Black Richmonders assumed different names.[43]
Further evidence of this flexibility abounds. Free Blacks frequently appear
in court records using more than one name.[44] George Quickley, a free Black
shipmaster, died in 1807 and left his estate to be divided between "Mary
Quickley my companion in life (though not legally married)" and their son
Peter Quickley. Three years later, when his former companion was arrested
for arson, she was styled "Mary Brown alias Quickley."[45] Perhaps aliases
sometimes represented free Blacks' efforts to evade oversight by unfriendly
authorities, but frequently they were invoked in situations that defy such an
explanation. Betty Hambleton, a free Black woman purchased her daughter
and freed her; in the deed of emancipation Hambleton referred to her daughter once as Betsey Grymes and once as Betsey Hambleton. A deed of emancipation presented a moment when precise identification would appear to
have been in the interests of all involved.[46] That aliases found their way into
such documents suggests that they had complex and plural meanings among
free Black Richmonders. On one level, they reflected free Blacks' disadvant-
aged position on the margins of Virginia society: norms regulating marriage,
inheritance, and parenthood did not easily apply to people who lived on the
cusp between freedom and slavery. Life on this margin was difficult and

children with the last name "Sabb" (HCCOB #13, 347); Angela Barnett registered her children as free under the name "Barnett," but when one of them was charged with felony,
the daughter was identified as "Sally Anthony alias Barnet." Angela Barnett's spouse was
William Anthony (HCCOB #13, 299; HCCOB #15, 140).
[43] It might also represent a practice that had evolved from plural naming patterns among
some West African peoples, but Africanist Paul Lovejoy does not recognize in these practices naming patterns common to any West African peoples (personal communication).
[44] Enslaved Blacks also used multiple names, but the sources I have relied on shed less
light on slave naming practices. For the classic study of slave naming practices that used
plantation records, see Herbert G. Gutman, *The Black Family in Slavery and Freedom,
1750–1925* (New York, 1976); for Virginia see Allan Kulikoff, *Tobacco and Slaves: The
Development of Southern Cultures in the Chesapeake, 1680–1800* (Chapel Hill, 1986),
325–6; and Sobel, *World They Made Together*, 154–8.
[45] RHCDB #5, 47–8; RHCOB #9, 79–80 and RSP Box 56, November 1810 Bundle, *Commonwealth v. Brown alias Quickley*. Among numerous other examples, see RSP Box 25,
March 1800 Bundle, *Thomas Gibson alias Mingo Jackson v. Amey Halestock*; and *Commonwealth. v. Daniel Dixon alias Hatcher's Daniel* in RHCOB #4, 635 and RSP Box 27, August
1801 Bundle.
[46] RHCDB #4, 67. Perhaps Betty Hambleton wanted to include both names by which her
daughter was known in the deed, but the casual and unexplained way in which she shifted
between names casts doubt on this interpretation.

oppressive, but liminal status provided some tools that could be used to fashion identity and gender.

The household remained the fundamental social unit for free Blacks just as it did for White Richmonders, but free Black households took a remarkable variety of forms and exhibited a marked fluidity. Many free Blacks lived in households organized around "standard" conjugal families. In 1782 Rebecca Jackson, a seamstress, purchased her freedom for £80; four years later she manumitted her husband "Toby commonly Toby Jackson" and her son David Jackson.[47] They and another son, Toby Jackson Junior, probably lived together in a house in Richmond until 1805. The senior Tobias Jackson outlived Rebecca, buried her in a private graveyard behind his house, and remarried a woman named Martha. Tobias Jackson was a shoemaker and presumably made and sold shoes in the household. If he employed other shoemakers, no record has survived. He and Rebecca Jackson did, however, take on Elizabeth Wallace as an apprentice seamstress in the household.[48] In short, the structure of the Jackson household appears to have been similar to that of most White craft households, with the possible exception that both Tobias and Rebecca Jackson were working artisans.

But even apparently traditional free Black households often worked according to rules that differed from those that governed rich or poor White households. Legally married free Black people were subject to the same laws governing property as were Whites, and in several cases free Black men were sued for debts incurred by their wives.[49] Because free Blacks sometimes opted against legally sanctioned marriage, such suits could cause confusion. On July 10, 1801, Fleming Russell, the constable of Richmond, attached and sold a walnut table and a tea chest from David Norton's residence in order to pay a debt on which Norton had defaulted. Catharine Evans "(alias Catharine Norman)" immediately brought suit against Russell, claiming that the table and chest were "her own absolute and bonafide property," and that Russell had no right to seize them. The case went to trial and created a headache

---

[47] Henrico County Deed Book (hereafter HCDB) #1, 41, LiVa; HCDB #2, 312–13. Toby and Rebecca Jackson also had a son named Toby, but I presume that the Toby Jackson freed in 1786 was Rebecca's husband, because the deed freeing David Jackson specified that he was her son, while that freeing Toby did not.

[48] RSP Box 37, June–July 1805 Bundle, *Commonwealth v. Jackson* (fight between David and Toby Jackson in their parents' house). RHCOB #8, 324, and RHCDB #5, 513 (Tobias Jackson Senior's will); RHCDB #1, 365 (for apprenticeship). She sued for her freedom dues (RSP Box 19, April 1795 Bundle, *Wallace v. Jackson*).

[49] RSP Box 30, November–December 1802 Bundle, *Patton v. Anderson*. Patton, a grocer and carpenter, sued Claiborne Anderson for debt and won on "a bond given by your wife who was then a free molatto" named "Sukey Pryor."

for all involved, because the court found it difficult to determine who had owned the seized property. That its confusion stemmed from questions about the status of Norton's relationship with Catharine Evans/Norman is suggested by one document that listed her not as Catharine Evans or Catharine Norman but as Catharine Norton.[50] Perhaps Norton and Evans lived together as a married couple but attempted to use Whites' lack of respect for Black marriages to protect their property from a lawsuit. Or perhaps Catharine Evans ran a boarding house in which David Norton was living, and she got caught in a legal system more interested in protecting the rights of White creditors than those of free Black owners of property. Or did Catharine Evans's relationship with David Norton lie somewhere between these two poles? The case illustrates White Richmonders' uncertainty about the legal status of free Black unions and suggests that free Black women and men formed households according to norms that often remained beyond the knowledge or general purview of town authorities. Denied the legal protection that marriage conferred on Whites, at least some free Blacks preferred to escape the legal limitations and obligations of formal marriage: free Black barber Ceasar Hope bequeathed most of his estate to Tenar Hope, who lived with him "as . . . [his] wife," regardless of whether he "ever marr[ied] her in form."[51]

Many free Black Richmonders lived in nonconjugal households. Like nonelite White women, they sometimes charged others for lodging and boarding in order to make ends meet.[52] Apparently they sometimes took rent from family members: in 1803 Mary Whistler sued Thomas Whistler, perhaps her brother, spouse, or other relative, for £5 for "board and washing etc." for $5\frac{1}{2}$ months. Boarders often lived in households that mixed enslaved and free Blacks, presumably on roughly equal footing.[53] Free Black women often

---

[50] RSP 28, March–April 1802 Bundle, *Evans (alias Norman) v. Fleming*. An 1801 trial ended in a hung jury; on March 9, 1802, a new jury dismissed the case, but then the court rescinded that order and the jury ruled in Russell's favor.

[51] Richmond Hustings Court Will Book #1, 165–6. Hope added "marr[ied] . . . in form" after the will was first written.

[52] RSP Box 19, December 1795 Bundle, *Whaley v. Butler*. The 1810 census provides further circumstantial evidence of free Black boarding houses. Forty-six households headed by free black women included more than five members. Surely many of these included boarders. Twelve households included between eight and ten members and thus are even more likely to have been boarding houses.

[53] RSP Box 30, January–February 1803 Bundle, *Whistler v. Whistler*. Mary and Thomas may have shared last names without being related, but Whistler was not a common name among the town's free Blacks. Pastry chef Nancey Bird's household included seven free Black and three slave members. Some almost surely were boarders. Samuel Mordecai, *Richmond in By-Gone Days: Being Reminiscences of An Old Citizen* (Richmond, 1856), 313–14 for Bird as pastry chef. 1810 census for household.

lived together in houses that appear not to have been inhabited by men. Some free Black men and women lived in households headed by Whites or shared households with slaves.[54] In short, these liminal people shared households with those on each of the borders that defined their status.

More interesting, however, than the variety of household types found in Richmond's free Black community is the relationship among the households that these people lived in and moved among. Perhaps because life was difficult and uncertain, free Blacks developed communal networks that cut across household lines. Some of this was hardly unusual. When Lucy Howell, "a mulatto orphan of Frank Howell" chose Frank Lewis, a free Black man, for her guardian, the free Black community responded to the death of a parent as White Virginians had been responding for over a century.[55] In other cases free Black Richmonders took further steps toward fluid households rooted in an urban Black community. Men and women living together did not always live harmoniously. Free Black women sometimes took their mates to court in search of physical protection, but courts could be intrusive, and the level of protection that they offered was doubtless low.[56] Free Black women could turn instead to one another for shelter against abusive men. Thomas Gibson "alias Mingo Jackson" was married to Lucy Gibson. Twice Thomas Gibson sued other free Black women, once for forcibly detaining his wife, and once for "seducing and detaining" her from his "bed and board."[57] Such language may suggest that Lucy Gibson was sexually involved with these

[54] RSP Box 19, December 1795 Bundle, *Whaley v. Butler* (Nancy Whaley sued Marian Butler – who was probably Black – for "boarding and Lodging.") According to the 1810 census, 133 Richmond households headed by White men included at least one free Black, and 76 households headed by free Black men or women included at least one slave. Also see RHCOB #3, 541.

[55] RHCOB #4, 363. For early White Virginians see Darret B. Rutman and Anita H. Rutman, "'Now-Wives and Sons-in-Law': Parental Death in a Seventeenth-Century Virginia County," in *Chesapeake in the Seventeenth Century*.

[56] RSP Box 24, September–October 1799 [1801] Bundle, *Commonwealth v. Anderson* provides one of many examples. In this case Suckey Anderson swore that "Clayborne Anderson did . . . assault Beat and kick her." The court forced Claiborne Anderson to post bond for good behavior toward his wife.

[57] RSP Box 32, Office Judgments and Dismissions 1797–1803 Bundle, *Gibson v. King*; RSP Box 25, March 1800 Bundle, *Gibson alias Jackson v. Halestook*. I am virtually certain that Amy Halestook (elsewhere Hailstock) was Black, and I suspect that Rachel King was Black. Lucy Gibson also turned to the courts for protection when she had Mingo Jackson arrested for a breach of the peace (RSP Box 49, January–April 1809 Bundle, *Commonwealth v. Jackson*). White women may have used similar strategies in response to physical abuse, but I found no evidence of it.

women; regardless, it indicates that she turned to them to escape her husband. Both times the court declined to intervene in what justices probably believed to be a private problem of a free Black Richmonder moving among households within her community.

Such fluidity among households was not limited to people: free Blacks also passed property among households. On October 13, 1800, a slave named Frank Bird was arrested for stealing a white hog from the house of Ellick Price, a free Black man, but the hog did not belong to Price. Instead, it was "the property of one Sally Sablong," wife of free Black barber Charles Sablong, who apparently kept her livestock at Price's house.[58] Sablong was not alone in keeping her property with someone else. Thomas Gibson, perhaps after a quarrel with his wife Lucy, deposited his trunk full of clothes and money with Charles Evans, a friend who lived at the mill house of John Harvie. And when Nancy Lewis, "a free woman of colour," left town for a visit to the country, she left some money that she had stolen with Lucinda Berry, a free Black neighbor.[59] If on one level households remained the fundamental unit of Richmond's free Black community, they were far from atomistic units. Free Blacks shared many of the legal disabilities and much of the social pressure that slavery and racism created. One response was to pool communal control over people and property among the town's Black population in order to limit the White community's influence. Court records provide conflict-ridden examples, but presumably the cooperative behavior that these unusual examples reveal extended to a range of everyday behavior.

No doubt kinship played a crucial role in shaping Black Richmonders' decisions about whom to trust with their property, with orphans, or with loved ones' personal safety. Unfortunately, only punctuated and incomplete free Black kinship networks can be reconstructed, making it difficult to document or measure the role of kinship in these interactions, but free Black Richmonders clearly turned to other Black Richmonders in these situations. The movement of goods and people among households helped to cement ties among Black Richmonders and reinforced the bonds of a distinct, though not a separate, community.

---

[58] RSP Box 26, September–October and December 1800 Bundle, *Commonwealth v. Frank Bird*. The court accepted Sally's ownership of the pig rather than referring to it as Charles's property.

[59] RHCOB #8, 242–4 (Gibson). RSP Box 46, February 1808 Bundle, *Commonwealth v. Lewis*; and RHCOB #7, 393. Similarly, when free Black Henry Cousins bought stolen goods from a slave of Samuel Paine, he left them with "a relation of his Rachel Cox," though Cousins denied knowing the goods were stolen (RSP Box 10, April 1788 Bundle, *Commonwealth v. Cousins*).

Work was the most ubiquitous aspect of everyday life for Black people
in Richmond. Many, like Toby Jackson, were artisans and lived in households organized around craft production.[60] Black women's work within those
households no doubt resembled that of nonelite White women; less evidence
survives about Black women's work in nonartisanal families. Some women
worked in the clothing trades. Others participated in other forms of household production for the market, working in gardens, spinning thread, and
caring for livestock.[61] Many, as mentioned earlier, took boarders and cared for
the infirm, either through private agreement or as part of early Richmond's
skeletal system of public relief. Such work could be a woman's contribution
to a traditional artisanal household or a primary source of income for households headed by unskilled women. Black women also did domestic work in
White households and worked as shopkeepers.[62]

Perhaps the most common form of work that Black women found in early
Richmond involved washing clothes. Almost all Black women, free and slave,
helped to wash clothes for those who lived in their households, and laundering clothes could serve as a complementary part of a household's market
activity. Keepers of boarding houses, nurses of elderly and sick people, or
needleworkers also charged for "washing."[63] Laundering clothes also served
as a primary economic activity. White Virginians' obsession with clean clothes
was "much celebrated by eighteenth-century visitors," and the demand for
cleanliness meant that enough women spent most of their time washing clothes
for the term "washerwoman" to become common. Customers took their laundry to washerwomen's homes and returned there to collect clean clothes.[64]

[60] For Black artisans, see Chapter 6 of this book and my "Slave Artisans in Richmond,
Virginia, 1780–1810," in Howard B. Rock, Paul A. Gilje, and Robert Asher, eds., *American Artisans: Crafting Social Identity, 1750–1850* (Baltimore, 1995), 48–62.

[61] RSP Box 11, May 1789 Bundle, *Grantland v. Sheppard*; RSP Box 48, September–October
1808 Bundle, *Commonwealth v. Ellis* (clothing trades).

[62] RSP Box 13, June–July 1791 Bundle, *Anderson v. Howe* (Sarah Anderson nursed the sick
James Howe); also RHCOB #6, 475; RHCOB #8, 365 (nursing sick). RHCOB #7, 438
(Frank Sheppard, a free Black painter received $20 to support a poor White man for six
months, but Sheppard's wife Jemima probably did most of the work). RSP Box 13, May
1790 Bundle, *Giffard v. Pryor* (debt owed housekeeper); RSP Box 22, 1797 Bundle, *Commonwealth v. Burgess* (Hannah Burgess for "retailing to negroes").

[63] RSP Box 24, March 1792 Bundle, *Hailstock v. Tatham*; RHCOB #8, 365; RSP Box 11,
May 1789 Bundle, *Grantland v. Sheppard*.

[64] Shammas, "Black Women's Work," 20–1 ("celebrated"); RHCOB #2, 351–2 (a White
woman assaulted one evening going "to her washerwoman's house after her clothes.")
Customers of washerwomen were not necessarily well off. Marcus Elcan's clothes were
stolen and he found them "at a Washerwoman's." Upon tracing them, he found they

This work was demanding and unpleasant, forcing women to work with harsh soaps, haul heavy water, and tend fires and hot water even during the hottest summer months. No doubt cleaning clothes for money was restricted to free Black and enslaved women – the least advantaged people in town.

Nonetheless, this hard and nasty work provided women an opportunity to come together during the work day. Much washing took place in public. Presumably these washerwomen "Boyle[d] . . . the cloaths with soap" over fires just outside their homes. Laundresses then gathered near the market house where Shockoe Creek approached the James River. They "washed [rinsed] in the stream," and then allowed clothes to dry on a nearby pasture, which was "considered a common" (between the courthouse and the river, Map 5). Surely they relieved some of their drudgery by meeting friends and talking with one another. In doing so, they laid claim to space adjacent to the town market and close to the center of Richmond's public life.[65]

A collective Black female claim to public space constituted a minor breach in the evolving standards governing race and gender in American cities. It seems unlikely, for example, that Sallie Rutherfoord would habitually have met with other elite Richmond women in public. One must not, however, mistake this public space for a privileged position. There was surely a connection between the ability of free Black women to claim this common and their roles in Richmond's market economy. Black women were working people, not "ladies," and the costs of such a designation greatly outweighed the advantages.

Understanding the nature of those costs and thus some of the meanings of gender for different Richmonders requires a distinction between the experiences of poor White women and those of free Blacks. Both groups operated in the geographical heart of Richmond's market economy. Both routinely engaged in a wide range of economic, social, and sometimes acrimonious activities in the public shops and on the streets of the town. When White women argued in the streets, called one another "mulatto whore[s]," or got into disputes in which they were called "transpourt[s], whore[s], and bitch[es],"[66] they implicitly rejected elite notions that women should be sheltered from

---

had been sent there by Isham Harris, his free Black servant. She may have been fencing rather than washing them, but she was not charged (RHCOB #4, 137).

[65] John Harrower quoted in Shammas, "Black Women's Work," 21. Harrower does not say where they boiled the clothes; that is my surmise. Mordecai, *Richmond in By-Gone Days*, 18 ("common"). The success of their claim is illustrated by the fact that Mordecai remembered the space as having been theirs over fifty years later.

[66] RSP Box 2, April–May 1785 Bundle, *Edy New v. William and Sarah Vaughan* ("whore"); RSP Box 33, May 1804 Bundle, *F. N. Guto v. James Custerlow* [Custaloe] ("transpourt").

the contentious, competitive world of the city. But when these White women appeared in court to adjudicate these disputes, they frequently found themselves represented by the males who headed their households. Similarly, when a nonelite White woman turned to the court system to recover money due her for market activity, her husband often filed the suit.[67] Free Black men sometimes appeared in court in their wives' stead. Because free Blacks often opted not to seek legal sanction for their marriages and because Whites paid less attention to marital ties among free Blacks even when such ties were legal, free Black women appeared in court on their own account more frequently than did their nonelite White counterparts.

It might seem that free Black women enjoyed a privileged position relative to nonelite Whites, but nothing could be further from the truth, for the assumption that Black women acted independently in the public realm rested in part on the effective denial of reliable legal respect for the private realm in which the sanctity of White Virginian families was protected. This was especially true for slave women, who could make no legal claim to private space without their masters' consent. It was almost as true for free Blacks. With little apparent excuse, constables and other White men felt authorized to violate free Black women's homes. John Tinsley and John Staple broke "down and destroy[ed]" the "pannel Doore" of Suckey Pryor's house in 1800. Three years later constable George Matthews committed an assault upon Mary Quickley. During the same month, he used a search warrant to gain entry to Suckey James's house. Having gained entry legally, he "made an Assault upon" Suckey Parish (probably the same person as Suckey James).[68] These free Black women's complaints never explicitly mentioned sexual assault, but it was sometimes – probably often – involved.[69] No doubt poor White women, and even wealthy White women, suffered sexual and other

---

[67] RSP Box 51, June–July 1809 Bundle, *Cornelius Johnston v. James Smith* (Smith failed to pay "Cornelius Johnsons wife in Richmond $15 in part of room").

[68] RSP Box 25, May 1800 Bundle, *Pryor v. Tinsley and Staple* (jury awarded $5); RSP Box 32, November 1803 Bundle, *Quickley v. Matthews*, and *Parish v. Matthews and Thompson* (jury awarded Quickley $30 and Parish $25 from Matthews and 1¢ from Thompson). Suckey James and Suckey Parish were probably the same person, because James was not among the five witnesses Parish summoned to testify. The damage awards in these cases indicate that the men crossed the line separating acceptable and unacceptable harassment. That Thompson was fined only a penny suggests that the court found much harassment acceptable.

[69] I found no complaints by free Black women of sexual assault by White men in Richmond between 1782 and 1810; an indeterminate number of the assault complaints surely involved rape or attempted rape. Perhaps free Black women found it easier to get White male jurors to award monetary damages for trespass, assault, and battery than to win criminal conviction and imprisonment for attempted or actual rape.

physical assaults, but there is no evidence that men who were unrelated to them could enter their homes with such impunity.[70] Attempts to deny free Black women's claims to their homes and bodies constituted assaults on their status as women as well as attacks on their humanity.

These assaults were primarily attacks on Black women's femaleness, but they also were attacks on Black masculinity. Prior to March 1800 a White man named John Howington "more than once . . . broke open" the door of William Goldman, a free Black man. After forcing his way inside, Howington treated Goldman's "sister . . . much amiss in a variety of instances." Having suffered this indignity too frequently, William Goldman finally "was so very imprudent as to strike Mr. Howington." Howington had him arrested, and the Henrico County court ordered Goldman to post $400 bond for good behavior. "Utterly incapable of finding security" for so much money, Goldman languished in jail "unable to render the smallest assistance to his wife and family" for eight months. During that time he was also incapable of helping his sister to resist Howington's assaults. Goldman finally won release by claiming to have become "truly and experimentally, sensible of the impropriety of lifting his hand against a White person."[71] County authorities forced him to recognize his legal incapacity to protect his home and his sister from a White man's attack. They simultaneously emphasized the degree to which, even when resting at home, Black women were in the court's eyes unworthy of protection from White aggression, and implicitly less "feminine" than White women.

Denied the protections accorded to both elite and common White women, free Black women necessarily developed an aggressive willingness to protect themselves. When two slavecatchers broke into the house Angelica Barnett shared with William Anthony, she responded to their assault by killing one of her attackers. In 1807 Suckey Smith, a free Black woman, was arrested for assaulting and beating a slave named Sam Sims in several places around town. A year later Paul Duke, a White man, visited Polly and Alcey Norman

---

[70] To have allowed that would have been to allow assaults on White men's property rights.

[71] Henrico County Court Judgments, Box 88–15, Bundle 1, Part I, William Goldman's Petition to be released from Confinement, LiVa. In 1802, Patsy Goldman, perhaps William's sister, sued a White man for assault and battery (HCCOB #10, 231). Another indication of the vulnerability of Black households came in 1806 when Averitt Gay and Basil Wood broke into James Plummer's "dwelling and violently and forcibly" took away "Sally Plummer," presumably James Plummer's enslaved wife, whom he had hired for the year. Plummer, however, could sue only on the grounds of her lost labor. Had he responded violently, he presumably would have met Goldman's fate (RSP Box 42, November 1806 Bundle, *Plummer v. Gay and Wood*).

to demand payment for some wood he had sold them. They asked him to walk around to the back door and then pushed him in the house and stabbed him about the face, head, and back with a knife and a fork. Such aggressive behavior was sometimes directed toward town authorities: Lucy Battles was jailed for "riotous disorderly conduct . . . in the street while in custody of the Watch." And it was sometimes directed at White women rather than White men: Polly Goleman, a mulatto woman, greeted Mary Ann Powers, a white woman, at the door of Powers's house and "assaulted . . . [her] with a Cow Hide."[72] Physically powerful, aggressive women violated the elite sense of femininity – a Richmond merchant called one free Black woman a "Brute of the fields" after watching her and her husband attack another free Black woman.[73] And Black femininity developed a different meaning from White femininity. It might appear that the space for Black masculine assertiveness contracted as that for Black feminine assertiveness grew, leaving Richmond's Black community without significant gender divisions, but such was not the case.

Race and gender on Richmond's streets

When Richmond-area Blacks joined together to overthrow slavery, their conspiracy formed almost entirely among men. If definitions of gender difference among African Americans were not identical to those among Whites in the Richmond area, they remained powerful nonetheless. To draw a fuller picture of those differences requires closer attention to what Black men and women did in early Richmond and to how they created markers of masculinity and femininity within the racial structures that circumscribed their lives.

Although, for example, Black men and women both worked in the town's burgeoning market economy, they did not do identical work. Black men worked overwhelmingly in construction, transportation, manufacturing, and craft

---

[72] Petition for Angelica Barnett [September 1793], Executive Papers, Box 81. See Chapter 5 of this for a discussion of this case. RSP Box 44, July 1807 Bundle, *Commonwealth v. Smith*. RHCOB #8, 42 (quotes from Duke's deposition; Normans were ordered tried at District Court). RSP Box 55, July, September, October 1810 Bundle, *Commonwealth v. Battles* (Lucy Battles was also called Sukey Battles in these papers). RSP Box 56, December 1810–February 1811 Bundle, *Commonwealth v. Goleman*. Goleman failed to post bond for good behavior and was committed to jail. Perhaps she was the sister whom William Goldman – spelling variations are common in the records – tried to protect from John Howington's assault.

[73] RHCOB #5, 462–3; RSP Box 33, May 1804 Bundle, *Eve Jones v. Daniel and Hannah Lewis* (Henry Banks's deposition).

production. Work of this sort brought them into contact with one another and with White craftsmen, supervisors, and employers on a regular basis. Wagoners and rivermen often traveled in and out of Richmond, carrying agricultural produce from the rural hinterland to the city and returning with manufactured goods. Construction workers often lived outside of town and were hired to urban craftsmen. Even when living in town, they often traveled from their households to various work sites. Black craftsmen working in more settled shops were less transient, but they interacted with these other men every day in town.[74] Enslaved and free Black men in and around Richmond developed a masculine culture of the road and the river. Black men who lived and worked in town knew others who lived and worked in the surrounding counties. They developed an easy camaraderie with other Black men whom they ran into on the road, in tippling shops, in disorderly houses, and in gambling dens after the work day, or more likely at the end of the week when many traveled to rural homes.[75]

Theirs was not an exclusively male world. One reason urban working men took to the road was to visit their wives and families who lived on plantations or farms outside town. No doubt some rural men also entered town to visit their families. But the road itself was an overwhelmingly male place: the fragmentary evidence that has survived from early Richmond strongly suggests that husbands, not wives, traveled to visit spouses and that they traveled back and forth in the company of male friends, while their wives remained at home caring for children. This was more true in Virginia, where Whites controlled urban markets, than in the Caribbean, South Carolina, and Georgia, where slave market women traveled between town and country.

Women were more likely than men to work as household servants, though most slave women in the Richmond area probably worked in the wheat, tobacco, and corn fields that surrounded the town. All apparently remained near their homes and, if separated from their husbands, awaited their visits. In town, Black women fought in the streets and in their homes; they worked in shops and in households; and they asserted claims to certain extralegal rights. They do not appear to have left town very often to visit in the countryside. The contentious and aggressive public world of town women did not extend into the countryside.[76]

---

[74] See Chapter 6 of this book.

[75] Evidence of this masculine culture of the road appeared in depositions from the trials of Gabriel's Conspiracy and is discussed in Chapter 2 of this book.

[76] Two exceptions should be noted: some women were arrested for hiring their own time in early Richmond (examples: RHCOB #4, 284, 328, 523), but three times as many men

Furthermore, town women who engaged in this public world do not appear to have been closely tied to the men who traveled back and forth to the countryside. They interacted with those men – gender was not an insurmountable barrier separating Black men and women in Richmond – but the bulk of free Black women's expressive interactions on the streets of Richmond involved other free Black women.[77] Breaches of the peace provide the clearest evidence. Free Black women hauled before the Hustings Court for breaking the peace were more likely to have assaulted – physically or verbally – other free Black women than members of any other group.[78] Though free Black women were probably the least economically privileged free people in town, they frequently lent one another financial assistance. People charged with assault or breach of the peace were required to find others willing to provide surety for a court appearance, and free Black women often signed bonds for each other when one was charged with such a breach.[79] When free Black women charged others with assault, they were, again, most likely to charge other free Black women.[80]

These records arose out of hostile interactions; such patterns of hostility, indicate those with whom free Black women interacted most frequently in emotionally intense settings. They suggest that free Black women were more likely to fight with one another and to support and receive support from one another than to fight with or support members of any other group. Divisions between women and men revealed through these disputes did not run along

were arrested for self-hire as women; female runaways sometimes left the city to return to their families or vice versa (example: *Virginia Argus*, December 20, 1805), but men were more likely to run away than women. This is not to say that rural women were passive (see n. 2 of this chapter), rather that they were less likely to exhibit aggression in a public sphere than were urban women, in part because they were less frequently in public space.

[77] Obviously it would be better to measure interactions involving slave women, but those interactions rarely showed up in court (or other written) records, so an examination of free Black women must suffice.

[78] Of 74 cases involving free Black female aggressors between 1782 and 1810, 40 of the identifiable victims were free Black women, 7 were free Black men, 8 were White men, and 1 was a White woman. Often no victim was listed.

[79] Of the 74 people recorded having signed bonds guaranteeing free Black women's appearance in court for breach of the peace, 23 were free Black women, 18 free Black men, and 25 White men. Two women and six men whose race I could not identify signed bonds.

[80] Of 89 cases, 37 of the aggressors were free Black women, 26 were free Black men, and 23 White men. The rest were people whose race I could not identify. This does not mean that free Black women faced greater danger from each other than from White men. The Hustings Court treated dismissively several cases in which free Black women charged White men with assault and surely discouraged such suits.

lines defined by a public-private dichotomy. Many of the disputes that led to legal suits took place in Richmond's streets. More important, to bring legal suit or to sign bonds before the court or a magistrate was to act within the public realm, and each time Black women voluntarily appeared before the courts they laid implicit claim to status as public people. Free Black women appeared frequently before the Hustings Court as plaintiffs and defendants in civil and petty criminal suits; the social world revealed in those cases was divided along gender lines, but the lines were different from those that separated White men and women.

Gender divisions extended to chronic violators of the town's petty criminal laws. From 1782 to 1810, the Richmond City Hustings Court charged many people with running illegal businesses by selling liquor without a license, allowing gambling, or more generally profiting from disorderly behavior. Authorities frequently charged men with either of the individual offenses or occasionally with operating a disorderly house.[81] Women, especially Black women, were more likely to suffer presentments for running disorderly houses.[82] The activities that occurred in disorderly houses probably were not much different from those that occurred in gambling and tippling houses. In 1804, when grand jurors presented Nancy Graves, a free Black woman, for running a disorderly house, they charged her with permitting "drinking, tippling . . . and misbehaving." Six years later Billy Blue was charged with "keeping a gambling and disorderly house."[83] The line separating these offenses is obscure.

The gendered nature of the jurors' presentments provides a clue to the difference. Nestled between the charges of tippling and misbehaving in the

---

[81] From 1800 to 1810 grand jurors issued 162 presentments against establishments run by one or more White men for selling liquor without a license; they issued 13 presentments against establishments run by one or more Black men; 5 presentments against White women; 2 against Black women; 1 against a man and a woman; and 1 against a woman whose race cannot be determined. They issued presentments against 76 establishments run by White men for gambling; 3 run by Black men; 2 run by Black and White men together; and 3 run by men whose race cannot be determined. No women were presented for running gambling houses (RHCOB #4–#9).

[82] From 1800 to 1810 grand jurors issued 18 presentments against disorderly houses run by one or more black woman; 5 by women whose race cannot be determined; 1 by a White woman (perhaps significantly, it was called a "riotous house" not a "disorderly house"; RHCOB #9, 68); 4 by White men; 3 by Black men; 1 by a Black man and a Black woman together; and 1 by a White man and a White woman together; and 2 by men whose race cannot be determined (RHCOB #4–#9).

[83] RSP Box 33, March 1804 Bundle, *Commonwealth v. Graves/Greaves*; RHCOB #8, 490 (Blue).

presentment of Nancy Graves was another offense written in larger letters: "whoring." Mary Gray, another free Black woman, was presented for permitting, "for her own lucre and gain . . . women as [well as] men of evil . . . fame and . . . dishonest conversation" to frequent her house. While there, they engaged in "drinking, tipling whoring quarreling and fighting."[84] Although there is no evidence that all establishments called disorderly houses by Richmond grand jurors were believed to be brothels, many were. No presentments against men for operating such houses, specifically mentioned prostitution, so Black women probably controlled early Richmond's commercial sex trade.

Black women were not the only people who practiced prostitution in early Richmond. Betsy Morgan, who was charged with "whoring" near the Old City Tavern in 1804, may well have been a White woman. And the Mrs. Eubanks who was presented for running a "riotous house" – presumably the same thing as a disorderly house – in 1810 was almost certainly White. Prostitution did not mean the same thing for White and Black women. White prostitutes clearly stepped outside of acceptable behavior and endangered their standing within the community. When Thurlow Richardson told Mary Bottomly that he could "have [his] will of her . . . whenever" he pleased, she sued for slander.[85] Sexual behavior that fell outside of prescribed boundaries could ruin a White woman's reputation and the reputation of the White man responsible for her. Thus, when Nancy Neale, reputedly a "town hore," had "a child by a negro," her father attempted to hide it. He refused to allow neighbors into the house while she was bearing the child, and after killing it, he put it down his well to conceal the birth. The body was found only after an anonymous informant addressed a letter to "som magerstrat of this . . . sitey."[86]

Nancy Neale's behavior violated several rules governing White women's behavior. Her father's shame was rooted in his daughter's status as "town hore," and in the race of the baby's father. Perhaps Nancy Neale's status as a whore resulted not from behavior that would currently be termed prostitution but precisely from the race of her lover. Regardless, her case illustrates some of the differences between behavior found acceptable for poor White and free Black women. While town authorities disapproved, at least officially, of "whoring" by both White and Black women, poor Whites and

[84] RSP Box 31, August 1803 Bundle, *Commonwealth v. Gray*.
[85] RSP Box 34, August 1804 Bundle, *Commonwealth v. Morgan*; RHCOB #9, 68 (Eubanks); RSP Box 33, May 1804 Bundle, *Bottomly v. Richardson*.
[86] RSP Box 15, April–May 1793 Bundle, *Commonwealth v. Neale*. The quotes are from the anonymous letter. The coroner's report on the infant's body is in the same Bundle.

free Blacks do not appear to have taken the same approach. While Nancy Neale's father believed that his daughter's sexual transgression cast so much shame on his family that he committed murder to hide it, free Black proprietors of disorderly houses continued to play active roles in the free Black community.[87] In short, although Black and White women participated in commercial sex in Richmond, such participation affected them differently. It placed White women beyond respectability within their community, while it appears to have been accepted, perhaps as an unpleasant necessity, by the free Black community.

Furthermore, patterns in grand jury presentments suggest that free Black prostitutes in Richmond developed communal bonds as they worked in disorderly houses. Free Black keepers of disorderly houses, unlike those who operated informal casinos or sold liquor without a license, tended to enter business partnerships.[88] This situation should not be romanticized. No doubt one reason so many women joined together in these enterprises was to pool the capital necessary for house rent or liquor purchases, and joint control over establishments in which they sold their bodies does not conjure up an idyllic image of empowered womanhood. Nonetheless, that these women chose to join with one another, rather than with Black men or with Whites, and that they occasionally formed partnerships with female relatives, suggests that they forged strong ties with one another out of the shared hardships that they faced.[89] Most important for this analysis, free Black women's preference for alliances with one another – rather than with Black men or Whites – suggests that even Black women who flouted White society's rules about feminine behavior observed a division between men and women.

The same is true of Black men who rejected the emasculation represented by Whites' attempts to retaliate against protectors of Black women.

[87] For example, free Black women known to have transgressed the sexual norms of elite Richmonders often signed for, or were signed for by, other Richmonders. For examples see RSP Box 31, April, June, July, October 1803 Bundle, *Tinsley v. Allen* and *Allen v. Tinsley*; RSP Box 38, October 1805 Bundle, *Commonwealth v. Barnett*; RSP Box 38, November 1805 Bundle, *Commonwealth v. Norman*; RSP Box 42, October 1806 Bundle, *Commonwealth v. Norman*.

[88] Of eighteen disorderly houses run by free Black women cited by grand juries from 1800 to 1810, seven were run by more than one free Black woman. In addition one was run by a free Black man and a free Black woman. Only 1 (of 4) of the disorderly houses run by White men was a partnership; only 1 (of 3) of those run by Black men was a partnership. Similarly only 20 of the 76 gambling houses run by White men, 12 of the 162 establishments in which White men sold liquor without a license, and 1 of 13 houses in which Black men sold liquor were partnerships. RHCOB #4–#9.

[89] RSP Box 43, March 1807 Bundle, *Commonwealth v. Winney Gabriel and her daughter Nancy*.

The Henrico County court would not have thrown William Goldman in jail had he not rejected the message that he should ignore White aggression against his sister. Other Black men left traces of their willingness to claim manhood by fighting for their families or their honor. In 1805 when Billy Buck's enslaved wife ran away from Edward Hallam after being whipped, Buck walked to Hallam's, put his wife's clothes in a cart, and headed home. According to Virginia law, Buck committed a robbery, but the open fashion in which he acted indicates that he believed himself to be asserting his rightful control over family property.[90] Authorities showed little respect for Buck's assertion of his rights as a man to contest White prerogatives, but they sometimes looked more favorably on Black men protecting their own masculine privileges against other Black men. When a slave named John broke into the house of "William Stewart (a free man)" to steal the clothes his wife had left while being harbored as a runaway, Henrico County justices had no choice under the law but to convict John of robbery. They accompanied the conviction, however, with a petition to the governor explaining the unusual circumstances and requesting a pardon, which was granted.[91] Less important than varying White attitudes toward these acts, however, is the responsibility assumed by Billy Buck and John for their wives' property and, presumably, well-being.

Black male Richmonders proved willing to fight for other ends as well. In 1805 a fight erupted between Toby Jackson Jr. and his brother David. They made enough noise to draw at least one spectator into their house from the street, and the fight ended when David "had a part of his nose bitten off." Witnesses did not comment on the cause of this fight, but they did note that Toby Jackson Sr. prevented spectators from separating his sons, asserting that they were "freemen and should not be disturbed." Apparently Toby Jackson Sr. understood the right and ability to fight to be attributes of manhood and freedom.[92] Before becoming famous as the leader of a slave conspiracy, Gabriel displayed a similar commitment to standing up and fighting for his honor by "biting off a considerable part" of the left ear of a neighboring

---

[90] RHCOB #6, 225–6. No doubt Buck had bought many of the clothes he "stole." Buck was also accused of hiding some of Hallam's silver spoons in the clothes. Whether he stole the spoons for revenge or they were planted in the clothes to lessen sympathy for Buck cannot be known. Buck was found guilty and bound over for trial at District Court.

[91] Executive Papers, Box 98.

[92] RHCOB #6, 165–7; RSP Box 37, June–July 1805 Bundle. Rebecca Jackson, the fighters' mother was examined with her husband for allowing this fight to go on, suggesting that she shared this vision of manhood. Kenneth S. Greenberg, *Slavery and Honor* (Princeton, 1996), ch. 1, discusses the abuse of noses during fights in the antebellum South.

White farmer.[93] People throughout the neighborhood could read of Gabriel's manhood through bodily mutilations – the branded thumb that he suffered as punishment and the farmer's semieaten ear – evident whenever either man was present. Black males established their manhood by proving willing to fight in defense of their families, their honor, or their friends.[94] This notion of masculinity influenced the conspiracy that Gabriel built soon after biting off Absalom Johnson's ear.

Gender and race

The legislator who thought Black women would be as ferocious and formidable as Black males in an insurrection was both right and wrong. Black women in Richmond often behaved in ways not in keeping with gender divisions that characterized the elite society inhabited by White state legislators. Black townswomen worked, fought, and had sex in ways and places that elite White women did not. They challenged Whites, Black males, and one another on the streets of the town. They asserted and defended claims to public and private space that Richmond authorities refused to guarantee.

The implication that Black women were less feminine than White women was true only from a perspective outside the Black community's. The worlds of both Black and White Richmonders divided along gender lines. Gender difference was not a single set of norms dividing men and women throughout the town. Instead, it was a sense of sexual difference continually created, challenged, and re-created in complex interactions among people of different classes and races. If much of the written record appears, to treat those who violated elite norms as unfeminine – as "brutes of the fields" – that is because elites controlled the terms in which the records were kept. Those records obscure the meanings of gender among Black Richmonders, but they show that Richmond Blacks built differentiated male and female spheres out of the traditions that they brought to the growing city and the conditions in which they lived – conditions over which they had only very partial control. They also reveal the ways that gender, race, and class interacted to create cultural margins along which Richmonders – female and male, Black and White, poor and rich – skirmished. Those struggles created the multifaceted meanings of gender in early Richmond.

[93] HCCOB #9, 94–5. See Philip Schwarz, "Gabriel's Challenge: Slaves and Crime in Late Eighteenth-Century Virginia," *Virginia Magazine of History and Biography* 90 (1982) for more on this incident. Also see Chapter 2, this book.

[94] See Frederick Douglass's famous description of his fight with Edward Covey in which "a slave was made a man" (*Classic Slave Narratives*, 294–9).

Enslaved and free Black women proved physically aggressive and willing to use force to defend themselves. They might have participated in an insurrection had guns been fired and a battle broken out. To join Black men in such a battle, however, would have been to surmount differences that divided them on a day-to-day basis.[95] Black men and women remained separated by the work they did, the people with whom they associated, and the lives they lived. They came together in families, in friendship, in religious congregations, and in social events, but their gender identities remained powerful determinants of the ways they experienced life.

There is little surprising in that. Gender divisions are among the most common in human societies, so it stands to reason that Richmonders of African descent would have conceived of differences along a male-female axis. More important than the existence of gender difference is the process through which differences were constructed. Tracing the ways gender shaped and was shaped by racial categories, legal status, and economic standing provides another glimpse at the social practice out of which the crosscutting identities so powerfully expressed in Gabriel's Conspiracy grew.

Social practice and racial identity

It has become almost a cliché to argue that assorted cultural categories – race and class as well as gender – are socially constructed. Perhaps because much of the best literature approaches the subject from a cultural studies perspective, however, quotidian interactions among people of different races, classes, and genders – the substance of social history – sometimes gets ignored in such analyses in favor of literary texts, psychological analysis, and theoretical inquiry.[96] As a result, the sophisticated studies of daily life and of social structure that have become staples of historical literature too often read as

---

[95] Viotti da Costa, *Crowns of Glory, Tears of Blood*, 192 for this happening in Demerara in 1823.

[96] Among the best examples of such analysis of African American and diasporic studies see Kwame Anthony Appiah, *In My Father's House: Africa in the Philosophy of Culture* (New York, 1992), esp. chs. 1–3; Paul Gilroy, *The Black Atlantic: Modernity and Double Consciousness* (Cambridge, Mass., 1993); Eric J. Sundquist, *To Wake the Nations: Race in the Making of American Literature* (Cambridge, Mass., 1993); Eric Lott, *Love and Theft: Blackface Minstrelsy and the American Working Class* (New York, 1993). None of these authors set out to analyze social history, so this comment is not a criticism of their work. But even David R. Roediger's important *The Wages of Whiteness: Race and the Making of the American Working Class* (New York, 1991) sometimes removes the insightful discussion of the language of race and labor too far from the lives and labor of those using the language.

if "regular" people had no intellectual lives, and brilliant reconstructions of popular cultures too often read as if those cultures developed independently of daily life. The enslaved Virginians who rallied behind Gabriel's call to overthrow slavery in 1800 inadvertently opened a window on their rich symbolic world. They left traces of an intense melding of received cultural traditions through which they forged their worldview and of a creative process through which they transformed that view into a weapon in a battle for liberation. Theirs was neither a culture shared with White Virginians, nor in any simple way, one separate from that of their masters. It was a creole culture that people of African descent living in Virginia developed over the course of the eighteenth century.

Gabriel's Conspiracy – or the evidence produced during the repression of Gabriel's Conspiracy – provides a fuller glimpse of this process than historians usually get. Nonetheless, it is a snapshot of a moment, and all of those who were engaged in producing the snapshot conceived of the moment as a special one. In reconstructing the meetings and discussions among alleged insurrectionaries during the summer of 1800, the courts inevitably ripped events leading up to August 30 out of their everyday context and freighted them with meanings rooted in the conspiracy.

By returning to the daily interactions through which Richmond's social structures and cultural norms developed, this rich snapshot can be contextualized. Richmond grew into a recognizably urban center during the 1780s and 1790s, and the influence of the urban social relations that developed there radiated out along roads and the James River into the town's agricultural hinterland. The Black and White working people who built the town developed complicated relationships, sometimes friendly and sometimes antagonistic, as they lived and worked on the town's waterfront and in its workshops. None of these developments was unique to Richmond – similar patterns of development had characterized growing towns in colonial and early republican North America throughout the eighteenth century – but they were relatively new to Virginians.

Urban life simultaneously offered Black Virginians enhanced opportunities for autonomous lives and the possibility of unusually egalitarian – or at least nonexploitative – relationships with some White Virginians. Racial difference did not lose its salience in the workshops and grog shops of early Richmond, but its meanings were constantly renegotiated as people worked and worshipped, drank and fought, relaxed and played together. The relative fluidity of racially defined roles was not unprecedented in Virginia; Black people in seventeenth-century Virginia found more avenues to social and

economic advancement than did those who lived after slaves came to dominate the colony's bound labor force.[97]

In many ways, the cracks that opened for Black people in very early
Virginia resembled those that urban Blacks at the turn of the nineteenth
century pried open. In both cases, though some found enhanced opportunity,
the vast majority remained subject to oppression. In both cases, the opportunities were tenuous, and the danger of being pushed back into servitude
(in the case of seventeenth-century blacks) or plantation slavery (for Black
Richmonders) was ever present. There was an important difference. Although
seventeenth-century blacks suffered through the difficulties that all bound
laborers experienced in Virginia, the patterns of specifically racial oppression
that characterized eighteenth-century Virginia had yet to develop. Black
Richmonders, on the other hand, carved out the spaces that allowed limited
autonomy at the very time that the new state was experiencing a substantial
hardening of its system of racial oppression. Blacks who lived in and around
the growing towns in Gabriel's Virginia struggled with and against various
White Virginians to win many small victories as individuals and as a community. These small day-to-day triumphs accumulated in ways that offered
important benefits to free and enslaved Black Virginians, but ultimately they
undermined neither slavery nor the system of racial oppression that it created and upon which it rested. In fact, they emerged at a moment when the
system of racial oppression was hardening.

By exploring this contradictory world of early urban Virginia, the crosscutting identities revealed in the course of Gabriel's Conspiracy can be
rooted in the complex interactions among women and men of African and
European descent as they lived their daily lives in early Richmond. Placing
the dramatic struggle of Gabriel and his followers within this broader context also reveals that, although the conspiracy represented a high point in
Black Richmonders' struggle against slavery's oppression, its repression did
not bring the battle to an end. Enslaved and free Black residents of early
Richmond struggled for personal, familial, and communal autonomy during
the decade following Gabriel's Conspiracy much as they had done during
the 1790s.

---

[97] T. H. Breen and Stephen Innes, *"Myne Owne Ground": Race and Freedom on Virginia's
Eastern Shore, 1640–1676* (New York, 1980).

EPILOGUE

Gabriel and Richmond in historical and fictional time

G ABRIEL AND HIS FOLLOWERS sought freedom in the Richmond of 1800, and understanding their struggle requires understanding their world. The meanings of their struggle, however, have not been limited to the time and place in which they lived and worked, built families and worshipped their God, resisted and accommodated to their oppressors. Gabriel's Conspiracy was defeated, but it was not destroyed. It lived on in the folk memories of Black Virginians, and, through those folk memories, it influenced the collective identity of Americans of African descent and the collective struggle against slavery and oppression. Stories about Gabriel were used to inspire resistance to slavery, and to support an argument for Black nationalism. Nor was the conspiracy's meaning limited to the antebellum period. During the 1930s Arna Bontemps wrote a novel based on Gabriel's Conspiracy, a novel that explored the relationships among literacy, traditional oral culture, and natural rights philosophy, while seeking to inspire a much later generation to heed Gabriel's call and struggle to complete the liberation of Americans of African descent.

8

Gabriel's Conspiracy
in memory and fiction

The period bounded by the American Revolution and the War of 1812 has long been portrayed as a high point in the history of White Virginians. During those decades, Virginians led Britain's thirteen mainland colonies into political independence, and, with a short Adams interlude, members of the fabled "Virginia Dynasty" presided over the new nation's government. The term "Jeffersonian Virginia" has come to signify an almost golden age of intellectual statesmen and "rational" politics.[1] If few historians now writing about Jeffersonian Virginia would subscribe to this image, much modern historical writing is infused with a palpable conviction of the power of the stereotype and the importance of qualifying or discrediting it.[2] Both the advocates of Jeffersonian mythology and its debunkers tend, however, to focus almost exclusively on the actions and beliefs of elites, even when criticizing those elites' own lack of concern for the enslaved.

Nineteenth-century African American writers and speakers developed a critique of Jefferson and the Founding Fathers that was more attuned to the meanings of the age for enslaved Blacks. One might logically suspect that the age that appeared golden from White Virginians' perspectives would have

---

[1] Charles S. Sydnor, *American Revolutionaries in the Making: Political Practices in Washington's Virginia* (New York, 1965 [1952]) is a classic representation of Revolutionary Virginia as a virtuous republic. More recently, Gordon S. Wood, *The Radicalism of the American Revolution: How a Revolution Transformed a Monarchical Society into a Democratic One Unlike any that Had Ever Existed* (New York, 1992), Part 2 discusses Jefferson in terms that match this characterization. As Wood points out in his introduction, this view has come under sustained attack during the past three decades.

[2] See, for example, Paul Finkelman, "Jefferson and Slavery: 'Treason Against the Hopes of the World,'" in Peter S. Onuf, ed. *Jeffersonian Legacies* (Charlottesville, 1993), 181–224. My thoughts on these issues were influenced by Peter H. Wood's comments on a paper Finkelman delivered at the 1993 annual meeting of the Society for the History of the Early American Republic (June 1993, Chapel Hill).

taken on a distinctly different hue for Black analysts. Such was in some ways the case, though condemnations of Jeffersonian hypocrisy voiced by African Americans were frequently interlaced with attempts to claim the authority of the Founding Fathers' ideas in the struggle for racial equality.[3] Nonetheless, in much of the public rhetoric of Black and White abolitionists, as well as that of other Americans, the spirit of Jefferson reigned over early republican Virginia, indeed over the early republican United States.

Conceiving of the state during the same period as Gabriel's, rather than Jefferson's, Virginia requires a reorientation in which many issues that appear central from one perspective (banks, debts, tariffs, and elections) become peripheral, and once-peripheral issues – work regimes, evangelical Christianity, family stability, and cultural autonomy – become central. Such a reversal also entails altering the relative importance of various events. Virginians of African descent presumably took little pride in Madison's role in writing the Constitution or in the succession of Virginians who held the White House. Recognizing this does not presuppose that Black Virginians lacked a sense of the state's history or of their history within the state, but it assumes that theirs would have been different from the more widely known White versions. Nineteenth-century Black Virginians had powerful incentives to conceal their vision of history from their masters, so few stories embodying this folk history have found their way into written sources.[4]

Stories about Gabriel's Conspiracy stand as a partial exception and permit some tracing of Black Virginians' changing understanding of their history. In the immediate wake of the conspiracy, enslaved Virginians constructed

[3] Frederick Douglass's famous July 5, 1852, oration in Rochester, New York (Philip S. Foner, ed. *Life and Writings of Frederick Douglass*, 5 vols. [New York, 1950–75], v. 2, pp. 182–8) executes the double move of condemning the Founding Fathers' hypocrisy while claiming the tradition. Eric Sundquist, *To Wake the Nations: Race in the Making of American Literature* (Cambridge, Mass., 1993), 112–39 discusses Douglass's complex appropriation of the patriotic language of American Revolutionary traditions. Also see James Forten Jr.'s speech to the Philadelphia Female Anti-Slavery Society, April 14, 1836, in C. Peter Ripley, et al. eds., *The Black Abolitionist Papers* (Chapel Hill, 1991), v. 3, p. 161. By the 1960s, Martin Luther King Jr., in his "I have a dream" speech, appealed to the Declaration without reference to Jefferson's failings.
[4] Most sources that have been recorded take either religious form – a form masters accepted – or are folktales. The best reconstructions of slaves' worldviews have relied on these sources and tend, as a result, to portray a static, timeless, ahistorical vision. See, for three important examples: Lawrence W. Levine, *Black Culture and Black Consciousness: Afro-American Folk Thought from Slavery to Freedom* (New York, 1977), esp. chs. 1, 2; Eugene D. Genovese, *Roll, Jordan, Roll: The World the Slaves Made* (New York, 1972); Sterling Stuckey, *Slave Culture: Nationalist Theory and the Foundations of Black America* (New York, 1987), ch. 1.

stories of the conspiracy that embedded Gabriel's struggle in a continuing fight to overthrow racial slavery.[5] During the first three decades of the nineteenth century, Black Virginians composed several songs about Gabriel's Conspiracy, traces of which have survived. Ultimately, these and other oral traditions regarding Gabriel did find their way into various literary texts, illustrating connections between African American vernacular and literary traditions that extend beyond the formal qualities that have been so brilliantly theorized to encompass more pedestrian questions of plot and content. Most important, these stories show the way that Gabriel's attempt to overthrow slavery in 1800 became transmuted into an important element in an oppositional culture that, while constantly changing, has supported continuing struggles for racial equality during the past two centuries.

Gabriel in folk history

Virginians of African descent had living oral traditions and told stories of Gabriel's attempt to overthrow slavery. White Virginians, in fact, counted on Blacks to tell stories about the conspirators. Condemned rebels were hanged in different places in Richmond City and Henrico County, so that unapprehended conspirators and other slaves who might be considering insurrectionary activity would witness the wages of the sin of coveting liberty.[6] Whites surely hoped that enslaved Virginians would retain a collective memory of what became of those who challenged slavery.

Authorities were aware that slaves might be disinclined to learn the "correct" lessons from Gabriel's unsuccessful plot. Around Easter 1802, just a year and a half after the failure of Gabriel and his followers, another insurrection scare arose in eastern and Piedmont Virginia. The trial depositions produced in this scare make little explicit reference to Gabriel, but Governor Monroe at least believed there to be a connection. He asked the local officials who investigated the scare to report their findings; on the back of several of those reports he scribbled "GI" (for "Gabriel's Insurrection").[7] It is difficult

---

[5] See Chapter 4, this book.
[6] Most slaves were hanged at the public gallows in Richmond, but some were hanged at "Watson's tavern, the property of Thomas H. Prosser, in Henrico County" where slaves from Gabriel's neighborhood could easily witness the executions (*CVSP*, (see ch. 2, n. 3 for full citation), v. 9, pp. 140–74 [152 for quotation]). Douglas R. Egerton, *Gabriel's Rebellion: The Virginia Slave Conspiracies of 1800 and 1802* (Chapel Hill, 1993), chs. 6 and 7 discusses the sites for different executions.
[7] Letters regarding the 1802 scare with "GI" written on the back in Monroe's hand can be found in Executive Papers, Boxes 119–20 (see ch. 2, n. 3 for full citation). See Egerton, *Gabriel's Rebellion*, Part Two for the argument that Monroe was right about the connection.

to say how "real" the Easter Conspiracy was, or how direct was its connection to Gabriel's Conspiracy, but Monroe recognized that Black Virginians retained memories of the radical implications of Gabriel's Conspiracy.[8]

Richmond's connections to the seafaring commercial world of the Atlantic helped to propel the story of Gabriel into the broader currents of African American oral traditions. In 1832 William Lloyd Garrison's *The Liberator*, claiming that Nat Turner's Southampton County insurrection made "every thing relative to" Africans' "projects for self-liberation" interesting, published "GABRIEL'S DEFEAT." The author of the piece claimed that incidents he related about Gabriel's Conspiracy were "embodied by some Africans in a song called 'Gabriel's Defeat'" that he had heard in Virginia. The song that was sung in Virginia must have been a marvelously complicated piece, for by the 1830s it had become a "favorite air in the dances of white people," and was also "popular among the colored *population of the South*."[9]

Like much oral culture, this song took different forms in different settings, and the various versions probably fell into two broad categories: those sung before White and mixed-race audiences, and those sung before all-Black audiences. Three surviving traces of "Gabriel's Defeat" – that in *The Liberator*, one collected by folklorists, and one in *Poor Jack*, a seafaring novel published in 1840 – reveal the ways Virginians of African descent changed the song for their different listeners. In *Poor Jack*, a Black fiddler who is confined in Britain's Greenwich Hospital and whose repertoire of songs originated "principally" among "those sung by the negroes . . . in Virginia and Carolina," sings a sea chantey that tells the story of "Gin'ral Gabriel," the "Nigger Gin'ral" who "almost ruined old Virginny."[10] This song closely resembles "Uncle Gabriel," a song anthologized by folklorists. The relation of these songs to the source for "Gabriel's Defeat" is revealed in an inaccuracy they share with the story in *The Liberator*.[11] In fact, it seems probable that

Chapter 4, this book, interprets some of the documents produced in the 1802 scare as implicit references to Gabriel.

[8] For contrasting interpretations of the 1802 incidents, see Bertram Wyatt-Brown, *Southern Honor: Ethics and Behavior in the Old South* (New York, 1982), ch. 15 (esp. pp. 427–34); and Egerton, *Gabriel's Rebellion*. Also see Chapter 4, this book.

[9] *The Liberator* I, 38 (September 17, 1831); 38. Emphasis in original. *The Liberator* credited the *Albany Evening Journal* with originally publishing the article.

[10] R. Brimley Johnson, ed., *The Novels of Captain Marryat* (Boston, 1896), v. 12, pp. 122–3. I am indebted to W. Jeffrey Bolster for finding this song, and for help in interpreting it.

[11] Richard Barksdale and Keneth Kinnamon, eds., *Black Writers of America* (New York, 1972), 236–7. This is a shorter and later (it conflates Gabriel and Nat Turner) version of the song in *Poor Jack*, so my comparison focuses on the other two versions. Both versions misidentify the person who turned Gabriel in to the authorities as a young nephew of his. I discuss this shared inaccuracy later.

the stories told by Opposition Bill, the fiddler in *Poor Jack,* and the report
in *The Liberator* represent some of the differences that characterized versions
of the song sung for White and Black audiences.[12] Thus, they provide an
imperfect but fascinating contrast between what anthropologist James Scott
calls the "public" and "hidden" transcripts in which Black Virginians narrated their memories of Gabriel.[13]

The contrasts between the two versions of Gabriel's Conspiracy begin
with the central focus of the two narratives. In the song sung for White ears
in *Poor Jack,* Opposition Bill ignores the conspiracy itself and begins his narrative with the White attempt to catch Gabriel: immediately after asking his
audience to listen to "a leetle 'bout Gin'ral Gabriel," the fiddler reports that
authorities offered "A dousand pound" reward for his capture. Already by
the third couplet of the song a "leetle boy" mistakenly "betrayed de Nigger
Gin'ral" in Norfolk, and Gabriel was on his way back to Richmond for trial.
Throughout the song, the focus remains on the measures used to control the
general – he is "chained," a "troop of light horse" is called out to guard him,
and it takes a wagon pulled by "four grey horses" to take him to the gallows. Opposition Bill's story of "de fate of de Nigger Gin'ral,/Who almost
ruined old Virginny!" is on one level a narrative of failure.

To a remarkable degree then, the narrative of Opposition Bill accepted
the terms in which Governor James Monroe had originally chosen to tell the
story of the conspiracy, by focusing not on the conspiracy itself but on its
repression.[14] Opposition Bill's song subverts Monroe's interpretation, however, by exaggerating the reward and by foregrounding the extent of state
repression aimed at a single man. This emphasizes White fear of slaves' potential power to ruin the state, rather than accenting the majesty of White power.[15]
This, then, was a song slaves could sing in front of Whites. It appeared to
focus on exactly what authorities hoped slaves would remember about the
conspiracy, but it did not accept a White version of the story. The song

---

[12] Not only was Captain Marryat, the collector of the song, White, but Opposition Bill
sings the song for a White audience in the novel.

[13] James C. Scott, *Domination and the Arts of Resistance: Hidden Transcripts* (New Haven,
1990).

[14] See Chapter 4 of this book for Monroe's report to the legislature.

[15] I am not implying that slaves read Monroe's letter to the legislature and wrote a
song with the conscious intent to refute Monroe's claims. Monroe's letter suggests that
discussions of the official response to the conspiracy were more acceptable to Whites
than were discussions of the conspiracy itself, and Opposition Bill's song suggests that
slaves took advantage of that fact to tell of the conspiracy through the story of its
repression.

reversed the meaning of the story, turning it into a tale of White anxiety rather than White power.[16]

The version of the song that served as at least a partial source for the article in *The Liberator* conflated Gabriel and the South Carolina insurrectionary leader Denmark Vesey in the figure of Gabriel. This Gabriel was a well-traveled and highly literate former slave who had bought his freedom before attempting to lead his brethren in a fight for liberty. All these qualities describe Vesey rather than Gabriel. But the story that the song told of the conspiracy itself was largely based on Gabriel's Conspiracy: it was set in Richmond and followed the basic outline of Gabriel's plan.[17]

Like the other version, this song subtly altered the story of Gabriel's attempted escape. While both effaced the Black crewmen who turned in Gabriel (see Chapter 3), the version that lay behind *The Liberator* story had Gabriel captured in Richmond rather than Norfolk. More important, the escaping hero was on board a ship "just ready to sail for St. Domingo." The *Liberator* also recorded what must have been a version of Black Virginians' memory of words Gabriel spoke at his trial:

I love my nation. – We have as good a right to be free from your oppression, as you had to be free from the tyranny of the king of England. I know my fate – you will take my life. I offer it willingly, as a martyr to liberty. My example will raise up a Gabriel, who will, Washington-like, lead on the Africans to freedom.

Gabriel probably made a similar speech at his trial, though authorities did not record it.[18] This remarkable passage reveals that Blacks sometimes encoded Gabriel's memory within a narrative of African American nationalism that fused the libertarian promise of the American Revolution with the millennial potential of Christianity. This story promises that Gabriel's Conspiracy

---

[16] The version anthologized by Barksdale and Kinnamon includes the story about the "four grey horses," but otherwise focuses much more explicitly on Gabriel's failure, closing with the line: "Hard times in old Virginny." Perhaps this more pessimistic version reflected disappointed hopes or increasing repression at the time of its collection, or perhaps it was a version sung before Whites thought to be particularly anxious.

[17] *The Liberator* I, 38 (September 17, 1831).

[18] Robert Sutcliffe, a White traveling near Richmond in 1804, heard that at the trial of some slaves "lately executed, on the charge of having an intention to rise against" their masters, a slave insisted "'I have nothing more to offer than what General Washington would have had to offer, had he been taken by the British and put to trial by them. I have adventured my life in endeavouring to obtain the liberty of my countrymen, and am a willing sacrifice in their cause'" (Sutcliffe, *Travels in Some Parts of North America in the Years 1804, 1805, and 1806* [York, England, 1811], 50). It seems unlikely that Sutcliffe was the source for the passage in *The Liberator*.

served merely as prologue for a coming victorious African American liberation movement, and it appropriates the figures of Washington, Toussaint
Louverture (in the reference to "St. Domingo"), and the angel Gabriel for
the use of that movement. Portions of this mix may or may not have been
added, either intentionally or inadvertently, by the abolitionist author of the
newspaper story. If that makes the story less certainly a direct reflection of
Black Virginians' memories of Gabriel, it emphasizes the ways in which the
memories of the conspiracy that slaves preserved in their oral traditions
remained living forces in the fight against slavery.

The difference between these two stories of the conspiracy – one presumably "tellable" before Whites and the other not – was not that one counten-
anced the justice of slavery while the other did not. Both versions contested
the stories of the conspiracy that had been constructed by White Virginians.
They do, however, provide a case study of the different levels at which Blacks
could contest White versions of history, depending on the audience for the
story. Veiled references to White fears of rebellion were acceptable, presumably because they included recognition of White power. The attempt to create and perpetuate in oral tradition a history of slave rebellion with African,
biblical, and American roots involved too open a challenge to slavery to be
acceptable in White ears.

These two versions of Gabriel's Conspiracy are also revealing for the events
that both proved incapable of representing. Neither alluded to the way
Whites learned of the conspiracy before it came about; in short, Pharoah's
betrayal disappeared from these narratives. Each also overstated the amount
of the reward offered for turning in Gabriel, and both denied the appeal of
that reward for Black Virginians. In each, a young nephew of Gabriel's
innocently revealed the rebel leader's hiding place out of youthful ignorance
rather than adult greed. Black Virginians' construction of a useful history of
Gabriel's Conspiracy necessitated the erasure of calculating adult informers
from the plot. Ultimately, it was not the brute effects of White power but
the way that White power undermined Black solidarity that most undercut
the radical potential of Gabriel's story and thus that story's usefulness in
slaves' struggle against their oppressors.

Although Black representations of Gabriel cannot be clearly situated in
the flow of Virginia's later history, they did in fact play a role. Most obviously they contributed to the subversive "hidden transcript" through which
enslaved Virginians and other African Americans rejected White versions of
Virginia's and the United States's, history of slavery. They also influenced
events considered important by traditional political historians. One of the
slaves' versions of the conspiracy found its way, after all, into *The Liberator*.

Nor was the story's influence limited to the small and northern readership of that newspaper. A correspondent for the *Richmond Enquirer*, gleefully indignant about the inaccuracies in the abolitionist version of Gabriel's Conspiracy, wrote a rebuttal more than twice as long as the original article. Making use of "the Message of Governor Monroe to the Legislature . . . with the accompanying Documents," the *Enquirer* retold the story for a White Virginia audience. While the intended point was to denigrate the conspiracy, it conceded that Gabriel's "combination was . . . sufficiently great to excite the utmost vigilance" and that Monroe did in fact offer a $300 reward for his capture.[19] It noted that Richardson Taylor, the White captain of the boat on which Gabriel tried to escape Virginia, had probably helped the fleeing leader. It told of the scythe swords that Gabriel and Solomon had made to arm their followers. In short, in addition to repeating *The Liberator*'s version of the story in order to refute it, the *Enquirer* repeated much of the story of Gabriel's Conspiracy for a Virginia audience. The newspaper sought to belittle Gabriel, but Black Virginians had ample experience in reinterpreting White versions of events, and there was much in this story that lent itself to such reinterpretation.

A suggestive but equivocal piece of evidence indicates that these songs contributed to a folk memory of Gabriel that survived among Black Virginians into the twentieth century. During the 1930s, a former slave named Cornelia Carney was interviewed near Williamsburg. She told the story of her father and of the brutal master who beat him viciously. Finally Carney's father "got beat up so much dat . . . he run away an' lived in de woods."[20] But Carney insisted that her father "wasn't de onlies' one hidin' in de woods."

Dere was his cousin, Gabriel, dat was hidin' an' a man name Charlie. Niggers was too smart fo' white folks to get ketched. White folks was sharp too, but not sharp enough to git by ole Nat. Nat? I don't know who he was. Ole folks used to say it all de time. De meanin' I git is dat de niggers could always out-smart de white folks. What you git fum it?

There is no way to be certain that Carney's Gabriel was the leader of the famous conspiracy or that "ole Nat" was Nat Turner; she spoke allusively

<hr/>

[19] *Richmond Enquirer*, October 21, 1831.
[20] Charles L. Perdue Jr., Thomas E. Barden, and Robert K. Phillips, eds., *Weevils in the Wheat: Interviews with Virginia Ex-Slaves* (Charlottesville, 1976), 66–7. Jesse Bolden kindly told me of an elderly African American living near Sparta, Georgia, during the 1980s whose family had been transported from Virginia to Georgia during antebellum times, and who mentioned the man who "blew a trumpet" and sought to free the slaves in Richmond.

rather than literally. The inclusion of both names in a narrative of resistance to slavery strongly suggests that enslaved Virginians kept alive stories of rebellion that countered their masters' texts.[21]

From collective memory to fiction

The memories that enslaved Virginians constructed of Gabriel's attempt to overthrow slavery were preserved during the first half of the nineteenth century by people telling stories and singing songs within slave communities. Not surprisingly, no factual accounts of such moments found their way into print and survived, but one Black Virginian's fictional account of Gabriel's legacy has survived. In *Blake or the Huts of America*, Martin R. Delany, a prominent abolitionist and a founder of pan-African nationalism, included an incident in which the hero Blake (at that point called Henry Holland) traveled to the Dismal Swamp attempting to foment a pan-African slave revolt, and spoke to a maroon who claimed to have known Gabriel. By furnishing one context – imagined by a Black man who lived part of his life in antebellum Virginia – in which stories about Gabriel were told, Delany provides the best surviving clue to what happened when Black Virginians spoke of Gabriel. Simultaneously, he illustrates the transmutation of oral traditions about slave resistance into more formal and polemical literature.

Delany's *Blake* was written during the 1850s and published serially (though incompletely) between 1859 and 1862.[22] It revolves around the efforts of the central character, born to free Black Cuban parents but kidnapped and sold into slavery in Mississippi, to rally enslaved men and women in Cuba and the American South to rise against their masters and overthrow slavery. After escaping from his Mississippi plantation and organizing slaves throughout the Lower South, Henry Holland, as Blake is called when in the United States, heads north to Charleston and then to Delany's home state of Virginia. He enters through the Dismal Swamp, where he finds several "old confederates of the noted Nat Turner" among others of "Virginia and North Carolina's boldest black rebels."[23] The maroons of the swamp hold "the names of Nat Turner, Denmark Veezie, and General Gabriel . . . in sacred reverence"

---

[21] Egerton, *Gabriel's Rebellion*, 178 provides another wonderfully allusive and elusive possible example of a folk memory of Gabriel.

[22] Floyd J. Miller, "Introduction," in Martin R. Delany, *Blake or the Huts of America* (Boston, 1970) reviews Delany's biography and the publishing history of the novel. Also see Sundquist, *To Wake the Nations*, 189–221.

[23] Delany, *Blake*, 112–14 for Blake's time in the Dismal Swamp. All quotes from *Blake* are from these pages unless otherwise noted.

and believe them to have been "the greatest men who ever lived." Gabriel's name is not just revered; unlike the others it is considered "a talisman."

Among those living in the Dismal Swamp are two "high conjurers" – Gamby Gholar, a "compeer of Nat Turner," and Maudy Ghamus, who has the "appearance of a centenarian." Ghamus recounts a story that places Gabriel, fighting "like mad dog!" in "de Malution wah." Gabriel's supposed heroism in the War for American Independence notwithstanding, Ghamus reports that there was "no sich fightin'" in the American Revolution like that which took place "in Gabel wah!" Delany's maroons, then, had developed a holy trinity of slave rebels, and they had constructed a history of Gabriel's Conspiracy that tied his efforts even more directly to Washington and the American Revolution than had the song that lay behind *The Liberator* story.

Neither Delany nor his character Blake represents Ghamus's tale as factually true: the text refers to stories told about "the pretended deeds of" Gabriel, Vesey, and Turner, some of which were "fabulous." Nonetheless, Blake treats Ghamus respectfully, calling him "father" and assuring him that he and his followers were the kind of fighting men needed for the coming revolution. The High Conjurers accept Blake's claim to kinship, anointing him a "conjuror of the highest degree known to their art," and sending him out of the swamp as their "son" to "go forth and do wonders." Though Blake lacks faith in the magic and culture of the folk, he accepts the proffered position and continues on his way, coincidentally following Gamby Gholar's instructions.

Delany's invocation of Gabriel and his location of the telling of this mythic narrative in what was Virginia's primary mythic locus of Black freedom – the Dismal Swamp – underscores his belief in the importance and vitality of folk traditions of resistance among enslaved Virginians. Delany never specified his source for these stories, but he did make a claim to personal knowledge of the region by inserting a footnote explaining that "the highest degree known to the art of conjuration in the Dismal Swamp, is Seven-finger High-glister."[24] Perhaps he had actually visited the swamp on his travels through the South; more likely he had heard about its residents from people escaping from Virginia slavery into the free Black communities of the North. Either way, his vignette provides as reliable an image as exists of Black Virginians

---

[24] Delany, *Blake*, 115. Throughout the novel Delany inserts short notes asserting the factual basis for certain events that he includes in the narrative. For example, when his fictional narrative includes a slave running away with hidden money, Delany adds: "This person had really $2,000 in gold, securely hid away unknown to any person but his wife, until showing it to the writer" (84), and on the next page he annotates another story with a note that reads: "a real incident which took place between a slave and a free black advisor" (85).

telling stories that placed Gabriel's Conspiracy within a counternarrative of Virginia's history.

Blake simultaneously structures this counterhistory developed by enslaved Virginians into Delany's very different conception of world history. The Dismal Swamp maroons of the novel revere Gabriel's name as a talisman and anoint Blake as the second (or perhaps the fourth) coming. If Blake is the hero that Gabriel's struggle prophesied, then he is a figure with grander ambitions than either the historical Gabriel or the conjurers in the Dismal Swamp had imagined. Blake seeks not just to take Richmond, or to end slavery in Virginia, or even merely to end slavery in the United States. He conceives of an enormous war in which the oppressed people of West Africa and all the slave societies of the Americas will overthrow their masters and create a new pan-African confederation.[25] Local struggles like Gabriel's and local traditions like those of the Dismal Swamp will play crucial roles in bringing this alternate history into existence, even if those leading the struggles and perpetuating the traditions remain only dimly aware of the broader movement.[26]

Interestingly, Black Virginians' understanding of Gabriel's Conspiracy as a precursor to future struggles found an echo in some White Virginians' representations of the state's past, suggesting that Black oral traditions influenced (though they certainly did not determine) White folk history. Marion Harland's *Judith: A Chronicle of Old Virginia* (1883) opens in 1831 on the eve of Nat Turner's rebellion when one of the "elderly women who loved to relate unwritten reminiscences" begins a story by announcing that she was in Richmond at the time of Gabriel's insurrection. Not surprisingly, the memory of the conspiracy passed along in White oral traditions differed in important respects from that perpetuated among Blacks. Harland's Gabriel is betrayed by a "body-servant" of Prosser's who risks his life to help his "easy master" escape the rebellious slaves; and Pharoah, animated by his love of Whites, braves swimming across the rising creek to warn William Mosby while Gabriel and his followers argue over the proper course. Harland also represents White Virginians as exemplars of Christian forgiveness: Aunt Betsy, a representative Christian slaveholding woman of Richmond, when praying for "the brave men who had gone out to meet the enemy, and for ourselves,

---

[25] In addition to the novel, see Sundquist, *To Wake the Nations*, 189–221.

[26] Ironically we too remain only dimly aware of the outlines of Blake's vision of world history, because the extant version of the novel is unfinished and ends on the eve of the revolution. Whether Delany chose to leave the end open – perhaps because the onset of the Civil War rendered his vision politically problematic – or whether the last of the serializations was lost is unclear.

our families, our homes, our churches, our beloved Richmond!" also includes a plea for "the poor, deluded creatures who had followed the lead of wicked men, and been taught to thirst for the blood of their best friends." All who are listening then echo her Christian plea with: "Father, forgive them! they know not what they do!"[27] White oral traditions subsumed the story of Gabriel into their contemporary understanding of slavery as a Christian institution in which the enslaved were treated benevolently.

More interesting, however, than these predictable differences in White and Black myths of Gabriel is the shared sense that his call to Black men to take up arms prophesied future struggles over slavery. Harland suggests that White traditions took seriously the religious basis of Gabriel's appeal, connecting the conspiracy both to the potential radicalism in slave Christianity and to Nat Turner's explicitly religious attempt to build a revolution. Whites appear to have shared with Blacks a sense that the name Gabriel carried a certain power: upon hearing that twin brothers had been named Michael and Gabriel after the archangels, one character insisted that, were they his chattel, he would force Gabriel to change his name "or leave the plantation."[28] Most telling, however, is the use of a story of Gabriel's Conspiracy to foreshadow Nat Turner's Rebellion. Though politicians and journalists preferred to discuss conspiracies or insurrections individually as separate and unrelated, Harland's novel suggests that many White Virginians shared with Blacks a notion of a living tradition of resistance to slavery, even while believing it to be a tradition of folly. Perhaps this belief was rooted in part in stories like Maudy Ghamus's that many White children must have heard slaves tell.

Marion Harland wrote *Judith* at a time when, in her own words, "the oral *raconteur*" was "going out of fashion" beneath the onslaught of "professional scribes," and she decried the "barren flat" that "our record of happenings not yet fifty years old" would become without the "elderly women who loved to relate unwritten reminiscences."[29] The professionalization and textualization of memory and history undoubtedly menaced traditions among White Virginians, but the de-privileging of oral traditions constituted a more fundamental danger to the historical consciousness of African Americans. The efforts of escaped slaves and abolitionists of African descent – Martin Delany

[27] Marion Harland, *Judith: A Chronicle of Old Virginia* (Philadelphia and New York, 1983), 9–29 (p. 9 for reminiscences, p. 23 for Pharoah, p. 12 for prayer).
[28] Harland, *Judith*, 21. Harland had one character claim that Gabriel copied his plan for government out of the Book of Daniel, an interesting tradition in light of Gabriel's use of the name Daniel when speaking to Billy and Isham on the sloop *Mary* (see Chapter 2, this book).
[29] Harland, *Judith*, 9.

prominent among them – notwithstanding, White Americans dominated the production, publication, and consumption of written texts. The displacement and marginalization of orally transmitted history, combined with the fragmentation of southern Black communities following emancipation and migration to the urban north and west, threatened to sever the descendants of slaves from their forbears' traditions.

African American intellectuals contested dominant interpretations of the nation's past along several different lines. Prior to the Civil War, escaped slaves had created the slave narrative, a specifically African American literary genre, and had used it to assert an alternate vision of Southern and American society. Central figures like Frederick Douglass, W. E. B. DuBois, Booker T. Washington, and Carter G. Woodson continued, during the late nineteenth and the first half of the twentieth centuries, to produce texts that aimed, in modern parlance, to cross over, winning a following and thus influence among White Americans in addition to offering the growing number of formally educated Black Americans a more convincing interpretation of their past. Many of these writers mastered both the social scientific languages and methodologies and the literary traditions of the dominant culture in order to confront the racist assumptions masked in White authors' – especially White scholars' – "objective" language.[30]

These approaches resulted in some of the most insightful social analysis produced during that era, analysis that, especially in the case of DuBois's work, continues to open new perspectives for the understanding of the culture and history of the United States.[31] By its very nature it was less successful, however, at preserving the folk memories and historical consciousness of once-enslaved African Americans. By the 1920s and '30s, increasing numbers of Black intellectuals sought to root their artistic work in the traditional forms and languages of Black folk culture, thus creating an organic link between the "high cultural" production of DuBois's "talented tenth," and the communities that had fostered that intellectual elite's development.[32]

---

[30] See Houston A. Baker Jr., *Modernism and the Harlem Renaissance* (Chicago, 1987) for his discussion of the "mastery of form."

[31] For a sense of the range and power of recent work inspired by DuBois's thought, see Paul Gilroy, *The Black Atlantic: Modernity and Double Consciousness* (Cambridge, Mass., 1993); and David W. Roediger, *The Wages of Whiteness: Race and the Making of the American Working Class* (New York, 1991). Also see Gerald Early, ed., *Lure and Loathing: Essays on Race, Identity, and the Ambivalence of Assimilation* (New York, 1993).

[32] Baker, *Modernism and the Harlem Renaissance*, analyzes these efforts and their historical precedents when discussing the "deformation of mastery." Also see the works of Zora Neale Hurston, especially (though not only) *Mules and Men* (Bloomington, Ind., 1978 [1935]).

Arna Bontemps, born in post-Reconstruction Louisiana but raised in Los Angeles, was one of the creative writers drawn to Harlem during the 1920s and influenced by these concerns. They may have taken on a particular meaning in his life because of the tension between his education in predominantly White schools in California, and the less formal education in folk culture provided by Joseph Ward, his "Uncle Buddy" from Louisiana, a tension exacerbated by his father's disapproval of Ward.[33] At any rate, in the wake of the stock market crash and "the gloom of the darkening Depression," Bontemps found inspiration in "the stricken slave's will to freedom," and began work on *Black Thunder*, a novel about Gabriel's Conspiracy.[34]

Bontemps's relation to the folk culture of the enslaved people about whom he wrote was complex and in many ways contradictory. In 1968 he explained that he had chosen to write about Gabriel rather than Nat Turner in part because Gabriel had "not depended on trance-like mumbo jumbo" and had thus based his movement on "a more unmistakable equivalent of the yearning" that Bontemps had "felt and . . . imagined to be general." In Gabriel he had found a pragmatic and calculating figure through whom to explore the "theme of self-assertion by black men whose endurance was strained to the breaking point." On some level this search for a Gabriel who could serve Bontemps's present fit snugly the oral traditions that had alternately fused the figures of Gabriel and Denmark Vesey, and then, assuming that Delany's fictional account grew out of slaves' stories, made of Gabriel a leader in the American Revolution. Nonetheless, in the rejection of Turner's " 'visions' and 'dreams,' " and the preference for a protagonist for whom "freedom was a less complicated affair," Bontemps revealed the ambivalence toward folk culture that one might expect him to have taken from the dual influences of his father and Joseph Ward (his Uncle Buddy).[35]

This ambivalence runs throughout the text of the novel. Gabriel is pushed and pulled toward freedom by divergent forces in the course of the novel, from the natural rights philosophy of the French, American, and Haitian Revolutions to Thomas Henry Prosser's brutal murder of an aging slave, to biblical readings offered by Mingo, an invented free Black character. The

---

[33] Kirkland C. Jones, *Renaissance Man from Louisiana: A Biography of Arna Wendell Bontemps* (Westport, Conn., 1992).

[34] Arna Bontemps, *Black Thunder* (Boston, 1968 [1936]). Quotation from Bontemps's "Introduction to the 1968 Edition," xxvi.

[35] Bontemps, *Black Thunder*, xxvi–xxvii, xxix (for quotations). For a reading of the novel that compares its meaning in the 1930s with its reception when reissued in the 1960s, see Albert E. Stone, *The Return of Nat Turner: History, Literature, and Cultural Politics in Sixties America* (Athens, Ga., 1992), 193–204.

languages of the Age of Revolution prove to be the weakest and least reliable inspirational sources for Gabriel.[36]

Bontemps does not, however, reject these Western traditions. Instead, he engages in a signifying act of revision by taking seriously the claim that liberty is rooted in nature rather than in the written texts that formulate such arguments.[37] Bontemps makes Gabriel "innocent of letters," but the rebel leader shows great interest in the "words" with which two Frenchmen living in Richmond discuss "the equality of man" and the need "to awaken the masses." Though "just words," these just words "put gooseflesh on Gabriel's arms and shoulders." They do not, however, explain Gabriel's attempt to overthrow slavery. As Biddenhurst, one of the Frenchmen, notes during this very conversation, the Blacks were already whispering, and Gabriel himself refers to the "strange music" of "Liberty, equality, frater-" as providing "words for things that had been in his mind, things that he didn't know had names." He remains open to learning more about these newly named concepts, responding to Biddenhurst's inquiry about whether he would like to "learn things like that," with "I reckon I would, suh."[38] But Gabriel never takes up Biddenhurst's offer to share a drink and conversation in a wine shop, and he had in fact been organizing his conspiracy for some time before hearing this discussion. His desire for freedom is so fundamental that it exists independent of a language with which to name it.

Gabriel does not need to hear Biddenhurst's explanation of natural rights philosophy precisely because in *Black Thunder* natural rights are truly rooted in nature. Bontemps continues a play on the word "just" when Juba, Gabriel's wife, warns him that "just thinking" will get him in trouble with the police. Gabriel makes clear that he cannot stop thinking about justice: "I ain't fixing to run away. . . . But I wants to be free. I wonder how it'd feel."[39] Just thinking is, after all, something human beings cannot help but do, and Bontemps

---

[36] Daniel Reagan, "Voices of Silence: the Representation of Orality in Arna Bontemps' *Black Thunder*," *Studies in American Fiction* 19 (1991): 71–83 argues that Bontemps gives preference to oral sources of Gabriel's inspiration. I think, however, that he overstates his case and understates Bontemps's ambivalence. The key to our different interpretations lies in the meaning of the note from Toussaint Louverture that Mingo discusses toward the end of the novel. For his reading see p. 79; for mine, which emphasizes the placement of Gabriel's Conspiracy into a prophetic mode of history, see pp. 271–4, this book. For the key incident see Bontemps, *Black Thunder*, 66 (for the message itself), 169 (for Mingo's reconsideration).

[37] Henry Louis Gates Jr., *The Signifying Monkey: A Theory of African-American Literary Criticism* (New York, 1988) for the theoretical definition of "signifying."

[38] Bontemps, *Black Thunder*, 20–2.   [39] Ibid., 30–1.

reinforces the natural basis for dreams of freedom through repeated invocations of animals' desire to be free. At various times slaves explain their insistence on freedom through reference to "a wild bird['s]" willingness "to break his neck" trying to get "out of a cage," the fact that "everything what's equal to a ground hog want to be free," and the claim that "anything what's equal to a gray squirrel want to be free."[40] Finally Gabriel makes the point explicit when answering authorities at his trial. They encourage him to implicate the "foreign agitators," the White men whose talk about "equality, setting the poor against the rich, the blacks against their masters" had "worked on" him to encourage his rebellion. Gabriel finds their belief that Whites had been involved "foolish." He had been "studying about freedom a heap," and had "heard a plenty folks talk," but the voice he could not ignore was that within him that kept telling him "that anything what's equal to a gray squirrel wants to be free. That's how it all come about."[41] Nature's language, not man's, compels the struggle for freedom, a revision of natural rights that works both to radicalize the concept by separating the struggle for freedom from philosophical traditions open only to people educated in Western traditions and to point to alternate sources for movements like Gabriel's in the "organic" development of local communities.

No doubt, on one level Bontemps intended this insistence on man's truly natural desire to be free as an answer to the claims he had heard, while living and teaching in Alabama, that the uproar over the Scottsboro boys case was caused by "outside agitators." But the relationship within the novel between formal philosophical defenses of natural right that originate from without and natural desires for freedom that spring organically from within the slave community has meaning beyond the specific political context within which Bontemps wrote. His written text inscribes not just a story of Gabriel but a hope for the reconciliation of the oral and the written in future struggles for equality.

The figure of "Toussaint l'Ouverture," leader of the world's only successful slave revolution, offers this reconciliation within the novel. Toussaint appears in the novel as a text – a handbill handed out by Haitian sailors in which Toussaint invited Black Richmonders to "unite with us" to ensure that "liberty and equality shall reign."[42] Toussaint's title on the handbill – "General for the Public Welfare" – and the absence of any specific reference

---

[40] Ibid., 69, 77, 91. For other references to animals and slaves' desire for freedom see pp. 93, 94, 119, 210, 211, 215. Stone, *The Return of Nat Turner*, 196–97, discusses natural imagery and natural law.
[41] Bontemps, *Black Thunder*, 210.   [42] Ibid., 66.

Epilogue

to Saint Domingue or Haiti, as well as the fact that he appeals through a written text, reinforce the universal appeal of his language. Bontemps, however, undercuts a simple reading of Toussaint as representative of a truly universal Western tradition of natural rights by twice having an elderly slave woman, a representative of traditional Virginia slave culture, explain Gabriel's failure by contrasting his approach to rebellion with that of the Haitians: "Toussaint and them kilt a hog in the woods. Drank the blood."[43] Gabriel's failure to learn from Toussaint's successful melding of traditional slave culture and natural rights philosophy weakened his movement.

Weakened it but did not destroy it. Toussaint makes another appearance in *Black Thunder*, an appearance in which Gabriel's Conspiracy gets inscribed into a prophetic mode of history reminiscent of that favored in the oral traditions of the enslaved in antebellum Virginia. This occurs near the end as Mingo, Gabriel's literate and free Black lieutenant, lies chained face down in prison listening to his comrades being hanged. Mingo thinks back on Toussaint's written appeal calling for his "brothers" to "come and unite with me." Suddenly Mingo is "awakened to a meaning he had not previously seen in" Toussaint's words, a meaning rooted in his realization that "Toussaint was in jail now, maybe dead." Mingo feels elated – "momentarily stronger" – rather than cheated by the realization that he had been called to sacrifice himself. "Do the dead combat for a common cause? Well, he thought, it was possible that they did, yes, quite possible."[44]

Mingo, Gabriel, and the other conspirators do not lose their struggle against slavery when executed, as Bontemps emphasizes by repeating his earlier use of smoke as an image. Smoke first appears in the novel at the funeral of Bundy, an old slave who had been dreaming of freedom when Prosser murdered him and whose murder helped to inspire Gabriel. The scene, narrated in the beginning by the collective voice of the slave community, includes a rejection of death's power.

Dying ain't nothing. You know how wood burns up to ashes and smoke? Well, it's just the same way when you's dying. . . . Dying ain't nothing. The smoke goes free. Can't nobody hurt smoke. A smoke man – that's you now, brother. A *real* smoke man. Smoke what gets in yo' eyes and makes you blink. Smoke what gets in yo' throat and chokes you.[45]

---

[43] Ibid., 166–7. 196.
[44] Ibid., 168–9. See Reagan, "Voices of Silence," 79 for a less hopeful reading of this incident.
[45] Bontemps uses language that signifies a Black character but never identifies the narrator in this sequence.

This chorus expresses scorn for White Virginians' ignorance – Prosser "don't even know a tree got a soul" – and warns that spirits will fight in this world: "Marse Prosser act like he done forgot smoke get in his eyes and make him blink. You'll be in his eyes and in his throat too, won't you, Bundy?"[46] Smoke is introduced as a powerful emblem of resistance and one tied to traditional slave spiritual practices rooted in an oral folk culture and in African animism.

Bundy is not the only slave whose murder creates smoke. Ben, who is the chief informer in the novel, watches the execution of Gabriel and sees the arc of the ax, "lingering . . . against the sky like a wreath of smoke." This becomes an image that he cannot escape: "Even when Ben closed his eyes, he could see that arc."[47] Gabriel's execution is also associated with music – the rope on the gallows "hummed like a violin string," and Ben continued to "hear that violin string" – a recurrent trope in the novel that is tied to the natural desire to be free.[48] And the novel closes with Ben heading into a storm fearing the vengeful "knives that waited for him with the sweet brown thrashers" – birds whose songs had repeatedly inspired conspirators – while trying to take solace in the "soothing tune" produced by the feet of a domesticated animal – a little mare – on cobblestone streets.[49] Though Gabriel's Conspiracy had been crushed, the desire for freedom continued to animate all natural men, and a storm was in the offing. Bontemps's text predicts that the memory of Gabriel's efforts, combined with an understanding of the mistake he made in paying too little attention to traditions rooted in traditional African American culture, would contribute to continuing efforts to win the freedom that nature promised.

Bontemps's text seeks to perform the reconciliation between folk and high culture that it suggests Gabriel's Conspiracy prophesied. As Mary Kemp Davis has shown, *Black Thunder* offers a retelling of the oral traditions preserved during the nineteenth century in enslaved Virginians' songs but carried into dominant literate circles by the White abolitionist Thomas Wentworth Higginson's essays on Gabriel's Conspiracy.[50] Bontemps read deeply in the surviving records of the conspiracy, and his narrative generally follows the known facts to be found there, with the addition of a richly

[46] Bontemps, *Black Thunder*, 52.   [47] Ibid., 223.
[48] Ibid., 13, 21, 33–4, 52, 53, 56, 61, 114, 117, 138, 164, 198 for uses of music, frequently birds singing but at least once (p. 21) the music of Western philosophical traditions, to call men to be free.
[49] Ibid., 224.
[50] Mary Kemp Davis, "Arna Bontemps' *Black Thunder*: The Creation of an Authoritative Text of Gabriel's Defeat," *Black American Literature Forum* 1 (1989): 17–36.

imagined fictional context.[51] At several key junctions in the novel – Gabriel's capture on board ship and his courtroom speech – "Bontemps consciously borrows material from the Gabriel legend."[52] Borrows but, as Davis points out, alters in the borrowing in order to construct a Gabriel for the struggles of the 1930s.

Bontemps's text not only offers the "theme of self-assertion by black men" that he thought crucial for "Americans, both black and white" in the 1930s and '60s.[53] It offers a model of the productive marriage of traditional forms of knowledge preserved in the oral traditions of African Americans who lacked formal education – people like the author's "Uncle Buddy" – and the modernist impulse central to the Harlem Renaissance and embodied in Bontemps's use of multiple narrative voices and perspectives. *Black Thunder* offers a vision of one of the great slave conspiracies in the history of the United States as an inspiring effort by enslaved people to win the freedom that it asserts to have been their natural birthright, and it advocates both in content and form a way to learn from Gabriel's temporary defeat in the continuing struggle.

Gabriel and Richmond in history and in time

Gabriel's Virginia stands for a time and place, but it also refers to a set of assumptions regarding what is most important about that time and place. To forge an understanding of Gabriel's Virginia requires something other than telling the story of Gabriel's Conspiracy. For the meaning of the conspiracy for those who joined it can be approached only through an attempt to comprehend the history that informed their sense of corporate identity – that is, through an analysis of the way that an identifiably Black Virginian worldview had come into existence over the course of the eighteenth century. Gabriel's, rather than Jefferson's, Virginia can emerge only out of an analysis that includes the meeting of various African peoples with one another and with creole descendants of other Africans, the formation of plantation-based communities centered around kinship and struggles over the labor process, and the broadening of these communities to envelop all Virginians of African descent as a result of migration, the Atlantic Revolutions, and the religious revivals

---

[51] The novel's first line – "Virginia Court records for September 15, 1800" – asserts Bontemps's familiarity with the documentary record (*Black Thunder*, 9).

[52] Davis, "Arna Bontemps' *Black Thunder*," 32.

[53] Bontemps, "Introduction to the 1968 Edition," in *Black Thunder*, xxix.

of the second half of the eighteenth century. In this history of Virginia, questions about creolizing elites, tobacco inspection, and relations to the British Empire are relegated to secondary importance, commanding attention only when they influenced the lives and self-perceptions of Virginians of African descent.

Gabriel's Conspiracy as an event takes on a profound but complex importance in unsettling the interpretation of Virginia during the Age of Revolution. Conceiving of Gabriel's Virginia does not mean placing Gabriel's Conspiracy at the center of Black Virginians' experiences any more than conceiving of Jeffersonian Virginia means placing the presidential election of 1800 at the center of White Virginians' experiences. It does, however, assume that Gabriel's attempt to end slavery represents a powerfully rendered image of the aspirations and perceptions of many Black Virginians. One reason, then, that the conspiracy must be carefully analyzed is for the process of appropriation that it reveals at the heart of the culture of resistance that animated slave communities, a process that underscored the complex crosscutting senses of corporate identity that characterized people of African descent in Gabriel's Virginia. The two Virginias – Gabriel's and Jefferson's – prove to have shared more than time and place: the interpenetration of the lives and values of enslaved and free, and Black and White, people proved so deep that Gabriel's attempt to combat White slaveholders used cultural idioms that Black and White Virginians had forged together – often in struggle with one another – over the previous century. Gabriel's Conspiracy reflected this shared past and became an important part of the shared past that later Black and White Virginians would use to forge their distinct but related identities.

An analytical danger exists in the stark clarity with which Gabriel's Conspiracy can be used to sketch the contours of the cultural world of Gabriel's Virginia. As valuable an image of shared values as was produced by enslaved men coming together to forge a rebellion against slavery, most of the daily struggles and experiences of enslaved people – struggles centering around things like work, family, sex, and religion – merited little attention in the records produced by the repression of the conspiracy. The rich crosscutting senses of identity revealed in the evidence produced in response to the conspiracy become more comprehensible when placed within the social context of Richmond – the growing town around which the conspiracy coalesced. Gabriel and his fellow conspirators were products of a specific part of their Virginia – a rapidly developing manufacturing and commercial center in which slave–master and black–white relations were in unusual flux. Urbanization and the adaptation of slavery to an urban economy form the social context in which the conspiracy must be understood. Richmond provides a key to

Gabriel and thus to Gabriel's Virginia, just as Monticello provides one key to understanding Jefferson and thus Jeffersonian Virginia.

Ultimately, however, neither the importance of Gabriel's Conspiracy nor that of the revision represented by Gabriel's Virginia lies solely in the Richmond or the Virginia of the turn of the nineteenth century. Understanding Gabriel's movement requires close attention to those contexts, but understanding his importance entails moving beyond the contemporary context and placing him and his world in time. Gabriel and his followers should be understood to have commented critically upon White Virginians' uses of natural rights philosophy and thus to have asserted an important alternate interpretation of the limited meaning and the broader potential of the American Revolution. Their assertion expands our understanding of the meanings of the American Revolution among the people of that era. They lacked, however, the military power to win recognition for their vision of racial justice, and their attempt had limited and sometimes negative immediate impact on enslaved people's struggle to win freedom.

To appreciate the deeper significance of the conspiracy, one must move beyond the temporal boundaries of Gabriel's Virginia and view the conspiracy not just as a moment that opened a valuable window on the conspirators' view of the world but as a key moment in the struggle for racial equality in America. It became a key moment not because Gabriel willed it so, but because Americans, most often African Americans, who survived him or were born after him found his attempt inspiring. Enslaved Black Virginians, and then African American and white abolitionist intellectuals, and then twentieth-century writers – from Arna Bontemps to Herbert Aptheker – sought to understand Gabriel's Conspiracy and his implicit critique of Jeffersonian Virginia. In doing so, they have used Gabriel and Gabriel's world to argue for a broader vision of America's past and to advocate greater justice in their own time.

Appendix
Richmond households in 1784 and 1810

The records available for household reconstruction in early Richmond, while rich in some regards, are far from perfect. The two most complete censuses were carried out by the city in 1782 and 1784. Each includes a listing of each free person, occupation, age, and the location of the household in which each lived. The censuses also include the names and ages of enslaved residents and the households in which each lived. These censuses were taken on the orders of the Richmond city government – the Common Hall Council – and were recorded in the Common Hall's Minute Book. Although the council continued to order that censuses be taken, for some reason the results were no longer recorded in the Minute Books, and I have not located later lists. While a comparison of the two lists reveals some interesting things about early Richmond – especially the transience of those who lived there – the structure of households remained quite similar in the two censuses, so I have summarized some of the most important data from 1784 in Tables 1 to 3. Tables 1, 2, and 3 are compiled from a census taken in 1784 under the order of the Richmond City Common Hall and recorded in the Richmond City Common Hall Minute Book (microfilm, VSL). Michael Lee Nicholls kindly furnished me with a computer printout that he compiled from the 1784 census. The film of the census is sometimes barely legible, and I have substituted my reading of the film for that of Nicholls in a couple of instances.

The federal government began taking censuses of the United States in 1790, but the raw returns of the 1790 and 1800 Virginia census-takers – the data necessary to reconstruct household composition – burned. The raw data from 1810 have survived and are given in Tables 4, 5, and 6. The source for Tables 4, 5, and 6 is raw census data from the 1810 United States census. The numbers yielded by my analysis of the raw data differ slightly from the reported numbers. The data reported in these tables differs a bit more because I have excluded listings that did not constitute households (e.g., the state penitentiary, the workhouse, and households headed by business partnerships). Including the 26 entities of these sorts would have added 82 slaves, 45 free Blacks, 21 White women, 182 White men, 21 White boys, and 8 White girls. Unfortunately, the 1810 census-takers did not record the locations of households on their returns, so I have not been able to provide breakdowns by neighborhood, but as I suggest in Chapter 5, the economic and demographic changes that Richmond experienced between 1784 and 1810 would probably have required a redefinition of the neighborhoods to reflect the ways people lived and worked in the city following the completion of the James River Canal. See Chapter 5 for my analysis of the growth and development of Richmond.

Table 1. *Population by area in Richmond in 1784*

Area	Households	White	Slave	Free Black
West Richmond	29	143	136	16
East Richmond	84	362	291	9
Warehouse Area	50	166	198	23
Totals	163	671	625	48

Table 2. *Adult sex ratios by area in Richmond in 1784*
(percentages of total Whites and slaves over 16 years old)

Area	White Men	White Women	Slave Men	Slave Women
West Richmond	60	40	59	41
East Richmond	64	36	48	52
Warehouse Area	78	22	53	47
Town totals	67	33	52	48

Table 3. *Occupations of household heads by neighborhood,*
Richmond, Virginia, 1784[a]

Area	Artisans[b]	Merchants	Professionals[c]	Others[d]
West Richmond	20	0	5	4
East Richmond	40	12	7	25
Warehouse Area	9	18	8	15
Town totals	69	30	20	44

[a] Almost half of the heads of households whose occupations are not listed were slaves who hired their own time and lived separately from their masters, or they were free Blacks. Three White women headed households but were listed without occupations. Only two householders were listed as laborers.
[b] "Artisans" includes skilled and semiskilled workers.
[c] "Professionals" include civil servants.
[d] This includes 23 people whose occupations were not listed, 8 tavern keepers, and scattered others. Many whose occupations were not listed were probably day laborers.

Table 4. *Slaves per household: Richmond in 1810*

Household Head	Total Slaves	Number of Households	Slaves per Household
White male	2,829	812	3.48
White female	397	166	2.39
Free Black male	69	94	0.73
Free Black female	87	171	0.51
Slave	51	13	3.92
Town totals	3,433	1,256	2.73

Table 5. *Free Blacks per household: Richmond in 1810*

Household Head	Total Free Blacks	Number of Households	Free Blacks per Household
White male	272	812	0.33
White female	41	166	0.25
Free Black male	292	94	3.11
Free Black female	514	171	3.01
Slave	—	13	—
Town totals	1,119	1,256	0.89

Table 6. *White children per White household: Richmond in 1810*[a]

Household Head	White Boys[a]	White Girls	White Children	White Women	White Children/ White Woman	White Children/ White Household
White male	768	706	1,474	909	1.62	1.81
White female	93	142	235	290	0.81	1.42
Town totals	861	848	1,709	1,199	1.43	1.75

[a] I count any White person under 16 a child, because that is where the census records made their first age division. Census-takers made no distinctions among free Blacks or slaves according to age or sex. The distinction among households headed by free Black males or free Black females made in the tables is based on name analysis.

Index

abolition, 135–6, 257, 262, 267, 273
Abrahams, Jacob, 169
Adams, John, 190
Adams, Richard, 159, 165
Adams, Thomas, 159
Africa, 5, 11, 18, 21, 29, 48, 51, 68, 72, 266
African, 8, 11, 15, 16–18, 20–3, 38, 44, 65, 68, 71–2, 82–6, 92–4, 154, 261–2, 272–3, 274
African American, 9–10
  as chosen people, 38, 52, 57, 74–5, 79, 93
  intellectuals, 267–74
African Baptist Church of Williamsburg, 37, 42
African slavery, 22
Afro-Virginian, 21–2, 34, 43–6, 48, 82, 93–4, 102, 139, 145, 206, 216, 274–5
Alexandria, Virginia, 153
Allen, David, 208
Allen, Jedidiah, 195
Allen, William, 198
Ambler, Eliza, 160
Ambler, Jacquelin, 160, 164, 206n
America, 5
American Revolution, 3, 6, 10, 11, 26–7, 41, 43, 137, 139, 149, 176, 256, 261, 265, 269, 276
  armies in, 33–4, 40, 159–60
  and Black Virginian identity, 32–5, 38–9, 49
  influence on Gabriel's Conspiracy, 87–8

Richmond and, 158–9
White Virginians' understanding of, 120
Anderson, Nathaniel, 204, 215–16, 218
Anderson, Nelson, 196
Andover, Massachusetts, 1
Angola, 18, 21
Anthony, William, 4, 177, 243–4
antislavery movement, 109, 175
apprentices, 7, 188, 190, 198–9, 236
Aptheker, Herbert, 60n8, 140, 276
Arrow, Rosi, 233
artisans, 61–2, 83–5, 88n68, 163–4, 171, 174, 190–7, 202–4, 209–10, 229
  slaves, 6, 7, 55, 61–2, 68–9, 82–5, 88n68, 89, 92, 164, 184–6, 188, 190–1, 194–9, 202–3, 205–10, 213–14
Atlantic world economy, 153, 154–5, 158–60, 184–6, 226, 259
Augusta County, Virginia, 158
Austin, William, 121
Ayton, Frederick, 207

Bacon, Nathaniel, 151
Bacon's Rebellion, 138, 151
Baptists, 36–8, 44, 74, 80, 96, 174–6
  White Baptists and Gabriel's Conspiracy, 129–30
Barbados, 14
Barden, John Randolph, 27n38, 28n41
Barnett, Angela/Angelica, 4, 176–82, 243–4
Barrett, Anderson, 204, 209–10
Bates, Moses, 191
Battles, Lucy, 244

Coles Point Quarter, 26–7
colonization of free Blacks, 130, 136
community, 3–5
 plantation-based, 16–28
 slave community, 2, 11
companianate marriage, 225–7
Cook, Moll, 233
corn (maize), 24
Couch, Daniel, 170
Courtney, Richard, 74, 175–6
Cowley, Robert, 67
Craven, William H., 213
Creese (slave of Martha Morrisett), 220–1
creolization, 6, 8, 14–17, 19–39, 48–9, 94,
 146, 155, 158, 274–5
Cringan, John, 198–9
Cross River (Africa), 21
Crouch, Richard, 204
Cowan, John, 192
Cuba, 264
cultural appropriation, 1, 8, 51, 57, 93, 275
 artisanal skills and, 61–2
 Christianity, 69–72, 74–81, 93
 defined, 5
 election rituals, 70–2, 93
 horses, 65–6
 literacy, 72–3, 80–2
 military titles, 70
 physical mobility and, 62–5, 91–2
 swords, 68–70

dance, 28, 156, 157–8, 169, 172, 173, 200,
 218
Darrous, John, 202
Davies, Samuel, 35–6
Davis, Mary Kemp, 273–4
DeGogue, Lewis, 169, 231
Delany, Martin R., 264–7, 269
Dismal Swamp, 189, 264–6
Dismal Swamp Company, 189
disorderly houses, 169–71, 173–4, 200–1,
 218
Ditcher, Jack, 7, 97, 103–4, 122, 127
domestic servants, 201–3, 240, 245
domestic violence, 228, 231, 238–9
double consciousness, 38, 45–8
Douglass, Frederick, 219, 268
Dover Baptist Association (Virginia), 175

Dublin, Ireland, 226
DuBois, W. E. B., 38, 45–8, 268
Duckingfield, Pharis, 218
Duke, Paul, 243–4
Dunmore, John Lord, 26, 27, 32–4
Dunmore's Proclamation (1775), 26–7, 34
DuVal, William, 179

Easter Conspiracy (1802), 142–5, 258–9
 Lewis's testimony, 143–5, 146
Eastern Shore (Virginia), 41, 233
Egerton, Douglas R., 57n2, 60n7, 67n24,
 74–5, 81n54, 83n57, 88n68, 106n21,
 113n44, 130–1n37, n38, 143, 181n80
election of 1800, 59–60, 81n54, 128–9,
 275
Equiano, Olaudah, 14–15, 18
ethnicity
 African, 11, 18–19, 21
 European, 11
Europe, 5, 8, 51, 68, 73, 82, 92
Evans, Charles, 239
Evans, Claiborne, 204, 206n49, 207, 218
Evans/Norman, Catherine, 236–7
Examiner [Richmond], 129–30
Executive Council, Virginia, 104, 122,
 127–8

family, 210–13
 Black family in Richmond, 210–13, 219,
  231–44, 250
 slave, 19–20, 91–2, 170–1, 187, 200,
  212, 245
 and slave hiring, 193–4
Farrar, Arthur, 143–5
femininity, 9, 220, 222, 251–2
 elite White conceptions of, 227, 251
 free Black conceptions of, 242–4
 non-elite White conceptions of, 228–31,
  241–2
First Baptist Church of Richmond, 175
Fithian, Philip Vickers, 155–8
Fleming, George, 203
Formicola, Serafina, 161
Founding Fathers, 256–7
France, 40, 41, 180–1
Franklin, Peter, 177–8
Fredericksburg, Virginia, 153, 156